W9-CEP-143

Circumstantial Evidence

BOOKS BY PETE EARLEY

Family of Spies
The Hot House
Prophet of Death
Circumstantial Evidence

Circumstantial Evidence

Death, Life, and Justice in a Southern Town

Pete Earley

BANTAM BOOKS
New York Toronto London Sydney Auckland

CIRCUMSTANTIAL EVIDENCE

A Bantam Book / September 1995

Grateful acknowledgment is made for permission to reprint 5 quotations used as epigraphs from *To Kill a Mockingbird* by Harper Lee. Copyright © 1960 by Harper Lee. Copyright Renewed © 1988 by Harper Lee. Reprinted by permission of HarperCollins Publishers, Inc.

Book design by Richard Oriolo.

Library of Congress Cataloging-in-Publication Data

Earley, Pete.
Circumstantial evidence : death, life, and justice in a southern town / Pete Earley.
p. cm.
ISBN 0-553-09501-3
1. McMillian, Walter—Trials, litigation, etc. 2. Trials (Murder)—Alabama—Monroe County. I. Title.
KF224.M36E17 1995
364.1'523'0976125—dc20 95-10271
CIP

Published simultaneously in the United States and Canada

Bantam Books are published by Bantam Books, a division of Bantam Doubleday Dell Publishing Group, Inc. Its trademark, consisting of the words "Bantam Books" and the portrayal of a rooster, is Registered in U.S. Patent and Trademark Office and in other countries. Marca Registrada. Bantam Books, 1540 Broadway, New York, New York 10036.

PRINTED IN THE UNITED STATES OF AMERICA

BVG 10 9 8 7 6 5 4 3 2 1

TO

Stephen Matthew Earley

Atticus did have deep misgivings when the state asked for and the jury gave a death penalty on purely circumstantial evidence. . . . "I mean, before a man is sentenced to death for murder, say, there should be one or two eyewitnesses. Someone should be able to say, 'Yes, I was there and saw him pull the trigger.' "

—Harper Lee
To Kill a Mockingbird

Contents

This is a true story about two white teenage girls who were murdered in rural Alabama and the black man who was accused of killing them and sentenced to death. When I began working on this book, I did not know whether the convicted man was innocent or guilty or whether he would be freed from prison or executed. Because of this, much of what you are about to read I personally witnessed, and the characters I describe did not have the advantage of revising their statements or smoothing over their actions after the fact, as is often the case when an author researches a past event. People lie, memories are imperfect, prejudices come into play, mistakes are made, wrong paths are taken. Those whose story is told here had to choose whom they would believe and then react accordingly.

I have written the book chronologically so that you too must weave your way through the conflicting accounts and confusing events. I have done this because I wanted to show just how difficult it can be in a death penalty case to discover the truth. More often than not, the murder cases we read about involve notorious figures, celebrities, or famous victims. Lawyers preen before the courtroom television cameras; judges choose their words with special care. This book is about two teenagers who were not famous and a defendant equally obscure. The victims could have been the daughters of an acquaintance; the accused a friend. I went to a small town because in a close-knit community, crime and punishment always wear a human face. Neither the victim nor the accused are strangers. Those responsible for dispensing justice—investigators, prosecutors, defense attorneys, the judge, and the jurors—cannot hide under a blanket of big-city anonymity, or forget the role they have played, when each day they encounter a victim's grieving parents or the distraught spouse of a condemned man. I chose a case in the Deep South because more defendants are sentenced to death there than in any other section of our country.

This book started out as the story of one murder, but it quickly grew into the story of two. At first these appeared to be entirely unrelated killings, each with its unique cast of characters, but investigators eventually linked them as the hunt for the murderer narrowed.

As this is written, we are averaging one execution per week in our country. Polls show that for the first time, a majority of whites *and* blacks approve of the ultimate sanction. We favor executions because we believe in our criminal justice system. If we didn't, we could not in good conscience condone a single killing. This book describes a simple death penalty case. I believe that what it has to say about our system of justice and how it is dispensed should frighten us all.

—PETE EARLEY

Part One

Slaughter of an Innocent

Maycomb was an old town, but it was a tired old town when I first knew it. . . . People moved slowly then. They ambled across the square, shuffled in and out of the stores around it, took their time about everything. A day was twenty-four hours long but seemed longer. There was no hurry, for there was nowhere to go . . . nothing to see outside the boundaries of Maycomb County.

—Harper Lee
To Kill a Mockingbird

Then he had grinned. Embarrassed, she had turned away. That night Ronda had mentioned to her mother what the black man had done, and Bertha had warned her daughter about being too friendly to strangers.

Unlike the modern stores in Mobile, Jackson Cleaners had no computerized system that kept track of each customer's laundry. There was no motorized chain that carried clean clothes along a track to the front of the store at the push of a button. Fetching clothes from the back workroom was Ronda's job, and in keeping with the small-town atmosphere, customers were never issued numbered claim checks when they brought in their clothing. Instead each person's name was written on a tag that was pinned to the garment. Once cleaned, the clothes were hung on a rack in alphabetical order. Ronda was expected to recognize each of the customers by name when they came into the store.

That was as easy for her as it would have been for her parents. She had been born and reared in Monroeville. Her daddy was from Burnt Corn, ten miles north, her mother from a family of twelve in nearby Peterman; both were active members of Eastwood Baptist Church. Before he had gone to work at a local manufacturing plant, Charles Morrison had driven a milk delivery truck, a job that made him a familiar face around town. And while Ronda did not actually know all 7,323 residents of Monroeville, she did know nearly all its white residents, either as friends or acquaintances or by name or family reputation. They accounted for sixty percent of the population. The remainder were blacks, and though whites and blacks intermingled daily at work and in the stores, the races lived largely segregated personal lives. Ronda knew few blacks, none well.

To an outsider Monroeville is unremarkable—just another off-the-interstate spot on the road map whose residents drive weatherbeaten pickups, turn to Heloise and Ann Landers respectively for household and moral guidance, and spend their Saturday mornings shopping at Wal-Mart. But the people who live in Monroeville are convinced that there is no finer place. On a map of Alabama the town sits isolated in the southwestern corner of the state, deep in the heart of its fertile Black Belt, two hours north of Mobile and about thirty miles west of the meandering Alabama River. The closest major road is Interstate 65, a divided four-lane highway that forms the spine of Alabama, linking the Gulf of Mexico to the state capital, Montgomery, and the state's two major northern cities, Birmingham and Huntsville. Travelers en route to Monroeville generally exit from I-65 at the Evergreen ramp and travel west on State Highway 84. The twenty-two-mile trip takes them past

Chapter 1

Ronda Reene Morrison was late. But then, she usually was. Customers at Jackson Cleaners expected to wait a few extra minutes on the Saturday mornings when it was Ronda's turn to open the store. One of her high school teachers had once chastised her for always being tardy. She promised to be on time the next morning, and she was. Just before the school buzzer sounded, Ronda zipped into her seat. Everyone stared. Her shirttail was out and she was holding her sneakers and socks in one hand and a can of hair spray and her brush in the other.

"I'm not late," she declared triumphantly, "but I really need to go to the bathroom and finish dressing!"

Even the teacher laughed. Ronda had a way of making people smile. Sometimes at school she would suck in her cheeks, pucker her lips, and blink her eyes. Her friends would swear she looked just like an old billy goat. Or she would crinkle her nose, squint, and snarl, transforming herself into one of the witches in *Macbeth*. Despite the faces she made, Ronda was beautiful. Naturally, that did not stop her from worrying about her looks. Was she too gangly at five feet, five inches? Were her vivid blue eyes, the envy of everyone else, too big and too pale? She called them bug eyes. And she fretted about her weight, even though it was only 120 pounds. She was particularly critical of what she called her hunker thighs. But her friends knew better. It really wasn't her athletic figure or the blond glint in her brown hair or her carefully chosen preppie clothes that made her special: It was her childlike innocence. She was the sort of teenager who felt sad whenever she saw a dead deer lying alongside the road; the sort who still enjoyed watching Walt Disney fairy tales; the sort who genuinely believed that deep down everyone was really a good person. Once Ronda's girlfriends told her that an unmarked sample tube of green toothpaste was a new brand of lipstick. "C'mon, Ronda," one dared, "put it on. It will turn red after you do that." Ronda had dabbed the green goop on her lips and waited expectantly for it to change. Only after her friends started giggling did she realize she was the butt of their joke. Ronda didn't get angry or run away embarrassed. She laughed at her own gullibility. At age eighteen, Ronda was, as an Alabama Circuit Court judge would later describe her, "a rose in the first flower of adulthood."

Exactly what happened at Jackson Cleaners in Monroeville, Alabama, on the morning of November 1, 1986, is a mystery. But this much is known. Shortly after nine o'clock, Ronda parked her gray Pontiac Sunbird, a gift from her parents, Charles and Bertha Morrison, under an old pecan tree growing next to the store and unlocked the front door of the building. Ronda had worked part-time at the cleaners for about a year, starting when she was still a high school senior. Now she was a freshman at Patrick Henry State Junior College, whose campus was less than three miles down the street the store was on.

Saturdays were always busy. Usually Randy Thomas, the young owner, was at the store to help, but he was spending the weekend with his parents in Tuscaloosa. It didn't worry Ronda to be alone. No one could remember the last time anyone had been robbed in Monroeville. A teenager might get nabbed shoplifting, a business might be burglarized at night, a vandal might break a store's windows, but a holdup at gunpoint on a Saturday morning was unthinkable—and especially at Jackson Cleaners. There was less than a hundred dollars in the register on Saturdays, and the shop's lobby faced out on the town's main thoroughfare. From her post at the waist-high counter, Ronda could glance through the large front windows and watch the traffic hurrying by. Occasionally a friend would honk a car horn and Ronda would wave.

The only excitement at the cleaners had occurred about one year earlier, when Ronda's close friend Lisa Odom had been working alone

one Saturday. A teenager had sauntered inside. Lisa didn't recognize him, so she asked what he wanted, but he just stood there. She suspected he was either high on marijuana or drunk. When he finally spoke he was friendly. He asked where she went to school and if working at the cleaners was fun. Then he began flirting. Lisa started to feel uneasy. She was a spunky, nationally ranked tennis player who was used to getting compliments and come-ons from boys, but this one was different. He was black. Lisa had just graduated from Monroe Academy, the private all-white high school formed by town parents in 1969 after the federal courts forced Alabama's public schools to integrate. Ronda went there too, and both girls felt uncomfortable around blacks. Lisa found herself wishing she hadn't worn shorts, though it was summer and hot.

"I really, really like white girls," the teenager announced abruptly.

Lisa could feel her face turning red. Luckily another customer came in and the youth hurried outside. After the customer left, he returned.

"Want some beer?" he asked.

"No."

"A joint?"

"You'd better leave before I call the cops."

"Now why ya wanna do that? Ain't done nothing."

He wasn't afraid. Lisa was. He seemed to sense it. Without warning he stepped behind the counter and boldly walked up to where she was sitting on a stool with her legs crossed. He reached down with his right hand and ran the tips of his black fingers along her white leg. She panicked. Pulling open a nearby drawer, she grabbed a pistol.

"Get out!" she ordered, pointing the handgun at his face.

He jumped back. "Be cool! I'm leaving! Be cool!"

As soon as he was gone Lisa telephoned the police. She was shaking. But later that night when she told Ronda, the two of them laughed about it. The gun hadn't been loaded. Randy Thomas was afraid to keep bullets in it because he said if he did Ronda and Lisa would end up shooting themselves.

Nothing that dramatic had ever happened to Ronda at the cleaners. But a few days before this November Saturday morning, she had felt jittery. A middle-aged black man had come into the store and asked to use the telephone. There were no pay phones close by. Ronda had said he could use the telephone mounted on the wall behind the counter, and he had walked over to it, stopping only a few feet from where she was standing. As he was dialing a number, the man had turned and stared at her, deliberately running his eyes from her head to her toes.

closed cotton gins, handpainted signs advertising Sunday-afternoon turkey shoots with a $25 prize to the best marksman, smoke-blackened roadside barbecue stands offering plates of sticky ribs and steaming collard greens for only $2.99, and modest farmhouses guarded by fat dogs sunning themselves out front. Much of the blacktop is edged by towering pines, and it is not uncommon for motorists to get stuck behind mud-caked and badly dented logging trucks. Semitrailers like these emerge from deep-rutted paths cut into the dense woods. The trucks plod along the highway, pulling freshly cut logs chained together and stacked like gigantic toothpicks on open steel-ribbed carts. Timber and cotton are Monroe County's cash crops and have made some rich. But not many.

A stoplight watches over the intersection of State Highway 84 and State Highway 21, the main northern route into Monroeville. As the highway enters the city limits, its name changes to South Alabama Avenue and it narrows into a winding street that follows the same path horses and wagons once used. Like all roads that enter Monroeville, it leads directly to the town square.

Monroeville is a pretty town. The southern edge is bounded by acres of cotton and corn, and when bird hunting season opens men and boys walk with their shotguns and bird dogs through the fields, occasionally flushing a covey of quail or pheasant. The northern edge of town rises amid gentle hills covered with poplar, pine, oak, and pecan trees. In 1832 Monroeville was declared the county seat of Monroe County, named after President James Monroe, and in keeping with its status, a county courthouse was erected in the center of the town square. Traffic moves counterclockwise around this quiet judicial island with its century-old shade trees, overgrown grass, park benches, and monument to war veterans.

Monroeville actually has two courthouses. The "new" courthouse, built in 1963, is a two-story, flat-roofed rectangular structure designed for function, not beauty. It houses various county officials, as well as a small courtroom. The "old" courthouse built next door is now a museum. Constructed of red brick and topped by a grand dome and a white tower with a black-faced clock, the courthouse reigns as the community's most famous landmark. In the summer tourists occasionally come to see the structure because it was the model for the courthouse in *To Kill a Mockingbird*, the 1962 movie starring Gregory Peck, which was based on Harper Lee's Pulitzer Prize–winning novel of the same name. Harper Lee was born in Monroeville, and though the characters in her novel live in the fictional town of Maycomb, Alabama, everyone acknowledges that she was describing her own hometown.

Lee's novel was not well received locally when it was first published. In it a black man is falsely accused of raping a white woman. No physical evidence links him to the crime; there is no proof the woman was raped. There are hints that she is lying and he is innocent. One brave white lawyer defends the black man, but the accused is found guilty and is killed. Lee set her story in the 1930s, but its depiction of racism in the town still offended many. It wasn't until after the novel became an American classic that the community began not only to embrace it but also to capitalize on it. The chamber of commerce now proudly advertises Monroeville's literary connection on interstate billboards, beckoning motorists to visit the "actual" site of the *Mockingbird* town.

Some of Monroeville's streets have not changed much from the way they were described in Lee's novel. While there are a few majestic houses off the town square, most homes are modest white frame 1950s structures, two stories tall, nearly all with enclosed front porches. They face each other across wide streets and spacious green yards bordered with gray concrete sidewalks made bumpy by the roots of towering elms and oaks.

There is another section of Monroeville known as Clausell, although it is always described as if it were a separate town. This is the black neighborhood. A string of badly weathered shotgun shacks sits at its entrance. Some have cracked or missing windows, the holes patched with cardboard. Others have front porches propped up on concrete blocks. The yards are barren of grass, filled with accumulations of junked cars, discarded bottles, broken bicycles, overgrown weeds. A handful of nicer, well-kept houses can be found farther into Clausell, which is named after one of the town's most prominent black families. These homes are owned by better-off blacks: the black undertaker, the preacher. Clausell once had its own downtown and segregated schools, but integration destroyed the need for blacks-only businesses and left the school buildings to vandals.

Ronda, Lisa, and the other MAGs (Monroe Academy Girls) avoided Clausell. For them it was a scary place, to be entered only on a dare. Blacks remained at the bottom of Monroeville's social order. You were polite to them, but they were never your friends.

Charles and Bertha Morrison had sheltered their daughter from many of the harsher aspects of Southern life, and because of that she saw Monroeville with an uncritical eye. To her it was a happy place where teenagers drove endlessly up and down South Alabama Avenue on Friday nights waving at one another. The weekly *Monroe Journal* published photographs of beaming white and black children on their birthdays without charge until they turned six. The Gideons continued to give away little red copies of the Holy Bible to all sixth-graders in the public schools, despite federal laws that ban such practices. No one chose to complain. It wasn't uncommon to see families bowing their heads in prayer before eating in public restaurants. Life followed a routine: work, hunting, school, church, interrupted only by the rivalry sparked by the annual Alabama-Auburn university football game. While some teens were quick to describe life in Monroeville as monotonous, Ronda told her friends she enjoyed the sameness. There was a comfortable feeling that came from knowing your neighbors, their pasts, their places in the community and your own. In one of her freshman classes Ronda had been asked to write an essay about her hometown. "I enjoy living in Monroeville because it is such a crime free city and people are able to go about their business without fear," she had written. "It is a place where teens can gather at night to visit until midnight and still feel safe walking home."

Some of Ronda's black classmates had criticized her essay, and this had upset her. She had always attended all-white schools until she had enrolled at the junior college. Two blacks complained that she was offering a Pollyanna view of Monroeville. They said it was a racist place where blacks were routinely oppressed. Ronda argued with them. Monroeville was only two hours by car from Montgomery, the birthplace of the civil rights movement, where Rosa Parks had refused to give up her seat or move to the back of a public bus. Yet during the 1960s, when Martin Luther King, Jr., was organizing a bus boycott and demonstrators were being beaten on "Bloody Sunday" at the Edmund Pettus Bridge in Selma, life in Monroeville had continued undisturbed. Not one angry black fist had been raised, not a single demonstration held. The community prided itself on the fact that no blacks had ever protested or marched outside the courthouse in anger. Clearly whites and blacks in town got along well. The black students replied that Monroeville had slumbered through the turbulent 1960s and because of that lagged far behind other integrated communities. There were no black clerks in Monroeville's banks, they complained; no blacks were ever hired as receptionists at local motels. Why did all the best jobs go to whites? Why were the best houses in town owned by whites, the most important community posts held by whites? Not much had changed, they argued, since Tom Robinson, the fictional black character in Harper Lee's novel, had been framed for rape based entirely on the lies of one white woman.

Ronda had been so upset by these accusations that she had spoken to her mother about them later that same night. Bertha had dismissed the disgruntled black students as troublemakers. If Monroeville was such a horrible place, why didn't they move?

By ten o'clock on November 1, several customers had come and gone at Jackson Cleaners. There was little time for Ronda to daydream or stare out the front window at passing friends. She spent her first hour at work greeting customers and darting into the back room to retrieve clean clothes. There was absolutely no hint of what the next hour would bring, no clue that after this particular Saturday morning, no one in Monroeville, black or white, would feel quite the same about their hometown or their own fate ever again.

Chapter 2

C'mon, Mama," Lee whined. "We got to go—now!"

No matter how hard she tried, Jerrie Sue Dunning couldn't seem to get started on her Saturday-morning errands until after ten o'clock. Today was particularly difficult because her husband was away on a business trip and fifteen-year-old Lee needed to get to the Monroeville Public Library before it closed at noon. She had a term paper due on Monday and she hadn't even started doing research. Dunning wanted to stop at the bank and at Jackson Cleaners, and she figured Lee would need at least an hour at the library. Her daughter was right. They needed to hurry. Dunning pushed four-year-old Beth, her other child, toward the door as Lee dashed outside, car keys already in hand. Now that Lee had her learner's permit, she expected to drive everywhere in town.

"Let's go to the bank first," Dunning said as soon as everyone was settled in the car, "and then Jackson Cleaners and then the library."

"Mama," Lee replied, "we got to get to the library before it closes at twelve!" She nodded toward the clock in the dash. It read 10:30.

"We'll have time," said Dunning. Although she did not elaborate, she knew the clock in the car was set six minutes fast. She thought it helped her get places on time. "We'll use the drive-through."

At the bank Dunning slipped her deposit slip and check into the window, but the teller sent both back. Dunning was trying to put her money into a special account that had been a temporary promotional offer. The last day for such deposits had been the day before. Dunning ordered Lee to park the car. She was going inside to complain. "This is not some big impersonal city, for goodness' sake! I'm sure they can make an exception." Lee groaned but did as she was told. A few minutes later Dunning returned to the car still holding the deposit slip and uncashed check.

"Let's get to the cleaners," she snapped. The clock in the dash read 10:46.

Florence Mason could feel the Holy Ghost inside her, and she couldn't help being happy. For three days she had been praising Jesus inside a big-top tent pitched in a grassy field outside Gulf Shores, an Alabama coastal town three hours away by car from Monroeville. Mason was twenty-three years old, but she joked that her real date of birth was only four years earlier. That was when she had been born again. Her rebirth had not been some mundane event. It had come like a jolt of lightning, surging through her with a hundred-thousand-volt intensity that she was certain had burned away her sins.

Mason had felt so enraptured at the revival that she hadn't wanted to leave it on Friday, and it was well after midnight when she finally returned to Frisco City, a tiny town just south of Monroeville. She had taken her five-month-old niece to the revival, and though the child had fallen asleep during the long ride home, she still was groggy on Saturday morning. It was after ten o'clock by the time Mason and the baby were finally ready to leave the house. Mason needed to pick up a dress at Jackson Cleaners and bring the baby back to her parents. As she rode north toward Monroeville, she hummed a gospel song. Because she didn't own a wristwatch, she would later be unsure exactly when she had reached the outskirts of town, but she would estimate that it was around ten-forty.

Coy Stacey tightened the tiny chrome ring on the lip of the kitchen faucet and turned on the water. Then he switched it off. The faucet did not drip. The *plop-plop-plop* he had heard Friday night was gone. Now that the leaky spigot was repaired, he had only one more Saturday-morning chore to perform. He needed to drop off his dirty laundry at Jackson Cleaners.

Stacey lived about seven miles southeast of town, in Excel, a community of three hundred fifty. He'd once served a term as mayor there. He glanced at his watch. If he left for the cleaners immediately, he could drop off his laundry and still make it over to the old carpet shop in Excel by eleven o'clock, which was when he and several other retired men were scheduled to begin their Saturday-morning domino game. He didn't want to be late. His buddies would start without him, and he'd have to sit around until someone gave up a seat at the table. Stacey gathered up his clothes. It was 10:42.

Jackson Cleaners occupied a one-story rectangular building made of concrete blocks painted a drab brown. Although the store was located on South Alabama Avenue, Monroeville's busiest thoroughfare, it was set apart from other businesses on the street. The commercial lots on either side of it were vacant, and at least fifty yards separated it from its closest neighbor. The front of the building, which looked east, was faced with brown bricks and had a pitched roof overhang made of dark wood shingles. This facade made the building look taller than it actually was and gave it a much-needed touch of flair.

Originally the owner had intended to rent space to two stores. Because of this, there were two separate front doors, built side by side in the center of the storefront, with plate glass windows on each side. But no tenant had ever been found to share the building with the cleaners so both front doors led into its lobby in the southeast half of the building. There was no door into the northeast half. It was used for storage. A passerby could look through the windows on the left of the front doors and see into the lobby, but the windows on the right were covered with straw blinds that made it impossible to peek inside. There was no sidewalk, and so many customers had parked in front of the cleaners over the years that they had killed the grass, packed down the dirt, and created an unplanned curving driveway.

The interior of the building was spartan. The lobby of the store was framed by two walls, one running along the back of the lobby parallel to the front of the building and the other at right angles to it. This wall separated the lobby from the northeast side of the building, and it was covered with cheap wood paneling. The southwest section of the building, directly behind the lobby, was where clean clothing was hung on metal piping suspended from the ceiling. Several hundred garments could be stored on this piping, which snaked its way across the room. The northwest section contained commercial washers, dryers, pressing tables, and other cleaning equipment. Unclaimed clothes were stored on metal racks in the northeast corner along with cardboard boxes filled with forgotten odds-and-ends.

When Jerrie Sue Dunning arrived the door to the store was open, the lobby empty.

"Hello," she called, "is anyone here?"

Silence.

"Hello!" she said, more loudly this time.

Again no response.

Dunning had assumed that it would take only a few minutes to drop off her laundry. Where was the clerk? She glanced around. There was a worn wicker chair near the front corner of the lobby, with old magazines tossed on its seat, and near it, against the south exterior wall, stood a bright red-and-white Coca-Cola vending machine. The floor was smooth concrete, painted dark brown. There were no draperies, no rugs, no plants. Three counters, with spaces between them, ran along the length of the lobby, separating the patrons from the employees. Dunning dropped her bundle of clothes onto the dull orange Formica top. A cash register sat on the adjacent counter. Next to it lay a notepad, a cigar box filled with small white tags and straight pins, a white plastic cup jammed with cheap ballpoint pens and pencils with chewed pink eraser tops, and a chrome bell with a button on top.

Dunning rang the bell twice. No one responded.

Against the left wall behind the counter stood a metal chair and a gray desk. A white electric clock, the square kind popular in kitchens in the 1950s, hung above the desk; its white cord had a brown stain on it where it had been scorched during an electrical short but had been repaired—a testament to the frugality of the store's owner.

"Hello!" Dunning called again. "Is anyone here?"

There was no reply.

The only decoration in the entire place was a large black-and-white calendar tacked on the wall directly behind the counter where Dunning had set down her clothes. It advertised a local bank and displayed a lithograph showing two large deer in a forest, both with heads raised as if anticipating danger. A black rotary-dial wall telephone and a chalkboard for messages hung near it. Dunning looked at the board. There were no notes on it.

"Hello!" she called out, now irritated. "Is anyone there?"

Dunning turned around and looked through the front windows at her daughters waiting in the car. As soon as Lee spotted her, the teenager began moving her mouth in silent exaggerated speech. Dunning recognized the words: *"Let's go."* She replied in similar fashion: *"I can't just leave my clothes here."*

Dunning turned back around. There was a double-width doorway cut into the lobby's wall. It led into the southwest rear of the building. It was dark back there, but from where Dunning was standing she could make out several women's dresses and men's shirts each hanging in clear plastic bags from the piping overhead. As she peered through the doorway, a beam of light caught her attention. She guessed correctly that it was coming from under the doorway of an employee bathroom at the rear of the building, beyond the hanging clothes. Maybe the clerk was using it and was too embarrassed to reply.

"Hello!" she yelled. "Are you back there?"

Dunning decided that she would simply write her name on a tag and leave it with her clothing for the clerk. She began to reach for one of the white slips of paper near the cash register, then jerked her hand back. The drawer of the cash register was open. Her eyes darted around the room as she quickly reviewed the scene. No clerk. No movement. No response to her calls. An open cash register. Had there been a robbery here? Was the thief hiding in the back room? Just then Dunning heard the front door opening behind her. Florence Mason walked in. She was carrying her niece in her arms. Dunning didn't recognize her. Mason was black.

"No one seems to be here," Dunning said, trying to sound calm. "I've called out several times but no one answers." She looked at the cash register, and Mason, following the direction of her eyes, also noticed the open drawer.

"Maybe we should go and look in the back room?" Dunning suggested halfheartedly.

Mason didn't move.

Coy Stacey came inside. His arms were full of clothes. "Good morning, Mrs. Dunning," he said cheerfully. He didn't know Mason, but he nodded politely to her.

"Coy, I've been here five minutes and no one answers!" Dunning said. "I think something is wrong!"

"Well, let's see if I can get someone," he replied confidently. He stepped behind the counter, walking to the doorway that opened into the back room. "Anyone home?" he called. He too noticed the light coming from under the bathroom door. "Maybe she's in the bathroom and just wants us to wait," he said to Dunning and Mason, keeping his voice low.

The threesome stood about awkwardly for another minute or so; then Stacey called out again, "Hello? You back there?" When there was still no response, he asked if either of the women had seen an employee's car parked outside. "Maybe she's off running an errand," he explained. The women followed him out the front door, Mason instinctively waiting for the two whites to go first. They found Ronda's Pontiac parked at the side of the building. When they returned to the lobby, Dunning mentioned the open cash register drawer. Stacey did not say anything, but as soon as he looked at the register, he suspected the cleaners had been robbed and assumed the clerk had been tied up, gagged, and left in the bathroom. Still, he was reluctant to telephone the police. He didn't want to look like a fool if the clerk was simply running an errand.

"Let's look around back there," he suggested, nodding toward the back room. As they moved toward the doorway behind the counter, the telephone rang. Dunning started to reach for it, then caught herself. Leaning down, she picked a piece of paper out of the trash can and used it to lift the receiver.

"Hello?"

"Is the girl there?" It was a man's voice.

"No. The only people here right now are customers and we don't know where the girl is who works here. You'll have to call back."

The caller hung up.

Stacey led the women through the hanging clothes toward the bathroom door. He gently tapped on it.

"Hello? Is anyone in there?"

Hearing no reply, he tested the knob. The door was unlocked. He began to push inward and suddenly felt something or someone pushing back. Lowering his shoulder, he gave the door a shove. There was a loud crunch, and when he peeked inside, Stacey had pinned a bag of trash against the wall. A naked bulb dangled from the bathroom ceiling. There was no one inside.

"Let's keep looking," he suggested. They turned to the right and walked slowly toward the northwest corner, where the various pieces of cleaning equipment sat. Every few seconds Dunning called out, "Is anyone here?"

By now at least ten minutes had passed since they had met in the lobby. At this point one of them realized that they had not searched the entire building. They had checked the lobby and the southwest and northwest areas, but not the northeast corner, at the front of the building. Stacey went first. Narrow beams of sunshine poked through the tears in the straw blinds covering the front windows. The space was crowded with rows of unclaimed clothes hung on chin-high racks made of metal pipe. Used cardboard boxes were stacked haphazardly amid the clothing. As they stepped forward Mason screamed out, "Here she is!"

Stacey and Dunning raced to her side. A tennis shoe was sticking out from under a rack. Bending down, Stacey could tell that it was a young girl, lying on her stomach. Her face was turned away from him, so he could not see who she was. She was not tied or gagged. There was no blood, but she was not moving.

"Call 911!" Stacey told Dunning, but she was already on her way outside.

"I'm going to get Dr. Lee!" Dunning yelled. Lee was a dentist whose office was across the street. She thought he might know CPR. Lee had just pulled into the parking lot and was stepping from his car when Dunning reached him. She opened her mouth, but nothing came out. She grabbed his arm, began to tug, and then found her voice: "Come! Quick!"

Back inside, Stacey was telephoning the Monroeville police department. "We need an ambulance and police at Jackson Cleaners," he reported, saying no more in case people were listening to police scanners. He didn't want to cause a panic or attract sightseers. Dunning and Lee hurried back inside. Stacey led the dentist to the body. Bending down, Lee felt for a pulse, then quietly nodded to Stacey, who understood the message: The girl was dead.

Lieutenant Woodrow Ikner had been on his way home for lunch when Stacey's call had come through the police switchboard. Ikner arrived at the cleaners at 11:12 A.M. William Gibson and Chuck Sadhue, two Monroe County sheriff's deputies, came rushing inside moments later. They had been less than two hundred yards from the store when the police dispatcher had asked for backup. Many of the town's police officers and sheriff's deputies got their uniforms cleaned at Jackson's. All three men knew the clerks there.

Stacey recognized Ikner. He had taught the police officer in Sunday school when Ikner had been just a boy. "She's back here, Woodrow," Stacey said. Just as Lee had done, Ikner felt for a pulse. Meanwhile Gibson and Sadhue located a light switch and began moving the racks of clothing. Ikner was the first to see the dead girl's face. He knew Ronda.

His son had been in her graduating class at Monroe Academy. He was speechless.

"Oh my God!" Gibson gasped. "What the . . ." His voice trailed off. Gibson's cousin Lynn was one of Ronda's closest girlfriends. He knew that the night before, Lynn and Ronda had gone together to the last Monroe Academy football game of the season.

Deputy Sadhue had been at the game too, and volunteered that he had seen the two girls together. "I was just talking to Ronda last night," Sadhue announced. "She was so happy."

Speaking into his two-way radio, Ikner told the dispatcher to call Monroeville Police Chief Bill Dailey and County Coroner Farrish Manning. He was careful not to tell the dispatcher why, but anyone listening to a police scanner quickly understood that something out of the ordinary was happening. Within ten minutes a crowd had gathered. A few people had stopped to pick up their clothing; others had been attracted by the police cars parked outside the cleaners. Several people actually came inside and looked at Ronda's body still lying facedown on the floor. Deputies Gibson and Sadhue decided to seal off the crime scene. They ordered the onlookers to leave and unrolled a four-inch-wide bright yellow tape that read POLICE LINE—DO NOT CROSS, which they stretched outside the front door. Gibson got his camera from the trunk of his police cruiser but noticed that he had only ten shots left on the roll of film. There was a grocery store less than a mile away, but he didn't want to leave to buy more film. Luckily Steve Stewart, the editor of *The Monroe Journal*, came running up with a camera and volunteered to take pictures for the police.

By this time a crew of paramedics from the hospital had arrived, but Ikner asked them not to touch Ronda until Stewart had taken photographs. The unnerved editor took four flash pictures and then realized that he hadn't set the shutter speed on his camera properly. The pictures were useless. He quickly made the correction and took two more shots before the crew rolled the body over.

When Ronda was turned faceup, everyone became silent. Not until then could they have known that her blouse had been unbuttoned, her bra had been pushed off her breasts, and her jeans had been unzipped.

Tears formed in Gibson's eyes. He stepped over to the lobby to regain his composure. Other officers were arriving. Gibson couldn't believe Ronda was dead. "I was just teasing her yesterday about her pet poodle, Tina," he said to no one in particular. Despite all that her disheveled clothing implied, it was her face that had gotten to him. The expression

Chapter 1

Ronda Reene Morrison was late. But then, she usually was. Customers at Jackson Cleaners expected to wait a few extra minutes on the Saturday mornings when it was Ronda's turn to open the store. One of her high school teachers had once chastised her for always being tardy. She promised to be on time the next morning, and she was. Just before the school buzzer sounded, Ronda zipped into her seat. Everyone stared. Her shirttail was out and she was holding her sneakers and socks in one hand and a can of hair spray and her brush in the other.

"I'm not late," she declared triumphantly, "but I really need to go to the bathroom and finish dressing!"

Even the teacher laughed. Ronda had a way of making people smile. Sometimes at school she would suck in her cheeks, pucker her lips, and blink her eyes. Her friends would swear she looked just like an old billy goat. Or she would crinkle her nose, squint, and snarl, transforming herself into one of the witches in *Macbeth*. Despite the faces she made, Ronda was beautiful. Naturally, that did not stop her from worrying about her looks. Was she too gangly at five feet, five inches? Were her vivid blue eyes, the envy of everyone else, too big and too pale? She called them bug eyes. And she fretted about her weight, even though it was only 120 pounds. She was particularly critical of what she called her hunker thighs. But her friends knew better. It really wasn't her athletic figure or the blond glint in her brown hair or her carefully chosen preppie clothes that made her special: It was her childlike innocence. She was the sort of teenager who felt sad whenever she saw a dead deer lying alongside the road; the sort who still enjoyed watching Walt Disney fairy tales; the sort who genuinely believed that deep down everyone was really a good person. Once Ronda's girlfriends told her that an unmarked sample tube of green toothpaste was a new brand of lipstick. "C'mon, Ronda," one dared, "put it on. It will turn red after you do that." Ronda had dabbed the green goop on her lips and waited expectantly for it to change. Only after her friends started giggling did she realize she was the butt of their joke. Ronda didn't get angry or run away embarrassed. She laughed at her own gullibility. At age eighteen, Ronda was, as an Alabama Circuit Court judge would later describe her, "a rose in the first flower of adulthood."

Exactly what happened at Jackson Cleaners in Monroeville, Alabama, on the morning of November 1, 1986, is a mystery. But this much is known. Shortly after nine o'clock, Ronda parked her gray Pontiac Sunbird, a gift from her parents, Charles and Bertha Morrison, under an old pecan tree growing next to the store and unlocked the front door of the building. Ronda had worked part-time at the cleaners for about a year, starting when she was still a high school senior. Now she was a freshman at Patrick Henry State Junior College, whose campus was less than three miles down the street the store was on.

Saturdays were always busy. Usually Randy Thomas, the young owner, was at the store to help, but he was spending the weekend with his parents in Tuscaloosa. It didn't worry Ronda to be alone. No one could remember the last time anyone had been robbed in Monroeville. A teenager might get nabbed shoplifting, a business might be burglarized at night, a vandal might break a store's windows, but a holdup at gunpoint on a Saturday morning was unthinkable—and especially at Jackson Cleaners. There was less than a hundred dollars in the register on Saturdays, and the shop's lobby faced out on the town's main thoroughfare. From her post at the waist-high counter, Ronda could glance through the large front windows and watch the traffic hurrying by. Occasionally a friend would honk a car horn and Ronda would wave.

The only excitement at the cleaners had occurred about one year earlier, when Ronda's close friend Lisa Odom had been working alone

one Saturday. A teenager had sauntered inside. Lisa didn't recognize him, so she asked what he wanted, but he just stood there. She suspected he was either high on marijuana or drunk. When he finally spoke he was friendly. He asked where she went to school and if working at the cleaners was fun. Then he began flirting. Lisa started to feel uneasy. She was a spunky, nationally ranked tennis player who was used to getting compliments and come-ons from boys, but this one was different. He was black. Lisa had just graduated from Monroe Academy, the private all-white high school formed by town parents in 1969 after the federal courts forced Alabama's public schools to integrate. Ronda went there too, and both girls felt uncomfortable around blacks. Lisa found herself wishing she hadn't worn shorts, though it was summer and hot.

"I really, really like white girls," the teenager announced abruptly.

Lisa could feel her face turning red. Luckily another customer came in and the youth hurried outside. After the customer left, he returned.

"Want some beer?" he asked.

"No."

"A joint?"

"You'd better leave before I call the cops."

"Now why ya wanna do that? Ain't done nothing."

He wasn't afraid. Lisa was. He seemed to sense it. Without warning he stepped behind the counter and boldly walked up to where she was sitting on a stool with her legs crossed. He reached down with his right hand and ran the tips of his black fingers along her white leg. She panicked. Pulling open a nearby drawer, she grabbed a pistol.

"Get out!" she ordered, pointing the handgun at his face.

He jumped back. "Be cool! I'm leaving! Be cool!"

As soon as he was gone Lisa telephoned the police. She was shaking. But later that night when she told Ronda, the two of them laughed about it. The gun hadn't been loaded. Randy Thomas was afraid to keep bullets in it because he said if he did Ronda and Lisa would end up shooting themselves.

Nothing that dramatic had ever happened to Ronda at the cleaners. But a few days before this November Saturday morning, she had felt jittery. A middle-aged black man had come into the store and asked to use the telephone. There were no pay phones close by. Ronda had said he could use the telephone mounted on the wall behind the counter, and he had walked over to it, stopping only a few feet from where she was standing. As he was dialing a number, the man had turned and stared at her, deliberately running his eyes from her head to her toes.

Then he had grinned. Embarrassed, she had turned away. That night Ronda had mentioned to her mother what the black man had done, and Bertha had warned her daughter about being too friendly to strangers.

Unlike the modern stores in Mobile, Jackson Cleaners had no computerized system that kept track of each customer's laundry. There was no motorized chain that carried clean clothes along a track to the front of the store at the push of a button. Fetching clothes from the back workroom was Ronda's job, and in keeping with the small-town atmosphere, customers were never issued numbered claim checks when they brought in their clothing. Instead each person's name was written on a tag that was pinned to the garment. Once cleaned, the clothes were hung on a rack in alphabetical order. Ronda was expected to recognize each of the customers by name when they came into the store.

That was as easy for her as it would have been for her parents. She had been born and reared in Monroeville. Her daddy was from Burnt Corn, ten miles north, her mother from a family of twelve in nearby Peterman; both were active members of Eastwood Baptist Church. Before he had gone to work at a local manufacturing plant, Charles Morrison had driven a milk delivery truck, a job that made him a familiar face around town. And while Ronda did not actually know all 7,323 residents of Monroeville, she did know nearly all its white residents, either as friends or acquaintances or by name or family reputation. They accounted for sixty percent of the population. The remainder were blacks, and though whites and blacks intermingled daily at work and in the stores, the races lived largely segregated personal lives. Ronda knew few blacks, none well.

To an outsider Monroeville is unremarkable—just another off-the-interstate spot on the road map whose residents drive weatherbeaten pickups, turn to Heloise and Ann Landers respectively for household and moral guidance, and spend their Saturday mornings shopping at Wal-Mart. But the people who live in Monroeville are convinced that there is no finer place. On a map of Alabama the town sits isolated in the southwestern corner of the state, deep in the heart of its fertile Black Belt, two hours north of Mobile and about thirty miles west of the meandering Alabama River. The closest major road is Interstate 65, a divided four-lane highway that forms the spine of Alabama, linking the Gulf of Mexico to the state capital, Montgomery, and the state's two major northern cities, Birmingham and Huntsville. Travelers en route to Monroeville generally exit from I-65 at the Evergreen ramp and travel west on State Highway 84. The twenty-two-mile trip takes them past closed cotton gins, handpainted signs advertising Sunday-afternoon turkey shoots with a $25 prize to the best marksman, smoke-blackened roadside barbecue stands offering plates of sticky ribs and steaming collard greens for only $2.99, and modest farmhouses guarded by fat dogs sunning themselves out front. Much of the blacktop is edged by towering pines, and it is not uncommon for motorists to get stuck behind mud-caked and badly dented logging trucks. Semitrailers like these emerge from deep-rutted paths cut into the dense woods. The trucks plod along the highway, pulling freshly cut logs chained together and stacked like gigantic toothpicks on open steel-ribbed carts. Timber and cotton are Monroe County's cash crops and have made some rich. But not many.

A stoplight watches over the intersection of State Highway 84 and State Highway 21, the main northern route into Monroeville. As the highway enters the city limits, its name changes to South Alabama Avenue and it narrows into a winding street that follows the same path horses and wagons once used. Like all roads that enter Monroeville, it leads directly to the town square.

Monroeville is a pretty town. The southern edge is bounded by acres of cotton and corn, and when bird hunting season opens men and boys walk with their shotguns and bird dogs through the fields, occasionally flushing a covey of quail or pheasant. The northern edge of town rises amid gentle hills covered with poplar, pine, oak, and pecan trees. In 1832 Monroeville was declared the county seat of Monroe County, named after President James Monroe, and in keeping with its status, a county courthouse was erected in the center of the town square. Traffic moves counterclockwise around this quiet judicial island with its century-old shade trees, overgrown grass, park benches, and monument to war veterans.

Monroeville actually has two courthouses. The "new" courthouse, built in 1963, is a two-story, flat-roofed rectangular structure designed for function, not beauty. It houses various county officials, as well as a small courtroom. The "old" courthouse built next door is now a museum. Constructed of red brick and topped by a grand dome and a white tower with a black-faced clock, the courthouse reigns as the community's most famous landmark. In the summer tourists occasionally come to see the structure because it was the model for the courthouse in *To Kill a Mockingbird*, the 1962 movie starring Gregory Peck, which was based on Harper Lee's Pulitzer Prize–winning novel of the same name. Harper Lee was born in Monroeville, and though the characters in her novel live in the fictional town of Maycomb, Alabama, everyone acknowledges that she was describing her own hometown.

Lee's novel was not well received locally when it was first published. In it a black man is falsely accused of raping a white woman. No physical evidence links him to the crime; there is no proof the woman was raped. There are hints that she is lying and he is innocent. One brave white lawyer defends the black man, but the accused is found guilty and is killed. Lee set her story in the 1930s, but its depiction of racism in the town still offended many. It wasn't until after the novel became an American classic that the community began not only to embrace it but also to capitalize on it. The chamber of commerce now proudly advertises Monroeville's literary connection on interstate billboards, beckoning motorists to visit the "actual" site of the *Mockingbird* town.

Some of Monroeville's streets have not changed much from the way they were described in Lee's novel. While there are a few majestic houses off the town square, most homes are modest white frame 1950s structures, two stories tall, nearly all with enclosed front porches. They face each other across wide streets and spacious green yards bordered with gray concrete sidewalks made bumpy by the roots of towering elms and oaks.

There is another section of Monroeville known as Clausell, although it is always described as if it were a separate town. This is the black neighborhood. A string of badly weathered shotgun shacks sits at its entrance. Some have cracked or missing windows, the holes patched with cardboard. Others have front porches propped up on concrete blocks. The yards are barren of grass, filled with accumulations of junked cars, discarded bottles, broken bicycles, overgrown weeds. A handful of nicer, well-kept houses can be found farther into Clausell, which is named after one of the town's most prominent black families. These homes are owned by better-off blacks: the black undertaker, the preacher. Clausell once had its own downtown and segregated schools, but integration destroyed the need for blacks-only businesses and left the school buildings to vandals.

Ronda, Lisa, and the other MAGs (Monroe Academy Girls) avoided Clausell. For them it was a scary place, to be entered only on a dare. Blacks remained at the bottom of Monroeville's social order. You were polite to them, but they were never your friends.

Charles and Bertha Morrison had sheltered their daughter from many of the harsher aspects of Southern life, and because of that she saw Monroeville with an uncritical eye. To her it was a happy place where teenagers drove endlessly up and down South Alabama Avenue on Friday nights waving at one another. The weekly *Monroe Journal* published photographs of beaming white and black children on their birthdays without charge until they turned six. The Gideons continued to give away little red copies of the Holy Bible to all sixth-graders in the public schools, despite federal laws that ban such practices. No one chose to complain. It wasn't uncommon to see families bowing their heads in prayer before eating in public restaurants. Life followed a routine: work, hunting, school, church, interrupted only by the rivalry sparked by the annual Alabama-Auburn university football game. While some teens were quick to describe life in Monroeville as monotonous, Ronda told her friends she enjoyed the sameness. There was a comfortable feeling that came from knowing your neighbors, their pasts, their places in the community and your own. In one of her freshman classes Ronda had been asked to write an essay about her hometown. "I enjoy living in Monroeville because it is such a crime free city and people are able to go about their business without fear," she had written. "It is a place where teens can gather at night to visit until midnight and still feel safe walking home."

Some of Ronda's black classmates had criticized her essay, and this had upset her. She had always attended all-white schools until she had enrolled at the junior college. Two blacks complained that she was offering a Pollyanna view of Monroeville. They said it was a racist place where blacks were routinely oppressed. Ronda argued with them. Monroeville was only two hours by car from Montgomery, the birthplace of the civil rights movement, where Rosa Parks had refused to give up her seat or move to the back of a public bus. Yet during the 1960s, when Martin Luther King, Jr., was organizing a bus boycott and demonstrators were being beaten on "Bloody Sunday" at the Edmund Pettus Bridge in Selma, life in Monroeville had continued undisturbed. Not one angry black fist had been raised, not a single demonstration held. The community prided itself on the fact that no blacks had ever protested or marched outside the courthouse in anger. Clearly whites and blacks in town got along well. The black students replied that Monroeville had slumbered through the turbulent 1960s and because of that lagged far behind other integrated communities. There were no black clerks in Monroeville's banks, they complained; no blacks were ever hired as receptionists at local motels. Why did all the best jobs go to whites? Why were the best houses in town owned by whites, the most important community posts held by whites? Not much had changed, they argued, since Tom Robinson, the fictional black character in Harper Lee's novel, had been framed for rape based entirely on the lies of one white woman.

Ronda had been so upset by these accusations that she had spoken to her mother about them later that same night. Bertha had dismissed the disgruntled black students as troublemakers. If Monroeville was such a horrible place, why didn't they move?

By ten o'clock on November 1, several customers had come and gone at Jackson Cleaners. There was little time for Ronda to daydream or stare out the front window at passing friends. She spent her first hour at work greeting customers and darting into the back room to retrieve clean clothes. There was absolutely no hint of what the next hour would bring, no clue that after this particular Saturday morning, no one in Monroeville, black or white, would feel quite the same about their hometown or their own fate ever again.

Chapter 2

C'mon, Mama," Lee whined. "We got to go—now!"

No matter how hard she tried, Jerrie Sue Dunning couldn't seem to get started on her Saturday-morning errands until after ten o'clock. Today was particularly difficult because her husband was away on a business trip and fifteen-year-old Lee needed to get to the Monroeville Public Library before it closed at noon. She had a term paper due on Monday and she hadn't even started doing research. Dunning wanted to stop at the bank and at Jackson Cleaners, and she figured Lee would need at least an hour at the library. Her daughter was right. They needed to hurry. Dunning pushed four-year-old Beth, her other child, toward the door as Lee dashed outside, car keys already in hand. Now that Lee had her learner's permit, she expected to drive everywhere in town.

"Let's go to the bank first," Dunning said as soon as everyone was settled in the car, "and then Jackson Cleaners and then the library."

"Mama," Lee replied, "we got to get to the library before it closes at twelve!" She nodded toward the clock in the dash. It read 10:30.

"We'll have time," said Dunning. Although she did not elaborate, she knew the clock in the car was set six minutes fast. She thought it helped her get places on time. "We'll use the drive-through."

At the bank Dunning slipped her deposit slip and check into the window, but the teller sent both back. Dunning was trying to put her money into a special account that had been a temporary promotional offer. The last day for such deposits had been the day before. Dunning ordered Lee to park the car. She was going inside to complain. "This is not some big impersonal city, for goodness' sake! I'm sure they can make an exception." Lee groaned but did as she was told. A few minutes later Dunning returned to the car still holding the deposit slip and uncashed check.

"Let's get to the cleaners," she snapped. The clock in the dash read 10:46.

Florence Mason could feel the Holy Ghost inside her, and she couldn't help being happy. For three days she had been praising Jesus inside a big-top tent pitched in a grassy field outside Gulf Shores, an Alabama coastal town three hours away by car from Monroeville. Mason was twenty-three years old, but she joked that her real date of birth was only four years earlier. That was when she had been born again. Her rebirth had not been some mundane event. It had come like a jolt of lightning, surging through her with a hundred-thousand-volt intensity that she was certain had burned away her sins.

Mason had felt so enraptured at the revival that she hadn't wanted to leave it on Friday, and it was well after midnight when she finally returned to Frisco City, a tiny town just south of Monroeville. She had taken her five-month-old niece to the revival, and though the child had fallen asleep during the long ride home, she still was groggy on Saturday morning. It was after ten o'clock by the time Mason and the baby were finally ready to leave the house. Mason needed to pick up a dress at Jackson Cleaners and bring the baby back to her parents. As she rode north toward Monroeville, she hummed a gospel song. Because she didn't own a wristwatch, she would later be unsure exactly when she had reached the outskirts of town, but she would estimate that it was around ten-forty.

Coy Stacey tightened the tiny chrome ring on the lip of the kitchen faucet and turned on the water. Then he switched it off. The faucet did not drip. The *plop-plop-plop* he had heard Friday night was gone. Now that the leaky spigot was repaired, he had only one more Saturday-morning chore to perform. He needed to drop off his dirty laundry at Jackson Cleaners.

Stacey lived about seven miles southeast of town, in Excel, a community of three hundred fifty. He'd once served a term as mayor there. He glanced at his watch. If he left for the cleaners immediately, he could drop off his laundry and still make it over to the old carpet shop in Excel by eleven o'clock, which was when he and several other retired men were scheduled to begin their Saturday-morning domino game. He didn't want to be late. His buddies would start without him, and he'd have to sit around until someone gave up a seat at the table. Stacey gathered up his clothes. It was 10:42.

Jackson Cleaners occupied a one-story rectangular building made of concrete blocks painted a drab brown. Although the store was located on South Alabama Avenue, Monroeville's busiest thoroughfare, it was set apart from other businesses on the street. The commercial lots on either side of it were vacant, and at least fifty yards separated it from its closest neighbor. The front of the building, which looked east, was faced with brown bricks and had a pitched roof overhang made of dark wood shingles. This facade made the building look taller than it actually was and gave it a much-needed touch of flair.

Originally the owner had intended to rent space to two stores. Because of this, there were two separate front doors, built side by side in the center of the storefront, with plate glass windows on each side. But no tenant had ever been found to share the building with the cleaners so both front doors led into its lobby in the southeast half of the building. There was no door into the northeast half. It was used for storage. A passerby could look through the windows on the left of the front doors and see into the lobby, but the windows on the right were covered with straw blinds that made it impossible to peek inside. There was no sidewalk, and so many customers had parked in front of the cleaners over the years that they had killed the grass, packed down the dirt, and created an unplanned curving driveway.

The interior of the building was spartan. The lobby of the store was framed by two walls, one running along the back of the lobby parallel to the front of the building and the other at right angles to it. This wall separated the lobby from the northeast side of the building, and it was covered with cheap wood paneling. The southwest section of the building, directly behind the lobby, was where clean clothing was hung on metal piping suspended from the ceiling. Several hundred garments could be stored on this piping, which snaked its way across the room. The northwest section contained commercial washers, dryers, pressing tables, and other cleaning equipment. Unclaimed clothes were stored on metal racks in the northeast corner along with cardboard boxes filled with forgotten odds-and-ends.

When Jerrie Sue Dunning arrived the door to the store was open, the lobby empty.

"Hello," she called, "is anyone here?"

Silence.

"Hello!" she said, more loudly this time.

Again no response.

Dunning had assumed that it would take only a few minutes to drop off her laundry. Where was the clerk? She glanced around. There was a worn wicker chair near the front corner of the lobby, with old magazines tossed on its seat, and near it, against the south exterior wall, stood a bright red-and-white Coca-Cola vending machine. The floor was smooth concrete, painted dark brown. There were no draperies, no rugs, no plants. Three counters, with spaces between them, ran along the length of the lobby, separating the patrons from the employees. Dunning dropped her bundle of clothes onto the dull orange Formica top. A cash register sat on the adjacent counter. Next to it lay a notepad, a cigar box filled with small white tags and straight pins, a white plastic cup jammed with cheap ballpoint pens and pencils with chewed pink eraser tops, and a chrome bell with a button on top.

Dunning rang the bell twice. No one responded.

Against the left wall behind the counter stood a metal chair and a gray desk. A white electric clock, the square kind popular in kitchens in the 1950s, hung above the desk; its white cord had a brown stain on it where it had been scorched during an electrical short but had been repaired—a testament to the frugality of the store's owner.

"Hello!" Dunning called again. "Is anyone here?"

There was no reply.

The only decoration in the entire place was a large black-and-white calendar tacked on the wall directly behind the counter where Dunning had set down her clothes. It advertised a local bank and displayed a lithograph showing two large deer in a forest, both with heads raised as if anticipating danger. A black rotary-dial wall telephone and a chalkboard for messages hung near it. Dunning looked at the board. There were no notes on it.

"Hello!" she called out, now irritated. "Is anyone there?"

Dunning turned around and looked through the front windows at her daughters waiting in the car. As soon as Lee spotted her, the teenager began moving her mouth in silent exaggerated speech. Dunning recognized the words: "*Let's go.*" She replied in similar fashion: "*I can't just leave my clothes here.*"

Dunning turned back around. There was a double-width doorway cut into the lobby's wall. It led into the southwest rear of the building. It was dark back there, but from where Dunning was standing she could make out several women's dresses and men's shirts each hanging in clear plastic bags from the piping overhead. As she peered through the doorway, a beam of light caught her attention. She guessed correctly that it was coming from under the doorway of an employee bathroom at the rear of the building, beyond the hanging clothes. Maybe the clerk was using it and was too embarrassed to reply.

"Hello!" she yelled. "Are you back there?"

Dunning decided that she would simply write her name on a tag and leave it with her clothing for the clerk. She began to reach for one of the white slips of paper near the cash register, then jerked her hand back. The drawer of the cash register was open. Her eyes darted around the room as she quickly reviewed the scene. No clerk. No movement. No response to her calls. An open cash register. Had there been a robbery here? Was the thief hiding in the back room? Just then Dunning heard the front door opening behind her. Florence Mason walked in. She was carrying her niece in her arms. Dunning didn't recognize her. Mason was black.

"No one seems to be here," Dunning said, trying to sound calm. "I've called out several times but no one answers." She looked at the cash register, and Mason, following the direction of her eyes, also noticed the open drawer.

"Maybe we should go and look in the back room?" Dunning suggested halfheartedly.

Mason didn't move.

Coy Stacey came inside. His arms were full of clothes. "Good morning, Mrs. Dunning," he said cheerfully. He didn't know Mason, but he nodded politely to her.

"Coy, I've been here five minutes and no one answers!" Dunning said. "I think something is wrong!"

"Well, let's see if I can get someone," he replied confidently. He stepped behind the counter, walking to the doorway that opened into the back room. "Anyone home?" he called. He too noticed the light coming from under the bathroom door. "Maybe she's in the bathroom and just wants us to wait," he said to Dunning and Mason, keeping his voice low.

The threesome stood about awkwardly for another minute or so; then Stacey called out again, "Hello? You back there?" When there was still no response, he asked if either of the women had seen an employee's car parked outside. "Maybe she's off running an errand," he explained. The women followed him out the front door, Mason instinctively waiting for the two whites to go first. They found Ronda's Pontiac parked at the side of the building. When they returned to the lobby, Dunning mentioned the open cash register drawer. Stacey did not say anything, but as soon as he looked at the register, he suspected the cleaners had been robbed and assumed the clerk had been tied up, gagged, and left in the bathroom. Still, he was reluctant to telephone the police. He didn't want to look like a fool if the clerk was simply running an errand.

"Let's look around back there," he suggested, nodding toward the back room. As they moved toward the doorway behind the counter, the telephone rang. Dunning started to reach for it, then caught herself. Leaning down, she picked a piece of paper out of the trash can and used it to lift the receiver.

"Hello?"

"Is the girl there?" It was a man's voice.

"No. The only people here right now are customers and we don't know where the girl is who works here. You'll have to call back."

The caller hung up.

Stacey led the women through the hanging clothes toward the bathroom door. He gently tapped on it.

"Hello? Is anyone in there?"

Hearing no reply, he tested the knob. The door was unlocked. He began to push inward and suddenly felt something or someone pushing back. Lowering his shoulder, he gave the door a shove. There was a loud crunch, and when he peeked inside, Stacey had pinned a bag of trash against the wall. A naked bulb dangled from the bathroom ceiling. There was no one inside.

"Let's keep looking," he suggested. They turned to the right and walked slowly toward the northwest corner, where the various pieces of cleaning equipment sat. Every few seconds Dunning called out, "Is anyone here?"

By now at least ten minutes had passed since they had met in the lobby. At this point one of them realized that they had not searched the entire building. They had checked the lobby and the southwest and northwest areas, but not the northeast corner, at the front of the building. Stacey went first. Narrow beams of sunshine poked through the tears in the straw blinds covering the front windows. The space was crowded with rows of unclaimed clothes hung on chin-high racks made of metal pipe. Used cardboard boxes were stacked haphazardly amid the clothing. As they stepped forward Mason screamed out, "Here she is!"

Stacey and Dunning raced to her side. A tennis shoe was sticking out from under a rack. Bending down, Stacey could tell that it was a young girl, lying on her stomach. Her face was turned away from him, so he could not see who she was. She was not tied or gagged. There was no blood, but she was not moving.

"Call 911!" Stacey told Dunning, but she was already on her way outside.

"I'm going to get Dr. Lee!" Dunning yelled. Lee was a dentist whose office was across the street. She thought he might know CPR. Lee had just pulled into the parking lot and was stepping from his car when Dunning reached him. She opened her mouth, but nothing came out. She grabbed his arm, began to tug, and then found her voice: "Come! Quick!"

Back inside, Stacey was telephoning the Monroeville police department. "We need an ambulance and police at Jackson Cleaners," he reported, saying no more in case people were listening to police scanners. He didn't want to cause a panic or attract sightseers. Dunning and Lee hurried back inside. Stacey led the dentist to the body. Bending down, Lee felt for a pulse, then quietly nodded to Stacey, who understood the message: The girl was dead.

Lieutenant Woodrow Ikner had been on his way home for lunch when Stacey's call had come through the police switchboard. Ikner arrived at the cleaners at 11:12 A.M. William Gibson and Chuck Sadhue, two Monroe County sheriff's deputies, came rushing inside moments later. They had been less than two hundred yards from the store when the police dispatcher had asked for backup. Many of the town's police officers and sheriff's deputies got their uniforms cleaned at Jackson's. All three men knew the clerks there.

Stacey recognized Ikner. He had taught the police officer in Sunday school when Ikner had been just a boy. "She's back here, Woodrow," Stacey said. Just as Lee had done, Ikner felt for a pulse. Meanwhile Gibson and Sadhue located a light switch and began moving the racks of clothing. Ikner was the first to see the dead girl's face. He knew Ronda.

His son had been in her graduating class at Monroe Academy. He was speechless.

"Oh my God!" Gibson gasped. "What the . . ." His voice trailed off. Gibson's cousin Lynn was one of Ronda's closest girlfriends. He knew that the night before, Lynn and Ronda had gone together to the last Monroe Academy football game of the season.

Deputy Sadhue had been at the game too, and volunteered that he had seen the two girls together. "I was just talking to Ronda last night," Sadhue announced. "She was so happy."

Speaking into his two-way radio, Ikner told the dispatcher to call Monroeville Police Chief Bill Dailey and County Coroner Farrish Manning. He was careful not to tell the dispatcher why, but anyone listening to a police scanner quickly understood that something out of the ordinary was happening. Within ten minutes a crowd had gathered. A few people had stopped to pick up their clothing; others had been attracted by the police cars parked outside the cleaners. Several people actually came inside and looked at Ronda's body still lying facedown on the floor. Deputies Gibson and Sadhue decided to seal off the crime scene. They ordered the onlookers to leave and unrolled a four-inch-wide bright yellow tape that read POLICE LINE—DO NOT CROSS, which they stretched outside the front door. Gibson got his camera from the trunk of his police cruiser but noticed that he had only ten shots left on the roll of film. There was a grocery store less than a mile away, but he didn't want to leave to buy more film. Luckily Steve Stewart, the editor of *The Monroe Journal*, came running up with a camera and volunteered to take pictures for the police.

By this time a crew of paramedics from the hospital had arrived, but Ikner asked them not to touch Ronda until Stewart had taken photographs. The unnerved editor took four flash pictures and then realized that he hadn't set the shutter speed on his camera properly. The pictures were useless. He quickly made the correction and took two more shots before the crew rolled the body over.

When Ronda was turned faceup, everyone became silent. Not until then could they have known that her blouse had been unbuttoned, her bra had been pushed off her breasts, and her jeans had been unzipped.

Tears formed in Gibson's eyes. He stepped over to the lobby to regain his composure. Other officers were arriving. Gibson couldn't believe Ronda was dead. "I was just teasing her yesterday about her pet poodle, Tina," he said to no one in particular. Despite all that her disheveled clothing implied, it was her face that had gotten to him. The expression was so terrible that Gibson would later recall he had never seen a look quite like it before or afterward. For years thereafter, as he was about to fall off to sleep at night, he would sometimes see Ronda's face. "Whoever killed that girl had scared her first," he said later. "Her face was frozen in fear—her mouth was open in a silent scream."

Charles Morrison was watching the kickoff of the Alabama University vs. Mississippi State football game on television when the phone rang. Bertha was not home. The caller was a friend. Had Charles heard that there had been trouble at the cleaners? No, Morrison said. The friend knew what had happened but suggested only that Morrison get to the store as fast as he could. Morrison bolted out the door. Jackson Cleaners was only a few blocks away. He drove there in three minutes but couldn't find a place to park because of the crowd. He stopped several hundred feet down the road and began walking. A friend ran to meet him.

"Don't go, Charles," the friend warned.

"What's happened?" Morrison demanded. "Is Ronda okay?"

The man shook his head. "Don't go up there."

Morrison quickened his pace. He had had an ominous feeling that morning before Ronda had gone to work. It was nothing he could really explain, just a gut feeling that something wasn't right and that he should not let Ronda out of his sight, but he hadn't said anything to her. Now that she was a college freshman, he was trying to give her more freedom. It wasn't easy for him or Bertha. Ronda was their miracle baby. They had wanted children desperately, but doctors hadn't thought Bertha could have any because of medical problems when she was young. She and Charles had been married eight years before she had finally become pregnant. It was the happiest day of their lives. They were convinced that God had blessed them, and they had never forgotten just how special Ronda was.

Several people encircled Morrison as soon as he reached the cleaners. "It's Ronda."

"Is it bad?" he asked.

"It's bad."

Police Chief Dailey and Coroner Manning had arrived a few minutes earlier, and as Morrison made his way to the front door the two officials stepped outside. Later Dailey wouldn't be able to remember whether he was the one who had told Charles Morrison that Ronda was dead or whether Manning had. All Dailey could recall was what he saw. Charles Morrison was a man's man—big, powerful, standing well over six feet, weighing more than two hundred pounds. He had worked at manual jobs all his life, and he was broad-shouldered, with huge rough hands. When he heard that his only daughter was dead, his entire body shook; his face melted. Charles Morrison seemed to shrink before their eyes.

"Can I see my daughter?" he asked, his eyes wet with tears.

"No," Dailey replied softly. "I don't think that would be a good idea right now."

Just then the paramedics came out the front door. They were carrying a body bag, which they pushed into the back of the waiting ambulance.

Charles Morrison didn't speak. He simply turned and walked back toward his car.

Chapter 3

Lieutenant Woodrow Ikner's head was spinning with whys. Why would someone rob such a cash-poor target? Why would someone attempt a rape on a busy Saturday morning in such a risky spot? And most of all, why had her attacker *killed* Ronda Morrison? Most armed robberies and attempted rapes don't end with a young girl lying dead on a concrete floor. It was Ikner's job to answer the whys. He had just been promoted to the newly created job of chief investigator for the Monroeville police department. This was his first major case, and he had never before been in charge of a murder investigation. Ikner knew he could depend on help from the county sheriff's department and the Alabama Bureau of Investigation, which made agents available to small towns whenever there was a murder. But he was eager to prove himself. For twenty years he had worked as a city cop, and he had pulled enough night shifts and investigated enough traffic accidents to have paid his dues. He also knew that some younger officers were convinced that his promotion at age forty-four had more to do with his friendship with Chief Dailey than with his investigative skills. Behind his back they were joking that he would have trouble solving a crime even if the perpetrator walked into the station and confessed. Ronda's murder was his chance to show them otherwise.

Murder is usually a messy business, especially if the victim has resisted or there has been a sexual assault. A piece of hair, a drop of blood, a fingerprint could expose the face of the killer. The first decision Ikner made was to begin gathering evidence without waiting for the Alabama Department of Forensic Sciences, commonly called the state crime lab. A few minutes before noon, Coroner Farrish Manning telephoned Michael Taylor, a medical examiner at the lab in Mobile, to report Ronda's murder and request an autopsy. In a summary Taylor would later write, he would note that he had asked Manning if the Monroeville police wanted the crime lab to send one of its evidence-gathering teams to the cleaners. Each team was composed of experts in fingerprinting, firearms, and the identification of hairs, fibers, and other substances. Taylor wrote in his report that he was told the local police were processing the crime scene and did not want outside help.

Ikner began by dusting for fingerprints in the lobby. Although neither of them said anything, deputies Gibson and Sadhue were startled. "I figured we'd wait for the state crime lab boys since they were the real experts," Sadhue later recalled, "but then I thought, 'Well, Woodrow must know what he is doing 'cause he's in charge.' " Gibson began helping Ikner, and while they were dusting the counter Steve Stewart took their photograph. The pictures he had taken of Ronda were much too gruesome for a local newspaper, but a shot of Ikner and Gibson working together to catch the killer would be perfect for that week's front page.

Ikner would later explain that he felt competent to collect evidence because he was, among other things, the first Monroeville police officer ever to have undergone a special police training course at the Federal Bureau of Investigation Academy in Quantico, Virginia. The FBI hadn't accepted him in 1981 when he first applied because he was seventy pounds overweight. But Ikner had been determined to enroll, so he had lost the weight and had been accepted. Unfortunately the short FBI program had not prepared him for the difficult task he now faced. Pinpointing fingerprints is easy if there are only a few, but hundreds of hands had touched the Formica counter at Jackson Cleaners, and differentiating among them proved impossible for Ikner and Gibson. Everything they found was smudged. After several frustrating minutes Ikner suggested that they continue their investigation in the back of the building. Gibson and Sadhue exchanged nervous glances. "Fingerprint powder was scattered everywhere," Gibson later remarked. "The place was a mess." It would now be impossible for anyone else to check for prints on the counter. "I was worried we were going to end up causing more damage than good," Sadhue remembered, "and that is exactly what we did."

Continuing their search, the three investigators found five spent shell casings. They were from a .25 caliber pistol. Ikner knew that most .25 caliber handguns are semiautomatics, which means they eject each shell after firing it, unlike a revolver, in which the shells remain in the gun's revolving cylinder after being fired. The location of each shell casing was therefore very important to document because it would show where the killer had been standing when he fired at Ronda. One casing was inside the bathroom, near the toilet. Another was found just outside the bathroom door. Two more were found about ten feet away, and the last was found about six inches from Ronda's head. When the locations of the shell casings were connected on paper, much as in a dot-to-dot puzzle, they formed a direct line that led from the bathroom in the southwest corner of the building to Ronda's body in the northeast corner. Ikner had been told by Coroner Manning that Ronda had been shot three times. Since they had found five spent casings, simple math told them that the killer had fired two shots that had missed. Where were those slugs?

Besides the brass shell casings, the investigators found an expensive gold necklace lying on the bathroom floor. The clasp was broken. Based on these preliminary clues, Ikner made a series of quick assumptions. He deduced that Ronda and the killer had fought inside the bathroom and that at some point during the struggle the killer had pulled off her necklace. He had also fired two shots, as evidenced by the two casings found there. Ronda had apparently broken free and run from the bathroom toward the northeast corner of the building. While pursuing her, the killer had shot twice more, ejecting two more shells. At that point Ronda must have fallen, because the killer had caught her and fired a final round. That last shot had been discharged at close range, because the shell casing had fallen to the floor within six inches of her head. Ikner tried to picture a man standing over Ronda and pulling a trigger as she struggled below him on the floor. The scene was too gruesome for him to imagine. Everyone had loved Ronda. Why had her attacker *murdered* her? The reason seemed obvious. He hadn't wanted her to identify him. He hadn't wanted to leave a witness. Suddenly Ikner found himself thinking: Why had the killer been so worried? Was it possible that Ronda had known him?

The sound of additional officers coming into the store jarred Ikner from his thoughts. His questions would have to wait. Nearly all of

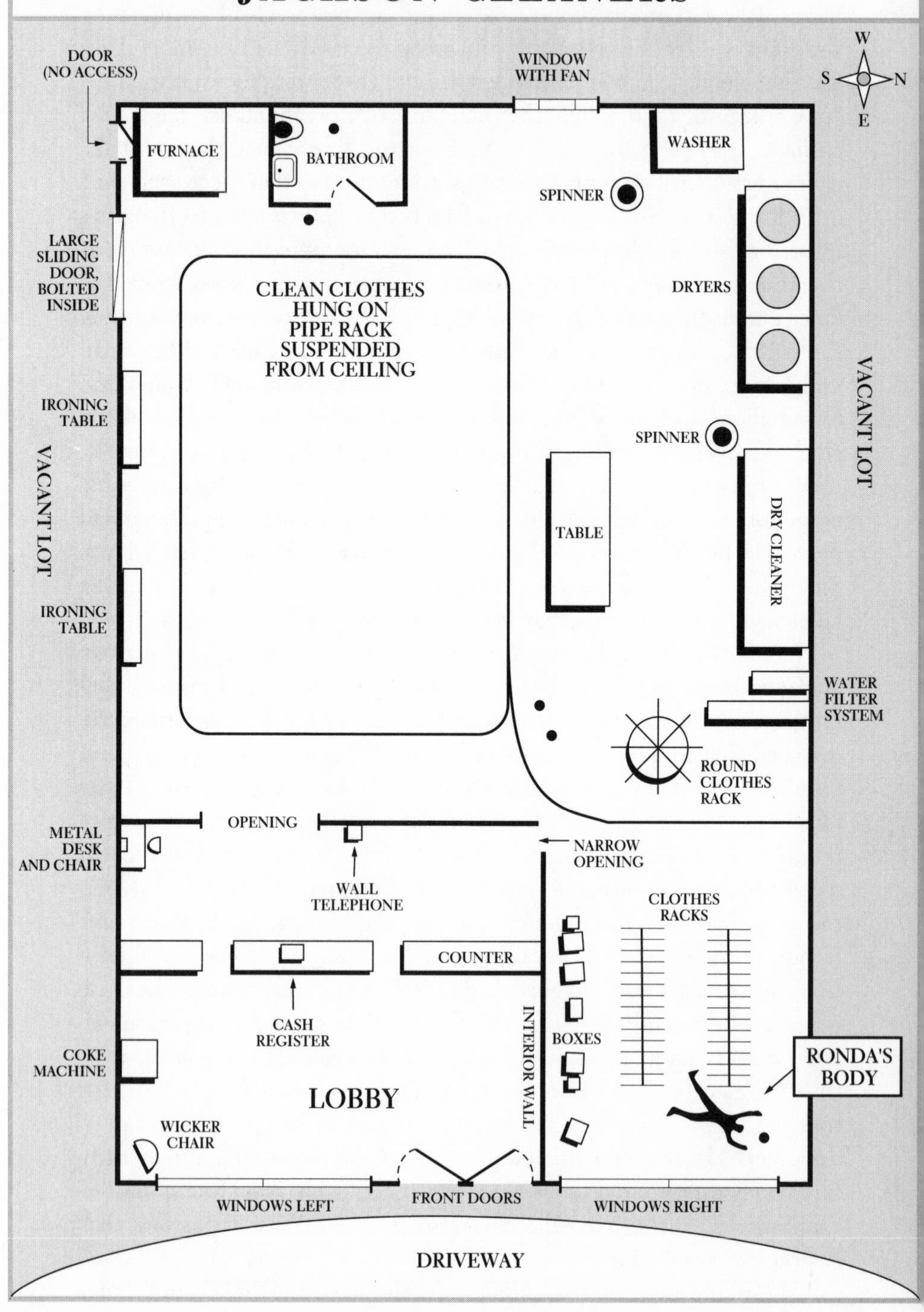

● SHELL CASINGS FOUND

Monroeville's twelve-member police force was now at the cleaners, along with most of the county sheriff's deputies. Someone needed to take charge. Coy Stacey, Jerrie Sue Dunning, and Florence Mason needed to be interviewed. For years Jackson Cleaners had been owned and operated by Miles and Doris Jackson, a prominent Monroeville couple. Ikner thought they still owned it, but another officer said the Jacksons had retired and sold the business to a newcomer in town named Randy Thomas. Someone needed to notify Thomas and, Ikner decided, to talk to the Jacksons too. Other merchants along South Alabama Avenue needed to be canvassed. Maybe they had seen something suspicious that morning. Finally someone needed to interview the Morrisons and Ronda's friends. During his FBI training course Ikner had learned that the first few hours after a murder were crucial. Time was on the killer's side. Later, when Ikner reconstructed his actions on that frantic Saturday, he would recall that the minutes had seemed to speed by, with events unfolding at a breathtaking pace. "It was impossible to keep track of everything going on. We were trying to check dozens of leads at once."

- Within minutes after Ronda's body was discovered, an excited caller telephoned the police to report that he had seen a man who matched the description of an escaped prisoner fleeing from the cleaners. The convict had broken out of a jail in an adjoining county a few days earlier and was wanted for murder.
- A gasoline station along Interstate 65 had been robbed shortly after eleven o'clock, and the police wondered if the two crimes had been committed by the same person.
- A nurse from the county hospital called the cleaners and announced that a patient had just come into the emergency room for treatment of scratches on his face and arms. She had heard the paramedics at the hospital talking about the murder and wondered if Ronda could have scratched her assailant.

Each tip, no matter how far-fetched, had to be logged and investigated, and as word of Ronda's murder swept the town, the police switchboard was jammed with calls. It was as if everyone in Monroeville stopped whatever they were doing as soon as they heard about Ronda and either drove to the Morrisons' house, went to the cleaners, called the police department, or congregated with neighbors and friends to discuss the murder. In the midst of this frenzy, Miles Jackson, the former owner of the cleaners, came rushing into the store. The police had been unable to reach Randy Thomas at his apartment in town, so they had called Jackson at his home and asked him to come down to the store. They had not told the sixty-seven-year-old Jackson that Ronda had been murdered, only that there was a "police emergency."

What happened next remains hotly disputed. This is how Miles Jackson remembers it: "I went inside . . . I said, 'Where is the girl?' I went in there thinking that the girl had fainted or something, that there had been a robbery. After saying that two or three times, Woodrow Ikner stepped up behind me and said, 'She is deceased.' I just went blank when I heard that. I have a heart condition and high blood pressure and I started to get faint. I needed to collect myself so I sat down in the wicker chair."

Deputy Chuck Sadhue was in the lobby when Jackson arrived, and he later recalled the scene differently. "Miles Jackson was on fire when he came in that morning. He comes in, runs over to that chair, sits down and immediately puts his hands over his face. He covers his face. He won't look at anyone and when Woodrow Ikner asks him a question, he says, 'I don't know! I don't know nothing! I've not been in this cleaners for two weeks!' "

Woodrow Ikner recalled Jackson's arrival this way: "Mr. Jackson came running in and immediately told me that he hadn't been inside the cleaners for six months. He told me that! Six months! He also told me he didn't know any of the girls who worked there, including Ronda."

After several minutes Jackson regained his composure and told the officers there was a way for them to identify who had been in the cleaners that morning. Whenever a customer left clothing to be cleaned, the clerk pinned a nametag on the garments and put them in a bin next to the washers. That tag stayed with the clothing until it was returned to its owner. At that point the nametag was removed and put into the cigar box next to the cash register. All the police had to do was collect the nametags from the soiled clothing that had been put in the bin that Saturday morning and gather up the tags from the cigar box where they were placed after customers picked up their clean clothing. Those two sets of tags would identify everyone who had patronized the store that morning. Woodrow Ikner quickly scooped up the cigar box and dashed into the back room to check the tags on the soiled clothes. Jackson, meanwhile, excused himself; he was feeling faint and wanted to go home. Before leaving, he told the police that Randy Thomas had gone to visit his parents in Tuscaloosa that weekend. Jackson promised to call him.

After Jackson left, three new investigators arrived separately at the cleaners. Larry Ikner, Simon Benson, and Thomas Tate would each play critical roles in the hunt for Ronda's killer.

As chief criminal investigator for the Monroe County district attorney's office, it was Larry Ikner's job to make sure the police didn't give a judge reason to release a suspect because of some legal technicality. Larry Ikner was a distant kin of Woodrow Ikner, but they had only a nodding acquaintance. A common joke in Monroe County was that if you looked back far enough, everyone was related. Despite their kinship, Larry Ikner felt uneasy about having Woodrow Ikner in charge of so important a case. He considered him a plodder and doubted his skills as an investigator.

The second newcomer, Tom Tate, had no official title but was soon to become sheriff. He was eager to get started, though he would not be sworn into office for three more months. Tate had won the Democratic primary, and since Republicans were rarely elected in Monroe County, the November general election was correctly being seen as a formality. Tate had never been a policeman or deputy, but he had spent eighteen years as a state probation and parole officer, and he considered himself "street smart" when it came to criminals. He also knew there was a natural rivalry between the police and the Monroe County sheriff's office. Like Larry Ikner, Sheriff-elect Tate did not have much confidence in Woodrow Ikner's ability, and he was certain that the sheriff's department, under his leadership, could do a much better job of investigating Ronda's murder than Ikner would.

The third investigator, Simon Benson, was one of only a handful of black agents who worked for the Alabama Bureau of Investigation. He had been assigned to the Monroe County region for only two years, but he had been born and reared in a nearby county and was familiar with southern Alabama and its often racist attitudes, especially those found in local police departments. In his early forties, Benson prided himself on being able to get along with everyone, regardless of whether they were white or black. He also believed that the ABI was better qualified and equipped to solve Ronda's murder than the Monroeville police *and* sheriff's departments.

Benson was the first of the three newcomers to arrive, and as soon as he entered the cleaners and spotted the fingerprint dust on the cash register, he assumed that a team from the state crime lab was hard at work. When he learned otherwise he quietly stepped outside, used his car radio, and told the ABI dispatcher to contact the state crime lab and have it send a forensic team to the cleaners immediately. When he came back in, Benson received a second jolt. He was told that Ronda's body had already been taken to the Johnson Funeral Home.

Benson knew that a victim's body was often the most important clue forensic scientists could use in their efforts to reconstruct a crime. The exact position, the condition of the clothing, the facial expression, the color of the skin—all could yield significant information. Moreover, the police were now going to have a tough time identifying clothing fibers, hairs, and other foreign objects found on Ronda. Had those items been left behind by the killer or by others, such as the paramedics or mortuary staff, who might have touched the body? Removing the body so quickly had clearly been a major blunder. Experience had taught Benson not to criticize local cops, especially white ones, so he didn't say anything—this was their case and the ABI was there by invitation. Besides, Benson realized from the reaction in the room when he asked about the body that a lecture wasn't necessary. "All of us knew better than to move Ronda," an embarrassed Chuck Sadhue admitted later, "but we *knew* Ronda, all of us did, and I think that made us block out our normal procedures. The truth was we all felt bad about having that little girl lying there on the cold floor like that, particularly with her bra pushed up and everything. She was someone we cared about."

A few minutes before four o'clock—nearly five hours after Ronda's body had been discovered—Michael Taylor and James Small arrived from the state crime lab. Woodrow Ikner showed them around. Taylor would later describe the cleaners as being in "complete chaos." Police officers, sheriff's deputies, and several persons who appeared to him to be curious onlookers were milling around the lobby and back room despite the yellow POLICE LINE tape near the front doors. Fingerprint powder was sprinkled everywhere. Taylor firmly believed that the best thing a poorly equipped police department could do whenever a murder was discovered was to simply close off the scene and call in the professionals from the state crime lab. But he also knew that in most murder cases local cops couldn't resist poking around. The scene at Jackson Cleaners was a sad reminder of that.

Ikner gave the specialists the five shell casings and showed them where each had been found. He also led them to the employee bathroom and showed them the necklace. A brick with a long brown hair on it was lying on the bathroom floor. Ikner had learned from Miles Jackson that the lock on the bathroom door was broken, so employees had used the brick to keep the door closed whenever they used the room. "Ronda might have hit the murderer with this brick," Ikner volunteered. "The hair might belong to the killer."

The two crime lab technicians listened politely but did not examine the brick or take the hair as evidence. Instead they drew a detailed diagram of the building and carefully noted where the body and shell casings had been found. They also found a tiny drop of what looked like blood on the wood paneling in the lobby. They cut around the spot, lifted out the piece of wood, and put it in an evidence bag. After dusting for fingerprints in the few places that hadn't already been checked, Taylor and Small left for the funeral home to claim Ronda's body. They were taking it back to Mobile for an autopsy.

"They didn't do much of anything," Woodrow Ikner grumbled once they were gone. "We gave them everything they found." The idea that the crime scene had already been contaminated did not enter his mind.

By five o'clock the number of investigators working on the case had grown to twenty. This included nine ABI agents sent from other parts of the state to Monroeville. They were under the command of Mike Barnett, a senior case agent, who had been dispatched to help Benson. It was obvious to Larry Ikner, the district attorney's representative, that someone needed to coordinate the investigation; otherwise they would all be stumbling over one another. Chief Dailey, Sheriff-elect Tate, and Agent Barnett quickly agreed. It was decided that Dailey and Woodrow Ikner would oversee the case, but no major decisions would be made without the approval of Larry Ikner or ABI agent Barnett. A command post would be established at the police department, and during nightly meetings everyone would share whatever information they had learned. Every witness statement and every interview transcript would be duplicated and handed out. Solving Ronda's murder was more important than any departmental rivalries, petty jealousies, personal ambitions, or politics.

At least on the day of the murder, that was what everyone said.

Chapter 4

Walter "Johnny D." McMillian would later claim that he was at home on the Saturday when Ronda Morrison was murdered. This is how the forty-five-year-old black man, his wife, Minnie, and their alibi witnesses would later reconstruct the events of that morning.

Johnny D. and Minnie were sleeping in the small farmhouse they owned about six miles east of Monroeville on Highway 84 when, at seven A.M., someone knocked on the back screen door. Still in his underwear and half awake, Johnny D. stepped barefoot across the worn red-and-white linoleum in the kitchen and glanced through the windows of the back porch to see who was there. He was greeted by the gap-toothed grin of Jimmy Hunter, a friend.

"Ain't you up?" asked Hunter. "You want to pull that transmission or not?"

"You don't need me to get started," Johnny D. replied in mock irritation. "Just get and never mind when I be getting out."

Hunter laughed and walked toward one of the several dilapidated wooden sheds behind the McMillians' house. He and Johnny D. had replaced the transmission in Johnny D.'s 1978 Chevrolet pickup a few days earlier. They had installed a reconditioned one that Johnny D. had bought secondhand, but it wasn't a perfect match, and now it was leaking fluid. Obviously they needed to reseal it. Johnny D. had asked Hunter to help with the job, but he had not expected him nearly so early. On the way back to his bedroom, he began warming up a pot of coffee.

"Don't you forget your sister is coming for a fish fry," Minnie reminded him as he slipped on a pair of worn overalls. As if on cue, the telephone rang, and when he answered it Johnny D. heard the hoarse voice of his sister, Everline Smith.

"Don't you go running off now, you hear?" she warned. " 'Cause I'm coming out your way real soon now."

"Well, I got lots to do today and probably won't be around," he replied, teasing her.

"Almighty God will strike you dead if you ain't there," she declared. "I'll tell Him too!" Smith was a self-trained holiness preacher, and she was not shy about threatening to call down God's wrath whenever it served her purposes. She and Johnny D. had always been close. They were two of ten children born to dirt-poor sharecroppers who had divorced when Johnny D. was ten. After their father left, every child had to work in the fields simply to earn enough to eat. Johnny D. had dropped out of high school to help. Those hard times had forged a bond between him and his siblings that Minnie could not rival, though she and Johnny D. had been married nearly twenty-five years and had three children of their own.

"I may need you to get me a bigger pot to cook in," Smith continued. "You got any?"

"No, maybe James got one," he replied, referring to one of their brothers, who lived a few miles down the highway.

Periodically Smith boiled fish and collard greens over a fire in the backyard at the McMillians' house. She sold the food to raise money for her all-black congregation. Its members were trying to save enough to build their own church. Even though Smith lived in Monroeville, as did most of her church members, she liked to cook fish at the McMillians' house because it was near a housing development known locally as the projects and by some as niggertown. During the 1960s the federal government had built about twenty brick houses on a plot of land next to the McMillians' property. These low-income, subsidized houses were rented to poor black families, and the McMillians knew everyone who lived there. Smith's cooking always attracted a good crowd from the projects, especially if Minnie contributed her specialty—barbecued ribs. There were no restaurants or other businesses close by. If there was any food left over, Smith knew she could always cajole Johnny D. into flagging down motorists on Highway 84. The McMillians' house sat close to the highway, and in the past Johnny D. had always managed to bring in additional customers by waving a cardboard sign that said FISH FRY at passing cars.

Shortly after nine o'clock, Smith and her oldest daughter arrived at the McMillians' carrying several packages of fresh fish and bags of collard greens. Johnny D. crawled out from under the pickup truck as soon as he heard his sister call him.

"You got my kettle?" she demanded. Obediently he drove in his car about a half mile down the road to his brother's house, but the cooking pot he found there was rusty, so he returned empty-handed. Fussing, Smith managed to find a suitable replacement and went to work. During the next three hours dozens of friends and relatives wandered into the McMillians' cluttered yard. Johnny D. loved to tinker with cars, trucks, and machinery. He was self-employed. With other blacks, he worked in the woods clearing land for local lumber companies. Consequently his yard served as a parking lot for an assortment of ancient semitrailers, rusty logging carts, old winches, and other metal scraps. Most of these relics stood surrounded by knee-high weeds or were hidden in run-down sheds with tin roofs. Although their property and house looked shabby, Johnny D. and Minnie were proud of it. They had bought the 1940s white clapboard farmhouse fifteen years before for $5,000 cash—at the time, their life savings. Both had always worked. Neither had ever accepted any sort of welfare.

The women who bought food from Smith sat in the backyard underneath a tall oak tree or on a rickety wooden picnic bench that had one leg at least an inch shorter than the others because it had been eaten by bugs. The men gathered around the pickup truck, now resting on cinder blocks, and swapped stories with Johnny D. and Hunter. Occasionally they passed a brown bag with a bottle of moonshine in it. In the kitchen Minnie supervised the cooking of the ribs and barbecue sauce, pausing periodically to chat with other middle-aged black women or shoo away a throng of neighborhood children looking for handouts.

Minnie would later remember that shortly after twelve o'clock, she saw Ernest Welch come into the yard. A rotund white man in his early forties, Welch was well known in the projects because he was the bill collector for Hainje's Furniture Company. Minnie's mother, Ida Bell Anderson, who lived behind them in a shack without electricity or running water, paid thirty-five dollars each month to the Monroeville store. Welch always came to collect on the first of the month because that was when the federal government issued its welfare and social security benefit checks. Minnie stepped from her kitchen into the back porch and watched Welch as he greeted Johnny D. and the others. He was one of the only white men in the area who ever came to a black person's home. Johnny D. got Welch to buy a fish sandwich from Smith, but Welch didn't unwrap or eat it. No one was surprised. Minnie assumed he was simply being polite. She didn't know many whites, but the few she knew didn't like the same foods blacks ate. Judging from the somber looks on their faces, it seemed to Minnie that Johnny D. and Welch were having some sort of serious conversation. Her husband came inside as soon as Welch left.

"Mr. Welch says his niece just got killed up there a while ago at the cleaners," he announced. "Mr. Welch says to me and Jimmy, 'My niece was murdered up there this very morning.' "

"Who be his niece?"

"A girl named Ronda Morrison. Says she was killed during a robbery at that cleaners on South Alabama Avenue up there in town."

"Well, I declare," Minnie replied, shaking her head in disgust. "What sort of evil person would kill someone like that?"

"Someone who is plumb crazy," Johnny D. said. "Only a crazy fool would do such a thing."

They would not mention the Ronda Morrison murder again to each other until six months later, when the investigation of the killing would suddenly focus on them and begin to ravage their lives.

Chapter

5

In the early 1800s Monroeville was not unlike most of its neighbors, communities with names such as Megargel, Uriah, Repton, and Mexia, which had been founded and had boomed when cotton was king and riverboats still steamed up the Alabama River to collect bales. That was before the Civil War, before outbreaks of yellow fever ravaged the county, before the First World War and the Great Depression. Over time nearly all these other towns had died, and by 1986 their downtowns were abandoned. Monroeville had avoided its neighbors' fate because of Vanity Fair Mills. In the 1930s the maker of women's undergarments, then based in Pennsylvania, came South in search of lower taxes and a nonunion workforce. It found both in Monroeville. The first mill employed a hundred people. Now the company operated four plants and had twenty-five hundred employees. Nearly everyone in town had a relative who worked at the mills.

Monroeville and Vanity Fair soon developed a symbiotic relationship. Vanity Fair built Monroeville's city park, golf course, and country club. Vanity Fair gave Monroeville economic stability. It was no accident that

Patrick Henry Junior College was built in Monroeville. Without the mills there would have been no money for tuition.

The improvements Vanity Fair provided helped draw another large employer to the county in 1976, when construction began on the Alabama River Pulp Paper Company thirty miles west of town on the banks of the Alabama River. It was reputed to be the biggest paper mill in the world, and once the plant opened Monroeville's population jumped from five thousand to seven thousand. While the newcomers and their money were welcomed, they were not really considered Monroevillians. People's roots had to go back at least four generations before folks stopped calling them outsiders.

Charles Morrison worked at the logging scales at the huge paper plant. Bertha Morrison was a seamstress at Vanity Fair. Their Alabama roots sank deep. They lived on Meadowbrook Road in a modest one-story rambler with a redbrick front, gray roof, and carport. Their lawn was neatly trimmed, their home well maintained. A similar house in their neighborhood had recently sold for $70,000, a price that was higher than the average home for sale in town but not lavish.

Six hours after Ronda's body was found, district attorney's investigator Larry Ikner and ABI agent Simon Benson went to interview the Morrisons. While driving from Jackson Cleaners to the Morrisons' house, Ikner asked himself the same question over and over again. What if it had been one of his daughters who had been killed that morning? How would he have reacted?

Ikner had a daughter only a few years younger than Ronda, and his wife was six months pregnant. Neither of them had planned on another baby, and the news had scared him at first because he thought he was too old to undertake the raising of another child. Ikner was forty and nearly bald; what brown hair he still had was turning gray, and his watermelon-shaped waistline seemed at constant war with the handmade leather belt he liked to wear, with LARRY tooled on the back. But after the initial shock Ikner found himself excited by the prospect of a newborn. Now he couldn't stop wondering: What would he do if he were Ronda's father?

As they turned onto Meadowbrook Road, Ikner found himself remembering another teenager's death. Just like Ronda, she was from a well-respected family. The way Ikner remembered it, she had been riding in a Jeep with a group of kids about a year ago when she fell off and was killed. "The girl's parents were religious and it was their faith that carried them through it," Ikner later said, recalling his thoughts. "There could have been accusations, anger, and hate, but there wasn't any of that." The family belonged to Eastwood Baptist Church, the same congregation as Charles and Bertha Morrison. "The girl's parents decided their daughter was really God's child and that God had let them have her for a certain period of time and then He had called her home. I always thought that was a wonderful way to look at it. But it takes an awfully strong faith not to be angry or hateful or to not want to reach out and get revenge."

There was another incident Ikner remembered as well. In the mid-1970s an unemployed drifter with mental problems got off a bus in Monroeville and began wandering down Highway 84. He came upon a house where two black children, ages four and five, were playing. Without warning the man picked up an ax at a woodpile and killed both children. Their grandfather heard their screams, but by the time he got outside it was too late. He saw his two dead grandchildren and then spotted the killer running away. The grandfather later claimed that he had been driving into town to get medical help when he accidentally hit the drifter, but the tire tracks told a different story. The old man had swerved off the highway in his truck and had struck the killer, throwing his body through the air. The vehicle had then followed its airborne target and had ridden over the body several times after it landed. Ikner had been a deputy then, and he could still remember the coroner and sheriff debating whether or not to arrest the grandfather. "The old man was never charged with any crimes," Ikner recalled. "The fellow's death was ruled a case of justifiable homicide."

Ikner had thought a lot about that incident over the years. "There was no apparent reason for those kids being killed. It was just a random, senseless act, just two innocent kids playing in their front yard, and although they were black, my heart went out to the family."

At first he thought it was the horror of the crime that made it stick in his mind. Later he decided it was something else. "Justice was served that day. Some may not see it that way, but I do. It was quick, and it was right." No lawyers, no legal wrangling, no plea bargaining—just an angry old man in a pickup truck doing what his heart commanded him to do.

Few knew as much about the inner workings of justice in Monroe County as Larry Ikner. Although he wasn't a lawyer and had only a high school education, most folks considered him the county's *real* prosecutor. In 1980 Ikner had been hired as the first and only criminal investigator ever to work for the Monroe County district attorney. If a defense lawyer wanted to arrange a plea bargain for his client, he telephoned

Ikner. If a business owner got a bad check, he called Ikner. If a liquor distributor got caught unloading booze in Monroe County, which was dry, it was Ikner who figured out a settlement. That didn't mean Ikner's boss, District Attorney Ted Pearson, was inept. Few Alabama attorneys could match Pearson's cleverness in a courtroom. But Pearson hated paperwork, was easily bored with pretrial preparation, had no interest in day-to-day operations, and loved to play golf. The gossip at the county courthouse was that Pearson sometimes didn't know anything about a criminal case until he rushed in from the golf course for a five-minute briefing by Ikner before the trial.

One reason Ikner was successful at his job was that he understood life in Monroe County. He was a "local boy," born and reared in nearby Frisco City. After high school he had served a stint in Vietnam, winning two medals for bravery and a Purple Heart. Back home he had gone right to work as a cop. There wasn't a county resident whose name Ikner didn't know. He also knew everyone's reputation.

As soon as Ikner knocked on the door on Meadowbrook Road, a friend of the Morrison family opened it. It was becoming dark outside, but it was even darker inside. All the curtains were closed. The house was crowded. A few men nodded as Ikner walked past them. Agent Benson followed respectfully. He was the only black. Most of the women had red eyes; many were weeping. Those who spoke did so in hushed tones. The largest group of mourners had gathered in the den at the rear of the house. Benson could see platters of food that neighbors had brought sitting untouched in the kitchen.

As an ABI agent, Simon Benson had been through this procedure dozens of times. He was used to dealing with people overcome with emotion. Yet as he and Ikner waited for Charles and Bertha Morrison to appear, he suddenly found himself feeling sad. This surprised him. He had seen grislier murders and he had never met the Morrisons or Ronda, but there was such an overwhelming sense of grief in the house that even the veteran agent felt it.

Benson had been taught as a child that there was a clear line between right and wrong, good and evil. His father was a holiness minister, and he had instilled in his son a firm conviction that sinners were required to pay for their misdeeds. Benson could still remember when he had decided he wanted to be a police officer. A crowd of angry whites had come to his family's house late one night, led by the county sheriff. A young black man had killed a white man, and the sheriff wanted Benson's father to use his ministerial clout in the black community to help find the youth and convince him to surrender. Otherwise vigilantes would hunt him down and lynch him. At first the sight of the mob had terrified Benson, but the sheriff had clearly been in control and had promised that the wanted man would be given a fair trial if he surrendered. A few days later the man turned himself in.

Benson had been in awe of the sheriff and the way in which he had defused the situation. He immediately told his parents he wanted to be a law officer too. They said blacks were not allowed to hold such jobs. In the 1960s that changed. The Alabama Department of Public Safety, the parent agency for both the State Highway Patrol and the ABI, was forced by the federal courts to integrate, and Benson was one of its first black hires. The department put him to work infiltrating black civil rights groups and reporting on their meetings. Later he was used as an undercover agent to buy illegal liquor, guns, and narcotics from blacks. Benson was often accused of being an Uncle Tom after making an arrest, but if such talk bothered him, he did not show it. His trademark was his grin. No matter how tense a situation might be or what sort of racial slurs were spat at him by whites or blacks, Benson never stopped smiling.

Over time Benson and Ikner had learned to use race to their advantage whenever they worked as an investigative team. Alone with a white suspect, Ikner would quietly refer to Benson as a nigger. With blacks, Benson described Ikner as a cracker. Both men said the terms meant nothing. Still, each understood the unwritten rules of south Alabama. They rode in unmarked cars together, ate together in restaurants, and together arrested both blacks and whites. They considered themselves friends, close enough to trust each other with their lives while on the job, but neither had ever invited the other to Sunday dinner in his home or stopped by at night to sit on the porch and share a beer.

In a murder investigation, Benson always began by questioning the family of the victim. Who knew Ronda better than her parents? He scanned the den where he and Ikner were now waiting. What had Ronda's life been like here?

When Charles and Bertha appeared, Benson instinctively let Ikner make the introductions and offer condolences. Everything that could be done would be, Ikner assured them. He and the other investigators would keep them informed, although there would be matters they might not be able to share until after an arrest was made. The Morrisons were going to have to trust them, and he hoped they would. Because Monroeville was a close-knit community, friends and others were bound to call the couple to confide in them. If either of them heard anything about the murder, no matter how insignificant it might sound, they should call the police.

As Ikner spoke Benson made mental notes. Bertha Morrison was petite and looked fragile next to her large husband, but she was in full control of her emotions and seemed almost guarded as she watched Ikner and listened intently to each word he said. Charles Morrison was not in control. He tried to speak as soon as Ikner finished talking but was overcome with grief. Bertha immediately took charge. She told Ikner and Benson about the essay Ronda had written for her class in junior college and how two blacks had argued with her. She then told them about the black stranger who had come into the cleaners and used the telephone. There were several black construction workers helping build a store near the cleaners, and Ronda had thought that the black man might have been working there. Bertha said she wanted them to know about both incidents, but she added that she and Charles didn't want to be misunderstood. At this point Charles joined in. He and Bertha did not believe their daughter's murder had anything to do with race, nor did they have any problems with Benson, a black man, investigating her death. They had simply been trying to think about recent events that struck them as odd, and both happened to deal with blacks. Benson told them he wasn't offended.

"I want you to do whatever needs to be done to find out who murdered my little girl," Charles said. He and Bertha would answer any questions, show the police anything they needed to see. They would even hire a private investigator if need be. "We're not wealthy," he told them, but he and Bertha were willing to sell their home to pay for any sort of lie detector tests, medical exams, or other tests the Monroeville police department couldn't afford.

Benson's gaze drifted. There was a comfortable overstuffed chair with a slightly sagging seat in the right corner. He guessed it was a favorite of Charles's. A console television sat diagonally across from it. On top of the set was an eight-by-ten-inch high school graduation photograph of Ronda. Because Ronda had looked directly into the camera when the picture was taken, her gaze followed you across the room. She was absolutely stunning and was wearing a gold necklace that resembled the one that had been found at the cleaners. In his mind Benson could see happier times: Morrison sitting in his favorite chair, watching television, his child's photograph proudly displayed above the screen.

"Just find out who killed my daughter," Charles Morrison pleaded. "Please."

Ikner began asking questions.

Did Ronda have any enemies?

None.

Did she have a boyfriend?

She had been seeing one boy, but it had not been serious.

Did she associate with anyone who might want to harm her?

Not that they knew of.

When Ronda was a baby, Bertha had dressed her as if every day were a Sunday. The moment Ronda had gotten dirty, her mother had washed her and slipped her into fresh clothing. As she grew older Charles and Bertha continued to watch over her. They always knew where she was, knew her friends, where she was going, what time she would be home. To them there was no one more precious. Whenever Bertha's brothers and sisters got together for a family reunion, Ronda didn't play with her cousins. She stayed close to her parents. Until her teenage years they were her best friends. Ronda had entered a beauty contest once, but only to please her father. He didn't think there was another daughter quite as lovely.

Had either of them recently noticed anything different about Ronda?

No. She hadn't seemed worried about anything that wasn't usual for a teenager.

As Ikner talked Benson continued to take an inventory of the room with his eyes. The den was tidy, without frivolous knickknacks, functional yet comfortable. There was a sense of warmth about it, of family. On a bookcase along one wall there were more photographs of Ronda—more pictures than books, in fact. A copy of the Holy Bible was nearby. It looked worn.

Was Ronda friendly with the other girls she worked with? Ikner asked.

Ronda had been good friends with Lisa Odom, but neither of them was close to Carol Jean Smith, the other clerk. She had attended Monroeville's public school, not Monroe Academy. It had been Carol Jean's Saturday to open the store, but she and Ronda had swapped at the last minute. "Ronda shouldn't have been there!" Bertha said. Both investigators noted an edge of bitterness in her voice.

Did Ronda or her friends use drugs?

No! The Morrisons were certain of that.

What did Ronda like to do when she wasn't working?

Normal teenage things. She was busy. In high school she had been voted wittiest in the graduating class. She had taken part in a slew of school activities. But it was Eastwood Baptist Church that had been at the center of her life, her parents said. Charles Morrison was a deacon there, and he and Bertha and Ronda rarely missed a Sunday service. Ronda had been baptized when she was nine years old. She had come home beaming from vacation Bible school one summer, Bertha told them. She quoted her daughter. "Guess what happened to me today, Mama?" Ronda had asked. "I gave my heart to Jesus."

Was there anyone who made Ronda feel uncomfortable sexually?

For a few seconds neither parent spoke, and then they both said Ronda had felt ill at ease around Miles Jackson. Sometimes Ronda and the other girls would run and hide in the bathroom when he came into the store and would stay there until he was gone.

"Run and hide in the bathroom" reverberated in both men's minds.

What was it about Jackson that made the girls uneasy?

He had never said or done anything—the girls just didn't like him.

How about Randy Thomas?

This time there was no hesitation. Ronda liked working for Thomas.

The two men had run out of questions, but as they started to leave, Charles Morrison stopped them. Because he had been working the night shift at the paper mill, he had not seen Ronda much during the last few days, he said. Now she was dead. Perhaps if he had not been away so much at night, perhaps if he had driven her to work, perhaps if he had . . . his voice sank to a whisper. The investigators thought they understood what he was trying to say. In his mind, he was asking himself over and over if there might have been some way he could have saved his daughter. Charles started to tell them about his feeling that morning that something bad was going to happen to Ronda, but he decided not to mention it. They were interested only in facts, not emotions.

Larry Ikner tried to comfort him. He was certain, Ikner said, that there was nothing Charles could have done. Ronda had simply been in the wrong place at the wrong time.

At about the same moment that Ikner and Benson were leaving the Morrison house, an eighteen-year-old black man named Bill Hooks, Jr., was urinating against the wall of a convenience store in Clausell. By the time he finished, he could hear footsteps approaching from behind.

"What the hell are you doing, Bill?" a voice demanded.

Turning around, Hooks spotted the blue uniform and badge of Monroeville police sergeant Danny Ikner. (Danny was a distant relative of Woodrow and Larry Ikner.)

"Aw, man, you ain't going bust me just for taking a piss, are ya?" Hooks asked.

Ikner could smell beer on Hooks's breath. "C'mon," he ordered. "Get in the car."

"Only had one beer," Hooks grumbled as they walked to the police car. "Where else a man supposed to pee? No one round here let a black man inside."

Ikner ignored him. An older black man called out to them.

"You taking him to jail?" asked William Tidmore, whom everyone called Nappy. Ikner nodded. Hooks and Tidmore had been washing clothes and drinking beer in a nearby coin laundry when Hooks decided to relieve himself.

"Get my clothes for me, Nappy," Hooks yelled as the cruiser pulled from the parking lot.

In the car Hooks began to fidget. "Hey, man, I needs to talk to somebody," he announced.

"Sure you do, Bill," the officer replied.

"No man, I means it. I knowed about the murder at the cleaners, sure do, no way you'll be wantin' to put me in jail after you hear me."

Ikner glanced at Hooks in his rearview mirror. "Hooks had a reputation for running his mouth," he later recalled. "He would do anything or say anything if he thought it would help him stay out of jail. I figured he was lying that night."

When they reached the jail, Hooks began pestering Ikner again. "You gots to gits me someones to talk to. I really knowed somethin'. I ain't lying."

"Sure, Bill," Ikner replied as he filled out the necessary paperwork to jail Hooks for "public lewdness/pollution." A few minutes later Hooks was led away. Ikner could hear him as he was being taken down a hallway to a cell. Hooks was still insisting that he knew something about Ronda's murder, still demanding unsuccessfully that someone listen to his story.

Chapter 6

Shortly after Saturday midnight, the investigators gathered for a brainstorming session at their newly established command post inside the Monroeville police station. They focused on two promising leads. At least four witnesses had seen an older-model green car parked outside the cleaners at ten-thirty A.M. This was suspicious because there were no nametags in the store that indicated customers had left or picked up clothing at that time. Woodrow Ikner had sorted through all the tags and had established that Jan Owen, a local resident, had been the last customer in the store before the murder. Owen told the police she had dropped off a blouse and skirt at ten-fifteen A.M. and that Ronda had been fine when she left. The investigators knew that Jerrie Sue Dunning had arrived at the cleaners at ten forty-five, followed by Florence Mason and Coy Stacey. That meant Ronda had to have been robbed, sexually attacked, and murdered sometime during the thirty-minute interval between ten-fifteen and ten forty-five. Why was the green car parked at the cleaners at ten-thirty? Did it belong to the killer?

The investigators had also learned that a young Hispanic couple had been seen walking toward the cleaners at about the time of the murder and had then disappeared. Nearly everyone in the City Cafe, a restaurant across the street and a tenth of a mile north of the cleaners, had noticed the pair when they first strolled past the cafe's front windows. It would have been difficult to miss them. The man was wearing dirty black trousers, a blue-and-white-checked jacket, and a vivid rainbow-colored checked shirt, but it was the woman who had caught the eyes of the all-male coffee drinkers. Hot-orange spandex pants, a black top so snug it looked as if it might burst open, heavy eye makeup, and black high heels were not the normal Saturday-morning garb of women in town. The fifteen or so men inside the cafe were still joking about the couple when Lieutenant Woodrow Ikner sped by in his police car and everyone hurried outside to see what was going on. The coffee drinkers assumed there had been a robbery at Jackson Cleaners, and that was when someone mentioned the Hispanic pair. Where had they gone? There was no sign of them on the street.

Pumped with adrenaline, many of the investigators stayed awake all night discussing the murder, but little new was learned until early Sunday morning, when Chief Dailey and Woodrow Ikner returned to Jackson Cleaners to make certain they hadn't overlooked any clues. This time they spotted a bullet hole in one of the white acoustical ceiling tiles in the bathroom and found a .25 caliber slug lying on the floor under racks of clothes. Dailey and Ikner could now account for all five shots. One bullet had been fired into the bathroom ceiling; another had missed Ronda completely and eventually fallen to the floor; and three had struck her from behind.

Shortly after the men found the bullet hole and slug, the police dispatcher told them the Hispanic couple had been located and were being brought into the station for questioning. Dailey and Ikner hurried out to their police cars, but before they could leave they were stopped by Lauren Jones, an elderly white man who lived across the street from the store. He demanded to know if an arrest had been made, and when Ikner said no, Jones asked if they had interviewed Miles Jackson yet.

"Why?" Ikner asked.

"Because I saw him at the cleaners yesterday morning just before all the commotion started."

"You saw him?" Ikner asked. "Are you sure?"

"Of course I am," Jones snapped. "I've lived in this town long enough to know who Miles Jackson is. I saw his green car parked there too."

Back at the police station, Ikner quickly determined from state motor vehicle records that Miles Jackson owned a car that matched the description of the older-model green sedan witnesses had reported seeing at the cleaners at ten-thirty. He took Chief Dailey aside.

"When I talked to Miles Jackson yesterday, he told me he hadn't been in the cleaners for *six months*. He never said a word about being in there earlier that morning."

Carlos Roquellera, a skinny Cuban in his early twenties, was visibly scared. Woodrow Ikner and Deputy Chuck Sadhue asked most of the questions, though the interrogation room was crowded with investigators.

"*No entender*, no speak English well," Roquellera kept repeating. Few of the lawmen believed him, but none of them spoke Spanish, so they could not be sure. It took them about an hour to piece his answers together into an understandable story. Roquellera had followed his girlfriend, Maria, to town around four months earlier. Her parents rented an apartment on South Alabama Avenue about two blocks north of the cleaners. He was living three tenths of a mile east of Jackson Cleaners at the Lynam Apartments, where he paid eight dollars per night for a room. When asked, he could not produce a driver's license, social security card, or any other identification. He said he was working as a laborer. Roquellera admitted that he and Maria had gone on a walk Saturday morning along South Alabama Avenue, a route that had taken them past the City Cafe at around ten-thirty. But he insisted that they had never crossed the street or gone into the cleaners. The reason no one had seen them later was that they had taken a shortcut back to the Lynam Apartments. They had crossed an open field directly behind the City Cafe, out of sight of the coffee drinkers inside. Roquellera said he and Maria had stayed in his room for a few minutes when they got to the apartments and had then walked over to the rental unit she shared with her parents. They had spent the remainder of the day there.

"Have you ever been inside Jackson Cleaners?" Sadhue asked.

"*No limpiador*, too much money," Roquellera replied.

Had he heard or seen anything strange coming from the cleaners during his walk?

No.

Had he seen a green car parked there?

No.

Woodrow Ikner noticed a tattoo of a crucifix surrounded by a circle of dots on Roquellera's left hand. There was a diamond turned sideways tattooed on his left arm and a heart on his right arm. All were amateurish scratches in the flesh made by a needle and then filled with blue ink. Ikner had read that Cuban gang members often put tattoos on their hands to signify their criminal specialty or rank. He asked Roquellera about the marks and whether he had ever been in any sort of trouble with the police.

"*No policia,*" Roquellera replied.

How long had he been in the United States?

In a broken mixture of English and Spanish, Roquellera explained that he had been born in Havana in 1965 but had lived in Miami since the spring of 1980.

As he studied Roquellera, Sheriff-elect Tom Tate spotted a reddish-brown stain that looked like blood splattered on the top of the suspect's right shoe. He asked him about it.

"*Pollo*—chicken," Roquellera promptly replied. "*Cena,* I eat, last night." He made a chopping motion with his hands.

The owner of Lynam Apartments had mentioned that Roquellera kept several scrawny chickens in a flimsy coop behind the apartment unit, Sadhue volunteered. The Cuban could have killed one for dinner. Roquellera then nervously offered a second explanation. Holding up his hand, he showed them a small cut and then pointed down at his shoe and shrugged. As the investigators were discussing his explanations in low voices, a clerk came into the room and handed Dailey a copy of a routine computer background check on Roquellera. According to the check, he was wanted in Naples, Florida, for violating his parole. In April 1984 Roquellera and a friend had been caught burglarizing a Kentucky Fried Chicken restaurant. He had been sentenced to three years in prison but had been paroled after spending only two months in jail. One of the conditions of his release was that he would remain under police supervision in Collier County, but he had fled two weeks after he was freed.

When the investigators confronted Roquellera with the report, he shrugged. He had not lied to them, he said. He simply had not understood their earlier questions. He was told to strip and was handed a pair of jail-issue overalls to wear. The investigators had noticed that he was dressed in the same clothes he had been seen in Saturday morning, and they wanted to send them to the state crime lab. Samples of hair from his head, armpits, and pubic area were also taken, and arrangements were made for a blood specimen to be drawn. If the Mobile lab could link Roquellera in any way to Jackson Cleaners, he would be charged with killing Ronda.

Maria, interviewed next, seemed surprised when told that Roquellera had not understood questions asked in English. She repeated the same story about Saturday morning that he had given until she reached the part about their going to her parents' apartment. After they took the shortcut back to the Lynam Apartments, Roquellera had noticed that he was out of cigarettes, she told them, so he had sent her on to her parents' apartment while he made a quick trip to a grocery store. She wasn't certain where he had actually gone because when he returned—some twenty minutes later—he still didn't have any cigarettes. He said the store had been out of his brand.

"Have you or Carlos ever been inside Jackson Cleaners?" Maria was asked.

No, she answered, but she *had* gotten angry at him recently because he had mentioned that an attractive blonde worked there. She had been jealous, and had teasingly referred to the blonde as his "new girlfriend."

The investigators hurried Roquellera back into the interrogation room and quizzed him about Maria's statements. Once again he insisted that he hadn't lied. He had not understood them and had simply forgotten about his trip to buy cigarettes.

"The closest grocery store is on the *same* side of the street as Jackson Cleaners," Sadhue said. "You had to cross South Alabama Avenue to get there."

"No, no, no," Roquellera replied. "*No dinero. No dinero.*" He had intended to cross the street but had realized at the last minute that he was short of cash, so he had simply returned to the apartment where Maria was waiting.

"Why'd you tell her the store didn't have your brand?" he was asked.

He hadn't wanted to admit in front of his girlfriend's parents that he didn't have enough money to buy a single pack of smokes.

None of the investigators believed him. It would have taken Roquellera only about ten minutes to do what he had just described, not twenty. But he stuck to his story and then suddenly offered them more.

"I hear noises from the cleaners."

"*What?*" asked Sadhue.

"Popping," Roquellera replied. "Popping noises come from the cleaners."

"What did they sound like?"

"Bang! Bang! *Fuegos artificiales!*"

"How could you have heard popping noises if you were standing across the street from the cleaners?" Sadhue asked. South Alabama Avenue was four lanes wide there.

Roquellera seemed unable to think of the correct words. "Bang! Bang!" he repeated. "I hear."

As soon as he was returned to his cell the investigators began discussing his alibi. Witnesses had seen him and Maria walking by the City Cafe. What happened next was easy to imagine. Roquellera had spotted Ronda through the front windows of the lobby and had noticed that she was working alone. He had hurried Maria back to his room, where he had secretly tucked a .25 caliber pistol under his shirt and then announced that he was out of cigarettes. After sending Maria to her parents' apartment, he had raced across the field behind City Cafe, run across South Alabama Avenue, and burst into the cleaners. He had quickly looted the cash register and then ordered Ronda into the back room. Perhaps he had planned on locking her in the bathroom, only to discover that there was no bolt on the door. Maybe Ronda had resisted. Maybe he had decided on the spur of the moment to rape her. She was, after all, beautiful. Or maybe he had always planned on killing her and had simply decided to rape her first. In the end, did it matter? For whatever reason, Roquellera had killed Ronda and then hustled back to his girlfriend's arms, thinking she would provide him with a perfect alibi. If they were lucky, the blood on Roquellera's shoe would match Ronda's blood type and they would have all the evidence they needed. In less than forty-eight hours they had come up with a prime suspect. There was only one skeptic in the room.

"If the Cuban killed that little girl," Woodrow Ikner wondered aloud, "what was Miles Jackson's car doing parked outside the cleaners at ten-thirty?"

Chapter

7

The next day, Sunday, investigators finally interviewed Randy Thomas, the owner of Jackson Cleaners. He had been out of town Saturday morning and had not learned about the murder until he returned to Monroeville later that day. When Police Chief Bill Dailey had told him Ronda was dead, Thomas had burst into tears and become so distraught that Dailey had decided to put off questioning him for a day. Thomas seemed to be in better emotional shape when he reported to the police station shortly after five o'clock. However, as soon as ABI agent Mike Barnett, who was conducting the interview, mentioned Ronda's name, Thomas broke down again. The agent gave him a few moments to compose himself before asking him another question, but Thomas continued to have trouble answering. His lower lip shook, and his puffy eyes floated in tears. Agent Simon Benson, who was helping Barnett, reached over and held Thomas's hand. That seemed to calm him enough for them to continue.

During their tape-recorded session, Thomas revealed that Miles Jackson had shown up unexpectedly at his apartment late Saturday night and had talked to him about the murder. "Mr. Jackson told me, 'I was the last one to see that girl alive! I was there at ten-thirty! . . . If I'd been there a few minutes later or hung around a few minutes longer, I might have been dead too or else maybe I could have stopped it . . .' "

Jackson had been certain of the time, Thomas said, because he had stopped at a local bank to deposit a check before driving to the cleaners. "Mr. Jackson showed me a bank deposit slip. He took it out of his pocket and it had a time marked on it." The time on the slip was 10:19 A.M. Jackson had estimated that it had taken him about five minutes more to drive from the bank to the cleaners.

Sliding the tape recorder forward across the table so that the microphone was only inches from Thomas, Barnett asked him if he was absolutely certain that Miles Jackson had admitted that he had been in the cleaners at ten-thirty on Saturday.

"Yes," Thomas answered. "He told me he was there."

Why then was there no record of his visit? Barnett asked. Jackson's name had not been found on any of the customer nametags in the store.

No one ever attached nametags to Jackson's clothing, Thomas replied, because all his garments were cleaned free of charge in accordance with the sales agreement they had signed when the store changed owners. Everyone knew that the clothes without nametags belonged to Miles or Doris Jackson.

During their meeting Thomas said he had asked Jackson if he had told the police that he had seen Ronda on Saturday. "Mr. Jackson said, 'Maybe I did. Yes, I did.' . . . And then he said, 'No, I didn't.' He said, 'They didn't ask me anything, so I figured . . .' He said they didn't ask him anything about it, so 'I guess it's not important.' "

"You asked Mr. Jackson if he had told the police that he was there at ten-thirty . . ."

"Right . . ."

". . . and his response was what?"

"That he didn't feel—he thought—he assumed that the police didn't think it was important because they hadn't asked him about it."

Barnett had one final question for Thomas. Had Ronda or the other girls ever told him how they felt about Jackson? Yes, Thomas said, nodding, all of them had felt "uncomfortable" whenever he came into the store.

At nine o'clock two deputies rang the buzzer at the Jacksons' house. Miles recognized one of them. He was a distant cousin. "Mr. Jackson," the other deputy said, "we need you to come down to the police department to answer a few questions."

. . .

On most Sundays Miles Jackson could be found singing in the choir of the First United Methodist Church, and when he had still owned Jackson Cleaners, his fellow parishioners had often joked that he enjoyed a "spotless" reputation. Jackson was proud of that.

He could trace his ancestry back to a brother of President Andrew Jackson. He himself had been named after his grandfather, a soldier in the Confederacy. His father, William Charles Jackson, had served on Monroeville's city council, and one of his uncles was president of a local bank. Jackson had never been in trouble with the police, never been associated with even a hint of scandal. He had been born and reared in Monroeville, had attended Auburn University, where he had met and married Doris, had joined the army at the outbreak of World War II, and had returned home in 1945 and bought Jackson Cleaners from his parents. Back then most white families in town hired black women to wash and iron their clothing, but with time that changed and Jackson Cleaners became the most prosperous laundry and dry cleaners in town. During the thirty-eight years when Miles and Doris owned it, the business had provided them with ample income to raise and educate three children, pay the mortgage on a cozy ranch-style home, and enjoy a comfortable life. Now that both were retired, Miles considered himself a proud and well-respected member of the community.

Lieutenant Woodrow Ikner had always thought Jackson was arrogant.

The two men had known each other most of their lives. But they had grown up under very different circumstances. Jackson could recall the time when Ikner was a boy, one of seven children being raised by a penniless widow who was forced to take in laundry and clean houses, just as black domestics did, to pay her bills. There were times when the Ikner family had been forced to accept donations: secondhand clothing and Christmas baskets from churches in town. Ikner had grown up being called "that poor little Ikner boy," and in a small town that was not quickly forgotten.

Jackson would later complain that as soon as he stepped into the police station, Ikner began treating him as if he were a criminal. "The first thing Woodrow did was read me my rights and tell me that I needed to hire a lawyer. I thought he was joking. I said, 'Why would I spend money on a lawyer when I know I haven't done anything wrong?' and he says, 'Well, we'll just see about that.' "

Ikner began spitting questions at Jackson without giving him time to respond. Why hadn't he told the police that he had been inside the cleaners on the morning of the murder? What had happened between him and Ronda? Why had she told her friends and parents she was afraid of him?

The accusatory tone of Ikner's grilling surprised the retired businessman. He hadn't actually realized until that moment that he was a suspect.

"I have never tried to hide anything from the police," he sputtered.

"Why'd you tell Deputy Sadhue that you hadn't been inside the cleaners for two weeks?" Ikner demanded. "Why'd you tell me you hadn't been there for six months!"

"I never said such a thing!" Jackson retorted. "I have nothing to hide. I can explain everything if you'd let me."

Ikner turned silent, and Jackson told the roomful of investigators what he had done on Saturday. He had driven to the bank at 10:19 A.M., which he could prove because he still had the deposit slip. From there he had gone directly to the cleaners to pick up a few items he had dropped off earlier that week. "Two women were coming outside carrying clothes. I always wear a hat. My daddy always wore a hat, and he tipped his hat to people, and so do I. I tipped my hat to the ladies as I passed."

Ronda had been sitting at the metal desk behind the counter reading a book when he had walked in. She hadn't bothered waiting on him. "They knew I had the run of the cleaners. I was management . . . so I went to get my clothes."

There was a blouse mixed in with his laundry and he knew it did not belong to his wife, so he asked Ronda if she recognized it. "She shook her head, indicating no. I took my clothes and said, 'See you later.' I remember those were my exact words because I never saw her again."

He had driven directly home and gone to work in his backyard, which was where he was when the police called and demanded that he hurry to the cleaners. He had been so upset when he was told that Ronda was dead that his mind had gone blank, he said. "I have a heart condition. I felt faint. I was so upset. I don't even remember who told me that little girl was dead."

"You're lying!" Ikner announced. "I told you about the girl! I told you she was dead!"

"I don't know if it was you or not!" Jackson snapped. "I simply heard a voice behind me say that the girl was deceased. It could have been you or someone else."

Jackson said he hadn't realized until he was driving home from the cleaners that he had forgotten to mention that he had seen Ronda earlier that morning. "It hit me like a ton of bricks. I was probably one of the last persons to see that little girl alive."

Ikner was skeptical. He forced Jackson to repeat his story over and over again. He was looking for discrepancies, but there were none. Several of the other investigators in the room began to grow weary of Ikner's repetitive questions. Finally he told Jackson he could leave, but rather than hurrying out the door, the elderly suspect asked if the investigators were interested in hearing his theory about the killing.

"Whoever went in there didn't go in to rob the cleaners," Jackson said, "because it is a well-known fact that the cleaners didn't have much money. The robbery was clearly an afterthought."

"Why did the killer go in there, then?" Ikner asked.

"It should be obvious. He went to sexually molest that little girl."

As soon as he heard himself saying those words, Jackson regretted it. He could tell from the reactions on their faces that his comments had only made the investigators even more suspicious of him. As soon as he left the station, Ikner and Sadhue attacked his story. His explanation about not remembering that he had been in the cleaners on Saturday morning seemed far-fetched to both men. Why hadn't he simply called the police as soon as he did remember? they asked. After all, he had gone to see Randy Thomas later that night and acknowledged then that he had been the last to see Ronda. And what about the two women who he claimed were coming out of the laundry at ten-thirty? No one had found any nametags in the cleaners verifying that the women had been there. Finally Jackson said the crime was a rape, the robbery a ruse. How could he be so certain? Ikner and Sadhue's criticism sparked others. Hadn't the Morrisons said that Ronda hid in the bathroom whenever Jackson came into the cleaners? Was it a coincidence that she and her killer had struggled there?

Just as they had done with Carlos Roquellera, the group of detectives began to imagine possible scenarios—only this time with Jackson as the killer. There was no evidence, of course, but within minutes they had built a plausible case against him based entirely on their own conjectures. It began with Ronda's running into the bathroom to hide as soon as she saw Jackson's car pull up in front of the store. He had walked into the lobby, had seen that it was empty, and had gone looking for her. Jackson had mentioned during Ikner's questioning that Thomas had asked him to keep an eye on the store while he was out of town. Obviously Jackson would have had a valid reason to wonder why the clerk wasn't in the lobby. When he spotted the light shining from under the bathroom door, he knew where Ronda was hiding. He also knew that the lock on the bathroom door did not work. Nearly all the investigators agreed that Jackson had a big ego. Maybe he thought Ronda would welcome his sexual advances. She was naive and friendly. Had he misread her smiles? Had he pushed open that bathroom door and surprised her? If so, Ronda would have panicked. Had she threatened to tell her parents, to call the police? Jackson would have known that the word of an innocent such as Ronda would be believed over his. He would have known that his "spotless" reputation would be ruined. Had that been enough to make him kill her?

Larry Ikner wasn't buying it. Why would a prominent retired businessman with absolutely no criminal record suddenly assault a teenage girl? Most rapists have a long history of sexual misconduct and no one in town, to his knowledge, had ever accused Jackson of even flirting. Besides, he was an old man with poor eyesight and unsteady feet. Couldn't she have pushed him aside? Even more important, if Jackson was the killer, that meant he had planned the rape and murder. Why else would he take a .25 caliber handgun with him into the cleaners? Did anyone in the room really believe that Miles Jackson was capable of premeditated murder?

"Lots of men carry guns for protection," someone countered. "Maybe things just got out of hand."

For the next several minutes the men argued about whether the killer's motive had been rape, robbery, or both. In the midst of this free-for-all there was a knock on the door. It was Charles Morrison. The room fell silent. In a quiet voice he thanked them for working such long hours. He knew they were doing their best to identify Ronda's killer, and he wanted them to know that he and Bertha appreciated it. Then, his words becoming a whisper, he explained that he had come to the police station to ask them for a personal favor. He was asking it as one man talking to other men, not as a victim talking to the police but as a father—someone they had known for years—speaking to other fathers.

"When you find out who did this," he was later quoted as saying, "I want a few minutes with him."

He was not going to harm or kill the person who had murdered his child, he explained. He wasn't going to take the law into his own hands. He simply wanted to meet the murderer face-to-face, to look into the eyes of his daughter's killer and ask him a single question: "Why did you have to murder my little girl?"

Deputy Sadhue felt tears building. He glanced around the room. He wasn't the only one fighting to hold them back.

Having said what he had come to say, Morrison left, but the room remained quiet for several moments. Sheriff-elect Tom Tate admired Morrison, but Tate said to himself that it would be dangerous putting Ronda's father in the same room as her killer. Still, he was struck by Morrison's plea. Like them, he was searching for an explanation. Rape? Robbery? Why did the intruder have to *kill* her? Why hadn't he simply tied up Ronda and left her in the back room?

When the debate began again, the investigators soon found themselves talking in circles. And then someone, no one would later remember who, suggested a new idea. What if both the rape and the robbery had been staged to cover up the actual motive? What if there was some other explanation for Ronda's death that they were overlooking? Suddenly ideas gushed out. Drugs? Gambling? Money laundering? Counterfeiting? Sexual escapades? Had the cleaners been used as a distribution point for crack cocaine? People said Randy Thomas liked to bet on football games. What if he owed the Mafia money and it had come looking for him and had killed Ronda as a warning? What if Ronda had seen or overheard something at the cleaners related to drugs and had had to be silenced? She wasn't supposed to be at work on Saturday, someone recalled. What if the killer had really been after the other girl? Randy Thomas owned a late-model BMW, another investigator pointed out. How could he afford such an expensive car? Wasn't that car popular with drug dealers? Why had Thomas chosen this particular weekend to be out of town? Had he known that Ronda was going to be killed? Maybe the store was used to launder drug money. Were Thomas and Jackson both involved? Had Ronda found out something so sinister about them and the cleaners that they had hired an outsider to murder her? Had she been killed by professional hit men who had then made it look like a robbery and rape attempt?

Talk about money laundering, the Mafia, and professional hit men would have been greeted with guffaws not too long before in Monroeville. Not anymore. The reason was drugs. In the late 1960s bootleggers were more of a problem than drug traffickers in southern Alabama, but that had changed in the early 1970s, when marijuana became more plentiful and federal and state agencies began beefing up enforcement in the larger port cities along the Gulf. When it became difficult to move drugs through cities such as New Orleans, Mobile, and Miami, dealers began choosing smaller harbors and journeying inland to sleepy towns where the local police were neither equipped nor trained to deal with them. A trafficker could easily unload his cargo into cars and trucks in the port of Pensacola, Florida, only forty miles south of the Alabama border, and then drive along back roads, crossing into Alabama in less than an hour. In addition to smugglers, sheriffs throughout southern Alabama suddenly began finding fields of marijuana plants growing freely in their counties. The soil and weather were conducive not only to cotton and timber, but also to the more profitable illegal weed. While it was impossible to calculate just how much drug activity there was in Monroe County in 1986, there were enough rumors to ensure that whenever there was a violent crime, drugs were mentioned.

As the night slowly became morning, the theories grew wilder and wilder. Innuendos were cited as facts, suppositions as the truth. When the session finally ended in the early-morning hours, no consensus had been reached, but plenty of seeds had been planted for motives other than rape and robbery. Deputy William Gibson would later recall feeling dazed by all the conjecture. "There was talk that Ronda had been murdered by the mob and professional killers." Inside the command post such speculation might have sounded plausible, but when Gibson stepped outside into the crisp morning air, reality returned. This was Monroeville, not Los Angeles, not Chicago, not New York City. He knew Randy Thomas. He knew Miles Jackson. He had known Ronda and he knew the other girls. He also knew who most of the drug peddlers in town were, and he had never known Ronda to associate with any of them. Less than forty-eight hours had passed since her body had been discovered, but Gibson already was beginning to believe that the murder investigation was slipping out of control. Mafia hits. Jackson-Thomas conspiracies. Drugs. Money laundering.

"It was nuts," he later recalled, "simply nuts."

Chapter 8

An autopsy verified that Ronda Morrison had died from three shots fired out of a .25 caliber handgun. One slug had hit her upper left arm, splintering the bone. Another had penetrated her right shoulder, going downward into both lungs. A third had entered the center of her back, where it had severed her spinal cord, ripped into her chest cavity, and punctured her right lung. Dr. Gary D. Cumberland and Dr. LeRoy Riddick, both state medical examiners, estimated that Ronda had remained alive for at least five minutes after she was shot. Her death had been neither quick, they concluded, nor painless.

Of the three gunshots, the one in Ronda's right shoulder was the most intriguing. Unlike the other two shots, it had been fired downward into Ronda's body, moving diagonally from right to left into her chest cavity. The shoulder wound also contained stippling, tiny bits of residue that were blown out of the pistol when the bullet was fired. Stippling is found in wounds only when a gun has been fired at close range, usually within two feet of the victim. Ronda's wound contained so much stippling that the medical examiners estimated the murder weapon had been only a few inches from her skin when it was fired. This discovery proved to be the key that the examiners needed to unlock the secret of what had happened inside the cleaners.

Drs. Cumberland and Riddick knew from reading the crime scene reports that Ronda had been in close contact with her killer only twice. They had clearly struggled in the bathroom, as evidenced by the shell casing on the floor and the broken necklace found there, and they had been close together when the killer fired his gun in the northeast corner of the building, as evidenced by the shell casing found lying six inches from Ronda's head. This meant that the shoulder wound with stippling had to be either one of the first bullets fired in the bathroom or the very last. But which was it?

The examiners solved that puzzle after studying the other two gunshot wounds. The one to Ronda's left arm could have been made at any time and was not lethal, but the bullet fired into the center of her back had severed her spinal cord. It was this wound that gave them the clue they needed. "Once Ronda's spinal cord was severed, she would have lost control of both legs," Cumberland explained later during an interview. Photographs of her body taken at the crime scene showed that her legs were spread apart when she was lying facedown, with the left leg bent slightly forward. Her left arm was hanging useless beneath her, but her right arm was extended. To even a casual observer it appeared as if she had been trying to push herself forward on the floor with her legs and right arm. Such an effort would not have been possible if her spinal cord had already been cut.

Based on what they had learned from the location of the bullets and what they had read in the crime scene reports and seen in the photographs, Cumberland and Riddick decided that the bullet that made the shoulder wound had been fired while Ronda and her attacker were struggling in the employee bathroom. This is how they accounted for the five shots fired that morning: One had gone into the bathroom ceiling and another into Ronda's right shoulder. Although she was wounded, Ronda had broken free and run toward the northeast corner. The killer had chased her, firing two more times. One of these shots hit her in the left arm; the other missed entirely. By this point enough blood had rushed into her lungs, both of which had been penetrated by the first bullet, that she fell to the floor. She was, however, still conscious, and as the killer rushed forward, she instinctively tried to crawl under a rack of clothes to get away. The killer had fired his fifth and final shot directly into her back while standing over her. This bullet had severed her spinal cord and stopped all movement.

Although the examiners believed their reconstruction was accurate, both felt frustrated. Cumberland later complained during an interview about the way the Monroeville police had handled the scene. Had he or another trained examiner been able to study the site before Ronda's body had been removed, Cumberland was confident, the firing order of the bullets could have been easily documented. During the autopsy he and Riddick also had found bruises on Ronda's face and neck where the killer had slapped and choked her. While it is difficult to obtain fingerprints from human skin, it is possible—if done by a specially trained technician within one hour of a murder. The state crime lab's team could have checked Ronda's face and neck for fingerprints, Cumberland said, but its technicians did not arrive in Monroeville until five hours after her body was found. By then it was much too late.

The remainder of the autopsy report was routine. Ronda had been a nail biter; her fingernails were chewed to the quick, so there was nothing underneath them, such as skin possibly scratched from the murderer during a fight. No semen or sperm was found on or in her body or on her undergarments or outer clothing. She had not been sexually molested. Her blood and urine samples showed no indication of illegal drugs or alcohol.

The autopsy had turned up several important clues, but what irritated Cumberland and Riddick was how many more there could have been if a state team had been called in earlier to do its job.

So many mourners crowded into Eastwood Baptist Church at two o'clock on Monday for Ronda Morrison's funeral that there were not enough seats. The Reverend William "Billy" Sunday, who had been pastor at the church for two years, estimated the crowd at eight hundred, making this the largest funeral service he had ever conducted.

The preacher had met earlier with Charles and Bertha Morrison and had prayed with them. "We don't understand Ronda's death now, but God never does anything foolishly," he had assured them. "He always has a reason for everything He does and He has a reason for this."

Near tears, Charles had confided that on the morning of the murder he had sensed that Ronda was in grave danger but had not acted on those feelings, and now he felt guilty. "God was sending you a premonition," Sunday declared. "The Lord was trying to prepare you for Ronda's death." There was no need for Charles to torture himself, the minister continued, because if God had wanted Charles to stop his daughter from going to work, then God would have made certain that he did exactly that. "We have to believe that something good will come out of this. God has a reason for allowing Ronda to die."

In his eulogy at the church, Sunday told the mourners that for a true Christian, death has no sting. "Heaven is a real and genuine place," he proclaimed, "and Jesus has promised us that Ronda and others who believe in Him will be with Him in paradise." Glancing down from the pulpit, Sunday saw that most of the congregation was in tears. But not Charles and Bertha. "They walked out of that service with their heads held high," he recalled later. "These good, decent, humble people, who were hurting inside so badly, knew that Ronda was with her heavenly father and their faith sustained them."

On Monday night Police Chief Dailey announced over Monroeville radio station WMFC that the city was offering a $3,000 reward for information leading to the conviction of Ronda's killer. Dailey also told *The Monroe Journal* that the hardware store on the town square had sold a record number of guns. "I know many many rumors are circulating around town," he explained, "but I would ask citizens to wait for us to determine the facts of the case." Meanwhile, he urged residents "to lock their doors and not walk alone at night."

Early Tuesday morning, the police asked Miles Jackson if he would take a polygraph test. Jackson was afraid to say no. "How is this going to look to the police, the gossips, and the public, if I refuse?" he asked Doris. The ABI had one of its polygraph examiners from Mobile meet him at the police station. After he was connected to the machine, Jackson was asked to pick a number between one and ten. He chose six. The examiner then counted from one to ten, pausing after each number to ask if that was the one Jackson had selected. Jackson answered truthfully, and when they finished the examiner showed him a graph paper filled with straight lines. He was then instructed to lie, and when they repeated the exercise the needles of the polygraph jumped wildly. "I just wanted to show you that you can't fool this machine," the examiner warned. During the next two hours Jackson was given three separate tests. Each time he was asked if he had killed Ronda Morrison or been inside the cleaners when she was murdered. Each time the tests showed that he was telling the truth when he denied knowing anything about the murder. When he returned home, he burst inside and hurried to tell Doris the results.

"I passed!" he declared.

"Well, of course you did," she replied.

Later that same afternoon Simon Benson and Larry Ikner stopped at Randy Thomas's apartment. A rumor was circulating around town that Thomas had wanted to date Ronda but that she had refused to go out with him. When Benson and Ikner knocked, Thomas opened the door a crack. He peeked out, then opened the door completely, but he did not invite them in. "I've hired an attorney," he told them, "and he said I wasn't supposed to answer any questions."

Taken by surprise, Ikner and Benson explained that they had simply stopped to give him a chance to put an end to a few rumors before people got the wrong impression.

"My attorney said not to talk to you unless he's with me," Thomas repeated. "Sorry, you'll have to call him." He shut the door.

Chapter 9

Woodrow Ikner felt like a man trying to hold smoke in his hands. The state crime lab sent word that it could find no physical evidence linking Carlos Roquellera to Ronda's murder. None of his hairs matched those found on her body or in the cleaners. While the reddish-brown spot on his right shoe was "consistent with human blood" and was thought to be type A, both he and Ronda had type A blood, and the sample was too small for the lab to determine whose it was. The lab noted that neither the soles of Roquellera's shoes nor his clothing contained any of sixty-seven substances found on the floor and elsewhere in Jackson Cleaners. It concluded that Roquellera had not been inside the building. Polygraph efforts also proved fruitless. He was given six tests. At first Ikner was encouraged, because each demonstrated that the suspect was lying. But the examiner noted that Roquellera seemed to have difficulty understanding English, and when he was given a new test and it showed that he was being "deceptive" even after he correctly answered such insignificant questions as whether or not the sun was shining, Ikner knew that the earlier results were flawed. The ABI spent a day searching for someone in the state who was qualified to give polygraph exams and also spoke Spanish, but it failed to find anyone. The police had no choice but to turn Roquellera over to Florida parole officials.

Miles Jackson, meanwhile, took refuge in his home. Even though he had passed a polygraph test, Ikner still considered him a prime suspect, and he remained the focus of gossip. Depressed, he and Doris talked about moving to another town.

Because of the cool reception Randy Thomas had given Larry Ikner and Simon Benson, the investigators added his name to their list of suspects, and for several days they questioned people about his background. Thomas had moved to Monroeville shortly after marrying into a well-to-do family in 1978. His in-laws had later helped him purchase Jackson Cleaners, but he had never really enjoyed running the place. He was reserved, didn't like fraternizing with customers, and had a tough time mixing with his wife's country club friends. In September 1985 his wife divorced him, and he started visiting his parents in Tuscaloosa nearly every weekend. Except for Ronda and the other two girls who worked for him, he had no real friends.

While Thomas's divorce, aloofness, and fondness for Ronda provided plenty of grist for the investigators at their nightly brainstorming sessions, they were unable to find a shred of evidence that tied him to the murder. Both his parents swore that he had been with them in Tuscaloosa when Ronda was killed. The fact that they were his only alibi witnesses struck some investigators as suspicious, but they could find nothing to challenge the parents' statements.

On December 6 the city held a cookout to raise money for a scholarship in Ronda's name at Patrick Henry State Junior College. The organizers' goal was to raise $23,000, the equivalent of $1 from every county resident. Picnickers ate hamburgers cooked atop portable grills erected in a park near the Vanity Fair outlet store. Most of the police, deputy sheriffs, and ABI agents investigating the case attended, and each assured the predominantly white crowd that it was only a matter of time before Ronda's killer would be caught. But privately they knew better. They were running out of leads. A week after the picnic, the nightly brainstorming sessions came to an end and the extra ABI agents assigned to help solve the case were reassigned to more pressing matters. Woodrow Ikner, who had initially worried about being elbowed out of the investigation, now found himself being pushed to the front whenever someone was needed to take the blame. Sheriff-elect Tom Tate was quick to remind everyone that he was not yet in office and that the investigation was being handled by the police department. Gradually the realization that the police were stumped seeped through the town.

Not knowing what else to do, Ikner decided to organize the dozens of witness statements that had been collected. The police had asked most of the witnesses to write their own statements, and many were in longhand. Ikner tried to find someone willing to type them, but no one at the station had time for so mundane a chore. He ended up taking them home for his wife to transcribe.

A few days before Christmas, District Attorney Ted Pearson hurried Larry Ikner into his office and showed him a letter he had just received. "I know who killed Ronda Morrison," the writer claimed, "and can lead you right to him." Neither man recognized the signature at the bottom of the page, but both were familiar with the return address on the envelope. The letter was from James Wally Peterson, an inmate at the Limestone Correctional Facility, a maximum-security state prison near Huntsville. Ikner contacted Benson and Tate and arranged for the three of them to interview Peterson the next morning. No one said a word about the letter to Woodrow Ikner. The time for cooperation was over.

Peterson greeted the three men as if they were close friends. The convict was in his early thirties, bone-thin, with ghostly white skin, the opaque color of a fish that lives so deep in the ocean that no sunlight ever penetrates its world. Since they had not taken time to read his prison file, he gave them a brief autobiography. He was serving the sixth year of a fifteen-year sentence for extortion. He was a recovering alcoholic, former drug addict, and sometime paid police informant. He was blunt. In return for his help, he wanted a parole.

During the tape-recorded session that followed, Peterson said he had learned about Ronda's murder during a telephone conversation with his girlfriend, a drug addict in Mobile. She had been in a rather seedy bar when, in Peterson's own words, "this dude starts hitting on her for sex and, uh, he's wanting to impress her and all, so he just tells her straight out that he's the one who robbed the cleaners in Monroeville and whacked the girl there." Peterson's girlfriend had discreetly grilled the man for more details, then followed him outside surreptitiously and written down the number of his license plate. All Peterson had to do was get in touch with his girlfriend again and she could finger Ronda's killer.

Tate had heard a lot of strange stories from convicts during his long career as a parole officer, and he knew that most were lies. If Peterson wanted their help, Tate said, he was going to have to convince them that he was telling the truth.

"Now that ain't no problem at all," Peterson replied, and for the next several minutes he spouted various facts about the murder. But he didn't say anything that had not already been widely reported in the media, and when he finished his spiel Larry Ikner pointed this out.

"I ain't read no newspapers or seen no television for weeks," Peterson protested, " 'cause I've been locked in the Hole and they don't got TVs and papers there. 'Tain't no way I could have read nothing about this case."

The three investigators remained unconvinced, and Peterson apparently sensed that. "My girlfriend," he informed them, "told me the murder weapon was a twenty-five-caliber semiautomatic pistol."

The caliber of the handgun was a detail that the police had withheld from the public. Only they and the killer were supposed to know it.

Peterson continued. "This dude tells my girlfriend that he fired off, now he himself wasn't sure, but maybe four or five rounds but, he says, maybe only three hit her."

Once again Peterson had just told them confidential information. The number of times Ronda had been shot had not been publicized.

"How much did the robber get?" Ikner asked.

Peterson laughed. "Hell, man, nothing but chump change. Even this dude, he says it weren't worth no killing."

During the next hour they tried to pry more from Peterson, but the only clue he volunteered was that the killer drove a late-model gray Mazda. "If you get me in touch with my girlfriend, Becky White, I can get her to answer all your questions, but if you try to question her without me being there, she'll disappear into the drug underground and I don't care if you are the ABI, FBI, CIA, or president of the United States, you'll never find her."

Since Peterson was a state prisoner, Ikner and Tate thought the ABI should handle him. Benson briefed Mike Barnett, who was still the senior agent in charge of the case. With help from prison officials, Barnett arranged for Peterson to take a polygraph test. He passed it. The examiner said his machine clearly showed that Peterson was telling the truth about his girlfriend's telephone call and her offer to help catch Ronda's killer.

Satisfied that his story was real, Barnett arranged for Peterson to have access to a telephone so that he could call Becky White. For several hours Peterson tried but failed to find her. "She's a junkie, y'see, so she spends her time with other addicts, going from one crack house to another," he explained. Barnett had Peterson moved into a special cell from which he could make phone calls at any hour. A few days later the agent was jarred awake at 3:20 A.M. by a ringing telephone. Peterson was on the line. His girlfriend was staying with friends in Tuscaloosa, he announced, and she was still willing to identify Ronda's killer—but only if Peterson was with her when she was questioned. "She don't trust cops," he said, "so if I ain't there, she ain't talking."

Transporting prisoners is always risky, particularly if they are going onto familiar turf. Peterson was from Tuscaloosa, and Barnett knew he could easily have been using his access to a telephone to arrange an escape. But Barnett was also desperate. He kept reassuring himself. After all, Peterson had known inside information about the murder and had passed a polygraph test.

Shortly after Christmas Peterson was taken in leg irons and handcuffs by car to the ABI office in Tuscaloosa, where he was handed a telephone and told to call White. All morning he tried, and each time Barnett listened in he could hear the convict pleading with his contacts, asking them to tell him where White was staying. By late afternoon Barnett was beginning to fidget, but Peterson assured him he was getting close. Soon afterward he reported word from a friend that White and some other addicts were spending the night in a trailer at Cedar Creek, a fishing spot some thirty-five miles away. Barnett hustled Peterson into the back of an unmarked car and, with a second carload of ABI agents following them, they headed there. Peterson gave directions, leading them through the woods and deeper and deeper into a swampy area that Barnett realized would be perfect for an ambush. When they finally located the trailer, Peterson slid down in the seat so that he couldn't be seen. While it was likely he had done this because he didn't want anyone to know that he was a police snitch, another thought also ran through Barnett's mind: "He's ducking down because someone is going to start shooting." The cars stopped fifty feet from the trailer, and the agents made their cautious way forward. The trailer was deserted. An angry Barnett raced back to the car.

"What kind of game are you playing?" he demanded.

"Hey, I never said she was here," Peterson replied. "I said she *might* be here."

Back at the ABI office in Tuscaloosa, Barnett gave Peterson an ultimatum: He had until midnight to find White or he was going back to prison. At 11:58, Peterson announced that White was in a nearby apartment complex, staying with a major drug dealer.

"Let's go," a jubilant Barnett declared.

"No way," said Peterson. "If the cops roll up there, this dealer will start shooting, and if he finds out I brought you, he will kill Becky."

"Then call her and tell her to meet us somewhere else," Barnett suggested.

"No," the inmate said. He had his own plan. "Becky won't come out of the apartment unless I go to the door and ask for her, so here's the deal. You take off the leg irons and handcuffs and let me walk up to the apartment door by myself. Then I'll go inside and get her and bring her out—as simple as that."

There was no way Barnett was going to turn Peterson loose. He figured Peterson would run. Besides, they could not know who might really be waiting in the apartment. He could have used one of his phone calls to arrange for a friend to meet him there with a gun. He could also be telling the truth about White.

"You are this close," Peterson said, holding his right thumb and forefinger less than an inch apart, "to catching Ronda Morrison's killer. All you got to do is trust me. I ain't gonna run. I want you to get me a parole."

Barnett offered Peterson a compromise. He would have an undercover officer go with Peterson into the apartment. No one would know he was a cop.

Peterson let loose a burst of profanity. "You are about to blow this big-time!" he threatened. "We go my way or we don't go. Now, do you want to catch Ronda's killer or not?"

Everyone was exhausted. In a final effort, Barnett appealed to Peterson's conscience. "Think about Ronda's parents. Think about that dead girl who didn't deserve to be killed like that. Think about how much good you will be doing. It's the right thing to do, James."

"Hey, man," Peterson replied coldly, "you're the man who is letting a killer go free."

A minute passed that seemed like an hour. Finally Peterson smashed out the remains of his cigarette. "Take me back to prison," he snarled.

When Barnett went to see Peterson the next morning, the convict refused to meet with him. It took Barnett two weeks, but he found Becky White on his own. She was not a junkie. She was married to a police officer and the mother of two small children. Before she had met her husband, she said, she had dated Peterson and he had become obsessed with her. For nearly nine years he had been harassing her. Had anyone bothered to read his prison file, White said, they would have found memos about his previous attempts to locate her. Barnett realized that

Peterson had indeed been trying to locate White over the telephone—but not because she knew anything about the Morrison murder. He had been stalking her with the help of the ABI.

Peterson would later admit in an interview that he had "run a game" on Barnett, Benson, Ikner, and Tate. He had not only been trying to find White, he had also been looking for a way to escape. Peterson had acquired a handcuff key in prison and had it hidden in his sock when the agents took him to Tuscaloosa. While they were making their cautious way from their cars to the abandoned trailer at Cedar Creek, he had been frantically trying to use the key to unlock his handcuffs and leg irons. The key had worked on the handcuffs but not on the other restraints, and he had been forced to abandon the effort. His phone call to the apartment of a "major drug dealer" was actually made to a friend, who had agreed to have a getaway car waiting near the apartment complex if the police were foolish enough to unlock Peterson's restraints and let him out of their sight.

When asked how he had known the caliber of the handgun used in Ronda's murder, Peterson laughed. "I did my homework," he bragged. He had been lying when he told Benson, Ikner, and Tate that he had not watched television or read newspaper articles about Ronda. "I read everything I could. If they had checked with the prison, which I figured they wouldn't, they'd've learned that inmates are allowed to get newspapers and watch TV while in the Hole." He had asked several armed robbers in prison what caliber of gun they would have used to rob a dry cleaners during a Saturday on a busy street. "Every one of 'em said something easy to hide, like a twenty-five-caliber." How had he known Ronda was shot three times? "Most twenty-fives carry five bullets and because them small guns ain't very accurate, I guessed three or maybe four had hit that girl." Beating the polygraph had been easy. "I lie so much, sometimes even I don't know when I'm telling the truth."

But even if Peterson had not deduced the correct caliber or had failed the polygraph, he insisted, the investigators would still have taken him up on his offer. "Those guys were desperate to solve that murder," he said. "They *wanted* to believe me."

One month after the ABI returned Peterson to prison, the con man watched a segment on television about an unsolved murder in another Alabama county. The next day he wrote a letter to the sheriff there, explaining that his girlfriend, Becky White, could identify the killer. He warned the sheriff, though, that neither she nor he would cooperate if the ABI was brought into the case. "The ABI framed me once," he wrote, "and I don't trust them." Shortly thereafter, the sheriff arranged for Peterson to be transferred to his jail and given access to a telephone. Becky White began receiving harassing telephone calls a few days later.

Chapter 10

The new year arrived with much grumbling. Pity for Charles and Bertha Morrison gave way to fear, suspicion, and anger. Why hadn't the police caught Ronda's killer? It had been two full months since the murder. "You can understand most killings," Larry Ikner said. "A person in a juke joint gets in a fight and kills someone or a shooting happens during a marital dispute. Ronda's murder was different. No one knew exactly why she had been killed. People thought, 'Hey, if it can happen to Ronda Morrison while she's at work, maybe it can happen to me while I'm in my home or working in my yard or driving my car somewhere. Maybe it can happen to my child.' " The Monroeville police continued to log two or three calls a week from people who had heard a noise outside at night and were afraid that "Ronda's killer" was on the prowl.

In late January Tom Tate was finally sworn in as the new Monroe County sheriff, and he immediately set out to calm the fears, restore the community's confidence in law enforcement, and breathe new life into the investigation. He announced over Monroeville's only radio station, WMFC, that the Peterman State Bank was adding $1,000 to the existing reward. He personally lobbied the Monroeville Telephone Company and got its directors to add another $1,000 to the pot. He began speaking at various men's groups and meeting with local businessmen and soon collected a total of $18,000 in pledged rewards. Posters advertising this sum blanketed the county, and Tate left standing orders at the jail that everyone arrested was to be questioned about the murder and told about the reward. With such a huge amount being offered—the equivalent of a year's salary for some county residents—Sheriff Tate felt confident that it would be only a matter of time before someone talked.

The new sheriff was a big man, basketball player tall, with a mop of sandy brown hair, a finger-crunching handshake, and mournful puppy-dog eyes. He refused to wear a uniform or coat and tie, didn't regularly carry a pistol, and presented himself as an aw-shucks, Andy Griffith sort of guy. This was deceiving. Tate had a master's degree in correctional counseling and among convicts had been known as an aggressive, tough, no-nonsense parole officer. He was extremely popular with whites, although many blacks were leery of him, in part because of his family background—Tate's father had worked for years in an adjoining county as chief deputy for a sheriff who was infamous during the 1960s for being a racist. Word also had reached the residents of Clausell that Tate often used the word "nigger" when talking in all-white circles. Still, none of this had been enough to keep black voters from helping to elect him. "If we got rid of every white sheriff who called us niggers," explained one longtime black resident, "there'd only be two or three left in the whole damn state."

At the City Cafe, arguably the town's most popular morning gathering spot for men, Sheriff Tate's initiatives were well received. The cafe was an institution in Monroeville, so well known that its owner had never bothered to put a sign on the front of the building. The interior was stark. Customers sat on metal folding chairs at tables with chrome legs and elbow-worn gray-and-white-speckled Formica tops. The floor was industrial-grade tile, the flatware cheap, including an occasional bent spoon or a fork with a missing tine. The air smelled of bacon grease.

None of this mattered. Beginning at four-thirty A.M. each day, the nondescript cafe came alive, and for the next six hours it served as a melting pot where men came to gossip, argue, and pontificate about the events that bound them together as a community. It was a diverse group. Paper mill workers smelling of fresh-cut pine; farmers with callused hands and walnut-shaped knuckles; a local attorney dressed in a J. C. Penney suit; a white-haired widower with two flesh-colored hearing aids;

a man wearing all black from his spit-polished cowboy boots to the Stetson still resting on his head; a real estate salesman with a pocketful of blue, red, green, and white pens each imprinted with his name and all neatly aligned inside a vinyl pocket protector; a retired teacher, a cattleman, a clerk, a shop owner—to an outsider who happened to wander into the cafe, the crowd looked like a motley lot brought together entirely by chance. This was far from true.

Over the years a morning ritual had developed at the cafe, and with it had come a number of unspoken do's and don't's. The men who had been meeting together for coffee the longest sat at the "long table," several small tables pushed together in front of the cash register. It was closest to the coffee urn and also within flirting distance of Hazel, the cafe's only morning waitress, although the flirting was always done good-naturedly and innocently, as in "Hey, darling, could you bring me a fresh cup," or "Gosh, Hazel, you sure are looking nice today." There were twelve seats around the long table, and if by chance one of the regulars missed a morning, someone new might be invited to come over from one of the other tables, which sat only two, three, or four. Few dared to simply walk into the cafe and sit uninvited at the long table, and anyone who did was met with hard stares.

Because most men stayed less than an hour, there were always new arrivals at the cafe, and with each came the chance for a fresh story, a differing point of view. The night crew from the paper mill was generally the first to arrive each morning, followed by cotton and bean farmers who had already finished an hour's worth of chores. The last to appear were the shopkeepers and the self-employed, who had not yet begun their workday. Despite all this coming and going, a regular could predict almost by the hour whom he would find inside, where they were likely to be sitting, and even the general nature of their conversation, whether sports, the weather, politics, or deer hunting.

While it would be impossible to pin this down, few doubted the subtle influence of the City Cafe. Friendships were reinforced, deals discussed, gossip exchanged. Most of the cafe's customers were married and were quick to report to their spouses any tidbits they heard. More than once the roots of a rumor or the inside scoop about a scandal could be traced to the eatery.

Before Ronda's murder, Charles Morrison had been one of the regulars at the long table, and although he had stopped coming in, his seat was kept empty out of respect, and his friends frequently spoke in somber tones about how he and Bertha were dealing with their daughter's death. "Neither of them have touched a thing in Ronda's room. It's like a shrine," a friend confided one morning. Another added that Bertha was calling all of Ronda's teachers and asking them to send her the essays and reports the girl had written. Bertha was making a scrapbook.

There was no City Cafe for blacks in Monroeville. A few met regularly at an auto repair shop near the projects, and some black employees at the paper mill were known to eat breakfast at an all-night truck stop south of town after they finished working the night shift. But none of Monroeville's established restaurants ever catered to blacks in the way the City Cafe did to its white customers. They met more often in Monroeville's black churches and in black nightclubs that operated in towns outside the dry county. It would be incorrect to say that Monroeville's black residents felt less concern about the Morrison murder than whites did, but some did wonder why her case was drawing so much attention. No one in Clausell could recall when the murder of a black teenager had ever prompted similar outrage or the posting of an $18,000 reward.

A significant portion of the regulars at the City Cafe were certain by late January that they knew who had killed Ronda and why. Randy Thomas had sold the cleaners in December and left town, and his departure was seen by many as prima facie evidence of guilt. The most widely heard theory was that Thomas had been laundering drug money at the cleaners for the Mafia and that Ronda had somehow found out and therefore had had to be killed. The allegations about Thomas were based on nothing but speculation, yet with each telling they seemed to gain credibility. A second suspect also was the subject of much talk. While it was widely known that Miles Jackson had passed a lie detector test, that did not protect him from persistent gossip.

Nonetheless, not everyone believed that Thomas and Jackson were involved, and one man at the cafe was particularly critical of the police department's handling of the case. Howard K. Denmar insisted that on the day of the murder he had actually seen Ronda's killer hurrying out of the cleaners, and the man he had spotted was definitely not Thomas or Jackson. The killer, he insisted, was a black man.

Four days after the murder Denmar, a thirty-three-year-old insurance agent, gave a handwritten statement to the police about what he said he had seen. He had been driving north on South Alabama Avenue en route to the City Cafe for breakfast when he had glanced at the cleaners. "I saw a man coming out the door. He was a black male, of slight build, maybe above average height, wearing a V-neck sleeveless sweater. I made eye contact with him," Denmar wrote, "and he looked right at me." Denmar pinpointed the time at 10:38 A.M.—only seven minutes before Jerrie Sue Dunning arrived at the store that Saturday morning.

Initially the police believed Denmar and went so far as to hire a hypnotist in Mobile to help him recall more details. But the hypnotist was unable to put Denmar into a trance, and when investigators could not find anyone to substantiate his story, they set it aside. Their failure to pursue his sighting outraged Denmar, so much so that he announced he was launching his own private investigation of the murder and began checking out tips on his own. Denmar had been one of Jackson Cleaners' best customers, often stopping there two or three times each week to drop off or pick up laundry, but he had not been a close friend of Ronda's or an intimate of the Morrisons; and his persistent questioning of their friends and on occasion even their relatives began to strike some Monroevillians as not only rude but odd.

One morning an excited Denmar arrived at the City Cafe and revealed that he had learned from a police source that Ronda had been shot with a .25 caliber pistol manufactured by Raven Arms. Such a handgun could be easily bought secondhand for as little as thirty-five dollars, and Denmar, an avid gun collector himself, thought the price was significant. Over the years he had learned at gun shows and from talking to the police that the brand of a handgun often told much about its owner. In Monroeville men were so proud of their firearms that they often kept their pistols and rifles on display in ornate gun cases in the living room or den. For some, owning an expensive firearm was the equivalent of a big-city yuppie's driving a BMW or Lexus. Because of this, many police officers adhered to a simple economic presumption: If the gun was expensive, the owner was white; if cheap, he was black. In Denmar's mind, the fact that the gun used to kill Ronda was one of the cheapest available gave credence to his claim that Ronda's killer was a black man.

Bill Hooks, Jr., had to spend only one night in the Monroe County jail after he was caught urinating on the wall of a convenience store on the Saturday of the Morrison murder. But the black youth didn't stay out of trouble long. He was arrested again in December and charged with burglarizing a house in a neighboring county. Just as he had done that November night when he was being taken to jail, Hooks again told the police that he had important information about the Morrison killing.

No one paid any attention to him, and he went to jail for the burglary. Three months passed before a deputy called the D.A.'s office to report what Hooks had said, and investigator Larry Ikner decided to drive to the jail in Evergreen, the county seat of Conecuh County, and interview him.

Ikner would later testify that Hooks claimed during their session that he had been passing Jackson Cleaners on the morning of the murder and had seen two men rushing out the front door. One was white, the other black. Hooks did not know who the white man was but said that his face was badly scarred from burns. He had recognized the black man. "He be John Dozier," he said. "All black peoples around here knows him."

Rushing back to Monroeville, Ikner ran a computer search of various state, county, and police records but could find no one in them named John Dozier. He decided Hooks was lying. Like so many other leads in this convoluted murder case, this tip too had turned out to be a sham.

Hooks would later testify that he had waited expectantly for the police to make an arrest and to reward him for his help. When that didn't happen, he began badgering the jailers once again, trying to get them to call Ikner or another investigator.

"I'm telling the truth," Hooks told them. "Johnny Dozier be the one I saw. He and this white dude. They killed that Morrison girl. That's the God's honest truth!"

By now it was February 1987, and the investigation was paralyzed. Charles Morrison was not the sort of man who lost his temper or banged his fist on a table and demanded answers, but he did stop periodically at the courthouse to ask Benson, Ikner, and Tate the status of their investigation. They were always reassuring, upbeat, confident that an arrest would be forthcoming.

Ikner dreaded these encounters. He could hear the hollowness in Morrison's voice, see the despair in his eyes. "You could tell that all of his hopes and dreams were wrapped up in that little girl. She had been his whole life."

And each time he saw Morrison at the courthouse, Ikner was haunted by the same questions that had initially nagged him on the day of the murder when he and Benson had driven to the Morrisons' house. What if Ronda had been my daughter? he asked himself. How would I feel? What would I do?

Ikner prayed that he would never have to grapple with those questions. He also knew that Charles Morrison was counting on him and his colleagues to bring his daughter's murderer to justice.

It was up to them. It was their job, and none of them had a clue about who was responsible.

PART TWO

A Second Murder

Atticus said the Ewells had been the disgrace of Maycomb for three generations. . . . They were people, but they lived like animals.

—Harper Lee
To Kill a Mockingbird

Chapter 11

Brewton, Alabama, population fifty-eight hundred, lies thirty-six miles southeast of Monroeville and is the county seat and largest city in Escambia County. At the turn of the century, it was also the richest boomtown in all Alabama. Opulent Georgian-style mansions still line Belleville Avenue, Brewton's most spectacular boulevard. They are the former homes of timber barons whose vast wealth was linked to two natural resources: yellow longleaf pine, a favorite of builders, and Murder Creek, so named because Indians once massacred a band of white settlers along its banks. The creek provided timber companies with a cheap way to transport lumber by barge from the sawmills to the Gulf port of Pensacola for export worldwide. In the early 1900s money poured into Brewton. The creek, however, proved a fickle partner. It overflowed its banks regularly, and with each new flood more of the town disappeared under mud. By the time the creek was finally tamed, the lumber companies had moved elsewhere.

Nonetheless, today Brewton still sits stubbornly on the west bank of Murder Creek, and the town continues to display a certain urbane flair missing from other county seats such as Monroeville. It is home to two modern shopping malls, an exclusive country club, two golf courses, and a slew of restaurants. On the opposite side of Murder Creek is Brewton's twin, a municipality called East Brewton, population thirty-one hundred. It is much the poorer of the two. There are no large malls within its limits, no private clubs, no fancy restaurants, not even any fast-food joints with huge red-and-yellow plastic signs. East Brewton is a relic left over from the "old South," an example of the way things were before strip zoning and national franchises. A visitor to East Brewton can still find a fishbait cooler sitting beside the screen door of a mom-and-pop grocery store. Children still swim in the "crick" and spend much of their time in bare feet. The town seems to have emerged naturally from the land it is set on: its houses built with local lumber, the gravel on its roads from nearby quarries, the people themselves the product of their environment.

Mozelle Arrant and Onzell Lisenby lived only a few houses apart in East Brewton. They were identical twins as unpretentious as their surroundings—hardworking women married to a diesel mechanic and carpenter, respectively, men who earned their livelihoods with their hands. As children the twins had known hard times. Their father, Cyzelle Pittman, was an alcoholic and violent man who frequently left his wife, Myrtise, and their five children without enough money to buy food. When he died in an alcohol detoxification center in 1978, few in town were surprised. Yet despite their difficult upbringing, all but one of the Pittman children had done well as adults. Only Victory Ward Pittman seemed to have inherited his father's addictions. He was forty-two, two years older than his twin sisters, and was a drunk, a thief, a sometime drug runner, an abusive husband, and an unfit father.

Early on the morning of Friday, February 20, 1987, Vic Pittman knocked on the kitchen door of Mozelle's house. She could tell he was upset, and she was not surprised. He often came to see her when he had a problem. She was startled, however, to see that this time he was sober.

"Vickie Lynn didn't come home last night," he announced. "I can't find that damn girl anywhere." He was talking about his eighteen-year-old daughter, the second of three children born to him and his first wife, Joyce Flowers Pittman, who had died in 1980. Vic had come to Mozelle's house because she had a telephone. Given his credit history, the telephone company had been unwilling to install a phone line in the rented house he shared with Vickie Lynn. "Can you call the school for me and see if she's there?" he asked.

Mozelle looked at her brother with a mixture of sadness and frustration. He had been a handsome man once, with coal-black hair, a muscular frame, and a quick grin. Not now. His eyes were watery; his cheeks were always ruddy as if he had stayed in the afternoon sunshine too long; his skin hung loosely on his bony frame.

"You been to the police?" she asked. Vic nodded.

Mozelle dialed the number of W. S. Neal High School, where Vickie Lynn was a senior, and asked if she had reported to her first-period class. She hadn't.

"What in the hell is going on?" Mozelle demanded as soon as she put down the receiver.

"I ain't done a damn thing!" Vic replied. "Why you always blaming me?"

Angry, he stomped out the kitchen door, calling over his shoulder that he was going to check with Onzell to see whether she had heard from Vickie Lynn.

Mozelle wondered if anyone could really understand what it was like to have a brother like Vic. She loved him, or at least she told herself she did, but he had caused her and the rest of her family nothing but heartaches. The low point had come five years ago when she and Onzell had joined Eunice Flowers, another relative, in petitioning the family court to take custody of Vic's children away from him. The children had then been fifteen, thirteen, and six. At the court hearing, the oldest daughter, Karen Ann, had described her father's drunken rages and told how he had physically abused and mistreated her. The judge had declared Vic an unfit parent, and his children had been farmed out to relatives. Vic had been so furious that he had threatened Mozelle and Onzell, although over time his anger had faded. Not that the problems had stopped. Karen Ann had shocked her aunts when she turned eighteen and began having a very public affair in East Brewton with a married nightclub owner and reputed drug dealer. Vickie Lynn, who until five months ago had always seemed to be a carefree and rather quiet teenager, had suddenly left the relatives with whom she was staying and moved out on her own without explanation, living first in a squalid mobile home park and then joining her father in a rented house on Grice Street. Mozelle and Onzell had begged her not to move in with Vic, but she had assured them it would be okay. "Despite everything," she had told them naively, "he's my daddy and he loves me!"

As Mozelle stood in her kitchen watching Vic back his old pickup truck out of her driveway, she remembered this and asked herself whether an alcoholic could really, really love anyone.

An hour or so later Onzell arrived in Mozelle's kitchen, poured herself a cup of coffee, and plunked down at the table. Sitting there together, the twins were mirror images of each other. Both were short, pear-shaped, with round faces, dark eyes, and throaty laughs made even deeper by the Marlboro cigarettes each chain-smoked. The only visible difference was that Onzell bleached her hair blond while Mozelle left hers brown. Despite their physical similarities, the women had strikingly different temperaments. Mozelle, who had been born five minutes before her sister, was quick-tempered, outspoken, fearless, aggressive, and determined. Onzell was quiet, shy, less confident; her feelings were easily bruised. Still, their lives had followed an amazingly similar path. Each had dropped out of high school to marry, eager to escape her violent home. They had wed men whom they had met on the same blind date. Each had one daughter and one son, and three of their children had been born on the fourteenth day of different months. The fourth had arrived early, on the thirteenth. The two sisters had lived their entire adult lives within a few blocks of each other in East Brewton and talked to each other every day. They were best friends.

Onzell seemed to have been the last one to see Vickie Lynn. The teenager had dropped in on her unannounced the night before.

"Was she acting funny? How'd she look?" Mozelle asked.

Onzell, remembering, broke into a smile. "Oh, Mozelle," she said, "I was so proud of Vickie Lynn when I saw her. She was the prettiest I've ever seen her. I didn't even recognize her at first."

It was easy to understand why Onzell was so tickled. At Christmas two months before, Onzell had invited Vickie Lynn to eat dinner with her family. This was not long after the girl had moved out on her own and was living in the trailer park. Her only income came from a monthly $125 social security check that she received because her mother was dead and her father had lost his custody rights. After she paid her $75-a-month rent, there wasn't much left for food and other necessities. She had been such an overweight mess when she arrived on Christmas Day that her aunt had marched her into the bathroom for a quick scrubbing and scolding. Vickie Lynn's hair had needed combing, her clothes had been filthy, and she had reeked of sweat. "You smell like a nigger," Onzell had snapped. "You can't let yourself go like this. Just because you're poor don't mean you can't keep yourself clean."

The Vickie Lynn who had arrived at Onzell's the night before was at least forty pounds lighter, although her five-foot, three-inch frame still looked somewhat overweight at 126 pounds. She had dyed her hair bright red, was freshly bathed, and smelled of perfume.

"Vickie Lynn was wearing brand-new blue jeans and she told me that her daddy had bought them for her," Onzell recalled. "They cost fifty dollars and had flowers embroidered on the front and back pockets and she was so proud of them that she lifted her sweater so I could see the flowers."

"Where'd her daddy get fifty dollars?" Mozelle asked. Vic hadn't held a regular job in years.

Ignoring the question, Onzell told her sister, "When she lifted her sweater, I saw her stomach and, Mozelle, it was pooched out! I thought, 'Oh my lands, she's pregnant or she was, and she has done had herself an abortion!' "

"Oh no, no, God almighty, no!" Mozelle protested. Both reached for cigarettes and had trouble lighting them because their hands were shaking.

Onzell continued, "She told me she liked waitressing." Only a few weeks earlier Vickie Lynn had started working as a waitress after school at Carol's Tasty House, a neighborhood cafe. "She said her daddy was going to help her buy a car once she saved enough money because he didn't like her walking around all over town at night by herself like she did. Then all of a sudden that child got the saddest look on her face and she says, 'Aunt Onzell, people just don't like me.' I said, 'Why's that, child?' and she tells me, 'My daddy is an alcoholic and my sister is a whore who runs with drug dealers and I'm having to live down both of them in this here town.' " Onzell paused, took a drag on her cigarette, and went on, "I told her, 'Vickie Lynn, you only have to live down what you do, not what someone else does,' and then all of a sudden she says, 'Well, I gotta go before Daddy comes hunting me. I don't want him getting mad.' "

They had walked out together onto the back porch. Onzell had wanted to offer Vickie Lynn a ride, but the gas tank in her car was nearly empty. Vickie Lynn had not complained. "She says, 'I can't lose weight if I don't walk.' "

But just before they said goodbye, Vickie Lynn turned and whispered to her aunt.

"She tells me, 'Aunt Onzell, I've been bleeding in my vagina. I've been to the county health department but the doctors there don't know what's wrong.' She didn't say nothing else about it, you know, whether it was because she was pregnant or had gotten an abortion and I didn't know what to say or do, so I just gave her a hug and said, 'I'm so proud of you, Vickie Lynn, you remember I'm always here for you and I'll stand with you no matter what.' "

Tears had formed in Onzell's eyes as she finished telling her story. Mozelle understood why she was upset. Both of them felt a bit guilty about Vickie Lynn. They knew she was a good kid who had never gotten any sort of break. Having grown up in an alcoholic and violent family themselves, they understood how tough it was for her, and over the years they had tried to help. But they had children of their own to raise, other obligations. There was only so much they could do. Despite their best efforts and those of other relatives, Vickie Lynn seemed doomed to be one of those kids who fell through the cracks.

"What time did she leave your place?" asked Mozelle.

"A little after ten o'clock," Onzell said. "I watched her walk down the street to the highway." And then, thinking out loud, she asked, "Do you think she might have run away from home because she's pregnant or she had an abortion?"

Mozelle wasn't sure, but she raised another possibility. About two weeks earlier Vic had arrived drunk at her back door blubbering about Vickie Lynn and drugs. Both the twins knew that their brother had once been involved in drug trafficking.

Now, recounting Vic's visit, Mozelle said, "He tells me he's found cocaine in Vickie Lynn's room. He tells me Vickie Lynn is selling drugs at the high school so he has ripped off her drugs to stop her. He says she and some other girl come home one night and tore the house upside down looking for them drugs and he didn't tell them that *he* is the one who stole them."

"Oh dear God," Onzell replied. "Not Vickie Lynn too! Not drugs!"

"I figured Vic was lying," Mozelle declared. "You know how he tells stories." The sisters were well aware of his tendency to exaggerate. Sometimes he would come to Mozelle's, read her a story from the local paper about a crime, and tell her that he knew all about it and that the police had arrested the wrong person.

"Dear Lord!" Mozelle said. "I just had the worst thought. What if Vickie Lynn *was* selling drugs and her stupid daddy stole them and the people who owned them drugs came looking for her and their money? What if they snatched her up and demanded that she pay them for them drugs? What if *that's* why she is missing?"

The sisters looked at each other. What had Vic Pittman gotten his daughter into now?

Chapter 12

Vic Pittman had not only gone to see his twin sisters on Friday morning, he had also telephoned his older daughter, Karen Ann, from a pay phone. He woke her up.

"Vickie Lynn didn't come home last night," he reported.

"She probably spent the night at a girlfriend's," Karen Ann replied. "It's not like this hasn't happened before."

"Well, when I catch her, I'm going to beat the hell out of that girl."

Karen Ann went back to sleep. She figured her sister had simply gotten tired of dealing with Vic and had taken refuge at a girlfriend's. Although Karen Ann was now twenty-one and recently married, her father still had a hold over her that she recognized yet could not understand. No one could get her so angry. She absolutely hated him. She also loved him. Over the years she had managed to forgive nearly all of his cruelty, but that did not mean many events weren't still fresh in her memory. She could still recall the smell of his alcoholic breath, the pain caused by his beatings, how he made her feel as if she were worthless. When she was only six, he had come home drunk and stomped her new puppy to death with his boot heels because it was yapping. When she was fourteen, he had pinned her against the refrigerator in the kitchen during an argument and had been about to throw hot grease in her face when she screamed at him, "Go ahead. I want to die! I hate you!" Her outburst had shocked him into putting down the skillet.

Karen Ann had learned to deal with all those awful memories, but there was one event she had never been able to pardon. During her darkest moments, she believed that her father was responsible for her mother's death.

From the start Vic's marriage to Joyce Flowers had been turbulent. Joyce came from a dirt-poor East Brewton family as dysfunctional as his. There were rumors in town of incest in the family. One of her brothers would later be sent to prison and would commit suicide after admitting that he had engaged in sex with his daughter. Joyce had fled her home at age seventeen, moving to New Orleans, where she was soon pregnant. The baby, born with spina bifida, died thirty-eight days later. With no money and nowhere to go, Joyce returned to East Brewton and became a waitress. That was when she and Vic had begun to date. By day he was an auto mechanic. At night he supplemented his income by turning back odometers at used-car lots for fifty dollars per vehicle and by delivering illegal whiskey to honky-tonks. "I liked walking both sides of the street," he later bragged. They soon married, and during those first years seemed to do well. They saved enough to buy a gas station. Karen Ann and Vickie Lynn were born, and the proud parents drew up plans to build a house. Still, there were always violent arguments, often sparked by alcohol. Both were heavy drinkers. Then in the early 1970s, the gasoline shortage hit and Vic began smuggling drugs to pay his bills. His years of running moonshine gave him an edge. "I knew which sheriffs you could pay to look the other way." But it wasn't enough. Vic eventually went broke, and he and his family, including a newborn son, David, settled in Evergreen, the Conecuh County seat, which borders both Monroe and Escambia counties.

If counties were people, Conecuh County would be a whore. It is where southern Alabamians, including many from Monroeville and East Brewton, went whenever they wanted to buy whiskey, gamble, or find a prostitute. Vic fit right in. Joyce got work as a waitress at the restaurant in the motel on Interstate 65. The bar there was known as a hangout for hookers.

In June 1980 Vic heard that Joyce had danced topless for a group of men at the bar. He stormed home drunk and began beating her. Neighbors called the police, and by the time they got there he had ripped off all her clothing. The children, who had huddled together in a bedroom, were trying to escape out a window. Karen Ann had been sure that her father was going to kill them. The sheriff called Mozelle, and she bailed her brother out of jail and took him home with her. But he refused to stay away from Joyce, and when the police caught him he was put in jail. Mozelle convinced the sheriff that her brother would be better off if he was committed to a state mental hospital, where he could receive treatment for alcoholism. Joyce, meanwhile, filed for divorce. "Once my daddy was gone," Karen Ann later recalled, "we were like a normal family. We were no longer afraid."

Two weeks later Karen Ann was awakened after midnight by her mother, pounding on the front door. Joyce had attended a going-away party for a coworker at the restaurant; she was drunk, she wasn't wearing any undergarments, and she was covered with her own vomit and feces. Karen Ann cleaned her up and put her to bed. The next morning she couldn't wake Joyce. Doctors in the emergency room suspected a drug overdose and pumped her stomach, but it didn't help. They told Karen Ann her mother needed to be rushed to a hospital in Montgomery so that the doctors there could perform a CAT scan. No one, however, offered to help the thirteen-year-old arrange the trip or pay for it, and the local ambulance service refused to take Joyce unless it received $172 in advance. The Pittman family had no health insurance and was known around town for not paying its bills. Karen Ann went to the motel where her mother worked and begged for donations. It took her four hours to raise the necessary cash.

At the Baptist Medical Center in Montgomery, doctors discovered that an artery in Joyce's brain had burst. They were helpless to save her. As soon as they heard what was happening, Mozelle and Onzell arranged to have Vic released from the state hospital, but he showed little interest. Joyce died in a coma four days later with her daughter at her side. Karen Ann made all the funeral arrangements. Vic told Mozelle, "I don't give a damn if they roll Joyce off the side of the road and let the buzzards eat her."

The doctors assured her that no one could predict aneurysms and that her mother's death had been unavoidable, but Karen Ann, who always suspected the worst about her father, decided with absolutely no evidence that he had paid his drug-dealing cronies to get Joyce drunk and slip her drugs. Now, nearly seven years later, she still blamed him.

After she awoke for a second time on the Friday morning when her father had called, Karen Ann began to feel uneasy. She found it suspicious that Vic was searching for her sister. Vickie Lynn was legally an adult, had lived on her own for a brief while, and had stayed out other nights without Vic's ever calling to check on her. Why was this particular Thursday night different? Why was her father, who had never showed that much interest before, now so concerned?

Though they had not lived together for several years, Karen Ann felt close to her sister. The court had sent them to different relatives after Vic lost custody, but both girls lived in East Brewton, and they talked nearly every day. An incident three years ago, however, had made Karen Ann wonder if there was a side of her sister she didn't know. They had gotten together for a Saturday-night sleepover, and for most of that evening they had munched on popcorn, watched television, fixed each other's hair, and talked about boys. Karen Ann had assumed that her sister was a virgin, but Vickie Lynn revealed that she had had sex with one of her married relatives shortly after her fourteenth birthday. She had also smoked pot with him. Furious, Karen Ann lectured her. Vickie Lynn was not as forthcoming after that.

All day Friday Karen Ann waited fruitlessly for Vickie Lynn to call. By Saturday morning she was worried. She drove to the house on Grice Street to see if either her father or her sister was home. The place was empty. As she backed her car down the driveway, Karen Ann noticed a package lying on the ground next to the mailbox. It was heart-shaped and the size of a hatbox, but it had neither a name nor postage on it, and the mail wasn't usually delivered that early. Karen Ann opened it. Inside she found a white formal dress that smelled of perspiration. It was too big for her, but it looked as if it was the size Vickie Lynn wore. She tossed the box and the dress onto the backseat of her car and decided to drive around town looking for her sister and her father. There was no sign of Vickie Lynn, but she spotted Vic's truck parked outside a downtown convenience store. As soon as he came out, she confronted him.

"Where's Vickie Lynn?"

"She ain't come home yet."

"What's this doing next to your mailbox?" she asked, showing him the dress.

A look of panic washed over his face. "We—We got to get this to the police!" he stammered. "We got to go right now, this very second!"

"Why?"

"Vickie Lynn's been kidnapped! The kidnappers left this as a warning!"

"Why in the hell would anyone kidnap Vickie Lynn?" Karen Ann asked. Although it was early, she could already smell alcohol on his breath.

"To teach me a lesson—about drugs," he blurted out. "You don't believe me, do you?"

"Hell no," she said. "You're drunk." She turned to leave, taking the dress with her, but he called after her.

"Karen Ann, we *got* to get this to the police right now," he pleaded. "This ain't no damn joke. Please come with me."

Giving in, she followed him in her car to the East Brewton police station. Inside, Vic grabbed the dress from her and hurried over to Chief Charles "Chuck" Adkins. Vic almost threw the dress at Adkins. Karen Ann could tell from Adkins's reaction that he didn't have a clue as to what Vic was doing. She expected her father to repeat his story about Vickie Lynn's being kidnapped because of something he had done involving drugs, but instead Vic spun around and pointed a skinny forefinger at her.

"My daughter's been gone since Thursday night and this morning Karen Ann shows up with Vickie Lynn's dress," he yelled. "Seems to me you should be asking Karen Ann about what in the hell is going on. What's she done to Vickie Lynn?"

Karen Ann felt her face flush. Without uttering a word, she turned and marched out of the police station.

Chapter 13

Mozelle was in her kitchen when Vic Pittman burst in. He had sped there from the police station.

"Them damn dopers is holding Vickie Lynn for ransom!" he shouted.

Wiping her hands on her apron, Mozelle tried to calm her brother. "Sit down and tell me what is going on," she ordered.

Mozelle would later recall Vic's telling her that Vickie Lynn had been kidnapped by a gang of drug dealers from out of town because Karen Ann and her drug-dealing pals had stolen some cocaine. If he didn't come up with $1,500 in ransom, Vickie Lynn would be murdered. Before Mozelle, stunned, could question him further, he had run out the door, yelling back over his shoulder that he was going to get a gun and "blow off Karen Ann's head!"

Near panic, Mozelle called Chief Adkins. He assured her that he would watch out for Vic, but she could tell from the tone of his voice that he wasn't taking her seriously. Everyone in town knew about Vic and his drinking.

Around ten o'clock that same night Vic returned to Mozelle's house, only this time he came sauntering into the kitchen as if he didn't have a care. Mozelle began pelting him with questions about Vickie Lynn and the kidnappers, and he laughed. His daughter hadn't been kidnapped, he said. She was staying at a friend's house out of town for a few days. In fact, he had come to use Mozelle's phone so that he could tell the police that she was no longer a missing person.

Mozelle felt so angry that she was ready to strangle him, but before she could say a word he grabbed the receiver, dialed the police department, and told the dispatcher that he could take Vickie Lynn's name off the missing persons list. "She's with a friend," he said.

Snatching the telephone from his hand, Mozelle yelled into the receiver, "Don't you dare take her off until someone actually sees her!"

The startled dispatcher said he had no choice. It was Vic who had reported his daughter missing, and, if he wished, he could report her found. Vic shot past Mozelle while she was still arguing with the dispatcher and sped off in his truck so fast that his tires threw gravel from the driveway against her house.

During the days that followed, Vic acted so strangely that his twin sisters started keeping daily logs of their encounters with him. Their handwritten notes would later reveal that he had offered them several contradictory explanations for Vickie Lynn's disappearance. At first he claimed that she had come home late one night and told him she was moving to another state. A day later he said he hadn't seen her for several days and had no idea where she was. When Onzell went to check on him one morning, she found the back door of the house kicked in and the interior in shambles. It looked to her as if someone had been searching the place. She found Vic passed out on a sofa. When he came to he said the Mafia had torn up the house looking for drugs. Helping him tidy up, she discovered a towel drenched in blood; he said he had cut himself shaving. Several days later Vic told Mozelle that Vickie Lynn had gotten pregnant and run away from home to have an abortion. Karen Ann didn't keep a written account of her encounters with her father, but she too would later recall that he had told her so many stories about Vickie Lynn that it was difficult to keep them straight.

Each time the twins heard a new account, Mozelle called Chief Adkins at the police department. When he wearied of taking her calls, she started telephoning Claude Cosey, a young deputy in the Escambia County sheriff's office. Some days she called him as many as twenty times, and she phoned him at home at such odd hours that his exasperated wife told her to leave them alone.

By now Vickie Lynn had been missing ten days. No one had seen or heard from her. On day eleven, a sober Vic walked into Mozelle's kitchen, poured himself some coffee, and, his voice serious, told Mozelle he wanted her to know the truth about Vickie Lynn: She had been abducted, tortured, and murdered because of a local bank robbery. Four months earlier the East Brewton branch of the First National Bank had been robbed by a man armed with a pistol. Vickie Lynn had happened to be walking past the bank when the robber ran outside and scrambled down an embankment leading to Murder Creek. Curious, the girl had followed him down the slope and under a bridge, where she had seen his face. "Vickie Lynn knew this person and promised not to tell," Vic said, "only a few weeks ago the robber saw her talking to an FBI agent in town. So she was murdered."

As strange as that story sounded, Mozelle believed it. She remembered the day of the bank robbery because Vickie Lynn had stopped by that night and told her aunts she had seen the robber hiding under a bridge. At the time, though, Mozelle and Onzell had thought Vickie Lynn, who was always hungry for attention, was exaggerating.

As soon as Vic left, Mozelle called Onzell and reported the latest. "My land, Vickie Lynn was just a sweet little teenager," Onzell replied. "She wouldn't have nothing to do with a bank robber. Why would that child even know a person like that or all these people selling drugs?"

Mozelle answered with a single word: "Vic!" She added, "I'm sure her damn daddy's got her in this mess."

Once again Mozelle telephoned Deputy Cosey. "Vic's just playing with you," he warned. "Stop listening to him. When Vickie Lynn wants to be found, she'll turn up." Cosey had heard rumors at the high school that Vickie Lynn was pregnant and had run away from home.

Mozelle felt like screaming. No one seemed to care that her niece had been gone eleven days. She didn't believe Vickie Lynn had simply run away. The owner of Carol's Tasty House told her the girl had not been in to pick up her last paycheck. Why would she leave town without cashing her check? What had she used for money?

The next morning the two sisters sat over coffee. "My God, what does it take around here to get people's attention?" Onzell cried.

"Let's face it," Mozelle answered. "No one gives a damn about Vickie Lynn. If anything is going to be done, we are going to have to do it."

They got out a street map and plotted the course Vickie Lynn would most likely have followed when she walked home from Onzell's house. Then they went from house to house knocking on doors. Mozelle did most of the talking, and Onzell carried an eight-by-ten-inch photograph of their niece. No one remembered seeing the girl. Ten fruitless stops later, the sisters were tired and discouraged.

"I'm sure everyone thinks we are loony birds," said Onzell, "and maybe they're right."

Mozelle nodded. Maybe Vickie Lynn had just run off the way her daddy claimed. Maybe she was pregnant. They decided to try one more house and then give up. An elderly woman came to the door. No, she said politely, she had not seen Vickie Lynn.

"Let's go home," Onzell said, but as they reached the street, the woman called them back.

"I didn't want to get involved," she whispered, "but you look so heartbroken." A teenage girl who looked like their niece had knocked on her front door several nights earlier, she told them. She was screaming and claiming that someone was chasing her, but the woman had been afraid it was a trick and had refused to open her door. She had glanced outside moments later, just in time to see the girl getting into a car with a white woman and speeding away.

Deputy Cosey wasn't in, so Mozelle telephoned Chief Adkins, and he promised to interview the elderly woman. Later that day he called back to say she was not a reliable witness; she could not remember which night the incident had happened. Besides, Adkins said, he suspected it had just been some kids playing a prank.

That same evening Mozelle reached Cosey and begged him to interrogate Vic. Finally he agreed, in part to get her off the phone.

Vic made no objection when Cosey and Adkins took him into the police station for a tape-recorded interview. In fact, he told them, he was as curious as his sisters about what had happened to his daughter. "A person just don't vanish, but this has just got me whipped." The officers had no choice but to let him go.

Mozelle stormed into the police station the next morning and demanded to know why Vic hadn't been arrested.

"For what?" Adkins asked.

"Think of something!" she replied. "You got to make him tell us where Vickie Lynn is!"

Wearily Adkins began arguing with Mozelle, and when she started to swear at him, Officer Mike Cain intervened and offered to buy her a cup of coffee. For the next hour he listened to her complaints and heard her fears. That afternoon after he went off duty, he went to Mozelle's house and sat in her kitchen for four hours talking to the twins.

Cain had been a member of the East Brewton police department for only two months, but he had already made a name for himself around town. The mayor had welcomed him and offered some advice on his first day as a city cop. There was no need to issue traffic tickets to anyone who lived in town; all other drivers were fair game. Cain reacted by issuing more summons to East Brewton residents on his first day than the other four officers on the force had issued collectively in an entire month. When the outraged mayor confronted him, Cain said, "I'm an aggressive officer. It's the only way I can do my job."

Cain was touched by the sisters' story, and he decided he would try to find Vickie Lynn on his own time. From that moment on, Mozelle and Onzell began telephoning Cain at the station and at his home whenever they had a tip or simply wanted to talk. He always made time for them. He was soon the butt of jokes at the station. His lieutenant told him the twins were "crazy—nothing but trouble." The entire Pittman family, he was warned, was "white trash."

On March 16 Cain reported to work about half an hour early as usual, and happened to meet Chief Adkins and Deputy Cosey coming out the front door of the station.

"We got a tip about a girl who's missing," Cosey volunteered. "Might be Vickie Lynn Pittman."

Without waiting to be invited, Cain jumped into the backseat of their car. Cosey briefed him during the ride. A deputy at the Conecuh County jail in Evergreen had called him the night before and told him a prisoner was claiming that he knew where the body of a teenage girl was hidden. The inmate claimed that the girl had been abducted while walking home in East Brewton one night and had later been murdered.

As they rode north along State Highway 31, Cain prayed for Mozelle and Onzell's sake that the dead girl was not the person all three officers suspected she might very well be.

Chapter 14

Ralph Bernard Myers had been caught three days earlier stealing three tire rims from the Big Three Tire Company in Evergreen, a minor theft but enough of a crime to require the posting of a $500 bond, which was more money than even the most intrepid bail bondsman in town was willing to gamble on him. He was an ex-con with a serious drug habit, a long history of mental illness, and an IQ that put him just a few points above what the State of Alabama considered mentally retarded and incapable of properly caring for himself.

Myers could neither read nor write. He had a face that was difficult to forget. Although he was only thirty, his hair was entirely silver, and he wore it slicked back like Elvis. His face was badly scarred from burns received when he was a child. Despite repeated surgery, his neck and chin remained disfigured. Skin grafts in both places were paler than the rest of his face, and his left lip drooped where the skin had been pulled too tight. He had an occasional lisp and found it difficult to close his lips evenly.

Like an applicant outlining his credentials, Myers began by bragging that he regularly fed information to ABI agent Simon Benson and had tried to call him first to give him information about the murder but had been informed that Benson was busy in Monroeville. He was willing to tell the three officers where a dead girl's body was hidden if they would help get him out of jail.

"If what you say checks out," said Cosey, "we'll see what we can do."

Myers didn't want to be tape-recorded, but Cain insisted, and they listened for thirty minutes as he told them a long, rambling story so confusing that the three men had trouble following it. Only with repeated questioning were they finally able to sort out what he was saying.

Myers had befriended a white woman named Karen Kelly who had moved to Evergreen from East Brewton about three weeks earlier. She was a cocaine addict and prostitute who, according to him, "is the kind of person who will walk up in your face and blow your damn brains out without a second thought."

Myers had overheard her talking to a black man about a white teenager in East Brewton who had been, in his own words, "a big threat because she knew a bunch on them and was going to tell the FBI." Kelly and the black man had abducted the girl while she was walking home in East Brewton and had beaten her to death with a pipe. Then they had driven into the woods and hidden her body next to an abandoned logging road. Myers stopped at that point; this was as much as he was going to tell them unless they agreed to free him. They were not yet ready for that and got up to leave, but as they did he dangled another piece of bait before them.

"Karen Kelly's boyfriend is a black man who lives in Monroeville and is a major marijuana dealer," he told them.

"How big?" asked Cosey.

"Well, one night Karen tried to bum two dollars off me and I said, 'Karen, I don't have it,' and she says, 'Why, that's okay, Ralph. I'll call my nigger boyfriend and he'll bring me all the money I want.' Later on that night I seen her again and, hell, buddy, if she wasn't sitting there counting out one-hundred-dollar bills—a damn stack of 'em. That's how big this dude is."

When they left the jail the three officers stopped for lunch at the Crispy Chick, a fast-food restaurant in Evergreen. As it happened, ABI agent Simon Benson was also eating there. He did know Myers but had never trusted him. "You're wasting your time talking to him," Benson warned. "He's a liar."

Cosey and Adkins agreed, but Cain wasn't so sure. Back in East Brewton, he reported what he had learned to Mozelle and Onzell. Neither of them had ever heard of Ralph Myers or Karen Kelly, but the next morning Cain got a call at work from a breathless Mozelle.

"Karen Ann knows this Karen Kelly woman!" she told him. "Her daddy introduced Karen Kelly to her—now get this, Mike—as his new fiancée a few months ago!"

"Is she sure it's the same Karen Kelly?"

"Oh yeah. Vic was dating her, but then she dumped him and got out of town in a hurry. And if Vic was dating her, then he probably introduced her to Vickie Lynn and that's what got her into trouble."

On March 23 Cain and Cosey convinced a judge to let Myers sign his own appearance bond. In exchange Myers told them that he had overheard Kelly and the black man saying that the body was hidden near Brooklyn, a loose-knit community about twenty miles north of East Brewton. "It's off County Road Forty-three," he said, "next to an old logging path."

"There's hundreds of logging roads in that area," Cosey protested. "It could take us months to search them."

Myers promised to telephone them after he checked "some facts with some people." Cosey figured he was lying, and as he and Cain watched Myers stroll away from the jail the deputy predicted that they would never see or hear from him again.

Technically Vickie Lynn was no longer a missing person because her father had asked the police to remove her name from their missing persons list. Moreover, Brooklyn was not in the East Brewton police department's jurisdiction. But Cain didn't care. He called Frank Dewberry, the head of the Escambia County rescue squad, and asked if he would pass the word informally among volunteer squad members that a body was hidden near a logging road somewhere off County Road 43. As always, Cain briefed Mozelle, and the next day she called him twelve times to learn whether he had heard from Myers. He hadn't. On the following day she called thirty-three times. When his telephone began ringing on the third day, he answered it expecting to hear her voice again. Instead, it was Myers. He had learned from "sources" that the dead girl's body had been stripped naked and buried under pine branches in the woods about two tenths of a mile from County Road 43, next to a logging path two miles south of the main crossroads in Brooklyn. The path was overgrown with weeds and covered with pine needles, and the killer had pulled a log across it to make it even more inaccessible. Cain passed the information on to the rescue squad.

Shortly after two-forty P.M. on Sunday, March 29, Frank Dewberry and his wife, Dorothy, found a badly decomposed nude body exactly where Myers had said it would be. Escambia County Sheriff Timothy Hawsey and Chief Adkins sped to the site, but no one called Cain. He didn't learn about it until he reported to work an hour later. He immediately asked for permission over his radio to come to the scene, but Adkins said no; there were enough officers there already. Cain was furious. Everyone had told him that he was wasting his time talking to Myers, yet it had been his directions that had led them to the corpse.

"Has anyone told Mozelle or Onzell?" he asked.

"No," Adkins replied. The body had not been identified. It was possible that it was someone other than Vickie Lynn.

Cain went straight to Mozelle's. She had bought a police scanner after Vickie Lynn had disappeared, and she rarely turned it off. He was afraid she had heard about the body and would be distraught, but her husband, Kenny, said she had been taking a nap.

"They've found a body," Cain told her when she appeared.

"Is it Vickie Lynn?"

"There is no way to know right now."

Mozelle began to cry. "I know it's her, Mike. I just know it. I got to call Onzell."

When his shift ended at midnight, Cain drove out to the site. Yellow police tape was strung across the entrance to the old logging road, so he parked along County Road 43 and went on foot. He could see lights shining through the woods. The two deputies who had been left to guard the corpse overnight had set up lanterns at the site. Cain had been told that the crime scene was being left undisturbed until the next morning because a heavy rain had started to fall during the afternoon and Sheriff Hawsey had wanted to wait until it cleared to begin collecting evidence. Unlike his counterparts in Monroeville, the sheriff had ordered his investigators not to touch anything and had called the state crime lab specialists right away for advice. They were scheduled to arrive the next morning. Cain also suspected that Hawsey had prolonged the search so that he could have a second chance to appear on the newscasts aired by the Mobile television stations. Hawsey liked being in the spotlight.

As Cain walked toward the glow of the lanterns, he could feel the pine needles on the logging road giving way under his shoes and the overgrown grass brushing wetly against his trousers. He thought of Vickie Lynn. The twins had shown him a copy of her high school graduation picture. It was a typical portrait of a smiling teenager.

Animals, birds, and maggots had feasted on the body, but remnants of flesh and hair still adhered to the exposed bones. What struck Cain first was the face. The girl had been beaten so savagely that her jaw had been broken into several pieces. Myers had said that she had been hit with a pipe. That seemed to fit the trauma Cain saw before him. It was impossible for him to look at the rotting corpse and match it to the smiling graduation photograph, yet he knew instantly that this was Vickie Lynn Pittman.

Cain walked back along the soft pathway to his car. It was starting to drizzle, and he zipped his thin jacket. Again he felt the pine needles giving way under his feet, and it came to him that every detail was exactly as Myers had said it would be. There was only one explanation for precision like this. Myers had not heard about this scene from "sources" on the street or by overhearing Karen Kelly talking to a black man. Myers had been here. He had walked down this path. He had felt the pine needles and wet grass just as Cain was feeling them now.

Questions flooded Cain's mind. He knew that every major case requires that an investigator submerge himself in a vast sea of details, suspects, and conflicting stories. It is the investigator's job to remember each detail, interview each suspect, listen to each story, knowing all the while that much of the information he is gathering will turn out to be useless, many or most of the leads false, several of the stories outright lies. There is no way, however, for a competent investigator to shortcut this process. Only after he has checked every lead, every suspect, and every story can he begin to sort out what has happened and find the truth. Right now everything was murky. Myers had identified the killers as Karen Kelly and a black man. But what would those two say? What role, if any, had Myers played in the murder? And then there was Vic Pittman. Why had he acted so strangely when his daughter had disappeared? Had he played a role in his own child's murder?

Cain felt a mixture of sadness and exhilaration. A teenage girl had been beaten to death. That was horrible. Now the hunt for her killer could begin. That was the thrill.

Chapter 15

Dental records showed that the sixty-three pounds of human remains found in the woods were indeed those of Vickie Lynn Pittman. Ralph Myers had said that Karen Kelly and a black man had killed the teenager. The next step was to find Kelly. That proved easy. She was being held on a forgery charge in the same jail in Evergreen where Myers had been. Mike Cain and Chief Adkins went to get her.

Cain wondered what Kelly would look like. What sort of person is it, he asked himself, who can beat a teenage girl to death with a pipe, hitting her so savagely that some of her front teeth are knocked down her throat into her lungs? A deputy brought a handcuffed Kelly out from her cell. Although she was only in her mid-twenties, she looked much older. She was short and gaunt. Her diet, a jailer told Cain, was mostly coffee, cigarettes, and painkillers. Her hair was dyed ink black, and her eyes were underlined by permanent half-moons. She looked as if she never slept. Once she might have been pretty, but not now. She struck him as someone who wore a perpetual scowl not only on her face but in her outlook.

As soon as Cain and Adkins led Kelly outside to their waiting squad car, she began talking. She was so jittery that both men suspected she was high on amphetamines. Afraid that she might say something incriminating during their forty-minute drive to East Brewton, Cain read her her constitutional rights before starting the engine. But there was not a word about Vickie Lynn. Instead Kelly chattered through the entire trip, bragging about her black boyfriend who lived just outside Monroeville near "the projects." Cain would later recall that this was the first time he heard of Walter McMillian, better known as Johnny D.

"Some folks don't go for white and black mixing, but I think it's a good thing, don't you?" the two men later quoted Kelly as asking them. But she did not wait for their replies. She launched into a long story about Johnny D.'s being a major marijuana dealer with important criminal connections. "He's too smart to get caught," she said. "He don't care if you know he sells drugs. He'll get me out of this. You just wait and see."

Since East Brewton had no jail, the two officers took Kelly across the river to the county jail in Brewton, which was under the control of Sheriff Hawsey. The day before, the sheriff and Adkins had gotten into a nasty dispute about which of them would be in charge of the case. Hawsey insisted it came under his jurisdiction because Vickie Lynn's body had been found in the county. Adkins argued that she had been murdered within the city limits, which made it his case. The two men had never liked each other. Adkins had once worked for Hawsey as a deputy but had quit in a huff after only one year. Now, as Kelly was being booked, a deputy informed Cain and Adkins that Sheriff Hawsey had left orders that no one was to interview her without him—and that specifically meant Adkins. The chief left in a snit.

The next morning when Hawsey and Cain interrogated her, Kelly was blunt. She knew all about the murder, she said, but she had not been involved and only learned about it after the fact.

"Tyrone Patterson did it," she declared. "I know because he told me he done it."

Patterson, she said, was a drug dealer, and she had an expensive crack cocaine habit. She had met him when she was living in an East Brewton trailer park, and when she couldn't pay for her drugs, he would give them to her in return for her cashing forged checks for him or doing tricks as a prostitute. He had another white girl working for him, too, and five or six black women. They were all part of "Tyrone's gang."

Hawsey recognized Patterson's name. He was a middle-aged black ex-con with a long criminal record.

"Why'd he kill her?" Hawsey asked.

" 'Cause he robbed the bank in East Brewton and she was going to tell the FBI about him," said Kelly.

Tyrone Patterson was also easy for the police to find. He was in jail in Monroeville, where he had been accused of writing several bad checks. The police had impounded his car when he was arrested, and now that he was a suspect in a murder case they decided to search it for evidence. There was nothing in the interior, but in the trunk were mud, pine needles, leaves, a shovel, a hammer, and black boots with what looked like bloodstains on them.

The police soon had more than Kelly's statement and the car to link Patterson to the murder. Ralph Myers also identified him as the black man whom he had overheard plotting to kill a white girl from East Brewton.

Exactly two weeks after Vickie Lynn's body was found, Sheriff Hawsey introduced Karen Kelly to Escambia County District Attorney Michael D. Godwin. The sheriff wanted Godwin to file murder charges against Patterson, and he thought Godwin should meet the woman who would be the state's star witness. Hawsey was not only the sheriff, he was an ordained Baptist preacher; and he believed that Kelly had undergone a religious transformation during the thirteen days she had been housed in his jail. As a matter of practice, he made certain that any inmate who requested a copy of the Holy Bible was given one, and during his rounds he often witnessed and prayed with prisoners. Kelly had become one of his most dedicated jailhouse converts.

Kelly's session with the two officials was tape-recorded and began with her proclaiming her newfound faith. "I have not been perfect in my lifetime," she said. "I was afraid to tell the truth when I was arrested, but that don't worry me anymore because I feel that the good Lord don't like wrong and that by me telling the truth that He'll protect me. I don't need the law to take care of me because He'll look out for me."

Godwin had been the district attorney less than two months and a lawyer only three years. This was his first murder investigation. It would also be one of his first criminal trials. He and Hawsey had been in the same high school class in Brewton, and he depended on Hawsey, who as sheriff had more experience, to advise him.

Hawsey assured Godwin that Kelly would make an excellent and credible witness. Kelly then repeated her story to them: Tyrone Patterson had robbed the East Brewton bank and had murdered Vickie Lynn to keep her quiet. Then she made a new revelation. On the day after the murder, she said, Patterson had driven to her house and had actually shown her the dead girl's body hidden in the trunk of his car, wrapped in garbage bags.

From a prosecutor's point of view this could be invaluable testimony; it meant that Kelly could tell jurors that Patterson had not only admitted the murder, but had actually shown her the corpse.

"Tell us exactly what happened," Godwin ordered.

"Tyrone . . . opened the trunk of his car and he had the girl's body in the trunk . . . I said, 'Tyrone, what did you do this for?' I screamed. He said, 'Shut up or I'll hit you in the back of your head with that pipe.' He said, 'Won't nobody know what happened to you.' And I didn't doubt it in the least because he was crazy. . . . I said, 'Why did you do this?' He said, 'Because . . . she knows about the bank robbery . . .' "

The prosecutor grilled Kelly for several minutes about the body, the car, and Patterson. He was trying to catch her in a lie because that was what a good defense attorney would do in a murder trial. Kelly never hesitated. None of her answers was contradictory. When he asked her what else she had seen in the car trunk besides the body, Kelly answered him immediately: "There was boots and a shovel in the trunk near the body."

"What did the boots look like?"

"To the best of my knowledge it was those water boots . . ."

"Rubber?"

"Uh-huh."

Kelly had just described two of the items the police had found in the trunk of Patterson's car. How could she have known they were there, Godwin asked himself, if she was lying?

"Why has it taken you so long to come forward with this testimony?" he asked.

"Wouldn't you kind of be afraid too to tell anyone?"

When they finished their interrogation, the sheriff took Kelly back to her cell and then returned to the courthouse to review her statement and the other evidence with Godwin. They felt good about what they had. Kelly was willing to testify that she had seen Vickie Lynn's body in the trunk of Patterson's car and that he had admitted killing the girl. Ralph Myers was willing to testify that he had overheard Patterson and Kelly discussing a murder. The police had found a shovel and bloody boots in the trunk of the car, and Kelly had just told them that she had seen a shovel and boots in the trunk along with the corpse. Finally there was

Patterson himself, an ex-con with a long record. As Godwin later put it, "A murder case couldn't look any better than this."

Two days later Mike Cain was riding in his squad car when Chief Adkins called him on the radio and told him to report immediately to the Escambia County Courthouse. When he got there Cain saw several trucks from out-of-town television stations parked in front.

"What's going on?" he asked Adkins when he was inside the building.

"Hawsey has called a press conference," the chief replied. "He's going to announce the arrest of Vickie Lynn Pittman's killer."

"*What?*" asked Cain, stunned.

"He and the district attorney are going to announce that the case has been solved."

Cain and Adkins were hustled into the room where the television cameras were waiting. Hawsey told the two officers to sit on his right side and Godwin on his left, and he sat in the center, directly in front of the cameras. He began by announcing that Vickie Lynn's murder had been solved in less than three weeks through the excellent cooperation of his department and the East Brewton police. He introduced and thanked both Cain and Chief Adkins. Then he announced that Tyrone Patterson was being charged with the murder of Vickie Lynn Pittman. Vickie Lynn had "found out things" about a criminal gang he controlled whose members were involved in writing bad checks, drugs, burglaries, and even prostitution. She had been about to expose Patterson and his gang, so he had beaten her to death. At least one woman, who had been a member of the gang, was cooperating with the police. There was no mention in Hawsey's prepared remarks about the East Brewton bank robbery.

"This is a terrible tragedy," Hawsey told the television cameras. "Vickie Lynn was a good girl who got mixed up with the wrong group doing the wrong things. It cost her her life. I hope young people will learn from Vickie's mistakes and stay on the right road. If not, they could easily end up like her."

Sitting there, Cain felt like a fool. Sheriff Hawsey had parroted nearly word for word what Karen Kelly had told him about Patterson, only he made it sound as if her accusations were documented facts. What other proof did he have that Patterson was the head of a criminal gang? None. And something else troubled Cain. As far as he knew, no one in law enforcement had even bothered to question Patterson. Shouldn't they at least have asked if he had an alibi before accusing him in public of being a gang leader and murderer?

Cain had other misgivings as well. Why had Ralph Myers known so much about where Vickie Lynn's body was hidden? Why had Vic Pittman acted so suspiciously when his daughter disappeared? And there was something more. During the trip from the Evergreen jail to Brewton, Karen Kelly had talked incessantly about how much she loved a black man named Johnny D. McMillian and how he was a major marijuana dealer. Had McMillian played a role in the murder?

As soon as the press conference ended Hawsey was mobbed by reporters, but Cain stuck around until they were gone. Then he hurried up to the sheriff and made a suggestion. There were still lots of questions that needed to be answered, he said. "I think we need to appoint a joint task force—someone from your office, the police department, and the ABI—to check every possible lead until we know everything that happened."

Hawsey brushed him aside. The sheriff's office was finished with its probe. "We have caught our man," he said. "Tyrone Patterson killed that girl."

Chapter 16

Accused murderer Tyrone Patterson sent word from his jail cell that he wanted to talk to ABI agent Simon Benson. He did not trust any of the white officers in Escambia County. Benson didn't want to be bothered—he was busy in Monroeville working on the Ronda Morrison case—but the prisoner was so persistent that he finally drove to the jail in Brewton. Patterson was being kept under tight security.

"I don't even know no girl named Pittman," Patterson blurted out as soon as he was alone with Benson. "I didn't kill nobody."

"If we didn't have a case on you, you wouldn't be here," Benson replied without sympathy. He had been briefed by Sheriff Hawsey and thought the state's evidence was convincing. Taking a tiny recorder from his pocket, he flipped a switch, and the voice of Ralph Myers could be heard identifying Patterson as the black man whom he had overheard plotting to kill Vickie Lynn.

For several minutes Patterson sat quietly, listening to the tape. "Mr. Simon," he said when it ended, "I don't know anyone named Ralph Myers. I know Karen and I know what she is doing. She is framing me."

"Why?"

Patterson grinned sheepishly. It was because he was responsible for her being in jail. When she was arrested in Evergreen, he told Benson, she had been cashing a forged $155 check he had given her. "I also ripped off some drugs she had," he added.

Benson was skeptical. If Kelly was lying about Patterson, then how had she known about the shovel and bloody boots in his car trunk?

"What date did Karen Kelly say this was, when I showed her this dead girl's body in my car trunk?" he asked.

According to Kelly's statement to the police, Vickie Lynn Pittman had disappeared on February 19, a Thursday, but had not been murdered until the night of February 22, a Sunday. Patterson had shown her the corpse in the trunk of his car early during the evening of February 23, a Monday.

Suddenly Patterson broke into a big smile. "Mr. Simon, I can prove Karen is lying. I got peoples who seen me and my car those nights—peoples you got to believe."

"Who?"

Patterson laughed. "The entire Evergreen police department. That's who!"

During the next few minutes he detailed his alibi. On the Sunday night when Vickie Lynn was murdered in East Brewton, Patterson said, he was thirty-five miles away in Evergreen being chased by the police. He had driven there with a friend to meet a drug dealer, but they arrived in town early and stopped to eat dinner at the Crispy Chick restaurant. Kelly had come inside and told Patterson that she and her boyfriend needed help. "She said he had a flat tire but didn't have no tire jack so I gave her my car keys and she went outside. I didn't go with her because I needed to go to the men's room." Kelly had returned a few minutes later and given him back his keys. "She told me I didn't have a jack in my car and, to tell the truth, I didn't know if I did or didn't because I had never looked." Patterson brightened. "That is when Karen must have seen my shovel and the boots in my trunk!"

After he and his friend finished eating, they met their drug connection and bought several hundred dollars' worth of cocaine. They had started driving back to Brewton when a police car fell in behind them and Patterson panicked. "I decided to outrun 'em because I didn't want them finding the cocaine." Within minutes several other police cars joined in the chase, but Patterson managed to turn off the main highway onto a logging road that led into the woods. He checked his rearview mirror. "I'd lost them, but only for a few minutes." Grabbing the cocaine, he had leaped from the car. His friend had taken the wheel and continued down the logging road. Patterson had stayed hidden in the woods until the police passed him. Then he dug a hole, buried the cocaine, and hitchhiked home. He found out later that the police had arrested his friend and impounded the car.

"My car sat out in front of the Evergreen police station all Sunday and the next day until real late that night."

Kelly had said that Patterson had been driving around with Vickie Lynn's corpse in his trunk from Sunday evening until Monday night and had then hidden the body in the woods with the help of a friend. "If my car was parked at the police station all Sunday night and Monday, then when did I have time to put a body in the trunk?" he asked.

Patterson said that on Monday night he had returned to Evergreen to get his car, but he insisted he had not gone to Kelly's house that night: "I went to get my cocaine." He drove into the woods, slipped on his rubber boots from the trunk, and used a shovel to dig up the cocaine. He tossed the shovel and boots back into the trunk without scraping off the mud and leaves.

"Are you willing to take a lie detector test about this?" Benson asked.

"Sure am," said Patterson, "because it's true. I didn't kill no girl. I was busy buying cocaine that night."

Benson arranged for an ABI polygraph examiner to test Patterson two days later. The machine showed that he was telling the truth when he said he knew nothing about the Pittman murder. It also indicated that he was being truthful about his alibi. A few days later Benson received a report from the state crime lab, which had been asked to examine the items found in Patterson's car trunk. The "bloodstains" the police had reported finding on the rubber boots were actually dots of red paint. The mud and leaves found in the trunk and on the shovel did not match any of the soil and leaf samples taken from the area in the woods where Vickie Lynn's corpse had been found. The lab not only concluded that there was absolutely no evidence that linked the items in the trunk to the murder, it went a step further. Based on the condition of Vickie Lynn's corpse, the lab's experts said it was highly unlikely that her body could have been driven around inside a car trunk without leaving traces of skin, blood, or hair, yet they found no such evidence in the trunk.

By this time Benson had also checked with the Evergreen police. Its records showed that officers had impounded Patterson's car and arrested his friend on February 22, just as he had said. The vehicle had been thoroughly searched and then parked in front of the station until late Monday, when Patterson claimed it.

Although Benson now believed that Patterson's alibi was valid, he did not share his findings with Sheriff Hawsey or prosecutor Godwin. He did, however, suggest that they delay their prosecution until after he had had time to finish his investigation. They ignored the warning. Instead they presented their evidence against Patterson to a grand jury, and, as expected, it indicted him for murder on the basis of the witness statements given to the police by Kelly and Myers.

The indictment terrified Patterson. "I'm being railroaded 'cause I'm black," he protested. Again he demanded to see Benson, and this time the agent asked whether he could think of any reason why Kelly and Myers were framing him. Patterson thought the answer was obvious. "They are trying to keep you from arresting them and whoever the real killer is," he said.

At about this same time, Karen Kelly was released on bond from Sheriff Hawsey's jail. The forgery case filed against her was being put on hold until after she testified against Patterson. An East Brewton police officer happened to be driving by the jail when Kelly came outside, and he decided to follow her. A few blocks from the jail, she ducked under a bridge that crossed Murder Creek. Curious, the officer parked his car and peeked beneath the structure. She was yelling at a man who had obviously been waiting for her there. The officer dashed back to his squad car and called Chief Adkins.

"Who's the man?" Adkins asked.

"Vic Pittman," the officer replied. "She's really giving him hell about something."

Chapter 17

From the day Vickie Lynn disappeared, Mozelle had suspected that her brother was involved. Now she was more certain than ever. Three days after his daughter was buried, Vic had showed up at the East Brewton police station holding a plastic bag with a bloodstained bone in it. He said it was a piece of Vickie Lynn's jaw that he had found lying in the dirt when he went into the woods to see for himself where her corpse had been hidden. As soon as Mozelle heard about Vic's discovery, she telephoned Deputy Sheriff Claude Cosey and asked him whether the state crime lab really had been that careless at the crime scene.

Cosey flatly denied it. "I saw them down on their hands and knees sifting through the dirt," he said. "There's no way Vic just walked out there and saw that bone."

In her daily log about Vic and all the different stories he told her, Mozelle now included questions she wanted answers to.

- Why did Vic have V.L.'s [Vickie Lynn's] jawbone?
- Why were Vic and Karen Kelly arguing beneath the bridge?

- Kelly told Sheriff Hawsey that she never met V.L., but Vic told everyone Kelly was his fiancée. They must've met.
- Why did Vic tell everyone V.L. was being held for ransom?
- Where did the white dress come from in the heart-shaped box at Vic's house the morning after she disappeared?

Mozelle called Mike Cain at work. "Vic and Kelly are lying," she said. "Vic's the key to finding out who killed Vickie Lynn. You got to get him to tell the truth."

Although Sheriff Hawsey had decided that his office had completed its investigation, Cain had no intention of stopping his. He decided to interview Mary O'Farrell, a woman who once had been married to Vic. Mozelle thought her brother might have confided in O'Farrell, though they were divorced. Cain taped the interview.

"I'm the one who left the white dress at Vic's house," she volunteered. "I figured Vickie Lynn might could wear it for her graduation dress. I told Vic I was going to leave it. He said he would try to meet me at their house, but he didn't show up."

"Vic *knew* about the dress—knew it was from you all along?"

"Oh yes, sir."

"What did Vic tell you about Karen Kelly and Vickie Lynn?"

"He just said that Karen Kelly and Vickie Lynn was close, you know —had got to be real . . . good friends, you know, when she and Vic were going together."

"Did Vic say or do anything suspicious when Vickie Lynn first disappeared?"

"He said he knew where Vickie Lynn was. I said, 'Where is she, Vic?' He said, 'She's in a field, but if I take them to her, they'll blame it all on me. . . . I said, 'Well, why don't you just tell them you didn't do it or whatever, you know.' He said, 'Oh, let's just forget it.' "

"When did Vic tell you that he knew Vickie Lynn was dead and her body was hidden in a field?"

"About March seventh."

Cain did the arithmetic in his head. That was nearly *three weeks* before her body had been found.

In interviews with the police, Vic had always insisted that he did not know anything about the white dress; that his daughter and Kelly had never met; that he had not known that Vickie Lynn was dead until her corpse was found on March 29. According to O'Farrell, he was lying.

"I think Vic was there when they beat his own daughter to death," Mozelle said after Cain told her and Onzell what he had learned. "I think they gave him her jawbone as a warning to keep his mouth shut."

"Oh no!" Onzell cried. "You can't believe that! Vic's our brother! Vickie Lynn was his own daughter!"

"I sure as hell do," Mozelle replied. "I think he stood there and watched them beat that little girl to death."

Cain found Vic sleeping on a discarded sofa in an abandoned one-car garage, where he was now living. Since Vickie Lynn's funeral, he had been on a drinking binge. Cain took him away, bought him some coffee, and then confronted him with what O'Farrell had said.

"She's lying to you," Vic declared. "I never said any of those things."

Cain argued with him, but Vic kept insisting he was telling the truth. Frustrated, Cain drove him back to his garage home. Black smoke was pouring from it, and the sofa where Vic had been sleeping was on fire.

"Don't you ever pick me up here like this again!" a shaken Vic shouted. "You gonna get us both killed! Leave me alone!"

A few days later Ralph Myers telephoned Cain in a panic and demanded that they meet in private on a secluded road outside town. Myers was late. Finally he roared up in his truck to where Cain was parked, slammed on his brakes, jumped out, and thrust both his hands in front of him.

"Look! Look! See how they're shaking!" he screamed. Cain tried to calm him. He knew from his past dealings with Myers how melodramatic he could be, but this time Myers couldn't seem to compose himself.

"Mike, you got to *do* something!" he said. "That bitch is going to get me killed!"

"Who's going to get you killed, Ralph?"

"That damn Karen Kelly. She got her boyfriend to threaten me. . . . Johnny D. called me up on the telephone and told me to keep my damn mouth shut about the murder because if I didn't, and this here is a direct quote, he said, 'We will kill you like we killed that Pittman girl and we'll kill your damn family too!' "

"What's he have to do with the murder?" Cain asked.

Myers jumped back in his truck. "I've already opened my goddamn mouth too much now but that damn Karen Kelly is the one behind all this. Tyrone Patterson ain't nothing but a damn scapegoat who's being framed up. He don't know nothing about that murder." Myers popped the clutch and sped away before Cain could ask him any more.

The meeting with Myers was not Cain's only secretive encounter.

Mozelle called him when he returned to the station and said Vic wanted to see him in a remote spot on the outskirts of town where he was hiding. Cain said later that this was the first time he had seen Vic show what he considered signs of genuine emotion. "Vic told me that he had known all along that O'Farrell had left the white dress at his house. He had lied about it, and he admitted that. He also admitted that he had known that Vickie Lynn was dead several weeks before her body was found, but he wouldn't tell me how he had found that out."

As they had talked, Vic had begun to cry. His daughter, he told Cain, had not been murdered because she had seen a bank robber and was going to tell the police. She had been kidnapped and killed because of a "bad drug deal." Cain pressed him for details, but he refused to say more.

"You and me will both be dead if I tell you what really happened," Cain later quoted Vic as saying. "These are heavy dudes."

Cain met Vic a second time the next morning, and the officer was blunt. "Vickie Lynn was your daughter, for God's sakes!" he said. "Someone killed her. If you know who, tell me. You owe her that much."

"I got another daughter," Vic replied. "I don't want her dead too."

"Vic," Cain said softly. "Who are you afraid of?"

Vic glanced around and then dropped his voice to a whisper. "Learn everything you can about Johnny D. McMillian, Karen Kelly's nigger boyfriend in Monroeville," he said.

Cain ran a computer background check on Johnny D. as soon as he got back to the police station, but there wasn't much there. The records showed that Johnny D. and his wife, Minnie, owned a Chevrolet pickup truck and a late-model Lincoln Continental. In 1982 he had been convicted of possession of marijuana and fined $100; in 1985 he had been charged with selling marijuana, but that charge had been dismissed; in May 1986 he had been charged with cutting another black man with a knife during an altercation outside a nightclub. He had been put on probation for one year. That was all.

As always, Cain kept Mozelle posted, and the following day he had a breathless call from her. She had just gotten a tip from a woman who lived at the Big Four Trailer Park in East Brewton, the same place where Karen Kelly had lived. "Mike, this woman said a girl was screaming bloody murder screams from Karen Kelly's trailer on a Friday night in February at just about the same time as when Vickie Lynn disappeared. The screams woke her up, and she told her husband that he needed to call the law because they was killing someone over there, but he told her that those dopeheads who lived in that trailer would kill them too so they didn't do anything."

The woman had also remembered looking out her trailer window the next day and noticing "a big fancy car" painted light blue parked outside Kelly's trailer.

"What color is Johnny D.'s Lincoln?" Mozelle asked.

Cain checked his computer printout.

"It's light blue."

"Oh, Mike!" Mozelle exclaimed. "All of them are in this together—Vic, Johnny D., Kelly, Ralph Myers. They picked up Vickie Lynn and took her to Karen Kelly's trailer and beat her there. I just know it. This is about drugs."

Cain wrote down the name of the woman who had telephoned Mozelle, and within the hour he and Chief Adkins were interviewing her. She told them the same story but acknowledged that she couldn't be certain on which Friday night in February she had heard the screams. Cain questioned other neighbors, while Adkins spoke to the trailer park's manager and learned that Kelly had moved out of her trailer on February 10—nine days before Vickie Lynn had been kidnapped. It would have been impossible for the girl to have been killed in Kelly's trailer.

Cain told Mozelle the tip was nothing but another wild-goose chase, but that did not stop her. She and Onzell went to the trailer park and interviewed the manager themselves, and he told them something he hadn't mentioned to the police: that Kelly had moved out of the trailer on February 10, but that her rent had been paid through March 1 and she had kept her door key until then. The two women had also found out that after Kelly had turned in her key, the trailer had been hauled away, gutted, and completely reconditioned. "I'm telling you, Mike, that is where they tortured and killed Vickie Lynn," Mozelle said. "That's why they gutted that trailer—to get rid of the blood."

"Mozelle, they probably gutted it because it needed to be redone. Those trailers are old out there," he replied. She was letting her imagination run wild, he thought.

Without warning, Mozelle began to cry. It shocked Cain. She had always seemed so tough. Only then did he realize what should have been obvious to him long before. Mozelle and Onzell had loved Vickie Lynn. Since her disappearance they had received dozens of telephone calls from people who had claimed to have information. They had carefully logged each call and had investigated many of the stories themselves, no matter how crazy they were. Not only did they have to deal with her disappearance and murder, they also had to deal with the uncertainty and mean-spirited gossip that had come with it. They had been told that Vickie Lynn was dealing drugs, was pregnant, had had an abortion, was a member of Tyrone Patterson's criminal gang. They had been told that she was murdered because she had seen a bank robber, because of a drug deal that had gone sour. One caller, a longtime friend, had told Mozelle that Vickie Lynn had been working as a prostitute; another claimed she was a cocaine addict. The twins didn't know what or whom to believe. Even their own brother, who should have been helping them, had deliberately misled the police about his daughter's disappearance. For the first time in his career, Cain began to understand, really understand, the reach of a killer. Not only had he beaten Vickie Lynn to death, but he had sent shock waves through the lives of everyone close to her.

"Mike," Mozelle said between sobs, "I will never be able to get on with my life until I find out the truth. I have to know who killed Vickie Lynn. I have to know why. I have to know if Vic was involved. You got to help me and Onzell. Please!"

He swore that he would.

Chapter 18

In Hollywood movies and mystery novels, detectives catch the villains by skillful deduction and the piecing together of clues. In real life, they depend on snitches.

On May 29 in Monroeville, ABI agent Simon Benson conducted a tape-recorded interview in the county courthouse with Karen Kelly, whom he suspected of lying about the Vickie Lynn Pittman murder. At first Kelly stubbornly stuck to her original story. "Tyrone Patterson done this killing," she said. Then Benson told her that Patterson had a solid alibi. Without a hint of embarrassment or explanation, she immediately changed her story.

Ralph Myers, she declared, had killed Vickie Lynn. She also offered Benson an entirely new motive for the killing: Myers had been paid to abduct and kill the teenager.

"Who paid him?" asked Benson.

"Walter 'Johnny D.' McMillian, my boyfriend," she replied.

"Why . . . did Johnny D. pay Ralph Myers . . . to kill Vickie Lynn Pittman?"

"Ralph said it was because of a bad drug deal that went down."

"Okay, do you know who was involved in the drug deal?"

"Karen Ann Pittman, old man Vic Pittman, and Johnny D. . . ."

"Did you, Karen Kelly, take part in the death of Vickie Lynn Pittman?"

"No, I did not. No way."

What happened next proved to be a major turning point in Benson's investigation. After the agent finished the interview and switched off his tape recorder, he and Kelly stepped out of the sheriff's office in the courthouse and walked down a hallway so that he could escort her out of the building. It was at that moment, Benson claimed later, that Kelly had blurted, "The Pittman girl ain't the onliest girl Ralph killed for Johnny D." According to Benson, as soon as Kelly let those words slip she became frightened and refused to elaborate, but he did manage to get a few cryptic clues from her. She said that Myers and Johnny D. had both bragged about how they had killed another teenage girl because of a drug deal, and that the murder had never been solved, even though a large reward had been offered. When Benson said he wanted to tape-record what Kelly had just told him, she cried "No!" and ran out of the courthouse.

Benson dashed upstairs to the district attorney's office and briefed Larry Ikner. Both men agreed instantly that Kelly had been talking about the Ronda Morrison murder. Neither had ever been convinced that the real motive behind it was robbery or rape. Both believed there had to be a more compelling reason for the senseless killing. Drugs fit.

There were other reasons why they were certain Kelly was talking about Ronda's murder. It was the only recent one that was still unsolved and the only one that involved a large reward. Moreover, the investigators were still suspicious of Randy Thomas. Why had he so quickly hired an attorney, sold the cleaners, left town? Finally both men remembered that Ronda was not supposed to be working on the Saturday when she had been killed. Separately these bits of information proved absolutely nothing. They were like pieces of a puzzle that seen apart made no sense. But that afternoon, when Benson and Ikner began moving them around —using Kelly's tips as their guide—they were able not only to fit them together but to create a recognizable picture. Myers and Johnny D. had murdered Ronda, they decided, because she had walked in on a drug deal at the cleaners that somehow involved Thomas.

Drugs seemed to explain not only the murder, but also the suspect. Everyone knew Johnny D. was involved in selling marijuana. It was hardly a secret. In 1987 smoking pot had become a rite of passage for many teenagers, just as drinking beer had been for their parents. Each weekend a regular clique of kids got high, and most youngsters knew there were two major suppliers. One lived in Clausell; the other was Johnny D. In fact, two years earlier the ABI had sent an undercover agent to purchase marijuana from him, but the agent had messed up the buy, making it inadmissible in court, and the charge had had to be dropped. As recently as three weeks ago, Sheriff Tate had sent deputies to search Johnny D.'s house for pot, but they had found none.

The fact that it was Karen Kelly who was implicating Johnny D. also was significant. She had been—and still claimed to be—his girlfriend. In May 1986 Kelly's husband had sued her for divorce on grounds of adultery and had identified Johnny D. as his wife's lover. Any divorce in Monroeville is subject for gossip, but no one could ever remember when a white man had accused his wife in public of having an affair with a married black man. A judge had awarded custody of the couple's only child to his father, and Kelly had been shunned by most whites. Even so, she had defiantly continued to brag about how much she loved Johnny D. If he *had* confessed a murder to anyone, the two investigators figured it would be Kelly.

That afternoon, as they discussed what she had said, the focus of Benson's investigation gradually shifted. Originally he had been trying to solve the Pittman murder. Now that case was put aside.

By nightfall they had arrived at a plan. Benson would arrest Myers for the murder of Vickie Lynn Pittman based on Kelly's taped accusations. However, he would not tell Myers *whom* he was being accused of killing. In fact, Benson and Ikner would imply that he was being charged with murdering Ronda Morrison. That way they could see his reaction. If he panicked, he might blurt out something incriminating.

They had come up with two perfectly legal ways to carry out this subterfuge. Instead of taking Myers to the jail in Brewton after they arrested him, they would drive him to the Monroe County jail. Myers had been in trouble enough times to know that the Pittman killing was an Escambia County case and had nothing to do with Monroe County. He was bound to wonder why he was being transported to a jail in Monroeville. They would also tell him that Sheriff Tate was going to help interrogate him. Myers would know that Tate had no jurisdiction in the Pittman murder—that was Sheriff Hawsey's domain. Tate was interested in solving the Morrison murder.

The next day Benson and Ikner drove to Evergreen to arrest Myers. Neither indicated whom he was being accused of killing, only that he was being charged with murder. They put him in the back of an unmarked car and headed west rather than south.

"Where we going?" Myers asked.

"Monroeville."

One of them mentioned that Tate would be waiting to help them interrogate him. Myers suddenly began to fidget.

When they reached the city limits, they turned north onto South Alabama Avenue and slowed down, until the car was barely moving when they reached the front of Jackson Cleaners. Benson watched Myers through the rearview mirror. Ikner was sitting next to him in the backseat.

"When we drove by the cleaners," Ikner said later, "Ralph Myers turned and looked over his shoulder at the building. He stared at it."

Both investigators reached the same conclusion: "He definitely had been there before. You could tell he recognized it," said Benson. "It was that obvious."

Chapter 19

Ralph Myers's arrest was reported that week in *The Evergreen Courant*, which also published his photograph. A few hours after the newspaper was delivered to the Conecuh County jail, Deputy Betty Baggett Salo called Benson in Monroeville and told him she had a prisoner standing next to her desk crying like a baby. "He claims he knows who killed Ronda Morrison. You better get over here quick!"

Benson and Larry Ikner sped to Evergreen and raced up the three flights of stairs to the jail. Bill Hooks, Jr., the black youth originally arrested for "public lewdness/pollution" on the date when Ronda was murdered, was still sobbing when they came through the door.

"This here is the man I seen coming out of Jackson Cleaners!" said Hooks, pointing at the photograph of Myers in the newspaper. Ikner and Benson led him into a nearby office and managed to calm him down. No tape recordings or notes were made that day, but all three later testified in court about their conversation. Hooks told the two investigators that he was absolutely positive that Myers was the white man whom he had seen fleeing from Jackson Cleaners. He had not known his name until he had read it in the newspaper, but he reminded them that he had first mentioned seeing a white man "with scars on his face" in February when Ikner had interviewed him at the jail.

"Him and Johnny Dozier is who I seen," Hooks said, again pointing at the photograph.

Ikner interrupted. No one in Monroeville knew any black man named John Dozier. He had run that name through every computerized police and state record available in February, and there wasn't a Johnny Dozier anywhere in Alabama.

"Got to be," said Hooks. "Black peoples knows him. He is Johnny Dozier. You know, Johnny D."

"Are you talking about *Johnny D.*?" Benson asked.

"That the man, Johnny Dozier."

"Do you mean Johnny D. McMillian?" said Ikner.

"Yeah! He the one!"

Ikner wanted to make certain Hooks understood what he was being asked. He repeated his question: "Are you saying Johnny D. Dozier is actually Johnny D. McMillian?"

Hooks nodded.

It was now clear to Ikner why he had never been able to identify Johnny Dozier. Hooks had given him a nickname.

Ikner and Benson asked Hooks to tell them once again what he had been doing on the morning when Ronda was killed. At that time, Hooks said, he had been working as an auto mechanic at Kenny Blanton's Used Cars, a few miles south of Jackson Cleaners. Shortly after nine-thirty A.M., he had been sent downtown to pick up some parts at Taylor Parts, a store on the town square. The return trip to the car lot took him directly in front of Jackson Cleaners, which he had passed sometime between ten-thirty and eleven.

"I seen two dudes coming out—Johnny D. and this white dude here in the paper," he said. They had gotten into a pickup truck and sped off. "The way they went spinning out in the truck let me know then that something was wrong at the cleaners."

Could Hooks identify the truck he had seen them in?

"I sure can," Hooks said, adding that he had once done some mechanical work on it for Johnny D. at his house.

The investigators asked Hooks if he was willing to testify against Johnny D.

"It's the truth so I gots to," he replied.

. . .

It was hot three days later, on Sunday, June 7, and Johnny D.'s pickup truck didn't have air-conditioning. He was driving home from Evergreen and was traveling only about thirty-five miles an hour because he had just converted the truck into a "low-rider" by removing its springs. That was a cheap way to lower the chassis so that the entire truck rode as close to the pavement as a car. Johnny D. thought low-riders looked sporty, but there was a price to pay. He was afraid to drive too fast because Highway 84 was bumpy and he didn't want the truck's underbelly to scrape the road.

He was about two miles away from his house when he noticed the flashing red-and-blue lights of a sheriff's car racing up behind him. He smiled. Sheriff Tate had been trying to bust him for selling marijuana ever since January, when Tate had taken office. During the election campaign, Tate had promised that as sheriff he would force every drug dealer to leave Monroe County. As popular as marijuana was, Johnny D. figured that if Tate carried out his pledge half the county's population would soon be running for the county line.

As he slowed to a stop, another sheriff's car spun sideways in front of his truck, effectively blocking his escape. Deputies jumped from the two cars with their shotguns and pistols pointed at him. Sheriff Tate ordered him to step out of his truck with his hands raised. Shocked by the show of force, Johnny D. opened the door warily and stepped out. Tate rushed forward, handcuffed him, and pushed him out of the way of several deputies, who immediately started to search his truck.

"There ain't no dope here," a deputy called out seconds later to Tate.

Johnny D. had known they wouldn't find anything. "What are you arresting me for?" he asked.

Tate didn't answer at first and then he said, "Sodomy."

"Sod-o-what?" Johnny D. couldn't pronounce the word and had no idea what it meant.

"Screwing a man in his ass."

"Who done that?"

"You did!" said Tate, who led him to one of the cruisers and pushed him into the backseat.

Like so many incidents in this story, what happened next is hotly disputed. Johnny D. would later claim that Tate threatened him and used racist language. "Tate was real, real angry 'cause I think he figured I was carrying dope in the truck and that's what he really planned to get me on, but there weren't none," Johnny D. explained. "I asked him who he was saying I had had sex with and he leaned in the car and says, 'You goddamn nigger. When I tell you to shut your goddamn mouth, you quit asking questions or I'll put one of these bullets through your goddamn head.' " Sheriff Tate later denied ever making such a statement. Nonetheless, both men agree that Tate drove Johnny D.'s pickup truck into town and parked it in front of the jail while a deputy followed behind in a police cruiser with Johnny D. in the backseat. For the rest of the day Johnny D. waited in jail for someone to tell him what was happening. Late that night he happened to see a black deputy putting a prisoner into a cell. He called him over.

"Hey, man, why're they locking me up like this?" he asked.

The deputy replied in a hushed voice. The sodomy charge was just something the sheriff had used so that he could put Johnny D. in jail and impound his truck. Pausing to make sure no one could overhear them, the deputy then said that the real reason Johnny D. had been arrested was because he was going to be accused of murdering Ronda Morrison as soon as the necessary paperwork could be drawn up.

"Ronda Morrison?" Johnny D. replied. "Why, I ain't never met that girl."

The deputy offered Johnny D. some quick parting advice. "Get yourself a damn good lawyer."

Within two hours after Johnny D.'s arrest, Benson and Larry Ikner went to see Karen Kelly at her mother's house south of town. They told her that Bill Hooks, Jr., was prepared to testify that he had seen Johnny D. and Myers running from the cleaners. They told her that both suspects were in jail, so there was no reason for her to be afraid of them. They asked her whether she would be willing to give them a sworn statement implicating Johnny D. and Myers. She said she would.

"Johnny D. told me he killed that Morrison girl in the cleaners," Kelly said under oath. On November 2, the day after the murder, she had met him at The Ranchero, a black nightclub. "I sat down at the table with Johnny D. and we were talking and I brought the murder up and he informed me that Ralph Myers drove the truck to the cleaners and he [Johnny D.] killed the girl—Ronda Morrison."

"Why did Johnny D. kill Ronda?" Benson asked.

"The girl knew too much. He had had some dealings with Randy Thomas . . . the man who owned the cleaners."

"Did he say what type dealings?"

"No, but Ralph Myers told me it was cocaine."

Although Johnny D. had not told her exactly what had happened inside the cleaners, Kelly said Myers had later bragged about the murder. She said Ronda was not supposed to be working at the cleaners that morning because a drug deal was "going down" in the back of the building. The girl had unknowingly "walked in on it," and Johnny D. had grabbed her. Ronda had broken free, and he had shot her as she tried to escape.

"Karen, were you at the Jackson Cleaners when the girl was killed?" Benson asked.

"No, I wasn't," she replied. "I didn't have nothing to do with any of this shit."

"Karen, is what you are telling us the truth?"

"Yes, it's the truth. What reason do I have to lie?"

The next morning, Monday, June 8, the investigators brought Bill Hooks, Jr., from the jail in Evergreen to Monroeville. Johnny D.'s pickup truck was still parked in front of the jail, and Hooks was allowed to examine it before he was taken inside. He then signed a sworn deposition identifying the truck as the one he had seen parked outside the cleaners on the morning when Ronda was killed.

"I seen [this] truck at Jackson Cleaners and the dude that I seen getting in it was Johnny D. McMillian and the dude that was driving the truck was Ralph Myers . . ."

"How do you know Johnny D.?" asked Ikner.

"I believe I worked for him once before . . . as a mechanic . . . at his house . . . on Highway 84."

"Are you sure the two people you saw was Ralph Myers, driving that vehicle, and Johnny D. McMillian, that got into it?"

"Yes, sir."

After talking to Hooks, Benson and Ikner checked with the manager of Taylor Parts, and he showed them a receipt signed by Hooks that proved Hooks had been in the parts store on the morning Ronda was killed, just as he had told them. It was while he was returning to work from the store that Hooks had spotted Myers and Johnny D.

On Monday night Benson, Ikner, and Sheriff Tate met to review their case. Hooks and Kelly had both given them sworn statements. Hooks had identified Myers and Johnny D. as the men he had seen running from the cleaners. He had also identified Johnny D.'s truck. Kelly had sworn that both men had admitted to her that they were involved in the murder. They had enough evidence, the three investigators agreed, to charge Johnny D. with murder, but they wanted something more. There was one more witness whose help they needed. If Ronda's killer was to be sentenced to death in Alabama's electric chair, as they hoped, they were going to need an eyewitness, someone who had actually seen Johnny D. pull the trigger.

The next morning Ralph Myers was brought from jail to the courthouse, where Benson, Ikner, and Tate were waiting. During this tape-recorded June 9 session, Benson was blunt. He told Myers he was about to be charged with killing Ronda Morrison. He was already accused of killing Vickie Lynn, and now he would be facing two possible death penalty charges. "Don't sit here and burn yourself away down to the electric chair," Benson said, "because that is where you're heading."

There was only one way for Myers to save himself from being executed, Benson went on. Cooperate. Tell the truth. Negotiate a plea bargain. He would still be charged with Ronda's murder, but if he agreed to testify for the prosecution, his life would be spared. "You is the onliest one that can save yourself . . . ," Benson warned.

It did not take Myers long to make up his mind. "Okay," he said. "I'll cooperate."

During the next hour Myers spun out his version of the murder. Like all his stories, it was a jumbled affair, but the basic facts were these: Myers had bumped into Johnny D. by accident at a car wash in Evergreen on the morning of the murder and had ended up driving him to Monroeville because Johnny D.'s right arm was hurting him. It was Johnny D.'s idea to drive to Jackson Cleaners, and he was the only person who had actually gone inside the store. Myers had waited in the parking lot. Thirty minutes or so later, he heard "popping noises," and Johnny D. came running outside carrying a small bag. He ordered Myers "to drive," but Myers was so flustered that he gave the truck too much gasoline and it stalled. Johnny D. jumped out, opened the hood, fiddled with the engine, and got the truck running. Then they drove away.

In his sworn statement, Myers insisted he had not known that Ronda Morrison had been killed at the cleaners that morning until he heard about it later on the news. He had thought about calling the police, but Johnny D. and a "heavyset" black man had come to his house and threatened him.

"Johnny D. told me, he says, '. . . I'll kill you . . . the same way that I've done over there at the Laundromat.' "

Benson, Ikner, and Tate were suspicious of Myers's account. "We figured Ralph was lying about not going inside the cleaners," Ikner said later. None thought he had told them, as they later put it, the "entire truth." But he had agreed to testify against Johnny D., and that was enough for now.

A few hours after Myers told his story, Johnny D. was led from his cell downstairs to another room in the jail, where Circuit Court Judge Sam Welch was waiting. Ordinarily a prisoner is taken to the courthouse, which is only two blocks away, to be charged and have his bond set. However, word already had spread through town that Johnny D. had murdered Ronda, and Sheriff Tate was afraid vigilantes might try to kill him. At Tate's urging, Judge Welch agreed to conduct the arraignment at the jail. Johnny D. was charged with capital murder, punishable by death, and his bond was set at $250,000. When he told them he couldn't pay it, he was taken back to his cell.

Afterward Sheriff Tate mentioned that someone needed to officially notify Charles and Bertha Morrison and to make certain that *The Monroe Journal* and the radio station were alerted. They had good news to report at last: Ronda's killers were behind bars.

Chapter 20

After he was charged with killing Ronda Morrison, Johnny D. was driven to Brewton and also charged with Vickie Lynn Pittman's murder. However, Escambia County District Attorney Mike Godwin told a local reporter that the Morrison case would take priority. It would be tried first, and if Johnny D. and Myers were convicted, then the charges in the Pittman case might be dropped. Why waste taxpayers' money, he asked, by going forward with a redundant second trial?

When she heard this, a furious Mozelle telephoned Godwin and demanded to know why Ronda's case was more important than Vickie Lynn's. The prosecutor tried to pacify her by explaining that the state had a stronger case in the Morrison murder, with "better evidence." But Godwin would later candidly admit that there had been another reason.

"In Monroeville the entire community was upset . . . but it wasn't quite like that here," he said. ". . . I'm not making any statement about the value of a human life, but with the Pittman girl, well, everyone knew she ran with the wrong crowd. Her death was just one of those things."

Mozelle had not needed Godwin's explanation. She already knew what was happening. Ronda had been beautiful, popular, a promising college student with loving, well-respected, and socially acceptable parents. Vickie Lynn had been dumpy, poor, an unsophisticated teenager with few friends. Her daddy was a drunk and her family was considered low-class. If the state did have better evidence in the Morrison case, it was because prosecutors had made solving it a top priority.

The differences in approach were real. The ABI had dispatched Benson and nine additional ABI agents to Monroeville on the day when Ronda was murdered. A short time later, Alabama Governor George Wallace had designated $10,000 of state money for the reward fund established to help find Ronda's killer. Wallace also expressed his personal concern and sympathy to the Morrison family. The Monroeville community had held a cookout to establish a scholarship fund in Ronda's name at the junior college. No such actions had occurred in the Pittman case. Mozelle and Onzell had been unable to interest anyone but Mike Cain in their niece's disappearance even when she had been missing for nearly a month. The ABI's Benson had been too busy in Monroeville to have any interest in the Pittman case until a desperate Tyrone Patterson had implored him to get involved. There had never been a reward offered, a community fund-raiser held, a word of sympathy articulated by the governor's office.

Even now the murders were being treated differently. Prosecutors were seeking the death penalty in Ronda's case. In Vickie Lynn's they were seeking life imprisonment at most. Even the terminology the state was using offended Mozelle. Ronda's alleged killers were charged with "capital murder," but for Vickie Lynn the charge was "simple murder," as if her death were an ordinary event that did not warrant so dramatic an outcome. In Mozelle's eyes murder was murder, justice was blind, a victim's social standing irrelevant.

One night when she was watching the national news on television, a network correspondent appeared on the screen, standing on the steps of the U.S. Supreme Court in Washington. Mozelle had not been paying much attention to the newscast until that moment, but she suddenly found herself leaning forward, peering at the screen. Right above the reporter's head, chiseled in stone across the entrance to the highest court in the land, were the words EQUAL JUSTICE UNDER LAW. Was that what Vickie Lynn was getting?

Mike Cain was just as angry as Mozelle and Onzell. He still believed that no one was taking time to investigate the Pittman murder adequately. Why had she been killed? Was it because she had seen the bank robber or because of a bad drug deal? Who had killed her? From what he could find out, the only evidence Benson had collected was Karen Kelly's sworn statement of May 29—the one in which she had said Johnny D. had paid Myers to kill Vickie Lynn because of a bad drug deal between him and "Karen Ann Pittman and old man Vic Pittman." Where was the corroborating evidence?

Cain had always considered the ABI the best investigators in the state of Alabama, but he wondered about Benson's eagerness to file murder charges based on a single statement by a proven liar. Kelly, after all, had originally claimed that it was Tyrone Patterson who had killed Vickie Lynn.

Cain decided it was time for him to talk to Vic Pittman again. He asked Deputy Sheriff Claude Cosey to join him, and the two of them picked up Vic. This time their taped interrogation lasted four hours. During the questioning Vic admitted that he had once smuggled drugs, but he denied he was still doing it, and he insisted he did not know Johnny D. "If you brought five niggers in here," he said, "I wouldn't be able to pick Johnny D. out." Over and over he blamed his older daughter, Karen Ann, for the murder. She was the one, he insisted, who was dealing drugs with Johnny D.

As it happened, Karen Ann came to see Cain the following day to pass along an unsavory tip she had heard. A truck driver had told her Vickie Lynn was murdered because she had been transporting drugs for Johnny D. and had lost a shipment of cocaine. "They use these big black guys to have sex with these white girls until their vaginas get big enough to carry a cylinder of cocaine in them," she quoted the truck driver as saying. Wild though the story sounded, Karen Ann reminded Cain that Vickie Lynn had complained of vaginal bleeding just before she was abducted. "I bet my damn daddy stole her cocaine and they killed Vickie Lynn because he wouldn't give it back."

By this time Cain had had his fill of Vic's blaming his daughter and her blaming him. In anger he accused Karen Ann of causing her own sister's death. She burst into tears and refused to answer any more questions.

Frustrated, Cain called Benson for advice. "I just don't know how to get the truth out of either of them," he said, adding with purposeful flattery, "but I'm sure someone with more experience could find out which one of them is lying. Would you come talk to them?"

It was late afternoon on a Friday and Benson said he was busy preparing for the Morrison murder trial, but he promised to drive to Brewton and interview Vic and Karen Ann on Monday morning. What happened next remains a matter of dispute. Benson would later say that he simply ended their conversation at that point. Cain would claim the ABI agent had offered him a parting suggestion: "Simon told me to put Karen Ann and Vic both in jail for the weekend. He told me, and this is a direct quote, 'A lot of people will talk if you just put them in jail for a little while and make them think about it.' "

Late Friday night Cain accused Vic and his daughter of withholding material evidence in a murder investigation and had them arrested. He had deliberately waited until after the county courthouse had closed for the weekend so that neither would be able to post a bond and be released. Benson arrived as promised on Monday morning to interrogate both father and daughter. He began with Vic. Ten minutes into the tape-recorded session, Vic told them that he and Karen Kelly had intentionally been misleading everyone. There never had been any "bad drug deal," he said. Vickie Lynn had been murdered because she was going to reveal the name of the bank robber.

"Vickie Lynn told me that Karen Kelly had robbed the bank in East Brewton. She said she knew because she had seen the money and Karen Kelly had told her that she had robbed the bank."

Kelly had not denied it, Vic said. "Karen told me, 'Yeah, I robbed the goddamn bank just to show these cops around here it could be done.' " But when he warned Kelly that Vickie Lynn was going to talk to the FBI, "She got very mad and said I had better tell my daughter to keep her mouth shut or else. When Vickie Lynn disappeared, I figured she had carried out her threat."

It was on the day when he and Kelly were seen arguing under the bridge that they had agreed to help frame Karen Ann, his other daughter, to divert attention from Kelly. He was afraid that if he didn't, Kelly would arrange his murder too.

A secretary typed Vic's statement, and Benson had him sign it. Vic was then released from jail, and the charge Cain had filed against him was dropped. Karen Ann was not so lucky. While in jail over the weekend, she began to cough up blood. A doctor said she had a bleeding ulcer and was suffering from extreme depression. She was released on bond. No one ever bothered to interview her, nor was she told that Vic had exonerated her. A short time later she and her husband moved away from East Brewton.

Cain was now ready to charge Karen Kelly with murder, but Benson balked, pointing out that Vic was a drunk who had already told the police dozens of stories—a good defense lawyer would easily discredit his statement.

"Well, Karen Kelly is a known liar, a dope addict, and prostitute who has told dozens of stories too," Cain protested. "Why are you believing *her*?"

Benson didn't answer, but Cain thought he knew. Kelly was one of the key witnesses in the Morrison case. Benson was not going to jeopardize that case by arresting her for the Pittman killing.

As before, Cain told Mozelle and Onzell, "Ronda's murder is taking precedence." But he promised to keep digging. "Eventually I am going to find out what really happened," he assured them.

He was wrong. He soon became embroiled in a nasty dispute with his lieutenant at the police department, and when their problems became public the city council fired them both.

Before leaving East Brewton, Cain stopped to see the twins and apologized. "I failed you. I let you down," he said, near tears.

Mozelle and Onzell hugged him and cried. "You did your best," said Onzell. "You cared when no one else did."

After he was gone, Mozelle took a deep breath. "It's up to us now," she said. "I want all of them—Simon Benson, Mike Godwin, Karen Kelly, and the rest of them bastards—to know one thing. Maybe Mike Cain is gone, but this ain't over until the fat lady sings." And then she added, "And darling, I haven't even got warmed up yet."

Part Three

Blind Justice

"Were you so scared that she'd hurt you, you ran, a big buck like you?"

"No suh, I's scared I'd be in court, just like I am now."

"Scared of arrest, scared you'd have to face up to what you did?"

"No suh, scared I'd hafta face up to what I didn't do."

—Harper Lee
To Kill a Mockingbird

Chapter 21

Walter "Johnny D." McMillian was not really worried when he was arrested on June 7, even after he learned that he was going to be charged with the Morrison murder. "Once I tells them they gots the wrong man, they will let me go," he assured Minnie over the telephone from the jail on the Sunday night he was arrested. "I remember exactly what I was doing the day that little Morrison girl was killed. Don't you? It was when my sister had that fish fry and Mr. Welch told us about the killing at the cleaners."

Minnie said she remembered it too, and she suddenly felt better. At least a dozen black people and three or four whites had seen Johnny D. at home that morning. "You is right, you is right," she said happily. "They gots to let you go."

All Sunday he waited for someone to ask him for his alibi. The next morning he waited for Benson, Ikner, or Tate to come and see him. By midafternoon he was beginning to feel impatient. He called Minnie again. "You need to talk to Everline," he told her, referring to his sister, Everline Smith. "Ask her to go to the courthouse and find out what is going on."

Johnny D. said he didn't want Minnie to go because she was too shy. That was fine with her. She had never been in any trouble with the law and didn't feel comfortable dealing with, as she later put it, "all those white officers and their badges and guns."

Johnny D. had another reason for sending his sister rather than his wife. He knew more about what was happening than he was telling Minnie or anyone else. Five days earlier Karen Kelly had warned him over the telephone that he was about to be arrested. "They are pressuring me and Ralph to lie about you," she told him. "They want us to say it was you who killed Ronda Morrison in the cleaners." He had asked who the people were who were pressuring her and she had told him: Benson, Ikner, and Tate. If Johnny D. sent Minnie to the courthouse, there was a chance that someone might mention Kelly's name, and that could lead to other talk. He didn't want that. Minnie did not know about his sexual escapades with Kelly despite the widespread gossip that had accompanied Kelly's divorce. Amazingly, he had been able to keep them a secret from Minnie. He wanted it to stay that way.

On Monday night Johnny D. called home for a status report. Minnie told him that Everline had gone to the courthouse but the meeting had not gone well. Instead of answering her questions, Benson, Ikner, and Tate, who knew she was a holiness preacher, had poked fun at her, asking if she really was a minister. "Everline says they is not going to let you go," Minnie reported.

Minnie was scared by now, but Johnny D. continued to reassure her. "They knows I didn't kill no girl in the cleaners. They ain't gonna have no other choice but to let me go. They just can't lynch a man no more 'cause he's black."

But when Johnny D. called home the next night, Minnie could tell from his voice that he was no longer so self-confident. He had been taken before Judge Welch that morning and charged with capital murder, punishable by electrocution. "I was so shook up I didn't understand nary a word they was saying," he said, "and they never did ask me what I was doing on the day that girl got killed! It's like they don't care one whit."

Then he said he was afraid that someone was going to harm Minnie or their daughter. Sheriff Tate had come to his cell later that afternoon, and Johnny D. had finally explained his alibi. "I told him I was at home when that girl was killed and I could prove it." At first he thought the sheriff believed him, because Tate had listened without interrupting. But when he finished, it was clear that Tate hadn't believed a word. Tate would later claim that he had simply walked away without comment after listening to the alibi. But Johnny D. said in subsequent court documents that the sheriff had threatened him and used racist terms. "Sheriff Tate says to me, real angry like, 'I don't give a damn what you say or what you do. I don't give a damn what your people say either. I'm going to put twelve people on a jury who are going to find your goddamn black ass guilty.' And then Tate says to me, 'How'd you like it if someone killed your daughter and threw her off the side of the road for maggots to eat?' " What he did not tell Minnie, Johnny D. would state later, was that Tate had made one further remark before leaving his cell: "He told me he was tired of niggers running around with white women."

Johnny D. wanted Minnie to move in with his relatives. Much to his surprise, she refused. "This is my house," she said. "Ain't nobody gonna scare me out of my house, especially when I ain't done nothing wrong." Two of their children still lived at home: Jackie, twenty-three, and James, twenty-two. A third, Johnny, who was twenty-five, was married and lived out of state.

After they finished talking that Tuesday night, Minnie telephoned Johnny D.'s brother Jesse, who hurried over to the house with a pistol. The fact that her husband was scared had alarmed her. He was the optimist in the family, the one who was always certain something good was about to happen. She was the chronic worrier. That night Minnie made up beds for all four of them on the back porch—the room farthest from the highway. She wanted everyone to sleep there in case someone fired a shotgun from a car speeding along Highway 84 or threw a firebomb. Before going to bed, she had James drive an old truck in front of the driveway to block it off.

Minnie was now forty-six, a quiet and unpretentious woman who savored her privacy. Like Johnny D., she had been born a few miles outside Monroeville, to sharecropper parents who had been even poorer than his. She could remember a time when the only things her mother bought at the grocery store were flour and sugar. Everything else they ate had to come from what the nine children and two parents raised themselves. She had been sent to work in the fields as soon as she was old enough to hoe, and she had been taught such essentials as how to make every last part of a pig into food.

There had been little time for school, and Minnie had quit in eighth grade, but she had forced herself to practice reading and was proud that her vocabulary and writing skills were better than those of most blacks, including her husband. She had grown up in a two-room shack without indoor plumbing or electricity. She was eighteen before she visited her first doctor, twenty before she went to a dentist. For the past two decades she had worked as a seamstress at Vanity Fair Mills, sewing bras. She rarely missed a workday, never was late, never sought a promotion. At home she picked and canned vegetables, washed and cleaned. She didn't own a microwave, automatic dishwasher, or clothes dryer. She rarely ate out at a restaurant and had traveled outside Alabama only twice. She had never ridden on a train or airplane. The only white people she spoke with regularly were her bosses at work. Her closest friends were her sister and her mother, who both lived in the projects. She spent her nights watching television and avoided gossiping over the telephone. She had no idea how the criminal justice system worked. She felt overwhelmed.

By midnight Minnie and the others were all in bed, but she could not sleep. She had turned on every light in the front of the house and had barricaded the front door with a big overstuffed chair. The door had a lock, but it did not work. Johnny D. had been promising to fix it but had never gotten around to it. He was not much good at household chores. The roof of their house leaked; several ceiling tiles were missing; the linoleum on the kitchen floor was badly ripped. Still, she considered herself lucky. This was their house, and that was important to her. Her father had died without ever owning property. He had lectured Minnie when she was little about the value of land. If a poor person owned property, even a tiny garden plot, he would never starve, but if he didn't own a bit of ground, he would always be someone else's slave.

Minnie had grown accustomed long ago to the sounds of night. There was the whooshing noise of cars hurrying past on the highway, the occasional clap-clap-clapping that large trucks made when their drivers downshifted in anticipation of the hill at the county line a few miles away, the occasional screech of brakes, the slamming of car doors at the projects when a gaggle of teenagers finally came home. But on this Tuesday night, all those familiar sounds frightened her. As she lay in her makeshift bed, her mind filled with images of what she most feared. She could see a long line of cars and trucks, their headlight beams leading the way, coming from Monroeville full of angry whites armed with baseball bats and shotguns. She could actually see them now as they burst into her house, grabbed her and the others from their beds, forced them into the muggy summer air, and led them one by one toward a hangman's rope. Minnie had lived all her life in Monroe County, and she had never heard of an incident that involved the Ku Klux Klan or white vigilantes lynching blacks. But she had never thought that her husband would be arrested for murder either. Why should she now think that she and her children were immune from racial violence simply because it had not occurred in the past? Each time a car passed, a truck downshifted, a car door slammed, she felt a pang of fear. She could not remember when she had been more eager to see a sunrise.

On Wednesday morning Minnie went to visit Johnny D. at the jail. He needed a lawyer, but he did not trust any of the nineteen lawyers identified in the telephone directory as members of the Monroe County Bar Association. All were white, and he assumed that white lawyers were automatically members of Monroeville's upper crust. He doubted that any of them would be willing to defend a black man accused of killing one of the town's most popular white teenagers. And if one did take the case, Johnny D. suspected he would do a superficial job.

One of his sisters had told him about a white attorney named Wyman Gilmore who had a reputation for defending blacks as vigorously as whites. Gilmore lived in Grove City, about forty miles west of Monroeville. Johnny D. told Minnie to go see him. Because she did not want to go alone, she asked Jackie to drive her there. As they rode along Highway 84, Minnie sat quietly gazing at the cotton fields that lined the blacktop. She and Johnny D. had been born and reared within ten miles of each other. They had picked cotton and hoed weeds in these very fields, meeting in them for the first time as teenagers. As adults they had remained in this same ten-mile radius. It was the center of their world.

Minnie would later recall the first time she had met Johnny D. She was eighteen years old and had never been kissed by a boy. She thought of herself as awkward, plain. He was hoeing weeds nearby, was seventeen, and had kissed plenty of girls. He considered himself one of the handsomest boys around. Whites called him Crazy Legs because when he worked part-time at the feed mill in Frisco City, he could empty a truck faster than any other black worker. He had been lean and strong and ambitious. At age forty-five, he still was. Many days Minnie had seen him work for ten hours cutting down trees for a logging company and then hurry home and play basketball for an hour or two with teenagers who lived in the projects. He was still handsome, she thought. He had a boxer's wide nose, a strong jaw, and a devil's just-dare-me eyes. She had fallen in love with him immediately. She had never met anyone who loved life more than he did. He was always running somewhere, doing something. When they met, Johnny D. owned a secondhand guitar, and even though he couldn't read music, he taught himself a few gospel tunes and convinced three friends to join him in a band. They named themselves the Jubilee Singers, and most Sundays they could be heard performing at local black churches. Minnie thought they sounded terrible, but he honestly believed they were on the verge of being discovered by a record company and would soon be rich.

In 1962 Minnie had discovered that she was pregnant. She was thrilled. He wasn't. His words had burrowed into her mind, and she still remembered them. His father had abandoned his children when he divorced his wife, Johnny D. told her. "I've always said, if I have children, I'm going to work and do the best I can for them. I know you ain't been fooling around with no one but me so I'll marry you." It wasn't a flattering proposal, but she believed that he would grow to love her. Even now, twenty-five years later, as she stared out the car windows at the cotton fields, she wasn't sure that he ever had.

Minnie tried to remember the good times.

Their first year together they had nearly starved. He had earned fourteen dollars per week as a field hand. They ate one meal a day and lived in a sharecropper's shack with wooden floors and a tarpaper roof. Minnie had been happy. Johnny D. had been miserable. He tried desperately to find better-paying work, but there wasn't any for a young black man. One day he told the white foreman of a logging crew that he had experience clearing trees. Within minutes after hiring him, the foreman knew Johnny D. had lied—he could tell by the amateurish way he handled a chain saw—but he worked so hard that the foreman kept him on. Still, only whites were allowed to work a full forty-hour week. When Johnny D. asked why, the foreman said, "They got families to feed."

Eleven months into the job, Johnny D.'s foot was crushed when a chain holding several logs broke and the logs fell on the foot. On crutches, without a job, he had become discouraged for the first time, and that had scared Minnie. As she remembered that low point, she also wondered if she was not now partly to blame for Johnny D.'s arrest. He had begged her to leave Monroe County several times. In 1964 they had moved to Cocoa Beach, Florida, where Johnny D.'s older brother, Andrew, helped him join a union and become a bricklayer's apprentice. He earned $150 per week, more money than any black man back home was getting, but Minnie hated the city. "You just knew there was crazy peoples outside," she later explained. "Peoples you didn't know. I was afraid to go out with the baby." After two months she and their son returned to live with her parents. Johnny D. lasted two more months in Florida before moving back home.

It was a pattern that soon repeated itself. Unable to find a decent-paying job at home, Johnny D. would convince Minnie to go with him somewhere else, but she would always become homesick after a few months and return to Monroe County. Most times Johnny D. would stick it out for a while by himself and then reluctantly come home and take a low-paying job in the woods cutting trees. As time passed he found himself training younger white men, only to see them promoted over him. "I could run my own logging business," he told Minnie one day. "I know as much as the white boss man." What he lacked was enough money to buy a truck and tools.

In 1970 Johnny D. heard that blacks were earning good wages working on fishing boats in the Gulf. This time he did not ask Minnie to go with him. He promised that their separation would be temporary. All he needed was to raise enough money to launch his own logging company. He had never been on a fishing boat, and he was seasick for days, but he stuck it out. The boats left port on Mondays and remained out until they caught their quota, usually returning on Fridays. Johnny D. would race home on weekends; Minnie and their three children would be eagerly waiting. He was earning $1,500 a month and was saving $500 of that for his future business. He thought it would take him only one year to save enough, but the one year soon stretched into two and then three. His weekend homecomings began to lose their luster. The children no longer waited. Minnie got used to living without him.

Then in 1975 an explosive charge used to make fish swim toward the fishing nets blew up in Johnny D.'s hand, taking off the tip of his right thumb and mangling his fingers. A seaplane flew him to a hospital in Pascagoula, Mississippi, but doctors there said he would lose his hand unless he was treated by specialists in New Orleans. For nearly a month he underwent rehabilitation at a Louisiana hospital. He was alone, bored, and often in pain. A nurse who worked at night and thought he was attractive introduced him to marijuana. When he was discharged, he paid $200 for a pound of it, which he brought home with him. He found his friends eager to experiment and ended up selling most of the pound for $400.

Johnny D. had grown up around moonshine, and he didn't think selling marijuana was much different from his mother's hiding mason jars filled with white lightning in the corncrib. After his hand healed he returned to work on the fishing boats, and each weekend he brought marijuana home to sell. Minnie disapproved, but he didn't care. "What's the harm in smoking a little weed?" he asked. "You always complaining about paying all these bills. Now I'm trying to get money to pay them and all you're doing is complaining, complaining, complaining."

By 1980 Johnny D. had saved enough to buy a used semitruck and enough tools to start his own land-clearing business. He moved back home. Because he was willing to work cheaply, a number of white timber company owners hired him and his crews. He was soon netting about $250 per week. It wasn't as much as he had earned on the boats, but he was his own boss and he was home. Whenever the work fell off, he supplemented his earnings by selling marijuana.

Once he got his business started, Johnny D. had thought, life would be perfect. But Minnie was now used to his being gone, and he was quickly bored with her listless home life. He pestered her about going out with him on weekends, and she finally agreed to visit a black nightclub in Mobile. Their evening out showed just how dissimilar they were. Johnny D. moved easily from table to table, meeting new people, telling jokes, laughing and dancing. Minnie sat alone, spoke to no one, and couldn't wait to get home. After that Johnny D. went out by himself on weekends. "The more he go," she later complained, "the wilder he got." They soon began to live almost separate lives. They shared a house, a bed, the children, and little else.

Defense attorney Wyman Gilmore looked frail when he greeted Minnie and Jackie in his Grove City office. He was already familiar with the Ronda Morrison murder—he had read about it in the newspapers—and he agreed to make some inquiries for them by telephone, but he warned them that he was not going to be able to take the case. His health was failing, and he did not have enough stamina for a long murder trial.

When Minnie and Jackie got home, Jesse told them that the telephone had been ringing nonstop. Most were calls from blacks who wanted to know what was happening. Everyone in the projects and Clausell was talking about Johnny D.'s arrest. Jesse said a few calls had been obscene. Minnie ordered him to leave the receiver off the hook.

The next morning she rose early. She knew she could not stay away from her job any longer. She did not want to give Vanity Fair a legitimate reason to fire her, although she was afraid that was going to happen anyway. She knew that Bertha Morrison also worked for Vanity Fair, and Minnie doubted the mill would want to keep the spouse of Ronda's accused killer on the payroll. How was she going to support herself and her family without a job? How was she going to pay an attorney's fees? She was too nervous to eat breakfast, so she thought about what she was going to say if her white boss called her into his office. By the time she was ready to leave the house, her hands were shaking so badly she was afraid she might not be able to steer the car. When she arrived at the plant parking lot, she turned off the engine and prayed. "Please, God," she whispered, and then, sitting there, she gave herself a pep talk. She had not done anything wrong, and neither had Johnny D. They were victims of this mess just like Ronda Morrison. There was no reason, she told herself, for her to be ashamed.

Minnie walked to the employees' entrance, took a deep breath, and went into the sewing room. It was enormous. She had counted the sewing machines once. There were fourteen rows of machines with thirty machines in each line. As always the room was noisy, but as soon as her coworkers spotted her they stopped talking. As she walked toward her machine the silence became painful. Minnie sat down and began assembling a bra. Her hands moved expertly and didn't betray her. No one spoke to her that day, and at quitting time she was quick to hurry outside and drive home. She had not been fired.

Jesse had put the phone back on the hook that morning as soon as Minnie had gone to work and had left it there, and late that night Wyman Gilmore called to report what he had learned. The district attorney's office was being completely inflexible. They were not even interested in checking Johnny D.'s alibi or talking informally about a plea bargain. They were intent on going to trial, and they were going to try to get Johnny D. executed.

Gilmore paused after he said that, but Minnie told him to continue; she knew it was possible Johnny D. might be put to death. Gilmore said the state had three witnesses ready to testify against her husband. Prosecutors were keeping the name of one witness a secret but had identified the other two.

"Who that be?" Minnie asked.

"A fellow named Ralph Myers says he drove Johnny D. to the cleaners that morning," Gilmore replied.

"He white or black?"

"White."

"And he say he was with Johnny D. at the cleaners that morning?"

"Yes."

"Well, he's lying then," she declared. "Who's the other one?"

"A woman named Karen Kelly. Do you know her?"

"Oh yeah," Minnie answered, "I knows her. She a white girl who was always coming around here chasing after Johnny D."

Gilmore hesitated, as if thinking about how to put his next comment. Kelly was more than just someone who had chased after Johnny D., he said.

Minnie didn't understand.

"They were boyfriend, girlfriend," the attorney explained, still trying to phrase his words with discretion.

Minnie felt foolish and sick. She was afraid she was going to vomit. She had heard rumors about Johnny D.'s chasing various black women. The stories had started shortly after he moved back home from the fishing boats. Minnie had been told that he had gotten one black girl from the projects pregnant. But she had always ignored the whispers. "If he is going to do that, he is going to do that and there isn't no sense in me trying to track him down or call around every weekend trying to find him," she had told her sister when stories about his womanizing first surfaced. Still, inside she had hurt. At one point she had even decided to divorce him, but after worrying about it for days, she changed her mind. She knew women whose husbands beat them, were drunks, couldn't keep a job. He was none of those things. Also, she was frightened. Where would she go without the house? Where would the children go? She had decided to say nothing about his affairs and simply wait for him to tire of his exploits. "He always comes home," she had told her sister. "He will this time too."

But despite those incidents, Minnie had never suspected that Johnny D. would dare cross the so-called color line. A married black man and a married white woman having an affair? "I didn't think Johnny D. was really that stupid," she later explained.

Gilmore told Minnie he would draw up a list of attorneys for her to review. As soon as she hung up, she ducked into her bedroom and began to cry. Then she became angry. She wasn't mad at Benson, Ikner, and Tate, although she was convinced that they were framing her husband. She wasn't even angry at Johnny D., although he had clearly lied to her. He had always told her that Karen Kelly was, in his words, "just a crazy white woman who wants to buy marijuana." Minnie was angry at herself, at her own blindness. She should have known better, she told herself. She had pegged Kelly for what she was the very first time Kelly had come to their house.

It had been a hot Alabama afternoon, and Minnie had been washing dishes at the kitchen sink and looking out the window at the clothes she had hung on the wire clothesline when she suddenly heard a woman's laugh. She followed the sound to the front of the house and peeked through a window. A petite white woman was standing in the dirt near the gravel driveway. Johnny D. was perched on the raised wooden porch near the front door. The woman was trying to buy marijuana, but he didn't want to sell her any. He had always made it his practice not to sell marijuana to strangers, particularly whites. "I don't know nothing about no weed," Minnie heard him say.

The woman laughed. She had always sent Thulani, a black girl who lived in the projects, to buy marijuana from him, she explained. "I've been smoking grass that Thulani's bought from you for years so don't give me any of that I-don't-sell-weed bullshit." They had both chuckled at her outspokenness. She told him her name was Karen Kelly and that she had gone to school with Thulani. "I tried to find that girl, but she's run off somewhere and I really need a joint. You can sell it to me," she purred. "I won't tell nobody."

Minnie eyed the woman. She was in her twenties, dressed in faded Levi's jeans that had been cut off at the crotch. They were so tight that Minnie wondered how the woman had gotten into them. She wore a white cotton blouse, sleeveless, with the top two buttons unfastened. It was scorching outside, and a warm breeze caused the blouse to open wider, exposing a snowy-white bra and pale skin. Minnie understood what the woman was doing. Women always recognized it, even if men were slow to catch on. It was obvious from the woman's laughter, the way she kept her eyes fixed on Johnny D. and listened as if his every word mattered. The heat. A bead of sweat gliding slowly along her neck and disappearing under the cotton collar. The warm breeze and the blouse that gently opened. Johnny D. had dashed into the house to fix her a bag of marijuana, like a hound that had just caught the scent of a bitch in heat. Kelly had laughed again when she paid for the bag and had driven away smiling.

When Johnny D. stepped inside, Minnie was ready.

"You go messing with that white woman and you'll end up in the penitentiary or you'll end up dead," she had warned him. Those had been her exact words. She could still hear herself saying them: "In the penitentiary or you'll end up dead." She could also remember exactly how Johnny D. had reacted.

He had laughed at her.

Chapter 22

Johnny D.'s arrest and reputation were chewed over among countless cups of coffee and $2.99 stacks of pancakes and eggs at the City Cafe. Everyone agreed he was guilty. Any black man daring enough to have an affair with a married white woman was certainly bold enough to strut into Jackson Cleaners on a busy Saturday morning and rob and sexually attack an innocent white teenager. His marijuana dealing was seen as additional proof, since most at the cafe were convinced that drugs had played some role in the killing.

If Johnny D.'s reputation needed any more tarnishing, it received it when *The Monroe Journal* reported that a judge had decided there was sufficient evidence to make him stand trial for sodomy as well as the two murders. On the night of his arrest, he had been told that the sodomy charge was simply an excuse that Sheriff Tate had used to arrest him. He had assumed it would be dismissed, but Benson, Ikner, and Tate produced a sworn affidavit from Ralph Myers in which he claimed that he had been repeatedly raped by Johnny D. and a "bushy-haired" black man three days after Ronda's murder. Myers's statement, said the judge, was compelling enough to warrant a trial.

Monroeville could barely accommodate all the rumors circulating about Johnny D. At the City Cafe one morning, a white banker recalled that Johnny D. had brought $500 in water-damaged bills into the bank to exchange for new ones. The money was smeared with dirt, and Johnny D. had explained that he had just "dug it up" from its hiding spot. Why would someone bury cash in a coffee can rather than put it in a bank? The answer seemed clear—it was profit from drug deals. Another diner said he had once heard Johnny D. called Easy Money, obviously a reference to drugs. A third thought it odd that he drove a 1979 Lincoln Continental. How could a black man who worked in the woods afford such a high-priced car? Within hours the white community was awash in talk about how Johnny D. had hidden drug money in coffee cans that he had buried all over Monroe County. What began as a story about $500 soon became a tale about $5,000 and then $50,000.

While whites were certain of his guilt, blacks were equally confident of his innocence. Members of the Limestone Faulk African Methodist Episcopal Church knew about his foolhardy affair with Karen Kelly and his pot selling, but they were also familiar with a less disreputable side of Johnny D. The McMillian clan was one of a handful of black families whose forefathers had founded the small white-framed church nestled in the woods southeast of town. Nearly all of its seventy or so members were related to Johnny D. either by blood or by marriage. Many of them had been to his house on the Saturday of the fish fry. None thought him capable of murder.

At the church the $500 in buried cash was easily explained. He had earned the money working overtime and had hidden it from Minnie because he knew she would spend it paying their monthly bills. He wanted to use it as a down payment on a new truck. The nickname Easy Money had nothing to do with drugs. One day when Johnny D. was driving home from the fishing boats in the Gulf, he happened to spot an elderly white man stranded by the road. Recognizing him, he offered to change the flat tire on the old man's car. The man noticed that Johnny D.'s car was newer than his own and asked if it was stolen. Laughing, Johnny D. showed his paycheck to the man. "I don't see how in the world a man raised on cornbread and collard greens can all of a sudden jump up and eat steak," the white man remarked. "From now on I'm calling you Easy Money."

Johnny D. had told that story to his friends over and over, especially the part where he owned a car better than a white man's. The Lincoln Continental, his friends added, had been bought secondhand from a dealer in Mobile, who had sold it cheap because the original engine had been replaced with one from a Chevrolet.

Of course, none of these explanations ever made its way into white circles, and if one had, chances were it would not have been believed. When Sheriff Tate was asked why he had not paid more attention to Everline Smith's claim that she had seen Johnny D. at home on the morning of the murder, he replied, "You expect a man's family to lie for him." When asked why he had not bothered to question Johnny D.'s neighbors about his alibi, Tate said, "There was no need to talk to anyone else. We already had three eyewitnesses putting McMillian at the cleaners. Besides, what do you expect those people to say? Of course they are going to stick up for one of their own."

When blacks were asked why they had not done more to challenge the gossip or defend Johnny D.'s alibi, their answers were based on equally cynical presumptions. "The sheriff and them others wouldn't believe us anyway," said a neighbor. "They needed some person to blame for that girl's murder and they decided that he be that one."

In all Monroeville only one white man stuck up for Johnny D. in public. Sam Crook, the cantankerous owner of a timber company, had worked with him in the woods clearing trees. "When the Morrison girl was killed, I mentioned it to Johnny D. I said, 'Johnny D., wouldn't you like to lynch the man who done that?' And Johnny D., why, he says to me, 'Mr. Sam, lynching is too good for him. They should treat him rougher than that.' Now that sure don't sound to me like something a murderer would say."

But few in Monroeville paid any attention to Sam Crook. He lived in a log cabin he had built outside town. It sat next to a separate cabin he had built for his wife. Each morning he raised the Confederate Stars and Bars on a flagpole he had erected next to a granite tombstone marking the grave of his favorite hunting dog, Monroe. Crook wore a handlebar mustache, liked nothing better than riding horses, and often quoted Plato in everyday conversation. Some in town said he thought he was the reincarnation of General Thomas "Stonewall" Jackson.

Besides Crook, there was one other white man who continued to show a keen interest in the case, so much so that some thought he was obsessed with it. Howard K. Denmar, the insurance agent who had been so certain only a few months earlier that Ronda's killer was a black man, had stopped coming into the City Cafe. He had become tight-lipped about his personal investigation. Whenever someone cornered him at the post office or caught him walking on the street, Denmar would look around to make certain no one could overhear their conversation and then drop a hint or two about his latest discovery. He told one acquaintance he was now confident that the killer was a white man who had become sexually fixated on Ronda and had been stalking her for weeks before the murder.

At the City Cafe, Crook and Denmar became the butt of jokes. Crook was a "nigger lover." Denmar was nicknamed Inspector Clouseau, after the bumbling Peter Sellers character in the Pink Panther movies.

Sheriff Tate kept Johnny D.'s whereabouts a secret. He claimed his prisoner would be killed by vigilantes if anyone learned where he was being housed. An incident a few weeks after the arrest seemed to justify Tate's fears. Ralph Myers asked to be moved from the jail in Monroeville to the one in Evergreen because his wife and children lived close by and could visit him there. Myers didn't know it, but Johnny D. was being held in Evergreen, and since the sheriff did not want them in the same building, he decided to make a swap. Late one night Johnny D. was secretly brought into Monroeville, and simultaneously Myers was transferred to the jail in Evergreen. The exchange went smoothly. In fact, Myers ended up in the same cell Johnny D. had occupied only a few hours earlier.

The next morning, a terrified Myers called Benson and Ikner.

"I almost was killed last night!" he screamed. "You gotta get me out of here!"

They raced to Evergreen to learn what was wrong. They found Myers chain-smoking and pacing the floor of his cell. Two white men wearing trench coats had appeared outside the cell shortly after midnight, he told them. Each was carrying a twelve-gauge shotgun, and they had demanded to know where Johnny D. was being kept. "If he'd been in this here cell, they would have blown his brains out for sure," Myers warned.

Conecuh County Sheriff Edwin Booker, who was responsible for security at the jail, promptly dismissed Myers's story. "It would be impossible for anyone to break in here at night without the jailer seeing them," he said, "and my jailer says no one got by him last night."

However, Benson and Ikner believed Myers. "You can fake a lot of things," Ikner said later, "but you can't fake the look of fear on Ralph Myers's face that morning when he told us what had happened." Benson notified the FBI, and one of its agents interviewed two other inmates at the jail who said they too had seen the armed intruders.

Ikner and Benson were quick to guess the gunmen's identities. They could not have been paid killers hired by the Morrison or Pittman family, Ikner reasoned, because they would have shot Myers if they were simply seeking revenge. After all, he too was charged with both murders. It seemed obvious that the gunmen had only one target—Johnny D. "He knows too much about how drugs are distributed in Monroe County," Ikner told a reporter. Benson added, "There are people out there who don't want Johnny D. telling what he knows about drugs." The gunmen were "professional killers," the two of them theorized, sent by the Mafia to murder Johnny D. before he had a chance to squeal.

That same afternoon Sheriff Tate arranged for his two prisoners to be transferred to different maximum-security state prisons. They were put into cells on the death row in each facility. Never before in Alabama history had anyone been confined to a death row *before* he was found guilty of a crime. Tate said it was for the men's own protection.

While everyone's attention was focused on Johnny D. and the Morrison killing, Escambia County officials silently released Tyrone Patterson from jail. He had spent five months behind bars. District Attorney Godwin told a local reporter that neither he nor Sheriff Hawsey had made a mistake in charging Patterson with the Pittman murder. "Patterson has not been acquitted of the murder charge nor has he been exonerated," Godwin said. ". . . We have just decided not to prosecute him at this time."

What Godwin did not reveal was that Patterson's alibi had turned out to be true and he was unquestionably innocent. Nor did Godwin mention that Myers and Kelly had clearly lied about Patterson in an unsuccessful attempt to frame him. The fact that these same two witnesses were now accusing Johnny D. of two murders gave no pause to Godwin or the investigators.

"If all we had in the Ronda Morrison case was Karen Kelly's statement implicating Johnny D., then that wouldn't have been enough to arrest him because we knew Karen was a liar," Larry Ikner later explained. "If all we had was just Ralph Myers, that wouldn't have worked either because he was a liar too. And if we had just had Bill Hooks alone saying he'd seen them at the cleaners, then that wouldn't have done it. But when you put all three of them together, well, that was strong enough. I thought we had a very, very strong case. I was also convinced he was guilty."

Godwin used similar logic when asked to explain why he had charged Johnny D. in the Pittman case. "We knew he was a shady character because he already had been charged with killing Ronda Morrison in Monroeville," Godwin said, "so we believed Myers and Kelly when they said he had killed the Pittman girl."

Ralph Myers couldn't stand being locked up. He had served a fourteen-month prison term for burglary in 1980 when he was only twenty-four years old, and it had nearly driven him insane. In a confidential evaluation written at that time, a prison psychologist noted that Myers had been sexually molested as a child and seemed preoccupied with the fear that he was going to be raped. He was especially afraid of black men, the psychologist wrote.

Sheriff Tate had asked prison officials to watch Johnny D. and Myers and to report occasionally on how each was adjusting to the death row cell to which he was confined twenty-three hours a day. After two months the officials noted that Johnny D. had adjusted without complaint. Myers, however, was showing signs of mental exhaustion and emotional stress. He was having trouble falling asleep at night and complained of recurring nightmares.

On September 8 Benson, Ikner, and Tate went to see Myers in prison. They got right to the point. None of them believed he had told them the truth in his June 9 statement. They did not believe he had sat idly outside the cleaners while Johnny D. had gone inside and killed Ronda. They felt certain that he too had been inside the building during the murder. They accused him of lying because he did not want to implicate himself. Unless he told them everything he knew about the killing, there would be no plea bargain, they warned. Myers would be put on trial along with Johnny D., and the prosecution would seek the death penalty for both of them.

Sheriff Tate told Myers in plain language what they intended to do next. If Myers didn't come clean, they were going to approach Johnny D. and ask whether he was willing to testify. There was a good chance that he would identify Myers as the triggerman in return for a lesser sentence. The first man to talk, Tate said, "is going to get some relief." The other would get a ticket to ride Yellow Mama, the nickname for the state's gaudy yellow electric chair.

Myers insisted that he had told them everything he knew. "I never went inside the cleaners," he declared. "I told the truth."

The next day, however, Tate got a telephone call from a clearly frightened Myers. He announced tearfully that he had changed his mind. If they would come see him again, he said, they would hear the "complete story." On September 14 the three investigators returned to the prison, and in a tape-recorded interview Myers admitted that he had actually gone inside Jackson Cleaners just as they had suspected. He also told them he had seen Johnny D. holding a gun and standing over Ronda's lifeless body in the lobby.

Much of what Myers said during the interview matched what he had told them on June 9. He had been approached by Johnny D. at a car wash in Evergreen and had volunteered to drive him to Monroeville on an errand. But this time Myers said that while he was sitting in the truck he had heard "popping noises" coming from Jackson Cleaners about "twenty-five to thirty minutes" after Johnny D. entered the store. Curious, he had gone inside.

"When I walked in, something was there that I didn't want to see—there was a girl laying behind the counter on the floor and also too, Johnny D. McMillian down there behind the counter and he had a little old bitty . . . brown satchel . . . he was putting money in the satchel . . ."

According to Myers, Johnny D. had jumped up, pinned him against a wall, jammed a .25 caliber pistol in his face, and threatened to kill him. It was at that point, Myers said, that he noticed someone else hiding in the back room. Although he couldn't make out the face, he saw enough to know that he was a white man with shoulder-length "black and gray" hair. Myers said Johnny D. had yelled out something to the white man and had called him Randy. The white man began cursing because his name had been used.

"I heard him, the white man in the back room, say . . . to Johnny D. . . . 'Well, goddamnit, go ahead and get rid of him too' and Johnny D. says something about 'I can't, I ain't got nothing else to shoot . . .' "

When Myers heard a door slam shut in the back room, he knew that the white man had ducked out the rear of the building. Johnny D. continued to hold him at gunpoint in the lobby for several minutes and then apologized. "He says . . . I didn't mean to get you off in this shit. I didn't know this was gonna happen but it was a businesslike thing . . . if you want to stay alive . . . the best thing for you to do is to keep your mouth shut and get the hell out there to that truck . . .' "

As ordered, Myers went out to the truck, where he waited for "two or three minutes" until Johnny D. came outside carrying the brown satchel Myers had seen him filling earlier with "wads and wads" of money. He ordered Myers to get going.

"Tell us what she—Ronda Morrison—looked like when you saw her," Ikner said.

"She was lying on the floor . . . I knew she was dead. I knew that, and I also knew that what I was seeing, I more or less didn't want to see it . . ."

Ikner interrupted. "Okay, what I am saying . . . was anything different about her face . . . was her eyes closed, or anything, or open, or what do you remember seeing about her face?"

"All I know was that her head, when I seen it, her head was laying back like and all I could see was her mouth was open and . . . the best I could remember, I think one of her eyes was open . . ."

Before the tape recorder was turned off, Myers asked if the three investigators were going to help him get "some relief." That would be up to District Attorney Ted Pearson, Ikner replied, but he was certain Pearson would help Myers if he was willing to tell a jury exactly what he had just told them.

"You have told us the complete truth now?" Ikner asked.

"Yeah," Myers replied. "I sure have."

The investigators thought so too. It had taken them nearly eleven months and they had wandered down numerous dead ends, but they believed at last that they had uncovered the facts about what had happened inside Jackson Cleaners. Myers was willing to testify that he had actually seen Ronda Morrison lying on the lobby floor with Johnny D. looming above her.

A short time after the three men left the prison, a guard stopped outside Myers's cell on death row.

"Pack your gear," the guard ordered.

Myers was being transferred to a less secure prison as a reward for his cooperation. No longer would he be kept in a tiny death row cell for twenty-three hours a day. He would be allowed to move around more freely, to attend chapel services, to buy goods at a canteen.

Johnny D. remained where he was, less than a hundred feet from Yellow Mama.

Chapter 23

J. L. Chestnut was reputed to be the most powerful black attorney in Alabama. Then fifty-seven years old, he was a founding and senior partner of Chestnut, Sanders, Sanders, Turner, Williams and Pettaway in Selma, the largest all-black law firm in the state. When Chestnut passed the bar in 1958, he was one of only nine blacks practicing law in Alabama, and many times he risked his life defending impoverished "Negro" clients in backwater courtrooms. His exploits were legendary in black communities. Early in his legal career, he often carried a gun to protect himself, not only from hoodlums but from racist sheriffs and police. He had been a confidant of the Reverend Martin Luther King, Jr., and an activist in Selma during the bloody civil rights demonstrations of the 1960s. Wyman Gilmore had been one of the first white attorneys to befriend Chestnut, so there was nothing unusual about his recommending Chestnut to Johnny D. and Minnie.

Afraid to take off any more time from work, Minnie sent her daughter, Jackie, and Everline Smith to meet with Chestnut in his office on Jefferson Davis Avenue, an address with ironic overtones for a civil rights activist. Chestnut rose politely to welcome the two women into his walnut-paneled office. He was a stubby, rotund, bespectacled man with nearly all-white hair that gave him a grandfatherly appearance. But it was his speech they would remember most vividly. His voice was deep, distinct, devoid of any trace of Southern twang. What poor-black articulation appeared in his sentences was put there intentionally, for impact. He bragged to them that he had defended more blacks accused of murder than any other attorney in the state, and although a good number of them had been convicted, none had ever been executed.

Although he did not tell his visitors this, Chestnut had no intention of defending Johnny D. He was simply too busy. It often seemed as if every poor black defendant in Alabama made his way eventually to Chestnut's firm, and while it performed thousands of hours of pro bono work, bills had to be paid, profits had to be earned. There was a limit to what he could do. Chestnut planned to shoo the women away once they had told him their story. A few minutes into the conversation, however, he began to change his mind. "The local banks were putting up rewards, the white civic clubs were holding barbecues to raise money for scholarships in this dead girl's honor," Chestnut pointed out later. "All of the white establishment in this small town was out to get the perpetrator, and the white community had decided that the perpetrator was Johnny D. McMillian. . . . How could he possibly get a fair trial? Who in this community was going to represent him? There were only white lawyers in Monroe County, and all of them were part of the white establishment. . . . For a white attorney to take this case would have been economic suicide. They would have been branded the worst sort of nigger lover and declared a traitor to their own race."

Johnny D.'s only hope was to find an outsider, someone not afraid of offending Monroeville's white majority. Chestnut saw himself as such a figure. "I've always felt that Monroe County was passed over by the civil rights movement in the sixties," he said later. "It was not subjected to the daily pounding that Selma and Montgomery were, and because of that, blacks were still being held down. I began to sense that this case could become a way to help push and nudge Monroe County forward. It could turn a spotlight on just how poorly blacks are treated there, and that excited me."

Chestnut also realized the publicity potential of a black-on-white crime in the hometown of *To Kill a Mockingbird.* It was bound to draw statewide attention, maybe even the national networks, and that would give Chestnut an opportunity to play a role he relished: that of an eloquent black attorney defending his underdog black client against the white racist establishment. "You had an innocent white teenager, possibly the victim of sexual attack, who was dead, and a black man accused of her murder. Many white Southerners think black men would like nothing better than to have sex with a white woman, when the truth is that I know of no black men who lust after white women. . . . Here was a case where that fantasy was bound to play a heavy role."

When the two women finished talking, Chestnut announced that he would take the case. He warned them, however, that he did not have time to do much pretrial preparation. "You must find someone else to be the lead attorney," he said. "My part will be showing up in court and using my skills at the actual trial."

Neither McMillian nor Smith had any idea whom to call, so Chestnut had his secretary telephone Bruce Boynton, a close friend and fellow black attorney in Selma. They met with him moments later. He was a tall, thin man, not nearly as polished as Chestnut but with a civil rights reputation just as impressive. His parents were considered the mother and father of Selma's civil rights movement. They had been among the first to protest the blatant racism practiced there, and both bore scars from beatings inflicted by angry whites. Boynton himself had been a law student when he first received national attention back in 1958, by going into a "Whites Only" diner in a bus terminal in Richmond, Virginia, and ordering a hamburger and a glass of tea. He was told to move to the "Colored" section of the diner and when he refused was arrested. Under the guidance of Thurgood Marshall, the case was appealed to the U.S. Supreme Court, where it was used to strike down segregation laws nationwide in all restaurants and waiting rooms that were connected with interstate commerce.

During the civil rights movement Boynton had been involved with radical black activists, and as he listened to Jackie McMillian and Everline Smith talk about Johnny D., he suddenly recognized a name from the past. In 1968 a young black civil rights organizer had been jailed in Wilcox County, next door to Monroe County. At that time the Wilcox sheriff was considered one of the worst racists in the state, and the leaders of SNCC—the activist Student Nonviolent Coordinating Committee—were afraid that the young man would be killed if he spent the night in jail. SNCC sent Boynton and two armed bodyguards to post bond for the worker, but when they arrived they were met by the sheriff, his chief deputy, and more than a dozen armed white men. Boynton tried to walk through the crowd, but the sheriff stopped him, and their conversation turned ugly. Suddenly the chief deputy reached over and slapped Boynton across the face. Everyone watched to see how he and the bodyguards would react. When they retreated to their car, there was laughter and catcalls but no more violence.

Back in Selma, Boynton and SNCC members began preparing for an armed attack on the jail. Boynton was given a white ten-gallon cowboy hat to wear as a signal. If he took it off, the armed men with him would know it was time to begin shooting. Fortunately, moments before they were about to leave the next morning they learned that the young organizer had been released from jail unharmed.

It had been nearly twenty years since Boynton had been slapped in the face, but he still remembered the last name of the chief deputy who had struck him. It was Tate. He was the father of Monroe County's present sheriff, Thomas Tate.

Boynton had not done as well financially as Chestnut. He was running his law practice from his house, a rainslicker-yellow frame structure in an area of Selma where unemployed blacks could be seen rolling dice on the sidewalk and drinking liquor from bottles hidden in brown paper bags. His wife, Alice, served as his secretary and researcher. Many of his poor black clients had no money to pay for his services, and he had recently been the subject of some bad publicity in *The Montgomery Advertiser.* According to the newspaper, Boynton had shown up in Selma's municipal court in April 1986 smelling of alcohol and had been ordered home by a judge after a breath test revealed he was above the state's legal limit for intoxication. Two months later the newspaper reported that Boynton was sent home again after a police officer complained that he could smell liquor on his breath. Boynton claimed the police were harassing him because of the clients he defended.

"Chestnut and I will represent Johnny D.," Boynton told the two women. The fee would be $20,000, payable in full before the trial began. McMillian and Smith were visibly stunned. Boynton quickly explained that this fee was a bargain. It would take him hundreds of hours to prepare for the trial; witnesses would have to be interviewed, motions filed, arguments made. The trial itself could take weeks. Besides, the two women would be hiring the state's two most experienced black attorneys. They signed a contract.

Back home, Minnie was stumped. "How we gonna pay them?" she asked. At Vanity Fair Mills, she earned $200 a week. All told, she and Johnny D. had about $5,000 in savings. She sent what money she could to the two attorneys and began selling her husband's equipment, including his much-prized logging truck. Johnny D.'s relatives chipped in. His oldest sister depleted her retirement fund, and the Limestone Faulk AME church began holding bake sales and taking up special collections. Minnie went to see Sam Crook, the white timber company owner who thought Johnny D. was innocent. He gave her $300. Another friend lent her $500.

As soon as Boynton received a down payment, he drove to prison to meet Johnny D. He wanted to determine for himself exactly what sort of client he and Chestnut were defending.

Chapter 24

A man in prison has plenty of time to think, to lie on the steel bunk in his cell and replay over and over again in his mind the incidents that have led him to where he is now. Johnny D. thought about Karen Kelly. He thought about that very first day when she came to his house to buy marijuana.

Until she explained that she usually sent Thulani to buy pot from him, Johnny D. thought Kelly was a snitch sent by Sheriff Tate to entrap him. He relaxed after he heard Thulani's name. He remembered her mentioning that a white woman named Karen was always asking her to buy pot.

By chance Johnny D. spotted Thulani about an hour after he had sold Kelly the bag of marijuana. He mentioned Kelly's visit.

"Well, I was home all morning," Thulani told him. "All that girl had to do was call me if she wanted some dope. She didn't need to come by your house."

"She say she couldn't find you."

"She's a liar, then, 'cause I've been home all day."

The next morning Johnny D. was standing in the front yard of a friend's house in the projects when Kelly drove into the driveway and waved him over to her car.

"I need some more weed," she announced.

"Damn, girl, you done smoked all that dope you bought yesterday?" he later recalled saying. "Good golly, you musta been smoking like a damn chimney pipe all night long!"

Kelly laughed. Her husband, Jake, was out of town, she explained. She was bored. Getting high helped her fall asleep at night.

"Most whites don't wanna come to the projects," Johnny D. said. "Why you not all scared and worried?"

"I'm not scared of nothin'," she replied.

Now it was his turn to chuckle.

"Are you afraid of me?" she asked him.

"Girl, you ain't nothing for me to be afraid of."

She made a face, mocking his bravado. She was sitting in the driver's seat and he was bent forward talking to her through the car window. Without warning, he leaned close and kissed her on the lips. Taken by surprise, Kelly stuttered a quick goodbye and backed the car from the driveway. As he watched, he saw her wiping her lips with her forearm. Years later, when she recalled that first kiss, Kelly too would remember rubbing her lips. "I kept thinking, 'My God! I just let a nigger kiss me! I let a nigger kiss me on the lips. A nigger! What the hell am I doing?' " But by the time she got home, she had calmed down. The phone rang a few minutes later.

"Who's afraid now?" a voice asked. It was Johnny D.

They agreed to meet the next night at Crabs, a black nightclub in Conecuh County. By chance her husband called from his out-of-town job a few minutes after she had finished talking to Johnny D. Rather than feeling guilty, she was exhilarated. She gulped down a couple of quaaludes and picked out what she would wear to Crabs. She chose a sexy outfit, just as she had done the day before when she had selected her shortest pair of shorts and had left her blouse unbuttoned. "I set out to seduce that nigger," she said later. "I sure did. I was a real mess."

Kelly had been born and raised in Monroe County. Her family was well regarded, but she had been seen as a troublemaker as far back as most could remember. When she was twelve she began smoking cigarettes. At thirteen she started drinking beer. The next year she began taking diet pills. At fifteen she decided no one loved her, so she swallowed an entire bottle of aspirin in an attention-getting suicide attempt.

A teacher told her mother and stepfather that Karen craved attention and was extremely resentful about her parents' divorce, which had happened when she was only two. She missed her father, who lived in Mobile but had little contact with her. She hated her stepfather. Miserable at home, she intentionally got pregnant when she was seventeen. A wedding was quickly arranged between Karen and her boyfriend, Jake Kelly, who was one year older. His parents rented a trailer for them in Monroeville, and Karen dropped out of high school. In early August 1977 she gave birth to a boy, Kevin. He was born one day before she celebrated her eighteenth birthday.

Jake Kelly graduated from high school that same year and went to work for a construction company. He moved Karen and the baby to a trailer park in Mobile near the job site where he was working. She was immediately bored. "I was smoking marijuana every day. I didn't have nothing to do 'cause Jake didn't want me to work and I didn't know nobody." One night she went with some other women from the trailer park to a bar for a "girls' night out." A man asked her to dance. She was high on marijuana. "Jake wasn't giving me the attention I needed at home so I figured I'd get it from someone else." The next day she had sex with the man at his house, and she began meeting him regularly. One of Karen's stepbrothers found out and told her husband.

Jake would later acknowledge under oath during divorce proceedings that he had struck his wife during their marriage, but he denied that he had ever beaten her. Karen claimed otherwise: "He locked me in the trailer and beat me every night for a week when he found out about the affair." She said she had begged her mother and stepfather to intervene but that they refused to get involved. "My mother said, 'You married him, you live with him,' and my stepfather says, 'He's only doing what's right after what you did.' "

Karen asked Jake for forgiveness. A few weeks later they returned to Monroeville, and for a while their marriage seemed to improve. They bought a brick home west of Monroeville for $40,000, and Jake began earning $16 an hour in construction work. They purchased matching motorcycles, went on a trip through the Blue Ridge Mountains in Georgia, and began to live what Jake considered a comfortable middle-class life. But Karen continued to be depressed and bored. Jake always seemed to be working, and when he wasn't he often spent more time hunting with his buddies than being with her. She began using uppers and downers. When Kevin started kindergarten she became even lonelier. "I was in my early twenties and the highlight of my day was supposed to be riding around on a lawn mower cutting the grass. I wanted more out of life."

In 1982 Kelly learned that Susan North, her best friend from high school, had returned to Monroeville. North had left town right after graduation, and Karen had been jealous. Both had been self-described hellraisers at Excel High School, with well-deserved reputations for being heavy drinkers and, as Kelly later put it, "as wild as you could get." Although she would later describe North as her best pal, North was not as kind. "Karen was always getting me into trouble in high school," she complained. "She was extremely jealous, and she had a real mean streak in her." Once North sneaked out of her parents' home and drove to a friend's house. She told Kelly about it the next day at school. That night North's parents were waiting to punish her. Karen had called them. She had been angry because North had gone to see someone else.

No mention of that incident was made when the two former classmates got reacquainted. During their talk North revealed that she was dating a black man. Kelly was flabbergasted. No white woman she knew in Monroeville had ever dared to date a black man. "My grandpa was a member of the Ku Klux Klan," she later explained. "I used to play in his white robes when I was a kid, and my family hated niggers. My mother used to tell me, 'Karen, the ugliest, meanest, dirtiest white man in the world is better than a nigger.' "

Kelly wanted to meet North's new boyfriend, so as soon as Jake left town a few days later the two women drove to a black club outside Evergreen. That was the night when Kelly first noticed Johnny D. "I remember saying to Susan, 'If I was going to go out with a nigger, then he'd be the one.' Susan asked me who and I pointed at Johnny D. She laughed at me 'cause I didn't know his name, but he was the one who I'd been getting my dope from [through Thulani] for years."

It was the next day that Kelly had gone to Johnny D.'s house to buy marijuana, dressed in her shortest cutoffs and unbuttoned blouse. She had lied about not being able to find Thulani. "I wanted to see what it was like to be with a black man, and I had decided he was the one I wanted."

Despite all her conniving, Karen was terrified when she met Johnny D. that first night at Crabs, and that made it even more exciting. It turned out that he was just as scared. He had never said more than a few sentences to a white woman, and he had certainly never dated one. She and Johnny D. had sex in the backseat of his car that night. A few days later they met in the woods. "Going out with Johnny D. was against everything I had ever been taught, everything my family had told me, everything that the good people of Monroe County stood for," she later recalled with a huge grin. "Jake hated niggers, and every time I made love with Johnny D., I thought about how my husband would just die if he knew a black man was having sex with me."

Johnny D. had felt no guilt about cheating on Minnie. "I worked hard all my life and I always provided for my family, but I'm a man and all men have vices. With me, it's always been women. They's my weakness. Getting drunk or smoking dope, uh-uh, them ain't really part of my nature, but women, foo-ey, they is just a weakness to me. Besides, all Minnie wanted to do was sit home. Karen, now that girl never wanted to stay at home. She was go, go, go and so was I."

After that first night Johnny D. figured he and Kelly might get together a few more times, but he never thought it was going to be anything permanent. "I never, never, never thought I'd be going to bed with no white woman," he said later. "No, no, no. I don't know why I did it. I must've been crazy, but I'd never known white people and being with Karen was, like, so *different*, you know."

Karen Kelly was twenty-three. Johnny D. was forty-one. She didn't plan on its lasting either. "It was just something I wanted to do at first," she explained, "but when we started to get to know each other, I began to fall in love with that man. He talked to me and listened to me. We could talk about anything and laugh, and it was funny because we were from two totally different worlds."

Karen felt safe when she was with him. "People respected Johnny D. and I knew he couldn't hit me," she said later. "No nigger had better hit a white woman in Monroe County. No way. We even laughed about it once. He said, 'You'd probably have me lynched if I hit you,' and I said, 'I would.' "

Johnny D. was discreet. Kelly wasn't. She told Susan North about her conquest and then got even more brazen. One week when Jake was gone, she was scheduled to undergo minor surgery in the Monroe County Hospital. The night before the operation, she called Johnny D. "I need cigarettes," she told him. He met her in the lobby with a carton. Kelly knew all the nurses were watching. That was part of the thrill.

A short while later Jake left town for a project that was to last three months. Kelly called Johnny D. from her bedroom. Her son was asleep in the next room.

"Come see me," she said.

"You crazy?" he asked, reminding her that she lived in an all-white neighborhood.

"Come see me."

He parked down the road from her house just before midnight and walked the rest of the way. They made love in her bedroom. Afterward she cooked him eggs and they drank coffee in the kitchen. He stayed until almost dawn.

"If Karen and me coulda gone away, started new someplace, maybe we coulda made it," he said later, "but we both knew it was too late for that, and Karen was getting deeper and deeper into drugs."

Six months after they began their affair, Kelly learned that Johnny D. was also seeing Thulani. She was enraged. "I began driving by his house five or six times each day," she later recalled. "If his car was gone, I figured he was with that black bitch. I couldn't get him out of my head. I loved him. I loved that nigger and he was seeing someone else."

One Saturday morning one of Johnny D.'s sons borrowed the Lincoln Continental, and when Kelly drove by the house on Highway 84 and didn't see it, she assumed Johnny D. was with Thulani. She called Minnie from a pay phone.

"You know where your husband is at?"

Minnie could see Johnny D. asleep in their bedroom. "Who is this?" she demanded.

"That don't matter none. What matters is your husband is screwing Thulani right now!" Kelly slammed down the receiver.

Upset, Minnie woke up Johnny D. "Who's calling me like this?" she asked.

He was honest. It was probably Karen Kelly. "That white girl's been chasing me around for weeks. She's crazy. Don't pay her no mind."

Later that day Karen saw Johnny D. at a service station near the projects and pulled up.

"Bitch," he snapped, "don't you ever call my wife again!"

Karen burst into tears. "I love you!" she yelled. Anxious to avoid a scene, he hastily asked her to meet in the woods to talk. Their argument lasted minutes at most. "We made love," she said later. "We couldn't stay angry at each other." Then Karen announced that she was going to divorce Jake and marry him.

Johnny D. was horrified. "I liked being with Karen, but I didn't want to marry her, no way. I said, 'Girl, I'm not leaving my wife and children for nobody and neither should you. You got a good husband. He a hard-working man. I got a good wife. We both needs to just keep on being married and just keep things the way they are.' "

One of Johnny D.'s sisters telephoned him a few days later to report that Kelly was calling his relatives and telling them how much she loved him. "That woman is gonna get you killed," she warned. A cousin told him that his wife had overheard Kelly bragging about how she was sleeping with Johnny D. The next day he saw her drive by his house eight times.

"Whenever I was with her, it was like she put a story in *The Monroe Journal*," he said later. "I didn't know how to shut her up. She was just so proud of it. I decided I had to get away from her. She was using so many drugs, she was just unstable."

One morning Kelly found a printed card stuck in her screen door. "The Knights of the Ku Klux Klan are watching you!" it warned. She drove to her mother's house, showed it to her, and accused one of her uncles of leaving it. "Karen, people are beginning to gossip about you and that nigger," her mother said.

Not long after that someone told federal tax investigators that Johnny D. had not been withholding payroll taxes for the three men whom he regularly hired to help him cut trees. The government leveled a $3,400 fine. A friend at the sheriff's department called him and said that an anonymous tipster had accused him of selling marijuana to white teenagers. "Somebody's after you," the friend said. "You better leave that white woman alone."

At the beginning of 1985 Johnny D. decided to end their relationship. He was dating Thulani, and the novelty of Karen had worn off. She had started calling Minnie again, and she was making threatening calls to Thulani. "She was taking all sorts of pills—speed, uppers, downers—anything she could get her hands on. She was getting deeper and deeper into drugs."

"Don't be coming around me no more," he told her one night. "We is done. I don't wanna see you again, ever."

Karen screamed curses at him, claimed she couldn't live without him, and threatened to kill herself and him. "I'll never let you go," she said. "You belong to me."

Johnny D. figured she was exaggerating.

Jake Kelly still had no idea that Karen was having an affair, but he had noticed that she was taking handfuls of pills each day. Her mood could change in seconds. Some mornings she couldn't bring herself to get out of bed. Jake convinced her to enter a private drug treatment program in Mobile, but during her third week there she was caught using drugs and was kicked out. They began to fight. In mid-1985 Karen moved with Jake and their son to a construction site in Louisiana. "I really wanted to get away and make it work for us," she recalled, but all she could think about was Johnny D. She wrote him a letter.

> Hello Baby,
>
> . . . I'd love to hold you and love you. I feel like I am a thing of the past and baby, I never wanted that. I wanted to be your's forever. . . . I am very unhappy down here and I want to come home. . . . I thought you might call but you haven't. Baby, I guess you have forgotten me. . . . But I don't want to love anybody but you. . . . Baby I will never stop loving you. . . . I've cried all week. I remember the nights we stood by the fireplace at my house, had coffee . . . have you forgotten Baby? It's time to build a fire again, but Baby will I have to sit there alone? . . . When you really love someone, it never goes away. Not forever. You will always be mine!
>
> Love Me!

She mailed the letter to one of Johnny D.'s sisters and asked her to hand-deliver it so Minnie wouldn't find out, but Johnny D. told his sister to send it back unopened. Karen wrote him three more love letters. Each was returned. What Johnny D. could not know was that Jake picked up their mail. Jake read Karen's letters, filed for a divorce, and asked for permanent custody of their son. In August and September 1986 Karen and Jake squared off in court. Her entire family testified on *his* behalf. She was described as a morally unfit mother. At the hearing Jake's attorney, Paul M. Harden, asked Karen if she had ever had sexual intercourse with Johnny D. McMillian. She pretended she didn't even know him.

"Have you ever had a date with a black person?" Harden asked.

"No sir, I have not."

"Have you ever been to Crabs nightclub?"

"No sir, I have not."

Harden waved a membership card from Crabs through the air. It had her signature on it. He had caught her in an obvious lie.

"You deny that Johnny D. McMillian has ever been in your home?" he continued.

"Yes, I deny it," she replied angrily.

"And under oath, ma'am, you're telling us you don't even know Johnny D. McMillian?"

"I know *of* him because his daughter was in school with me," Kelly said. "That's all."

Harden produced the four letters Karen had written to Johnny D. Jake had saved them. The attorney started to read from one of them:

> Hi Honey, I was hurt to hear you would talk about me the way you have to Thulani. She told me you said I had the coldest pussy in Monroe County. . . . She said you said all I liked to do was suck your dick. . . .

That was enough, the judge declared. He could read the letters in private.

Harden called Johnny D. as the next witness.

"Have you ever been out with Karen Kelly?" he asked.

"No sir."

"Ever been drinking with her?"

"No sir."

"Ever been to bed with her?"

"No sir."

"You realize you can go to the penitentiary for lying on the witness stand?"

"No."

"Well, let me ask you again. Have you ever been out with this girl in any shape or fashion? Remember now, you are under oath."

"No sir."

Harden had assumed Johnny D. would lie, so he called a close friend of Karen's as his next witness.

"Karen told me she was going to have Johnny D. McMillian kill my husband and me if I didn't lie for her today," the woman testified, her voice trembling.

"What was she worried you'd talk about?" asked Harden.

"She didn't want me to tell the judge about her and Johnny D. . . . the black man Karen was sleeping with."

On September 15, 1986, the judge awarded custody of the Kellys' son to Jake and publicly chastised Karen Kelly. She was outraged. "I'd given up my husband and my child for Johnny D., and after the trial he still didn't want anything to do with me. No one did. My family disowned me. Everyone wanted me to leave."

She moved to Greenville, a town an hour's drive north of Monroeville, where she had a brief sexual relationship with another black man. She called Johnny D. and told him about it, hoping to make him jealous, but he didn't care. Only after she threatened to begin telephoning his house again did he agree to come see her. Kelly would later claim they made love during his visit. "If he really wanted to be rid of me, why'd he always come see me when I called?" she asked later.

Just before Halloween Kelly moved to East Brewton. She now had a new black boyfriend, Henry Jones. His brother, Clyde Jones, was dating a white girl named Allison Parker, and the brothers suggested that Kelly and Parker become roommates, since both were looking for a place to stay. The two women moved into the Big Four Trailer Park, and on their first night in the trailer they got high smoking marijuana and drinking beer. Later Parker would be able to remember only bits of their conversation, but she did recall that Kelly kept repeating how much she loved Johnny D. McMillian—and not Henry Jones—and how that love had cost her everything. There was one other comment that Parker would recall Kelly's making over and over again that night. "I'm going to teach that nigger a lesson," Kelly swore. "He's going to pay for what he's done to me."

Parker, who was in her early twenties, was a big woman, weighing more than two hundred pounds. She was both naive and extremely insecure. She would later claim that Kelly had gradually seized control of her life. "I idolized Karen at first and she really was kind, and then she began to take control. She told me what to wear, what to eat, who I could talk to—everything—and I did what she said because I wanted her to like me."

Kelly stopped seeing Jones at that point and convinced Parker to dump his brother. "We don't need anyone but each other," she told Parker one night.

During the day Parker worked at a fast-food restaurant, but Kelly hadn't been able to find a job, so she stayed home and did the housework and cooking. One night Parker invited a coworker home for dinner. When she introduced the woman as "my best friend at work," Kelly's face flashed with anger. She practically threw their plates of food at them. Later Parker woke up with severe stomach cramps and began to vomit. A supportive Kelly wiped her forehead with cold washcloths and suggested it was a twenty-four-hour virus. The next day, however, Parker discovered that her coworker had been just as ill. They decided that Kelly had poisoned their food. When Parker confronted her about it that night, Kelly pleaded innocent and blamed their dinner guest. "If anyone put something in your food it was that bull dyke you brought home," Kelly charged. "She is trying to ruin our friendship and get into your pants." Astoundingly, Parker believed her.

On Thanksgiving Day, 1986, Kelly took fourteen lithium tablets, six

Valiums, and twenty aspirins in an attempt to kill herself. Parker, who had been out running an errand, returned to find her lying on the floor of the trailer surrounded by empty pill bottles. "Johnny D. don't love me anymore," Kelly said. After her stomach was pumped in the emergency room, Kelly begged Parker to call Johnny D. and tell him about the suicide attempt. He came to the trailer a few days later with gifts: a bag of pot and a jar of moonshine. The three of them got high and drunk. Parker had never seen Kelly so happy. The next morning Parker was drinking coffee in the kitchen when Johnny D. came out of Kelly's bedroom and joined her.

"You need to get away from Karen," he told her softly. "She'll get you into a mess of shit you don't know nothing about. She's poison."

Later that afternoon Parker found Kelly drinking whiskey from a bottle and popping pills. "The only reason Johnny D. came over was because I tried to kill myself," she complained. "He's in love with that black bitch."

"He loves his wife," Parker volunteered. "Johnny D. told me he loved her this morning."

Kelly's eyes narrowed. "That man loves me," she said adamantly, "and only me."

For two weeks Kelly waited for Johnny D. to telephone or stop by. He didn't. Finally she and Parker drove to Monroeville to see him. They took a large plastic garbage bag filled with men's clothes that Kelly had shoplifted from the Kmart store in Brewton. Kelly wanted to give the bag to him as an early Christmas present, but he refused to take it. He asked her to leave him alone.

"I told her, 'Karen, I don't want to see you no more. I don't want you telling people we are going together. We is done. Leave me alone,' " he later recalled.

Kelly drove Parker to a crack house and spent every dollar the two women had on crack cocaine.

"When I asked her how we were going to pay our electric and water bills and rent," Parker said later, "Karen told me to call Johnny D. She says, 'He still owes me. Let him pay the damn bills.' I called Johnny D. the next day and he gave me the money."

Over the Christmas holidays Kelly began using crack cocaine several times a day. To feed her habit, she began turning tricks at the trailer park. She got Parker to use crack too. "I was trying to be just as bad as Karen was, but I couldn't keep up. Karen was going crazy. It was like she wanted to destroy herself."

Kelly began having sex regularly with Jerome "Pumpkin" Turner, a black ex-con who lived in the trailer next door. It was Turner who introduced them to one of his drug connections, Tyrone Patterson, the black man she and Myers would later try to frame for the Pittman murder. Patterson began giving the women crack in return for their shoplifting merchandise and cashing forged checks for him.

By January 1987 a new face appeared at the women's trailer. Vic Pittman had started coming around. "Behind his back, Karen laughed at him and called him a nasty old drunk," said Parker, "but I think that old fool really planned on marrying her."

During the first week of February 1987 the Brewton police raided Pumpkin Turner's trailer and found traces of illegal drugs and a pistol. Because he was an ex-con, his parole was revoked and he was sent back to prison. Parker would later insist that Kelly had tipped off the police. "She was angry at him because he had started seeing another woman and Karen was jealous," Parker said. "She told me that she was going to fix him good. No one dumped her."

By this time the two women had worn out their welcome in East Brewton. They moved to Evergreen, where Kelly soon attracted another admirer: Ralph Myers.

What happened next is difficult to determine. By this time Kelly and Parker were both addicted to crack cocaine and both had become paranoid, a side effect of the drug. What is known with certainty is that in mid-February 1987, Parker deliberately got herself arrested by lighting a marijuana joint in front of an officer and then racing her car through a red light. ABI agent Simon Benson was among the officers who finally forced her to pull over. "She told us she wanted to be put in jail," he later recalled. "We could tell she was on drugs."

Two days later Vickie Lynn Pittman was abducted in East Brewton.

No one paid much attention to Parker, and she was eventually turned loose, but after Myers and Johnny D. were charged with the Pittman and Morrison murders, she resurfaced in Evergreen. In an interview Parker would later recall that she had contacted Benson and told him she had gotten herself arrested because she was terrified of Karen Kelly. She claimed Kelly had tried to stab her one night with a knife because she had figured out a secret in Kelly's past.

"When we were living together in East Brewton, I took the trash out one night and found a perfectly good black wig and a pair of black sunglasses in the trash can," Parker said later. "I figured someone had thrown them away by mistake, so I took them back into the trailer and showed them to Karen. She freaked out and told me to throw them away . . . I found out the next day someone had robbed the East Brewton bank and that's when I put two and two together. Karen had been really broke and then all of a sudden she had lots and lots of cash for drugs. I decided she had robbed the bank or helped rob it. That was why she really wanted us to get out of East Brewton. She was afraid Pumpkin Turner was going to tell on her because she had told the police about him. She is the bank robber."

After Parker told Benson her theory about Kelly, the agent asked whether Parker had ever met Vickie Lynn Pittman or had ever heard Kelly and Johnny D. discussing ways to abduct and kill her. Parker denied knowing anything about the murder and said she had never met Vickie Lynn. A short time later she was arrested on drug charges.

A guard brought a letter to Johnny D.'s death row cell a few weeks after he had been moved into the prison. He wasn't expecting mail. He could barely read, and Minnie and his relatives were coming to visit him regularly on weekends. He didn't have any idea who might have written to him until he saw the writing on the envelope. He recognized it. He slipped the letter out and read the brief message:

> Hello baby,
>
> I'm sorry you're in prison. . . . You know they forced me to lie about you. . . . Just remember, I LOVE YOU! I always will. You will always be mine. You and me, forever.

It was not signed, but he knew who had written it. His mind immediately called up his favorite memory of her. She had been so pretty when she had first come to his house to buy marijuana. It had all seemed so innocent back then.

Not now.

He decided to give the letter to his attorneys when they came to meet him.

Chapter 25

"Pimpish," defense attorney Bruce Boynton said. "Johnny D. is pimpish." J. L. Chestnut nodded. Boynton had just returned from meeting their new client, and he was describing him to his cocounsel. "He is a womanizer, but I don't think he's a murderer."

Before a criminal trial the prosecution is required to disclose whatever evidence it plans to use against the accused. Boynton had stopped at the Monroe County Courthouse and picked up a packet from Larry Ikner that contained copies of sworn statements made by Ralph Myers, Karen Kelly, and Bill Hooks, Jr., whose name was now being made public by the prosecutors. The two defense attorneys had read them, and both agreed that the most damaging testimony was Myers's. The defense would have to find a way to undercut his credibility, particularly because he was prepared to testify that he had seen Johnny D. standing over Ronda's body with a pistol in his hand.

"We got to emphasize that Myers told the police two different stories," said Boynton, referring to Myers's June 9 and September 14 statements. In the first, Myers admitted that he had driven to Jackson

Cleaners but denied that he had gone inside. That admission had not come until September 14.

"Myers is the key to this whole thing," Chestnut decided. "We will have to focus the trial on him and off our man."

They talked briefly about possible reasons why Myers would lie about Johnny D. and decided that the most obvious was to save his own neck by being the first to cut a plea bargain. "We have to make certain that jurors understand Mr. Myers is receiving a payoff," Chestnut said. Then he switched subjects and asked, "Now, what about this Hooks character?"

"He's a nobody," Boynton replied. "My guess is he's doing this for the reward."

"And Karen Kelly?"

Boynton shook his head, and Chestnut laughed. "She's a piece of work, isn't she?" he asked rhetorically.

According to the prosecution, Kelly was prepared to testify that Johnny D. had bragged to her about killing Ronda. But both attorneys knew that prosecutor Ted Pearson was going to have a tough time controlling her as a witness. In fact, she had telephoned both Chestnut and Boynton shortly after they had agreed to defend Johnny D. and had assured both men that she would change her story and help him if she was called as a witness. She would claim that she had been forced to lie about him.

"What do you think Ted is going to do about Kelly?" asked Boynton.

Chestnut wasn't sure. Calling Kelly was dangerous, but Pearson might take the risk just so that the jury could see her. The savvy prosecutor would assume that the defense would portray Johnny D. as a good, honest, wrongly accused family man. If Kelly was summoned into court and skillfully questioned, jurors were sure to learn about their sexual relationship, and that would destroy the defense team's carefully cultivated image. Suddenly Chestnut had an idea. "Let's subpoena Karen as a *defense* witness and scare the hell out of Ted."

His logic was simple. By listing Kelly as one of Johnny D.'s witnesses, the defense would be sending Pearson a clear signal: She is now on our side. "Old Ted will have to think twice about calling her if he believes she is going to get up there and talk about how the police forced her to lie about Johnny D."

Boynton liked the idea, but he wasn't sure that even if Kelly promised to help them her testimony would benefit Johnny D.

Chestnut told him not to worry. "We sure as hell aren't going to call her," he said, "even if we put her on our witness list. It's just a ploy." There was no way Kelly could help their client. Even if she defended him, she would still come across as a married white woman who had committed adultery with a married black man. "The last thing we want jurors to know is that Kelly was having sex with our man."

Chestnut asked about Simon Benson.

"He's black," Boynton said.

"Oh," Chestnut replied, "one of those."

Boynton nodded.

Chestnut later explained his comment. "Whites are always going to feel better when they have one black man accusing another black man of a crime. It makes it look less racist when, in fact, this whole case was clearly racist. Do you think a white man would have been charged with murder in Monroe County if the only evidence against him were statements by three black people with reputations the likes of Ralph Myers's, Karen Kelly's, and the Hooks boy?"

"We're going to have to work on Mr. Simon Benson," Chestnut told Boynton. "We'll have to remind him who his people are and bring that brother back into the fold."

Within an hour they had decided on a strategy. At the trial they would focus their attack on Myers, trying to ruin his credibility. They would belittle Hooks, painting him as a drunk whose only motive for testifying was greed. They would preempt Kelly by listing her as one of their witnesses and hope that Pearson would not risk calling her. For their own witnesses they would call Minnie, Everline Smith, and some of the other blacks who had seen Johnny D. at the fish fry. Meanwhile they would launch some pretrial attacks. They would tell the media that Johnny D. was the victim of a racist prosecution. They would also file as many pretrial motions as possible. "Each time a judge rules," Chestnut later explained, "there is a chance that he will rule incorrectly, and that increases our client's odds at getting his case overturned during an appeal and winning him a new trial."

Circuit Judge Robert E. Lee Key, a sixty-nine-year-old white jurist who had dispensed law in Monroe and Conecuh counties for nearly thirty years, was scheduled to preside at Johnny D.'s trial. "Key will often rule from the hip and worry about the law later," Chestnut told Boynton. "All we have to do is get him to make one error." If they could catch the judge making a mistake, then they could tie up Johnny D.'s case for years in the appellate courts. They might also force the state to retry him, and both men knew that an accused's chances of an acquittal were always better at a second trial. There was always a chance that a witness would change his story or simply forget over time.

While the defense worked on its plan in Selma, prosecutor Pearson plotted his strategy on the second floor of the Monroe County Courthouse. Tall, lean, with thick glasses and what seemed like a perpetually stuffy nose, Pearson had been district attorney since 1969, nearly all his professional career. He was in his mid-forties, recently divorced, and bored with his job. The Morrison case was the first in a long time to catch his interest. Although he had never heard of the defendant, Benson and Ikner assured him that Johnny D. was a drug kingpin and ruthless killer.

"You know Chestnut and Boynton are going to play the race card," Pearson warned the two investigators. "They always do."

"Race has got nothing to do with this," Ikner said. "We got one black witness [Hooks] and two white witnesses [Myers and Kelly], and that should help."

"What sort of witness is Myers gonna make?"

Benson shrugged. Ikner said, "He should do okay on the stand."

"And Karen Kelly?"

Benson and Ikner looked at each other nervously.

"She still loves Johnny D.," Benson warned.

Pearson had a habit of mentally switching roles whenever he reviewed a case. *What would I do if I were defending Johnny D.?* It didn't take him long to spot a potential flaw in the prosecution's case. In his September 14 statement, Myers said Ronda was lying on her back near the cash register in the lobby when he rushed into Jackson Cleaners. Yet her body had been discovered lying facedown in the northeast corner of the building. How had she gotten there? If Boynton and Chestnut investigated, they would discover there was no mention in the police reports of drag marks or bloodstains being found in the lobby. Worse, the autopsy said that Ronda had probably died exactly where her body was found, a conclusion based on the locations of the shell casings and the severity of the various wounds. How was the prosecution going to explain this obvious discrepancy?

There was another problem as well. The state's two chief witnesses disagreed about the killers' getaway. Hooks said Myers and Johnny D. had sped away from the cleaners—that was why he had noticed them. But Myers said he had been so flustered by the murder that he had stalled the truck before they left the parking lot. Johnny D. had been forced to get out, lift the hood, and tinker with the engine. Hooks also claimed that he had seen both men coming out of the cleaners together, but Myers said that after the murder Johnny D. had sent him out to the truck, where he had waited for two or three minutes more. Finally Myers said that he had seen Johnny D. stuffing a small satchel with "wads and wads" of cash. Where had that money come from? Everyone knew the cleaners had less than a hundred dollars in the register. Pearson assumed it was drug money, but there was no evidence at all that a drug deal had taken place.

Benson and Ikner predicted that the defense would call several witnesses to back up Johnny D.'s alibi, but most would be blacks from the projects, and they would probably not make very good witnesses. "What about Johnny D.?" Pearson asked them. "What sort of witness is he going to make?" Benson and Ikner could only guess.

As he reviewed the case, Pearson reached the same conclusion his opponents had. Myers was going to be the key to winning a conviction. It was all going to boil down to whom the jurors believed: Johnny D. or Ralph Myers.

On November 17, 1987, Judge Key held a hearing to review the myriad pretrial motions Chestnut and Boynton had filed. Ronda Morrison had now been dead one year. Among the motions was a demand that the trial be moved outside Monroe County because of unfavorable pretrial publicity. Chestnut made an impassioned plea for the change of venue, arguing that most county residents—especially whites—had already decided Johnny D. was guilty; but neither defense attorney expected the judge to move the trial. He was an elected official, and although he was about to retire, they doubted he would rob Monroeville's residents of the right to judge someone accused of killing one of the town's sweethearts. In fact, Chestnut and Boynton were privately hoping Key would deny the request. "The evidence was so overwhelming that our man couldn't get a fair trial that if Key denied our motion, then Boynton and I both knew we had him," Chestnut later explained. "We would have our reversible error and we could get Johnny D. a new trial if we lost the first one. All Judge Key had to do was say *'No!'* But old Judge Key outsmarted us."

Key understood what Chestnut and Boynton were plotting because he had been outmaneuvered once before in a sensational murder case. In March 1977 two black convicts escaped from a North Carolina prison, stole a car, abducted a sixteen-year-old girl, and took turns raping her as they drove across Georgia into Alabama. They kept her locked naked in the trunk of their car without food or water during their three-day trip. Entirely by chance, they stopped in Monroe County to kill her. They ran over her with the stolen car, and when that did not do the job, they used a hatchet to chop through all but a sliver of her neck. Both men were caught. Both confessed. Judge Key sentenced both to death.

But neither man was executed. Their cases were repeatedly appealed, chiefly by the NAACP Legal Defense Fund, which argued that the men's right to a fair trial had been violated because there were no blacks on their juries. In one of the appeals defense attorneys accused Judge Key of being racially biased. He had been so outraged by that charge and the delay in executing the men that he had written a letter of complaint to the Alabama Supreme Court. It still galled him that two individuals who in his opinion were clearly guilty were still filing death row appeals. He was determined not to have that happen in Johnny D.'s case.

"I'm going to grant your motion," Key announced. Chestnut and Boynton were stunned. To ensure that Johnny D. received a fair trial, Key said, he was moving the case completely out of the Thirty-fifth Judicial District, which contained Monroe and Conecuh counties. The trial would be held at the Baldwin County Courthouse in Bay Minette, some sixty miles southeast of Monroeville. The defense attorneys' shock turned to horror. Nearly forty-three percent of Monroe County's population was black, but only sixteen percent of Baldwin County's residents were. Even more disheartening was the county's reputation as a stronghold of racism.

Chestnut and Boynton huddled with Johnny D. If he could come up with more money, they could appeal Key's ruling. They would claim that his rights were being violated because his case was being moved from a county with a sizable black population to one with few blacks. But Johnny D. told them he didn't have any more cash. Minnie still was trying to raise the final $6,000 of their original $20,000 fee. The attorneys dropped the idea. Johnny D. would have to take his chances in Bay Minette.

Chapter 26

The trial of Johnny D. was scheduled to begin in December 1987, but a series of procedural delays pushed it back to February 1988. As the date grew closer Chestnut and Boynton began reminding Minnie that their entire fee was due before the trial started. Minnie was having trouble sleeping and was so nervous that she couldn't eat. She had lost forty pounds. Boynton's telephone calls about the money began bothering her. " 'Where's the money? Do ya got the money? Ya got to get the money.' That's all them lawyers asked me," she later said. "They didn't want to talk about the case—only the money, money, money!" When Boynton called five days before the trial, Minnie finally erupted. "I'm telling you there ain't no more money," she snapped. "I wish Johnny D. *was* some big-time dope dealer so we could have enough to pay you."

Minnie would later claim that Boynton had become gruff when she protested. "He says, 'Now don't you let your husband go to the electric chair just because you couldn't come up with the money. You don't want to be responsible for him being killed, do you?' "

Minnie felt overwhelmed and cheated. Johnny D. had lied to her about his affair with Kelly. The police, she was convinced, had framed her husband. And now the lawyers, who were supposed to be helping her, were telling her it was going to be *her* fault if Johnny D. was sent to the electric chair.

After talking to Boynton, she began to cry. Then she began to pray. The next morning she drove to a bank in Frisco City, south of Monroeville. She and Johnny D. were not customers there, but she had already borrowed as much as she could from their own small bank. She had thought about approaching one of the bigger banks in Monroeville, but she doubted any of them would run the risk of irritating Ronda's parents or members of the white community by giving her a loan. The white manager at the Frisco City bank listened politely when Minnie explained why she needed money. She admitted that everything she and Johnny D. owned was already mortgaged. There was nothing she could offer him as collateral. But she had been born in Monroe County and had worked for Vanity Fair Mills nearly twenty years. "I'm not a lazy person," she said, mustering her pride. "It may take me a pretty good piece of time, but I will pay you back. If I give someone a promise, I always keep it." There was something else she needed to tell him, she said. "What peoples is saying ain't true. My husband didn't kill no girl in that cleaners. He was home. I saw him there."

The manager left her alone for several minutes. When he returned, he handed Minnie a check for $3,000. She said a prayer as she walked outside. "Thank you, God, for them white peoples who ain't all bad."

Minnie sent the check to Boynton and Chestnut, who agreed to continue representing Johnny D. even though another $3,000 was still owed them. Both knew they probably were not going to get any more, particularly if their client was found guilty.

When Johnny D.'s trial date finally arrived, the McMillians' oldest son, Johnny, drove Minnie to the Baldwin County Courthouse. He had moved back home from out of state to help his mother. A friend sat with them in the courtroom and pointed out Charles and Bertha Morrison. Minnie thought about trying to talk to them but was afraid to say anything. She had heard that they were convinced Johnny D. was guilty. She had never been in a courtroom before, and she felt as if everyone there was staring at her, particularly the whites. Minnie was sure each of them knew about Johnny D. and his affair with Kelly and she felt ashamed, even though she kept telling herself she had done nothing wrong.

As soon as Judge Key entered the courtroom, Ted Pearson rose from the prosecutor's table and sheepishly announced that the state was not ready. Ralph Myers had decided a few minutes earlier that he was not going to testify against Johnny D. as promised.

"What are you saying?" asked Judge Key, startled. "Are you moving for a continuance . . . ?"

"Yes sir," Pearson replied. "I'm going to have to because the only evidence I have is Mr. Myers."

Chestnut jumped to his feet. Johnny D. had been lingering on death row for more than six months, he said. The prosecution had no physical evidence linking his client to the murder. The state's entire case consisted of statements from three "questionable" witnesses, and now the prosecution's most important one was refusing to testify. Chestnut demanded that the court either proceed immediately with the trial or dismiss the murder charge against his client. Judge Key was clearly irked. A panel of potential jurors had been summoned to the courthouse and was waiting to be questioned. Both sides had been told to be ready to proceed. Now a single witness was stymieing the entire process. Glaring at Pearson, the judge announced that if the state could not prosecute Johnny D., then it needed to bring Myers into the courtroom and put *him* on trial for Ronda's murder. Surprised, Pearson protested, saying he was not prepared to prosecute Myers. The district attorney's office had focused on making its case against Johnny D. Besides, he added, Myers's court-appointed attorney had not been given adequate time to prepare a defense.

"Well, you should have been ready to try either defendant," Judge Key grumbled. Reluctantly he announced that the court had no choice but to postpone the trial until Myers could be evaluated at a state mental hospital to determine whether or not he was mentally competent to testify or himself be put on trial. The Morrisons, Minnie, and all their supporters were told to go home.

Myers was immediately confronted by his court-appointed attorney, who demanded to know why he had balked at testifying. The reluctant witness said he wanted a better plea bargain. All he had been promised was that he would not be sentenced to death for his part in the Morrison murder, and that wasn't good enough. He could easily end up being killed in prison if he helped the state convict Johnny D.

In exchange for his continued cooperation, Myers expected the following concessions: He wanted the capital murder charge filed against him to be dismissed. He would then plead guilty to a much lesser crime and would receive a light prison sentence, which, he said, would be automatically suspended by a judge. Simply put, Myers did not want to spend one day in jail because of the Morrison murder. That was the price of his cooperation.

Pearson laughed when he heard these demands. The district attorney wasn't about to be blackmailed by someone who had admitted taking part in a killing. "Tell him no deal," Pearson told Myers's attorney. "No way he walks away free."

Neither side budged during the next few days, so Myers was taken under guard to the Taylor Hardin Secure Medical Facility for evaluation.

Although she had kept out of sight in Bay Minette, Karen Kelly had been at the courthouse when Myers refused to testify. She had caught a glimpse of Johnny D. through a small window as he was being led from the building and she had waved, but he hadn't seen her. He had not replied to any of the letters she had mailed to him in prison, and his relatives had refused to pass along her oral messages to him. She had heard that he was angry at her, even though she had begged him to forgive her. His continued refusal to talk to her made Kelly angry herself. Her life had not been easy since his arrest. In fact, as far as she was concerned, she had been having just as rough a time of it as he had.

Kelly had moved to Mobile after Johnny D. and Myers were jailed. Initially she had lived with her natural father, but he had tossed her out after she was accused of using someone else's credit card to buy herself new clothes. As usual, her mother posted her bail. Then she got a job in a fast-food restaurant, but it didn't pay enough to support her drug habit, so she went to work as a dancer in a topless bar. Her crack cocaine habit was now costing her close to two hundred dollars a day. She soon discovered that even with tips, she could not earn enough to feed it. "All I thought about was getting high. When I was stoned, I was happy because I didn't think about any of this mess with Johnny D."

Desperate for cash, Kelly went to work in a Mobile "movie house" where men paid forty-five dollars to watch thirty minutes of a pornographic film in a private booth with a "hostess." The owners of the movie house pocketed the admission price; whatever Kelly did in the booth was her business. She would later brag that she had routinely charged men two hundred dollars for sexual intercourse, but other girls who worked there laughed at those figures. "Most men just want to pay you ten bucks for a hand-job," one explained. Kelly tried to cut her expenses by substituting for crack a cheaper narcotic drug called Dilaudid, which she crushed, mixed with water, and injected. She rubbed vitamin E on her skin to hide the needle marks. Soon she was shooting up so often that both her arms were black-and-blue and her veins had started to collapse. She returned to using crack, and once again began looking for a better-paying job. A coworker told her about a "lock-in" whorehouse in Abbeville, Louisiana, that needed white hookers, especially if they were willing to have sex with blacks. Kelly took the bus to Abbeville. She lived in the house twenty-four hours a day and serviced as many men as were sent her. Kelly told her customers that her name was Hope. "I had hit rock bottom. I was stoned all the time . . . I was just sorry as hell." Her days became a blur of men, intercourse, and drugs. "I didn't care about anything or anybody. I remember thinking, whenever I got sober, 'You stupid bitch, if you had stayed home with Jake and not run off with that nigger, you wouldn't be in this mess.' " She sent Johnny D. a letter and accused him of making her a whore.

After a few weeks in Abbeville, Kelly had returned to Mobile and gone to work for an escort service, which was a front for prostitution. She had been working there when Simon Benson called to say that Johnny D.'s case had been scheduled for trial. He had told her that she was being subpoenaed by both sides, which was why she had gone to the courthouse in February. Even a glimpse of Johnny D. had reminded her how much she still loved him and how miserable her life had become. When she returned to Mobile, she began having nightmares. They were not about him or Myers or the Morrison murder. They were about Vickie Lynn Pittman. As soon as Kelly fell asleep, the girl appeared in her dreams. She could see the teenager's face and hear her as she pleaded for someone to help her. The dreams always ended the same way. Vickie Lynn would begin to scream and Kelly would know that the beatings had started. "She would just keep screaming and screaming and screaming until I woke up." After several sleepless nights, Kelly began hearing the screams inside her head even when she was awake. Already alarmed, she now began to panic. "I couldn't sleep. I couldn't eat. She would scream and scream and only I could hear her voice."

In March 1988 Benson called Kelly at the escort service to make certain she was ready to testify once Johnny D.'s trial was rescheduled. During their brief conversation Kelly mentioned that she was having nightmares about the Pittman murder. Benson telephoned a few days later and began asking her questions about the killing. By this time Officer Mike Cain had been gone from the East Brewton police force for several months, and Mozelle and Onzell had assumed that no one was pursuing their niece's death, but Benson would later insist that he had never stopped his investigation. He had simply been moving at a slower pace than Cain and the twins had wanted. His calls made Kelly even more jittery. "Benson tells me, 'Ralph says you were there. Ralph says you were at the Pittman murder. Ralph says you helped kill her.' Every time he calls me, he tells me this." The screams in her head began getting louder. "The only way I could get them to stop was by smoking crack."

Then came one night in June when Kelly used crack and found for the first time that it didn't work. She could still hear Vickie Lynn. She panicked, considered killing herself, and then called Benson. "You're right!" she cried into the phone. "I seen 'em kill that Pittman girl. I was there when she was killed." As soon as she uttered those words, the screams in her head went away.

Benson drove to Mobile with Escambia County Sheriff Hawsey and interviewed Kelly on June 18, 1988, at the ABI's office there. During the tape-recorded session, she frequently contradicted herself and at times had trouble answering basic questions. She would later recall that she had taken several amphetamines just before the interview and was not fully aware of what she was saying. Despite her erratic replies, Benson and Hawsey pushed her for further answers.

"I don't know if I'm imagining this," she told them, "so y'all are going to have to help me put this time together, but I know that I was there when the Pittman girl was killed. There's no doubt in my mind because I can remember the screams. I was not in the same room, but, uh, I can't get it together—I don't know—now I know I was there. I know that I was there when the girl was killed. But, uh, I wasn't in the room. I wasn't where I could see. I could hear now, but I wasn't where I could see. . . . Now I know who was there but, uh, I was doped up. . . . I can't put it all together in my mind because like I said, I was messed up."

Although most of her answers were just as disjointed, she eventually told the two investigators that she had been with Johnny D., Myers, Tyrone Patterson, and several other black men on the night when Vickie Lynn Pittman was abducted and murdered. She said they had all met at the trailer rented by Jerome "Pumpkin" Turner in the Big Four Trailer Park. Kelly had arrived late, and as soon as she stepped inside, she had heard Vickie Lynn screaming. The teenager was being held in a back bedroom because "everyone" was afraid she had told the FBI about drug trafficking in East Brewton.

When she got to this point in her story, Benson asked Kelly for the names of everyone in the trailer. Rather than answer his question, she began talking about the "screams" that had started to hound her. Even now, as they were speaking, she could hear them.

"I know these screams would not keep coming back to me if they weren't real," she said. "I could go on and forget it. It wouldn't keep nagging at me and nagging at me . . . but these screams, I keep hearing them. I keep hearing these screams."

Why had Vickie Lynn been screaming? Benson asked.

"She was screaming because they were torturing her. She told them to give her a chance—that if they wouldn't kill her, that she wouldn't tell nothing."

"Who was she talking to?"

"Ralph and Johnny D."

Fifteen minutes into the interview, Kelly abruptly asked Benson to turn off the tape recorder. When it was turned back on an hour and a half later, Benson said on the tape that Kelly had "needed some time to kinda get the information correctly in her mind." Now, he said, she was thinking more clearly. What Benson did not explain on tape was that during the break, he had accused her of lying. Vickie Lynn had been kidnapped in late February, several days *after* the police had raided Turner's trailer, revoked his parole, and returned him to prison. There was no way he could have been at the trailer as Kelly had claimed.

When the interview resumed, Kelly told Benson and Hawsey an entirely new story. This time there was no mention of any trailer. She said she had been washing clothes at a coin laundry when Johnny D., Myers, and Vickie Lynn arrived and invited her to go on a ride. The foursome had driven into the woods and started to drink moonshine.

"Johnny D. and Ralph got out of the truck and they talked for a few minutes and then they come and got Vickie Lynn out. . . . They had a tire tool and a knife and Ralph had, ah, it looked like a billy club and they started beating the girl and the girl started hollering and I got out of the truck and I went back there and I watched them beat the girl and Johnny D. slapped me and put me back in the truck. . . . But I stood and I watched them beat the girl for a while before she died. Ralph was kicking the girl in her face and all. They were hitting the girl in the mouth and in the nose and in the legs and they put me back in the truck."

Kelly said Johnny D. and Myers decided to hide the body in the Brooklyn area. They planned to remove the girl's clothing and burn her body, but when they got to the site they discovered that Vickie Lynn was still breathing.

"Johnny D. leaned down over the girl to stab the girl. I grabbed the butt of the knife and tried to grab the knife from Johnny D., but he stabbed the girl anyway and she made a gurgling noise. Ralph and Johnny D. covered the girl up with stems and leaves and straw. . . ."

It had started to rain, Kelly said, so they decided to leave the body for animals to eat rather than trying to set it on fire. Even though Kelly had now admitted to Benson and Hawsey that she had been present during the murder, neither lawman arrested her. Instead they sent her home. Kelly had told so many stories to the police that no one could be certain which, if any, were true. But this was not why Benson had decided not to charge her. She had just given him something he desperately wanted, something that was even more important to him than arresting her. She had furnished him with a lever to use on his reluctant star witness in the Ronda Morrison case.

Ralph Myers was still refusing to testify, still demanding that he be freed from jail in return for identifying Johnny D. as Ronda's killer. Kelly's statement gave the prosecution a sudden edge in the ongoing plea negotiations. Up until this point the evidence against Myers in the Pittman murder case had been fairly weak. But not anymore. The prosecution now had an eyewitness who was willing to testify that she had actually seen Myers beat Vickie Lynn to death. Kelly might be reluctant to testify against her former lover, but Myers was different. Benson knew she hated him and would not hesitate to name him as a killer. The fact that Myers had led the police to Vickie Lynn's body would add enough corroboration to her statement to get him convicted.

Benson hurried back to Monroeville. It was time for the prosecution to have another chat with Myers and his court-appointed attorney. Karen Kelly wasn't going anywhere. Benson could always deal with her later.

Chapter 27

Sheriff Tom Tate carefully watched the spectators as they walked through the metal detector that had been erected outside the Baldwin County courtroom solely for Johnny D.'s trial. Inside the chamber there were twelve rows of hard wood pews. The spectators divided themselves instinctively as they walked down the center aisle. Those who thought Johnny D. guilty sat in the rows behind a table at the front of the courtroom used by the prosecutors; those who thought him innocent sat behind the defense table on the other side. When Chestnut glanced over his shoulder, he was not surprised to see only black faces in the pews behind him.

The judge's chair was on a dark wood platform with an American and an Alabama flag perched on either side and a clock built into the wall above it. To his left was the jury box: two rows with seven chairs in each, enough to accommodate twelve jurors and two alternates who would serve should any of the jurors become ill.

Ralph Myers's refusal to testify in February and a series of other delays had pushed Johnny D.'s trial back still further. It was now August 1988, some twenty months since Ronda's murder. Johnny D. had spent nearly fourteen months locked in a one-man cell on Alabama's death row. Now he was finally going to get the chance to prove he was innocent.

There had been a time when Chestnut would arrive in a town a few days before a murder trial, go to the courthouse, and obtain a list of residents who had been called for jury duty. He would take the list to a local black preacher, and in return for a donation to his church, the minister would identify each juror by race, age, sex, and, based on his opinion, attitude toward blacks. When the trial began, Chestnut would already know those he wanted to decide his client's fate and, even more important, those he didn't. In this case, Johnny D. didn't have enough money to pay for any special services, and Chestnut didn't have any free time. They would choose jurors based on their answers to a series of short questions asked during the voir dire portion of the trial and hope for the best.

The prosecution, meanwhile, was receiving help from Baldwin County District Attorney David Whetstone and his assistant, Lynn L. Stuart, who had been assigned to help Ted Pearson prosecute the case. They knew most of the thirty-nine potential jurors and were quick to advise Pearson on whom to choose.

Under the rules of the court, the prosecution could "strike" fourteen persons from the pool. The defense could strike thirteen. The remaining twelve would make up the jury, with the last two jurors struck from the list serving as alternates. Although it is illegal for either side to exclude a juror solely because of race, all the attorneys understood that Pearson would try to keep blacks off the jury. He would also try to stack the panel with older white men and middle-aged white women, especially those with teenage daughters or granddaughters. The defense would push for blacks.

Within minutes after the jury selection started, Chestnut was objecting. He accused Pearson of eliminating blacks without any valid reason. Judge Key asked the district attorney to explain why he had just removed a young black woman from the jury pool. It was because of her age, Pearson explained. Chestnut laughed aloud. "He's kept a fair number of young jurors, Judge. White ones, that is." Judge Key ordered the bailiff to put the black woman's name back on the list. For more than an hour the two sides slowly whittled down the roll, until there were twelve jurors left. Two were black, ten were white, eight were women, four were men. Chestnut and Boynton told Johnny D. to look each juror in the eye. Only someone who is guilty refuses to make eye contact with the people deciding his fate, they warned him. Johnny D. glanced over at them. None seemed sympathetic.

Before the first witness was called, Chestnut announced that he wanted the race of everyone who testified noted in the court record. "Why is that necessary?" Pearson asked. Because the only reason Johnny D. is on trial, Chestnut declared, is because he is black. The two sides began arguing, but Judge Key cut them off. He would decide on a witness-by-witness basis whether or not a person's race needed to be recorded. Chestnut felt good about the ruling. A defense attorney not only had to defend his client in the courtroom, he also had to think about the impression the court record was going to make when it was read later by an appeals court. Chestnut planned to mention race as often as he could. Few issues slowed down the federal appeals process as much.

The prosecution's first witness was Ray Owens, a Frisco City resident who testified that on the Saturday of the murder he had been waiting outside Jackson Cleaners for the store to open. Ronda Morrison had arrived late and had been the only employee on duty, he said. Next Pearson called Jan Owen, who told the jury that she had dropped off a skirt and blouse at the cleaners at ten-fifteen that morning. Owen said Ronda had seemed happy and carefree when she had last seen her. Pearson's third witness was Jerrie Sue Dunning, who described how she had arrived at the cleaners at ten forty-five and found the front door ajar and the lobby empty. Under gentle prodding, she told the jury about the search that had been made for Ronda and the discovery of her corpse in the northeast corner under a rack of clothes. Her testimony was followed by Coy Stacey's, which buttressed everything Dunning had said. Chestnut and Boynton questioned each of the witnesses, but only briefly. They assumed that Pearson was using them simply to establish several rudimentary facts: that Ronda had been the only employee at work in the store; that she had been fine when seen at ten-fifteen; and that she was found dead shortly after ten-forty-five. The defense attorneys saw no need to attack these points and possibly irritate the jury by nitpicking.

Lieutenant Woodrow Ikner and Deputy William Gibson were the next to be called, and they testified respectively that money had been stolen from the cash register and that Ronda had been sexually attacked. Near the end of Gibson's testimony, he was asked if he had noticed anything unusual about the floor in the northeast corner of the store.

"Up near her body," he explained, "there was dust and it appeared to be where somebody—apparently where something was drug, you know, through that dust."

"Did that area where you say there were drag marks, did that lead to Ronda's body?"

"Yes."

The prosecution did not call special attention to Gibson's answer or ask him to elaborate, but what he had just said was critical. He had just given the state a plausible explanation for the flaw in the prosecution's case that Pearson had first noticed months earlier. Ronda's body had been found lying facedown in the northeast corner of the cleaners, but Myers had claimed in his September 14 statement that he had seen her lying faceup on the floor in the front lobby. Jurors were bound to wonder how the body had gotten there, and Gibson had just told them: It had been dragged.

Pearson watched Boynton as he rose from the defense table to cross-examine Gibson. Few in the courtroom realized how important this moment was. If Chestnut and Boynton had read Gibson's original police reports, they would know that he had never mentioned anything about drag marks before this moment. If they had studied the autopsy, they would know that the state medical examiner had concluded that Ronda had collapsed and died exactly where her body had been found. All Boynton had to do was challenge these facts to raise doubts about Gibson's statement and, later, to discredit Myers's eyewitness testimony.

"Mr. Gibson," Boynton said politely, "how long have you been employed by the Monroe sheriff's department?" Gibson answered the question, and Boynton asked him a second one that was just as innocuous.

The defense didn't know! Chestnut and Boynton had not spotted the flaw. Despite evidence that suggested otherwise, the jurors now believed that Ronda's body had been dragged from the lobby into the northeast corner, where it had been found.

Day two of the murder trial began the next morning with Pearson asking for permission to call a surprise witness. Chestnut was outraged. Johnny D. had a constitutional right to know in advance who was scheduled to testify against him and what each witness planned to say. The rules of the court prohibited the addition of any last-minute witnesses unless there were extraordinary and legitimate reasons for bringing them into court. Chestnut reminded the judge that Johnny D.'s trial had been postponed for more than one year. That was plenty of time, he argued, for the prosecution to have interviewed all the witnesses it needed. Pearson acknowledged that his request was unusual, but he explained that Sheriff Tate had just learned about the surprise witness four days earlier and had been able to convince him to step forward and testify only within the past twenty-four hours. Judge Key told Pearson to proceed.

Joe Hightower was a twenty-seven-year-old welder from Frisco City whose hands shook and whose voice cracked nervously as he answered assistant prosecutor Lynn Stuart's questions. Hightower explained that he had been driving by Jackson Cleaners on the Saturday when Ronda was murdered.

"I happened to notice Johnny D. McMillian's truck sitting there, at the cleaners. . . . It is a late-model Chevrolet. It was . . . kind of a low-rider truck," he declared.

"Had you ever seen that truck before?"

"Yes . . . a great number of times . . . a hundred, one hundred and fifty times or more. . . ."

Chestnut and Boynton shot each other nervous glances. Up until now, Bill Hooks, Jr., had been the only witness they were aware of other than Myers who could place Johnny D. at Jackson Cleaners on the day of the crime. Hooks was a petty thief, a known liar, and a drunk. The defense had felt fairly confident that it could convince the jury that he was after the $18,000 reward. Now the prosecution had found a witness who did not have a criminal record and had apparently been reluctant to step forward. Moreover, he was white. Both attorneys began scribbling down notes as Hightower continued testifying.

"How did you know that this truck belonged to Johnny D. McMillian?" assistant prosecutor Stuart asked.

"Because I had been to Johnny D. McMillian's house with other people," replied Hightower, "to purchase marijuana."

Chestnut leaped up. "Objection!" he yelled. "Objection!"

Without waiting for Chestnut to explain the reason for his objection, Judge Key told the jury that it was to ignore Hightower's reference to marijuana. Johnny D. was not being accused of selling drugs, nor had any evidence been introduced that showed he had ever sold them. Key ordered his clerk to strike Hightower's reference to marijuana from the court transcript. But Chestnut was not satisfied. "Judge," he protested, "I move for a mistrial." How could his client get a fair trial now that he had been branded a drug dealer? Judge Key again admonished the jurors, "You must disregard what the witness has just said." He then told assistant prosecutor Stuart to continue with her questions. She immediately asked Hightower why he had waited so long to come forward.

"I was scared of Johnny D.," he answered. "I just—I don't know—just because [of] the reason I have been to his house."

"Objection!" Chestnut yelled again. "Judge, I move for a mistrial." Once again the witness had suggested that Johnny D. was a drug dealer. He had now implied that he was dangerous as well. Key overruled Chestnut. "Continue," he said.

Stuart asked, "Why were you scared to come forward with this information?"

"Because when you fool with drugs—you just don't know—if you get involved with something like that it could cost you your life," Hightower replied.

"I object to that answer!" Chestnut thundered, leaving his seat.

"Overruled," snapped Key.

"I ask that his answer be stricken from the record," added Boynton.

"Overruled," said Key.

"Move for a mistrial," said Chestnut.

"Overruled," said Key.

When it was time for Hightower to be cross-examined, Chestnut asked, "Mr. Hightower, you are very much alive here this morning, aren't you?"

"Yes sir."

Chestnut then forced Hightower to admit that he had never been threatened or harmed by Johnny D. or anyone associated with him. Nonetheless, Chestnut knew he had failed to undo the damage the state's surprise witness had caused. Regardless of Judge Key's admonishments, the jurors were still going to think of Johnny D. as a drug dealer and someone whom Hightower had feared.

The prosecution's next witness was Dr. Gary Cumberland, the state medical examiner who had performed the autopsy on Ronda. His testimony should have been routine, but Pearson made a procedural mistake when he began questioning him, and Boynton objected. Under the rules of the court, the prosecution could not introduce new evidence unless it first established how the police had obtained it. Simply put, Pearson could not begin asking Cumberland questions about the autopsy until the witness first told the court how Ronda's body had gotten from the floor in Jackson Cleaners to the state crime lab in Mobile. This procedure is called establishing the chain of custody, and it is required so that the court can be certain that unauthorized persons have not tampered with a piece of evidence before it is introduced in court. Once Ronda's body was discovered, it was up to the police to keep track of it and everyone who had access to it.

Judge Key knew Pearson was skipping the chain of custody step. He also knew that he had no choice but to sustain the defense's objection. However, the prosecutor's mistake was something that could be easily remedied, so Key ordered the bailiff to take the jury outside the courtroom and then subtly tried to tell Pearson that he needed to go back and establish how Ronda's body had ended up at the crime lab. "It is not up to me to conduct the prosecution," Key explained carefully, "but it seems to me like a whole lot of preliminary questions need to be asked first here. . . . I think you understand what I'm talking about."

Pearson said he understood, but he began to argue with the judge. He wanted to ask some other questions about the autopsy first and then establish the chain. His response irritated Key because what he was doing was against the rules. "You haven't just got out of law school," Judge Key said. "Let's do this correctly."

Pearson promised that he would, but as soon as the jury was brought back into the courtroom, he again started questioning Cumberland about the autopsy without going back to establish the custody chain. Judge Key began to worry. Unless Pearson followed the correct procedure, he was going to give the defense a legitimate reason to get Johnny D.'s case overturned on appeal if he was convicted. Interrupting Pearson, Judge Key told his bailiff to take the jury outside the courtroom once again.

"Do I have to write you a book about this?" Key asked Pearson. "You got to connect all this up, you know."

Pearson still didn't seem to understand what Key was telling him, so an exasperated Judge Key spelled it out. He told him exactly what he needed to do. He then addressed Chestnut and Boynton. "We need not get hung up on little details like this," he said. "I am going to tell all the lawyers this—this case is not going to be reversed on some technicality. Whatever the verdict, if it has to be appealed, I want it upheld in the appellate courts." Judge Key had the jury brought back into the courtroom and ordered Pearson to go ahead, assuming that the prosecutor was finally going to follow the proper procedure. Incredibly, he didn't. Totally ignoring Key's instructions, Pearson began questioning Cumberland once again about the autopsy without first establishing how Ronda's body had gotten to the crime lab.

"Objection," said an amused Chestnut.

Judge Key stared at Pearson. "Overruled," he said. "Let's get on with it!"

Minutes later Pearson tried to introduce a photograph taken during the autopsy. Chestnut objected. Because Pearson had never established the chain of custody, the defense attorney argued, any additional evidence he wanted to introduce about the actual autopsy was tainted. Judge Key banged his gavel.

"Overruled," he said. "Let's proceed."

Now it was Chestnut's turn to become peeved.

"Not only did we have Ted Pearson to deal with," he later said. "We also had Judge Key doing everything he could to help the prosecution."

Chapter 28

Judge Robert E. Lee Key was a native Alabamian with a thick accent and pure white hair. His great-grandfather had owned a plantation and thirty slaves. His grandfather had been in the Sixth Alabama Infantry of the Army of the Confederacy, which had fought in nearly every major battle of the Civil War. His father had been superintendent of schools in Evergreen and had named his son in memory of the Confederacy's greatest general. Key considered himself a Southern gentleman of high moral character. During World War II, when he was serving in China, the navy gave him $1 million in cash to deliver to a remote military outpost. It was the payroll for the entire post, and Key carried it several hundred miles across China hidden in the lining of his coat. When someone later asked him if he had considered, even for one second, stealing the money, Key replied honestly that the thought had never entered his mind.

During a brief recess on the second day of the murder trial, Karen Kelly sent the judge a note asking for permission to visit Johnny D. in private that night at the jail. Judge Key knew Kelly. He had presided over her divorce, and he could still recall the love letters she had written to her black lover and how she and Johnny D. had both lied under oath about their affair. The judge considered Kelly's love letters pornographic and her repugnant. Neither the prosecution nor the defense was aware that he had been the judge in Kelly's nasty divorce, but Key did not think that mattered. He had lived all his life in the same judicial district where he now administered the law, and it was not unusual for him to know the defendants who came into his courtroom. In his own mind, he was satisfied that he could be impartial.

"You tell that woman that she is not to show her face in this courthouse," Key instructed his bailiff. "If she does, I'll throw her in jail."

The bailiff explained that Kelly had been subpoenaed as a witness by both sides, even though she had not yet been called to testify. She was required to report each morning to a room where witnesses were being sequestered during the trial. Key had no choice but to let her into the building. "Okay," the judge replied, "but you make certain that woman is not allowed to communicate with the defendant in private under any circumstances."

When the trial resumed later that day, the prosecution called Bill Hooks, Jr. He took the witness stand looking even more terrified than Joe Hightower had been. Pearson coaxed Hooks through his testimony, and the jurors listened intently as he told in often wretched English how he had spotted Johnny D.'s truck parked outside Jackson Cleaners and had seen Myers and Johnny D. leave the building and speed away.

"What kind of truck was it?" Pearson asked.

"It was low down to the ground," Hooks replied, "with chrome rims on it. . . ."

Pearson asked Hooks to tell the jury when he had first told the police about what he had seen. "That very night," Hooks declared. He testified about his being arrested for urinating in public on the evening of the murder, and that he had tried to tell the police when he got to the jail about what he had seen at the cleaners, but no one had believed him. Pearson knew that the defense would claim that Hooks was lying about Johnny D. to collect a reward, so he quickly pointed out that on the night of the murder no rewards had been offered. Those had come later. Pearson also emphasized that Hooks had told the police within twenty-four hours of the murder that he had seen a white man with burns on his face and a black man he called John Dozier fleeing the cleaners. He had to be telling the truth, the prosecutor concluded. How else could he have identified two men on the very night of the murder who were dead ringers for the suspects arrested six months later?

Before the trial began, Chestnut and Boynton had agreed that they would take turns cross-examining witnesses. Boynton had drawn Hooks, and for the next half hour he asked Hooks to recount his story in excruciating detail. Trying to catch him in a lie, he failed. Hooks repeated his story flawlessly and thereby got a second opportunity to stress to the jury what he had seen. Switching tactics, Boynton tried to ridicule Hooks, but this too seemed to work in the witness's favor. Boynton was coming across as a bully, while Hooks gained sympathy. Again Boynton changed his approach. He asked Hooks the name of the investigator who had interviewed him on the night of the murder. Hooks didn't know. Was there anyone at the police station who could verify that he had been interviewed that night? Hooks said he had talked to several deputies and investigators, but only one had taken his story seriously. Ironically, that deputy was Hooks's cousin.

"What is your cousin's name?" Boynton asked.

"I don't know. . . ."

"He is your cousin but you don't know what his name is?"

"No sir. All I know—his first name is Robert—I don't know his last name. . . . I didn't even know he was my cousin until he told me he was some kin to me. . . ."

". . . Can you describe the way he looked?"

"No sir, I can't describe him. . . ."

"You can't describe your own cousin?"

"I done told you, I ain't knowed Mr. Robert was my cousin until I went to the jailhouse that night."

Boynton looked at the jury and grinned. Hooks could not remember the name of the investigator who had interviewed him at the jail. What proof did the court actually have that he had spoken to anyone that night about the murder? Furthermore, Hooks could not describe what his own cousin looked like, yet he claimed that he could positively identify two men whom he had seen only for a few seconds as he was driving past Jackson Cleaners. When Boynton looked at the jurors' faces, he sensed that he had finally found a weakness in Hooks's testimony. The defense was scoring points. But then an unexpected thing happened. In a voice that was clear, eloquent, and loud enough to resonate throughout the courtroom, Hooks defended himself. "The only thing I can do," he said, "is just tell the truth exactly like I see it. Don't add nothing to it, don't take nothing away, and that is what I been doing—just telling the truth."

Boynton sat down and Pearson called the state's next witness: Ralph Myers.

Unlike Hooks and Hightower, Myers strutted in with a cocky grin. With little prompting, he told the jury that he had driven Johnny D. to Jackson Cleaners on the morning of the murder and had waited patiently outside the building for around forty minutes while Johnny D. was inside. He said he had rushed into the cleaners as soon as he heard "popping noises—like firecrackers."

"When I got in, I observed a girl laying on the floor of the lobby," he said softly.

"Can you describe what she looked like?"

"Well, not really clearly, I cannot, but there was a young girl laying on the floor and it looked like her mouth was about half open and half closed."

Bertha Morrison, who was sitting in the front row, began to cry. Charles Morrison tried to comfort her. Judge Key announced that it was nearly noon and a good time to break for lunch. As soon as the jurors were safely out of the courtroom, Chestnut sprang to his feet. "I would like the court to declare a mistrial," he said. Nodding toward Bertha Morrison, he explained that several jurors had noticed her emotional outburst and that had clearly made them feel prejudice against his client. Key looked angry. "I didn't hear anything," he said. But even if Mrs. Morrison had sobbed out loud, he added, he was not going to punish her for it. Under Alabama law, a victim's family could sit at the prosecutor's table if it wished, and Key said he saw nothing improper about a mother's shedding tears for her murdered child. With a bang of his gavel, he emptied the courtroom for lunch.

That afternoon Myers continued with his description of what had happened inside the cleaners. With much drama, he told how he had seen a white man hiding in the back room, and he gave a word-for-word account of how Johnny D. and this mysterious "third man" had debated whether or not they should kill him. Finally he recalled how he had been sent out to wait in Johnny D.'s truck for several minutes and how, when Johnny D. came outside, the two of them had tried to speed away, only to have the truck stall in the driveway and require Johnny D. to open the hood and fix it. Myers was clearly enjoying himself, and Pearson was satisfied when he sat down with how well Myers's testimony had gone.

It was now Chestnut's job to prove that Myers was lying.

"Are you a truthful person?" he asked.

"Yes, I am," Myers replied.

". . . Didn't you give the police two different statements?" asked the attorney, referring to his confessions on June 9 and September 14.

"That's right, I did," Myers answered candidly.

Chestnut pointed out that in the first statement, Myers vehemently denied that he had ever been inside the store. In the second one, he admitted that he had hurried into the lobby. "So you lied in the first statement?" Chestnut concluded.

"One statement was almost completely the truth," Myers replied. "The other was the whole truth."

"Does 'almost completely the truth' amount to a lie?" Chestnut countered.

"Not by my definition," said Myers. "A lie is telling something that didn't happen or telling something that is not true. I simply did not tell the whole truth the first time around."

For more than an hour Chestnut and Myers argued back and forth about his testimony, but the veteran attorney did not catch him in any perceptible lies. Having failed at that, Chestnut tried ridicule. He suggested that Myers's testimony was nonsensical—at one point, Myers had said that he had barely known Johnny D., yet he claimed that the defendant had invited him on a robbery that had ended in murder.

"Mr. Myers," Chestnut said, ". . . you were an eyewitness right after the murder of this young lady—you saw Johnny D. and this white man inside the cleaners . . . and you are telling us that they both let you leave the cleaners alive? Just walk out? That is your testimony?"

"Yes," Myers replied solemnly. "That is my testimony."

Chestnut shook his head in disbelief, but Myers didn't flinch, and the defense attorney knew he was losing ground. He thought for a moment about what he should try next and came up with an idea. Myers had told the police in his September 14 statement that Johnny D. had given Karen Kelly the .25 caliber pistol used in the murder and that she had later shown it to him. Although the police had questioned Kelly and searched through her belongings, they had been unable to find the murder weapon, and when they confronted Myers he admitted that he had been lying to them about the gun. Obviously if he had lied to the police once, he might also have been lying when he claimed that he had gone inside the cleaners and seen Johnny D. standing over Ronda's body. Chestnut decided to quiz Myers about the handgun.

Much to his surprise, Myers admitted before the jury that he had lied to the police about the gun. He said he had been trying to get Kelly into trouble because he was angry at her. His admission was a small victory for the defense, but Chestnut believed it was an important one. If nothing else, he had gotten Myers to acknowledge that he had lied to get someone else in trouble. Chestnut ended his cross-examination.

Assistant prosecutor Stuart shot from her chair. "I have a few follow-up questions for the witness," she announced. "Who is this Karen Kelly?"

Chestnut felt queasy. He had mentioned Kelly's name, and now the prosecution was going to take advantage of it.

"The best I can answer, Karen Kelly was a friend of Mr. McMillian," Myers replied.

"And can you describe her?"

This was the question Chestnut and Boynton had most feared. Chestnut began to rise to his feet, but before he could object Myers answered, "Why, she is a white woman."

"And was she his girlfriend?" Stuart asked.

"Yeah, at one time . . ."

"Objection!" Chestnut shouted. "Objection! This is hearsay."

". . . She was a girlfriend?" Stuart repeated at the same moment that Chestnut was voicing his objection.

"Yeah," said Myers before Judge Key could rule. "She was."

"Sustained," said Key. But it was too late. The prosecution had made its point without having to risk calling Kelly as a witness. The jury had now been told that Johnny D., a married black man, had a white girlfriend. "Nothing further, Your Honor," said Stuart.

For the prosecution, everything was going better than Pearson had expected. Joe Hightower had testified that he had seen Johnny D.'s truck parked at the cleaners. Hooks had testified that he had seen Johnny D. and Myers fleeing the cleaners. Myers had testified that he had driven Johnny D. to the cleaners and had seen him standing over Ronda's corpse in the lobby. On that evidence alone, Pearson figured a jury would convict Johnny D., but there was even more. The prosecution had been able to let the jury know that Johnny D. was a drug dealer and that he had a white girlfriend even though he was married.

The prosecution had also gotten a big boost because Chestnut and Boynton had failed to point out several glaring inconsistencies in the testimony. No one had ever asked Myers how it was possible for him to have seen Ronda lying faceup in the lobby when her body had been found lying prone in the northeast corner of the building, where she had fallen after being shot. Nor had Chestnut or Boynton pointed out that Myers and Hooks had described the getaway as if it were two different events. Hooks testified that Johnny D. and Myers had walked out of the cleaners together and had "speeded away" in the truck. Myers said he came out first, waited two or three minutes for Johnny D., and then was so flustered when they were ready to drive off that he had caused the engine to stall.

Furthermore, the defense had failed to notice that Myers's testimony had not matched what he had said in his September 14 statement about seeing Johnny D. stuffing "wads and wads" of cash into a brown satchel. This was bound to have raised questions in the jury box, because no one knew of any evidence indicating there were large sums of cash at the cleaners. In court Myers had carefully edited his story. There was no mention of wads of cash. Instead he suggested that Johnny D. had been carrying a .25 caliber pistol in the satchel.

For a second Pearson debated whether or not he should call Karen Kelly as a witness. But he couldn't think of a thing she could add, and there were plenty of ways she could hurt the state's case. Pearson decided he was done. The prosecution rested its case.

Chestnut looked at Johnny D. and forced a smile. "I knew our man was going to go down unless we came up with something pretty spectacular," he said later. "I also knew that we didn't have anything spectacular to put on."

Chapter 29

Minnie McMillian was worried. She was about to testify, and no one had told her what to say or do. Neither Boynton nor Chestnut had interviewed her beforehand. What if she said the wrong thing? Wasn't an attorney supposed to know what his witnesses were going to say before he called them? On television they always did. As she walked toward the witness chair, her hands began to sweat and her heart pounded. Why did she have to be the first defense witness?

Boynton gently led her through the events of the morning of the murder. Minnie chose her words carefully. She spoke slowly. Jimmy Hunter had come to the house around seven A.M. and gotten Johnny D. out of bed so that they could repair the transmission in the pickup. Everline Smith had called and then had come over and started cooking for the fish fry. Minnie said Johnny D. had left the yard only once. At nine-thirty he had gone to fetch a pot to cook fish in, but it was rusty. He had been gone only about five minutes, and he had driven in a car because the pickup was on blocks.

"What makes you certain that this . . . occurred on the same date that Ronda Morrison was killed?" Boynton asked.

"Well, for one thing, Mr. Ernest Welch came out there to pick up my momma's furniture money and he comes the first of every month. He have never missed the first since Momma has been dealing with him." Minnie explained that Welch was a bill collector for Hainje's Furniture and that her mother lived in a house behind hers. "Jimmy Hunter and Johnny D. was out there working on the truck and Mr. Welch stopped out there where they were and he said, 'My niece just got killed up there a while ago up there at the cleaners.' "

Boynton sat down. Minnie took a deep breath. He really hadn't asked her many questions at all. So far, so good, she thought. She braced herself for Pearson's cross-examination.

"Now you say Mr. Ernest Welch came out there?" Pearson began.

"Right," she answered cautiously.

"You remember because he always came on the first of the month?"

"Right," she said, and then she decided to elaborate, thinking that he might be trying to trick her. "I ain't talking about I remember him because he came—because he came on the first. I say I remember him because he the one that came and told them about the girl getting killed. . . ."

"Are you just positive it was on this day that Johnny D. . . . was home all day?"

"I sure am," she replied confidently. "It ain't every day somebody get murdered. I remember."

Much to Minnie's shock and relief, Pearson said he had no more questions. As she walked from the witness chair, she decided that testifying had not been as difficult as she had feared.

The defense called Jimmy Hunter, and he repeated the same story Minnie had told. He too recalled seeing Welch. "I have an account with Hainje's Furniture, and the guy that picks up my payment, he came by there that day. He seen my car out there and I told him, I said, 'I haven't been to the bank yet but maybe I will come by there Monday . . . and pay you,' and then he asked me, he say, 'You heard about what happened this morning? . . . My niece got killed up there at Jackson Cleaners."

Changing subjects, Boynton reminded the jury that Hightower and Hooks had both described Johnny D.'s truck as a low-rider. He asked Hunter if the truck was a low-rider in November 1986, when Ronda was murdered.

"No, it wasn't. . . . He had the work did in April or May . . . in 1987 . . ."

"To make it a low-rider? That was done in '87?"

"Yeah. It sure was. Not until then."

On cross-examination, Pearson ignored Hunter's revelation about the truck and instead focused again on Welch. Was Hunter absolutely positive that the bill collector had come by the McMillians' house that morning?

"Yes sir, he was there," said Hunter.

Pearson had no further questions.

Chestnut and Boynton were becoming suspicious. Why was the prosecutor so interested in whether or not Welch had been at Johnny D.'s house?

The defense called a neighbor of the McMillians, who said he too had seen Johnny D. at home that Saturday. Then Everline Smith testified that she had seen him at the house all that morning. She added that Welch had stopped by too, as well as two other white men. They identified themselves as police officers, she explained. "They said they were FBI . . . but I don't know who they were."

That surprised Pearson. "FBI? Did these people who said they were the FBI show you any FBI identification?"

"No," Smith replied, "but they were there that day. I seen them! They stopped for a minute and then left."

The defense called two more witnesses, who both said they had seen Johnny D. at home working on his truck. That brought the total number of alibi witnesses to six. Minnie had tracked down each of them and had asked them to testify. All but one were relatives. Chestnut and Boynton thought six was enough.

For a few seconds the two defense attorneys whispered between themselves, trying to decide whether or not they needed to call Karen Kelly as a witness. The prosecution had already made it clear that she was Johnny D.'s white girlfriend, so that damage was done; and Kelly had promised them that if she was called, she would accuse Benson, Ikner, and Tate of pressuring her to lie. They decided against it. It would not be worth the risk. It would be obvious from her answers that she still loved Johnny D., and that would make her testimony suspect to the jury. Besides, Kelly was so unpredictable that there was no way to know in advance what she might claim once she took the stand.

That left only one more defense witness: Johnny D. himself. Chestnut glanced at the clock on the wall behind Judge Key. It was late in the afternoon. They told the judge they were ready to quit for the day. A few hours later the two attorneys met with Johnny D. in the jail to review their defense. He was eager to take the stand, but Chestnut was against it. What good would it do? he asked. Johnny D. wouldn't be able to say anything that Minnie and the five other witnesses had not already said. "If the jury didn't believe them," said Chestnut, "what makes you think they will believe you?" There was also a risk. If he testified, Pearson could ask him all sorts of potentially embarrassing questions, particularly about Kelly. "I'm against you getting up there," Chestnut concluded. Johnny D. glanced at Boynton, who nodded in agreement. "It's not worth it," said Chestnut. "Trust me."

The next morning Boynton announced that the defense was resting without calling any additional witnesses. Prosecutor Pearson was stunned. "I just couldn't believe that they were not going to put their man on the stand," he said later. Pearson knew, of course, that a defendant is not required to testify. Nothing in the law requires it. In fact, the jury would be specifically told by the judge when he issued his final set of instructions that the accused should not be penalized for remaining silent. But Pearson had learned during his long tenure as a prosecutor that jurors always expected a defendant to testify. "I knew right then and there that Johnny D. was going to be convicted. A jury wants to hear an accused man say, 'Hey, I didn't do it.' "

Pearson told Judge Key that the prosecution wanted to call one rebuttal witness. Key nodded, and Pearson called out the name: Ernest Welch. Chestnut and Boynton spun around and watched as a portly white man in his early forties made his way through the courtroom. Suddenly they understood what was happening. During his questioning of their witnesses, Pearson had been setting the stage for just this moment. Obviously he knew something they didn't. Pearson reminded the jury that every one of Johnny D.'s alibi witnesses had testified that Welch had been at the McMillians' house on the morning of the murder. That was why they were so certain that the fish fry was on the same day.

"Did you go to Johnny D.'s house on that Saturday?" Pearson asked.

"No sir," Welch said.

"And are you positive of that?"

"I am positive."

Welch said he always collected furniture payments on the first day of the month, just as Minnie McMillian had testified, because many of the poorer customers of Hainje's Furniture received their welfare checks on the first and he wanted to get the money they owed the store before the checks were spent. But Welch explained that the government always mails welfare checks *one day early* if the first of the month falls on a

Saturday. The first day of November 1986, he continued, was a Saturday, so he had gone to the McMillians' house on Friday, October 31—not on Saturday.

Pearson asked Welch if he had given Minnie's mother a receipt, and the bill collector handed him two thick books. Both contained records that showed she had paid Welch $42 in cash on October 31, 1986, the day *before* the murder.

". . . You are absolutely positive you did not see Mr. McMillian or Mr. Hunter on that Saturday?" Pearson asked.

"I am positive," Welch declared.

Pearson sat down triumphantly. He had made all Johnny D.'s alibi witnesses look as if they were lying. Minnie was dazed. Why did his records show he had been there the day before? Suddenly she realized that she had made a terrible error during her testimony. She had said that Welch had come to her house on Saturday to collect money from her mother. But that was wrong. The receipt book was correct, but so was she. Welch had been there on Friday *and* on Saturday too! On Friday he had stopped to collect from her mother. But he had also stopped on Saturday to talk to Jimmy Hunter and collect his payment. There was no receipt to confirm that visit because Hunter had been broke and had not paid it—he had suggested that he stop by the store later in the week to do that. In near panic, Minnie tried to explain to Chestnut and Boynton what had happened. Although the two men listened to her whispering, she wasn't sure either really understood the significance of what she was saying.

"Was Ronda Morrison your niece?" Chestnut asked Welch during the cross-examination. He wanted the jury to realize that Welch was related to the Morrisons and therefore could be a biased witness.

"Yes sir," said Welch. His wife was Bertha Morrison's sister.

Chestnut then grilled Welch about how the store kept its books, particularly the receipt books. It sounded as if Chestnut was trying to imply that the books could have been doctored, but Welch assured him that there were too many safeguards for them to have been changed.

Was it possible that he had stopped at the McMillian house on both Friday and Saturday? Chestnut asked, finally getting around to Minnie's point.

"No," said Welch flatly. On Saturday he had been on the west side of Monroeville collecting money. The McMillians lived on the east side. He had never gone near their house that day. Chestnut rephrased his question. He was trying to get Minnie's explanation into the court record.

"There was some testimony, Mr. Welch, that on November first you did not come to the McMillian household to collect from the McMillians, but in fact, you had passed the house, saw Jimmy Hunter, turned around, and came back to collect from him," Chestnut continued. "That is not true?"

"That is not true," said Welch. "No."

". . . There is the testimony of at least two, maybe more, persons here on their oath that they saw you at the McMillian house on the Saturday in question," said Chestnut, his voice firm. "All of these people are mistaken about that?"

"I guess so, because I wasn't there."

Once again Chestnut reminded Welch that six witnesses had said they had seen him at the house on Saturday. Why was he so certain he had not stopped there on the morning of the murder? Welch said again that he had not been there.

Frustrated, Chestnut sat down.

Prosecutor Pearson and assistant prosecutor Stuart divided up their closing statement. Stuart's summation was brief and stuck to the facts. How could anyone doubt that Johnny D. was guilty? she asked. Two witnesses had seen him leaving the building; the third had seen him standing over the dead victim.

Defense attorney Bruce Boynton spoke next and tried to undercut Stuart's remarks. The police had found no physical evidence that linked Johnny D. to the crime, he declared: "Fingerprints—we no got!" He then attacked the credibility of the state's witnesses. Hooks and Hightower were testifying, he charged, because they hoped to collect some of the $18,000 reward, and added that both had been caught lying. They had described Johnny D.'s truck as a low-rider, but according to Jimmy Hunter's testimony, at the time of the murder it had still been a standard pickup truck. Ernest Welch was Ronda's uncle and was surely put under tremendous pressure from family members not to do anything to help Johnny D. The attorney did not comment on Ralph Myers. He was leaving him for Chestnut. Instead he began praising the defense's witnesses. All six of them were decent, law-abiding folks who were not the type to lie, and all had testified that Johnny D. had been home that entire Saturday morning.

Once Boynton finished, Chestnut rose from the defense table. "Ralph Myers is lying," he said. "His testimony doesn't make sense. . . ." He reminded jurors that Johnny D. lived only a few miles from Monroeville, yet Myers had testified that the two of them had met at a car wash in Evergreen some thirty miles away. "What fool, what retarded fool, would set out to rob a cleaners on a busy Saturday morning in a small town like Monroeville . . . and then drive all the way over to Evergreen to get an additional witness to take to the robbery? . . . People getting ready to rob don't go about adding additional witnesses to the act."

Having made that one specific point, Chestnut launched into an hourlong diatribe about the evils of racism and about various miscarriages of justice in Alabama that he had encountered during his career. He talked mostly about himself, but also about how wonderful a judge Robert E. Lee Key was. He even complimented Ted Pearson—but he said nothing further about the accused. Finally he apologized to the jury. He and Boynton, he explained, should have brought in other alibi witnesses besides people related to Johnny D. They should have brought in records that proved Johnny D.'s truck had been converted into a lowrider six months after the murder rather than relying solely on Hunter's testimony. They should have found and identified the two white FBI agents who Everline Smith insisted had stopped at the fish fry. "We ought to have got them in here and I'm hot because we didn't," he shouted. And then, pointing a finger at Pearson, Chestnut added, "but he ought to have had them here too!" The prosecution, he argued, should have done a better job investigating the murder, because if it had, the police would have discovered that Johnny D. was innocent.

Chestnut looked as if he were about to sit down, but he decided to take one final jab at the prosecution. "They say 'practicing law,' " he said slowly. "After all these years, I'm not practicing. . . ." Shooting a glance at Pearson and Stuart, Chestnut added sharply, "Ted and them practices law, but I *know* what I am doing."

Several blacks in the gallery laughed, and Judge Key banged his gavel. "Some of you might think this is funny," he warned. "But it is not funny. . . ."

Unlike Chestnut, Pearson spoke succinctly. He began by recalling what a lovely teenager and daughter Ronda had been. He then offered an answer to Chestnut's question about "what sort of fool" robs a store on a busy Saturday morning. "The defendant very likely did not go there with the intent to rob somebody," Pearson theorized. Although he couldn't be certain why Johnny D. had gone to Jackson Cleaners, Pearson suggested it probably had something to do with drugs. But why he had gone there was not really important. All that mattered was what had happened at the store after Johnny D. walked in there.

"What did Johnny D. see?" Pearson asked. "I think he saw Ronda Morrison there in the bathroom. You saw the condition of her clothes. Pants half down, blouse unbuttoned. Did he decide he was going to take advantage of that pretty young lady? You saw what she looked like."

Pearson then offered the jury his scenario of what had occurred, and it proved amazingly simple: A black man had gone into the cleaners, where he had spotted a beautiful white teenage girl half undressed in the bathroom. He had been overcome with lust and had attacked her. Ronda had been alive at ten-fifteen A.M., Pearson said. She was found dead shortly after ten-forty-five. "That is about a thirty-minute period." There was plenty of time for Johnny D. to attempt a rape, particularly since he had Myers standing guard outside the building.

Chestnut and Boynton seethed as they listened. They both believed Pearson was intentionally hitting the hottest of all race-baiting buttons by implying that black men, if given the chance, would rape white girls. As he neared the end of his speech, Pearson acknowledged that Johnny D. was not required by law to testify. "That is his right," he said. "But there is one person . . . who doesn't have any rights. She is laying in her grave now . . ." He paused and looked directly at the jury. "The evidence is abundant that Johnny D. is the guilty party. Only you, only you . . . can say . . . we, as civilized people, we don't tolerate this kind of behavior." Glancing at Johnny D., the prosecutor uttered only one more word: "*Animals!*"

At two o'clock the jury began its deliberations.

Chapter 30

As soon as they were alone in the jury room, one of the men said he thought Johnny D. was guilty. Several others quickly agreed. Only one juror felt uncomfortable with what was being said. "Shouldn't we choose a foreman before we discuss the case?" Doris Hansen asked. She was white, forty-six, had four children, ran her own flower shop, and was a self-described nut about following procedure.

"Why don't you just do it?" another juror asked her. "We already know how everyone feels."

Hansen insisted that they vote for foreman by secret ballot. No one had any paper, so they took some from a copying machine in the corner. She tore a piece into several neat strips, and everyone took one. She was elected, even though she had written down someone else's name. That struck her as funny. She had not even expected to be on this jury. She and her husband lived next door to David Whetstone, the Baldwin County district attorney. They were friends, and she had figured she would be disqualified as soon as the defense found out they were neighbors. But no one had asked her. Another juror's father was a cop. He hadn't expected to be chosen either. As they talked, the jurors decided that Chestnut and Boynton hadn't done a very good job of screening them.

Hansen insisted that everyone discuss the case, though they had already said Johnny D. was guilty. She didn't think it was right for them to hurry back into the courtroom so quickly. The jurors agreed, but rather than discussing the evidence, most talked about how poor a job the defense had done. "All of us realized that these black ladies were simply lying about this fish fry to create an alibi," Hansen remembered later. "The furniture man said he wasn't there that Saturday morning, and his records proved that. What we couldn't figure out was why these witnesses got up there and told such an obvious lie and why their attorneys let every one of them say it. Didn't they know the furniture man was going to testify? We decided those attorneys were just not too bright."

Though it wasn't supposed to matter, several jurors grumbled about Johnny D.'s not testifying. "I thought, 'Gosh, if someone accused me of doing something like that and I had six ladies who were just proven to be lying, wouldn't I come back with some sort of rebuttal and defend myself?' " Hansen said. "We would have liked to have heard him say he was innocent. And when he didn't, well, we all figured we knew why."

None of them believed Johnny D. had gone to the cleaners to rob it, though he was accused of committing a murder during an armed robbery. They figured he had gone there to make a drug deal. "We kept wondering why the owner of that place was never called to testify." The fact that Hooks and Hightower were scared convinced them drugs were involved: "That little Hooks boy was so terrified, you just had to know that Johnny D. was a dangerous man." Judge Key had told them to disregard Hightower's comment about buying marijuana from Johnny D., "but how could we?"

After an hour or so of discussion, Hansen suggested they vote by secret ballot. The results were unanimous. Wanting to make certain she had done everything correctly, Hansen polled each juror. One by one, each said Johnny D. was the killer, including both black jurors. As they started back into the courtroom, Hansen tucked the twelve slips of paper marked "guilty" into her purse. She had saved every birthday, Mother's Day, and other holiday card her children had given her. She thought Bertha Morrison might want to have the ballots as a keepsake.

At 4:42 P.M., Judge Key called the court back into session and warned the spectators that he would deal harshly with anyone who reacted emotionally either by clapping or booing. When the jury entered the courtroom, Key had his bailiff retrieve the written verdict slip. Hansen was relieved. She didn't want to have to stand up and read it. She was afraid that Johnny D. and his supporters might try to come after her later. The sheriff's department had told the jurors it would give each of them a ride home if they were afraid. Key read their decision: "We, the jury, find the defendant guilty of the capital offense of murder during robbery in the first degree."

Hansen felt happy for Charles and Bertha Morrison. She looked over at them. Everyone on the jury had seen Bertha when she broke down and sobbed. They felt sorry for her. But Hansen was afraid to look at Johnny D. She didn't want him to remember what she looked like. Judge Key explained that the first part of the trial was now over. Now the jury had to decide whether it would recommend life in prison for Johnny D. or the death penalty. He asked the prosecution if it wanted to call anyone to testify. A prosecutor will often put someone from the victim's family on the witness stand to demand an eye for an eye, but Pearson said he didn't wish to call anyone. Key asked the defense, and Chestnut said he had only one witness. He was calling the defendant.

Johnny D. was irritated. He now wished he had ignored his attorneys' advice and testified earlier. As soon as he was sworn in, he began to explain that he was innocent and didn't even know Ralph Myers. Judge Key interrupted. "I don't want to cut you off," he said, "but we are not going to try this case again." If Johnny D. wished to ask for mercy, then he could admit his guilt and beg for forgiveness, but the jury had already decided that he was a murderer and there was no point in arguing about that now. Johnny D. didn't know what to say, and Chestnut too seemed unsure about what to do next.

"Wait a minute," Chestnut said, and then, after whispering to Boynton, he announced, "Your Honor, that is all."

Johnny D. didn't move. He wanted to tell everyone that he was innocent and that this entire trial was one big mistake, but he didn't know how. Judge Key asked Pearson if he had any questions for Johnny D., and the prosecutor said he didn't. Johnny D. was dumbfounded. Everything seemed to be whirling past. The jury didn't know anything about him, how he had always been a hard worker, how he had tried to provide a good life for his family, how he had started his own business, how he loved to play basketball: His hopes, his dreams, his past meant nothing. A jury of complete strangers was about to decide whether or not he should live or die based entirely on what Hooks, Hightower, and Myers had said about him. As he walked toward the defense table, he thought about standing still and screaming out, "Stop! Wait a minute! Let me explain!" Instead he sat down quietly.

Jury foreman Hansen also felt frustrated. For three days the jury had waited to hear Johnny D. explain what had actually happened inside the cleaners. She had dozens of questions. Had Myers told the truth? None of the jurors had been sure. Had the two men gone into the cleaners because of drugs? Most of all, why had he had to *kill* Ronda? Was he afraid she would identify him or be angry because she had spurned his sexual advances? Hansen felt angry herself. She and the others deserved to know!

Judge Key announced that each side would now make a closing statement, beginning with Pearson. "Ladies and gentlemen, this is a cruel crime, an especially cruel crime," he said in a soft voice. "This victim was a young lady just starting out in life . . ." For several minutes Pearson talked about Ronda. He wanted to make certain the jury understood that she was an important person whose life mattered, not some faceless victim. Several times he turned and pointed at Johnny D. He knew that if he were shy about labeling him a killer, they would be reluctant to seek his death. "Ronda died a lonely death laying on the floor of that Laundromat in the dirt . . . her last breath perhaps choked with the dirt on that floor, caused by that man right there . . . ," he said. "He didn't have to kill her. He didn't have to kill her. He did *not* have to kill her. He could have gotten what he wanted without harming that lady a bit, but no, he consciously chose to snuff out her life, just like you blow out a candle . . ."

By the time Pearson finished, most of the white women in the courtroom were crying, and many of the white men had tears in their eyes. The blacks sat stony-faced, staring straight ahead.

Chestnut spoke next. "A day will come, a morning will come . . . it is always some ungodly hour . . . the moment of an execution . . . and I will be sitting in my office by the telephone . . . and I will be at the eleventh hour trying to save McMillian's life. And the reason I will be trying to do that goes far beyond any legal duty, any duty imposed on me by laws created by man. I do that because I understand that capital punishment is a misnomer. Death transcends punishment." Chestnut quoted scripture and spoke about how only God has the right to decide who lives and who dies. Only once did he mention Johnny D. He attacked the death penalty and talked about how hard he had fought against it in previous cases.

Back in the jury room, Hansen handed out slips of paper for another

Slaughter of an Innocent

Ronda Morrison, in her graduation photograph. (COURTESY OF CHARLES AND BERTHA MORRISON.)

Charles and Bertha Morrison considered Ronda, their only child, to be a gift from God. The family posed for this portrait shortly before her murder. (COURTESY OF CHARLES AND BERTHA MORRISON.)

Jackson Cleaners. (AUTHOR'S PHOTO.)

Within minutes after finding Ronda's body, sheriff's deputy William Gibson and Monroeville police officer Woodrow Ikner searched for fingerprints on the counter of Jackson Cleaners. Later Gibson himself would wonder if their hasty efforts had destroyed valuable evidence. (STEVE STEWART, *THE MONROE JOURNAL*.)

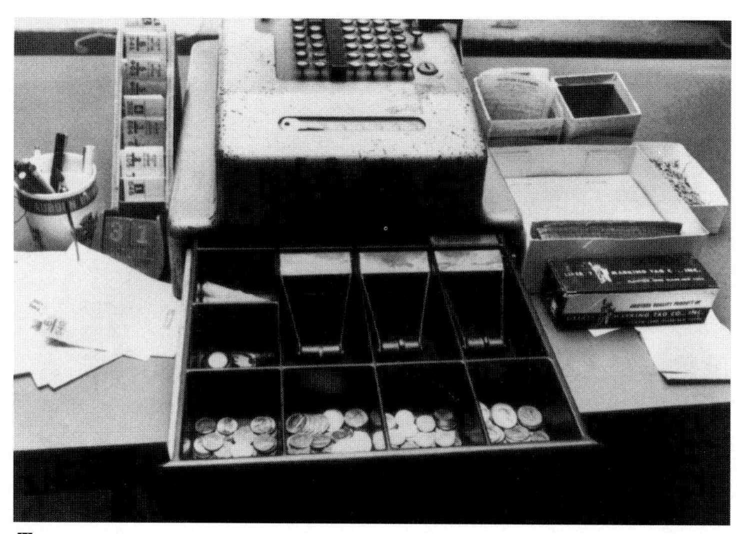

The cash register at the cleaners contained only $100, yet the robber left $25 in coins behind. (STEVE STEWART, *THE MONROE JOURNAL.*)

Monroe County sheriff Thomas Tate liked to describe himself as "a simple country boy," but he quickly shed his easygoing manner after the murder. (AUTHOR'S PHOTO.)

Larry Ikner, in a photograph taken in the early 1980s, knew everyone in Monroe County by name and by reputation, which gave him an edge as the district attorney's chief investigator and troubleshooter. (*THE MONROE JOURNAL.*)

A Second Murder

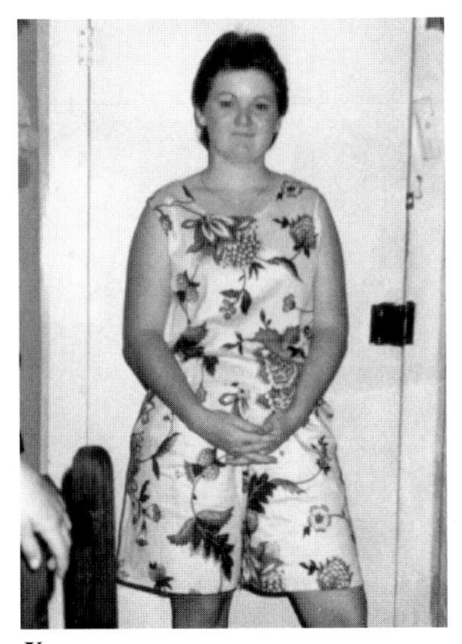

Unlike Ronda Morrison, Vickie Lynn Pittman was considered "white trash," and her murder received short-lived attention until investigators decided that both young women had been killed by the same man. (COURTESY OF KAREN ANN PITTMAN.)

Karen Ann (*left*), David, and Vickie Lynn Pittman in a family portrait taken in the summer of 1986. (COURTESY OF KAREN ANN PITTMAN.)

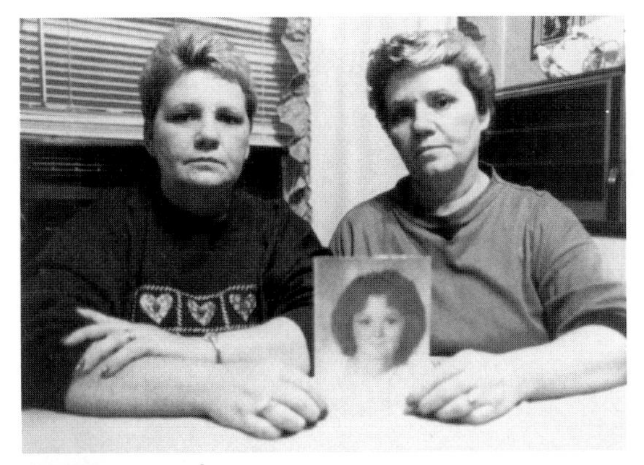

Afraid that local officials were not doing enough to catch Vickie Lynn's killer, twins Onzell Lisenby (*left*) and Mozelle Arrant launched their own probe of their niece's death. Their first suspect was their own brother. (AUTHOR'S PHOTO.)

Vic Pittman was living in the same house with his daughter Vickie Lynn when she disappeared. (AUTHOR'S PHOTO.)

Watched over by her aunts Onzell and Mozelle, Vickie Lynn was buried in a family plot in the Elim Baptist cemetery. Since no one knew precisely when she died, the date on the headstone read Feb. 22-23. (PHOTO BY RUTHOMPSON FOR CLEAR IMAGE PHOTOGRAPHY.)

Karen Kelly pleaded guilty to Vickie Lynn's murder, then claimed she was innocent as she was being taken from the courtroom. (SHIRLIE LOBMILLER.)

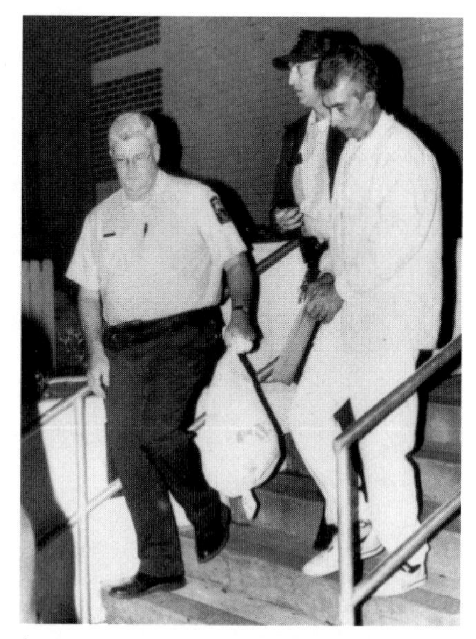

After Ralph Myers, here being escorted from jail, was charged with murdering Vickie Lynn Pittman, he offered to help the police catch Ronda Morrison's killer—and led them to Walter "Johnny D." McMillian. (MARILYN HANDLEY, *THE MONROE JOURNAL*.)

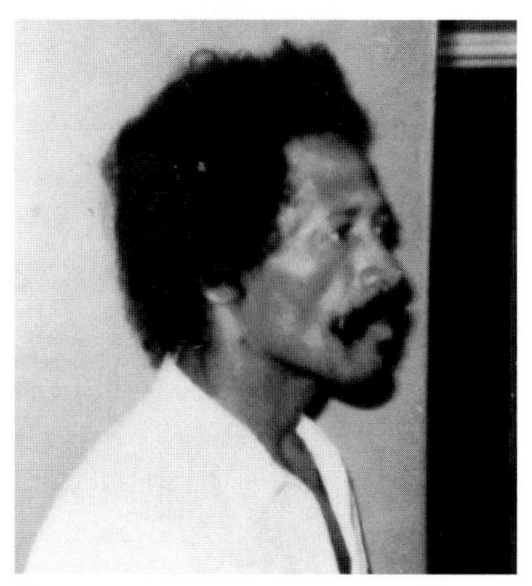

Prosecutors said they could tell by looking at this police mug shot taken of Walter "Johnny D." McMillian that he was involved in criminal activities. (MARILYN HANDLEY, *THE MONROE JOURNAL*.)

Minnie Belle McMillian never doubted her husband was innocent because she had been with him at home on the morning of Ronda's murder. (AUTHOR'S PHOTO.)

When hired by McMillian's family to defend him, attorney J. L. Chestnut boasted that he had defended more black men accused of murder than any other lawyer in Alabama. (AUTHOR'S PHOTO.)

Bruce Boynton served as McMillian's lead defense attorney in his first trial. (AUTHOR'S PHOTO.)

In his closing arguments, Monroe County district attorney Theodore Pearson called McMillian an "animal." (*THE MONROE JOURNAL*.)

Conecuh County sheriff Edwin Booker warned investigators that Ralph Myers was a natural-born liar who could not be trusted to tell the truth about Ronda's murder, but no one listened to him. (AUTHOR'S PHOTO.)

Although Tommy Chapman admitted in private that he had serious misgivings about McMillian's guilt, he felt obligated to defend the conviction vigorously after he succeeded Theodore Pearson as district attorney. (AUTHOR'S PHOTO.)

Black, brilliant, and Harvard-educated, Bryan Stevenson could have gone to work for any number of high-priced New York law firms. Instead, he elected to defend death row inmates for a meager wage. (AUTHOR'S PHOTO.)

Attorney George Elbrecht (*right*) and Alabama Bureau of Investigation agent Simon Benson confer during a court hearing. (MARILYN HANDLEY, *THE MONROE JOURNAL*.)

The Alabama Capital Representation Resource Center team, better known as the death row defenders: Mike O'Connor, Eva Ansley, and Bryan Stevenson. (AUTHOR'S PHOTO.)

ABI investigators Thomas Taylor (*left*) and Thomas Greg Cole were told to reopen the Morrison murder probe after *60 Minutes* raised questions about the case. (ALABAMA DEPARTMENT OF PUBLIC SAFETY PHOTOS.)

After spending six years on death row, Walter "Johnny D." McMillian is released. A smiling Minnie is at the left. (CLAUDE GLADWELL, *THE MONROE JOURNAL.*)

An admirer embraces McMillian moments after he steps outside the Baldwin County courthouse. (ALVIN BENN, *MONTGOMERY ADVERTISER.*)

Walter "Johnny D." McMillian, Minnie, and a beaming Bryan Stevenson. No one from the prosecution or the state ever apologized to McMillian for his wrongful imprisonment. (CLAUDE GLADWELL, *THE MONROE JOURNAL.*)

McMillian was certain on the day of his release that his problems were over, but a jubilant Bryan Stevenson knew better. (ALVIN BENN, *MONTGOMERY ADVERTISER.*)

secret ballot. She repeated what Judge Key had told them. Before the death penalty could be imposed, at least eight people had to vote for it. Otherwise Johnny D. would spend his life in prison with no chance at parole. Hansen read the results of their vote as she opened each slip. "Death . . . Life . . . Death . . ." Five voted to kill him. Seven voted for life. Hansen felt relieved. She had not wanted his execution on her conscience.

After the jury's decision was announced, Judge Key informed the courtroom that it was merely a recommendation. Under Alabama law, he could either accept it or impose his own sentence. He asked Johnny D. if there was anything he wanted to say. He was giving Johnny D. one final chance to beg for mercy.

"I didn't kill that girl," Johnny D. declared. "Me and Ralph Myers ain't been no friends and Ralph Myers never been in my truck, no kind of way. Ralph Myers . . . told some of the biggest lies. Ralph Myers don't know a bit more about me than a man in the moon. . . ." He paused. He was trying to think about what to say next. What could he add that would sway Judge Key?

"Do you have anything else?" Key asked him.

"It's a pity and a shame for an innocent man, hard as I worked, let a man, a tramp like that, put me in the penitentiary for nothing," Johnny D. said. "That ain't right."

Judge Key announced that he would sentence Johnny D. after reviewing a standard investigative report about the defendant and his past that would be prepared by a state probation office. The trial was over. Charles and Bertha Morrison both felt relieved. Their daughter's killer had been caught and convicted and now was going to be punished. Several of their friends nodded their approval and thanked Pearson and Stuart.

As she watched her husband being led away, Minnie fought back tears. Her oldest son, Johnny, took her hand. He was furious. "You're gonna pay for this," he said as he passed Sheriff Tate on the way out of the courtroom.

When Minnie and Johnny got home forty-five minutes later, the telephone was ringing. Minnie thought it was probably a pesky reporter, but she recognized the voice as that of a black deputy sheriff. Sheriff Tate had issued a warrant for her son's arrest. Tate was accusing Johnny of verbally threatening a police officer because of what he had said as he left the courtroom. It would be better, the deputy explained, if Minnie brought Johnny in rather than having a squad car come after him. Minnie drove her son to jail. She was heavily in debt and had no cash for his bond, so she left him there. On the way home she finally broke down. Tears gushed from her eyes. As usual she got angry at herself. Why was she carrying on like this? she wondered. She had known that Johnny D. was going to be found guilty as soon as Welch testified. "Who was going to believe a bunch of blacks when there was one white man saying we was liars?" she later asked. She was scared. She thought she knew what Judge Key was going to do next. She tried to stop crying, but she couldn't.

One month later Johnny D. was taken into the Monroe County Courthouse before Judge Key for sentencing. The judge said he had reviewed the required presentence report. It contained a short biography of Johnny D. and statements by people who knew him. The judge also said that he had studied a Victim Impact Statement filled out by the Morrisons. They had not written much, but the few lines they had jotted down were filled with emotion: "Our life had centered around our daughter. Now that she is gone we have no goal in life." Before filling out the report, the Morrisons had asked their minister at Eastwood Baptist Church what they should do, and he had told them that God required them to forgive Johnny D. and pray for him. God also required them to demand Johnny D.'s execution, the pastor said. God expects justice, and that includes punishment. If the Morrisons asked the court to show Johnny D. mercy, they would be denigrating the "sanctity of life" and committing a sin. With that advice in mind, the Morrisons had written in the report, "This man took our daughter's life and should pay with his own."

Chestnut asked to address the court before Judge Key sentenced Johnny D. No white person had ever been sentenced to death in Monroe County for murdering a black person, he said. He asked Key to consider one question: If Johnny D. were white, would the judge have treated him differently when he sentenced him?

Chestnut's comments irked Key, and he did not bother to reply. Instead he stated that Ronda's murder had been heinous, atrocious, and cruel. "The only appropriate sentence," he declared, "is death by electrocution. . . ."

One last time, Key asked Johnny D. if there was anything he wished to say.

"I am not guilty," Johnny D. replied. "I'd like for the girl's parents to know that I did not kill their daughter. I want them to know that."

Chapter 31

Six weeks after Johnny D. was sentenced to death, Simon Benson arrested Karen Kelly for the murder of Vickie Lynn Pittman. "You used me!" she screamed when he took her to jail in Brewton. "As soon as Johnny D. was out of the way, you came after me."

Mozelle and Onzell were thrilled. They had assumed that Benson had forgotten the case. Mozelle called the courthouse. "When are you going to put Karen Kelly on trial?" she asked prosecutor Michael Godwin. "When are you going to try Ralph Myers and Johnny D.?" The twins were not only seeking vengeance, they wanted answers. They still did not know why Vickie Lynn had been killed. Was it because of a bad drug deal? Did it have something to do with the bank robbery? Had she been kidnapped and held for ransom? Was her father involved? Godwin told Mozelle he had decided to prosecute Kelly and Myers, but since Johnny D. had already been sentenced to death, there was no point in trying him too.

"Well, at least two of them bastards will have to pay for what they've done," Mozelle told her sister.

Karen Kelly's mother couldn't find anyone willing to defend her daughter. After being rejected by nearly a dozen local attorneys, she finally convinced Tommy Chapman, an attorney in Evergreen, to take the case. He agreed because Christmas was coming up and he needed the money. Chapman was thirty-nine and politically ambitious. He already knew a considerable amount about Kelly, her former black lover, and Ralph Myers. In 1986 he had defended Johnny D. after he was arrested for slashing another black man with a knife during a fight outside a nightclub. Chapman's brother, Terry, had sent Johnny D. to him. Terry owned a lumber-cutting business, and Johnny D. had worked for him periodically.

Although he was considered a fairly good trial lawyer, Tommy Chapman's specialty was negotiating plea bargains. He had been born and reared in Evergreen and had been befriended early in his career by Judge Key. The judge had served as his mentor, and the friendship had helped Chapman become established in local legal, social, and political circles. In Johnny D.'s case, Chapman had been able to get the charge reduced and also get his client a suspended sentence and probation. "It was a black-on-black cutting, so it was easy to negotiate," he explained later.

By coincidence, during the same year he defended Johnny D., Chapman was assigned by the court to represent Myers at a sanity hearing. Myers had been arrested by the Evergreen police for his own protection after he jumped in front of a semitrailer truck that barely missed hitting him. He had been trying to kill himself because he and his wife had been arguing. Chapman arranged for Myers to be examined at a state hospital and then released.

Besides Johnny D. and Myers, Chapman also knew the Vic Pittman family. Chapman's mother had been a manager at the motel where Joyce Pittman had worked before her death, and Chapman's father had been counseling Joyce about her alcohol problems. To an outsider this web of connections might seem surprising, but Chapman did not think it odd. Links like these came with being a lawyer in a small town. If an attorney lived in the same place long enough, he joked, there was a good chance that he would end up representing everyone in the entire community in some capacity, sometimes twice.

As soon as Kelly's mother paid a deposit on his fee, Chapman drove to Brewton and met with prosecutor Godwin. What evidence did the state have that Kelly had killed Vickie Lynn? he asked.

Godwin laughed. The murder charge against her was based almost completely on evidence that Kelly had given the ABI against herself. She had admitted in three separate interviews that she had been present at the murder. Of the three, the most damning statement was her June 18 confession to Benson and Sheriff Hawsey. This was the one she had given them while she was high on drugs at the ABI office in Mobile. Chapman skimmed all three.

"She tells a different story in each one of these. Her stories contradict one another, and all she says is she was there," he told Godwin. "She doesn't admit killing anyone. You don't have much of a case."

"There's another witness," Godwin replied. He handed Chapman a typed statement taken from Ralph Myers.

> MYERS: Karen looked like she was high on coke or LSD or something. She was making smart remarks about how it was this girl's time to die. . . . Anyhow it looked like Karen had a knife in her hands . . . Vickie Lynn had been beaten and was in the back of my truck. All the sudden, Karen got on top of Vickie Lynn and started making a motion like if you had a waffle on top of a table and was stabbing a knife in it, that same kind of motion . . .

Chapman tried to brush the statement off. "Myers could be saying this just to get the blame off himself. This isn't much."

Godwin smiled again. "Your client admits that she was there and I believe her. If people lie, they usually lie about *not* being at a murder scene. They don't lie and put themselves at one. Trust me, a jury is going to find her guilty."

Chapman went to see Kelly at the jail. "They're punishing me because I go with niggers," she charged. "I ain't killed that girl." Chapman thought she looked terrible. Her hair was uncombed; her skin was yellow; her hands shook so badly that it looked as if she were suffering from some muscular disorder. Chapman suspected she was in the midst of a drug withdrawal. He told her they would talk later.

Over the next few weeks Chapman met with Kelly several times. Some days she would be articulate and friendly; at other times she would act crazy. One afternoon she mailed him an envelope filled with cockroaches.

"I don't really know if I was even there when they killed that girl," Kelly told him during one of their talks. "I think I was, but I might only believe I was there because Benson and others have told me I was there. I really can't remember. I was using so many drugs back then, I'm not sure of nothing."

Chapman suggested that she be examined by a psychiatrist, and her mother paid for one to interview her, but he couldn't tell whether she was suffering from amnesia or simply lying.

Three weeks before Kelly's murder trial was scheduled to begin, Chapman found a weakness in the prosecutor's case. He had sent Vickie Lynn's autopsy report to a highly regarded pathologist, who decided the teenager had died from blows to her head while being beaten. This was crucial because in his statement Myers had said that Kelly had stabbed Vickie Lynn *after* she had been beaten. That meant Vickie Lynn was already dead by the time she was stabbed, Chapman decided, so it was impossible for his client to have committed a murder. "You can't kill someone twice."

Chapman arranged for Kelly's mother to meet him at the jail. He wanted them both to hear his theory. He also warned them that it might not work, especially if the state's pathologist disagreed about when the girl had died. During their talk Chapman suggested that they use his discovery as a lever to negotiate a plea bargain rather than risk going to trial. If Godwin thought there was a chance that he could lose the case, he might be interested in cutting a deal.

"No way!" Kelly said, but when Chapman began explaining what could happen at a trial she began to weaken. Her past was going to be made public: her drug use, her prostitution, and her affair with Johnny D., a black convicted murderer. Moreover, if she was found guilty there was a good chance that she would be sentenced to life in prison without parole. Did she really think a jury was going to feel sorry for a cocaine addict and whore who had committed adultery with a black man? Chapman asked. Her mother was horrified at the idea of a public trial. Hadn't Kelly caused her family enough shame? "Your son has to grow up in Monroeville," she lectured Karen.

"But I didn't kill that girl," Kelly said, "or if I did, I can't remember it." But half an hour later she gave in. "I agreed to just go ahead and take a deal," she said later, "because I was tired of listening to them. My mom said it was time for me to pay the price for running around with niggers. Maybe some jail time would do me good, she said."

When Chapman met with Godwin the next day, he found the prosecutor eager to negotiate. "Every time I spoke to Ralph Myers," Godwin said later, "he wanted to add a new name to the list of people who had supposedly been at the Pittman murder. He kept changing his story, so I didn't know what Myers might say if and when we finally went to court."

On August 23, 1989, Mozelle and Onzell were told over the telephone that Kelly's trial was being canceled. Instead she was going to plead guilty the next morning at the courthouse. The twins got there early. Both thought they would have a chance at the hearing to tell the judge how they felt about Kelly before she was sentenced. They knew that Charles and Bertha Morrison had been allowed to write down their comments in a Victim Impact Statement, but no one had offered them any such document.

Mozelle wondered if Vic would show up. "You think he still wants to marry her?" she asked spitefully. He wasn't at the courthouse when they arrived.

The twins expected that Godwin would require Kelly to tell the court why she had helped kill their niece. Since they both assumed that she was going to be sentenced to prison for life without parole, it was her explanation that interested them most. They would finally learn the truth.

When Kelly was brought into the courtroom, she looked directly at the sisters. Embarrassed, Onzell turned away, but Mozelle glared at Kelly. She was trying to let Kelly know just how much she hated her. With Chapman standing at her side, Kelly told the judge she wanted to plead guilty. She was ready to admit that she had helped kill Vickie Lynn. In return for her plea, prosecutor Godwin said he was willing to recommend a maximum sentence of ten years for the murder, as well as five more years for the check forgery charge filed against her, which had never been resolved.

"Did he say *ten* years?" Mozelle, stunned, whispered to her sister.

Onzell nodded.

Before either twin could say anything more, the judge banged his gavel and the hearing was over. No one had asked them to speak.

Once again Mozelle turned to Onzell. "Johnny D. is gonna fry for killing Ronda Morrison, but that bitch only gets ten years for killing our Vickie Lynn." She jumped from her seat and marched toward Godwin. "This ain't right," she said, loudly enough for everyone in the courtroom to hear her. "Mike Godwin, you sold us out!"

Kelly glanced over her shoulder as deputies escorted her out of the room. Mozelle was certain she saw Kelly grinning at her, but as soon as Kelly was taken outside the courthouse she broke down in tears and nearly collapsed in front of a local photographer and a newspaper reporter. "I did not kill that girl," she said. "I am innocent."

The next day a deputy called Mozelle. "Karen Kelly wants to see you, but you'll have to get down here quick because she is leaving for prison at three o'clock." Mozelle glanced at her watch. It was one P.M. She called Onzell, and they drove with their mother to the jail, where they were searched for weapons and then taken into a tiny room to wait. Sheriff Hawsey was praying with Karen, they were told. Once he finished she would be brought in to them.

Onzell was scared. "What in the hell are we doing here?" she asked.

"I'm going to make that bitch tell us the truth," replied Mozelle.

Hawsey entered the room. There had been a schedule change, he said. Kelly was going to be taken to prison within the hour. The most time they could have with her would be fifteen minutes. Knowing how quick-tempered Mozelle could be, the sheriff made the sisters promise they would not try to hurt Kelly. He then had a deputy bring Kelly into the room. She sat on the opposite side of a table from the three women. Hawsey told her she could stop the meeting whenever she wished simply by calling to the deputy who would be stationed outside the door. She thanked the sheriff and, as he turned to leave, added that his prayers that morning were really helping her cope.

Mozelle was so irritated that she could barely speak. "My family has walked through a living hell because of you," she said at last. "Now I want to know the truth. What happened to Vickie Lynn? Why was she killed?"

"I didn't really even know your niece," said Kelly, "except that I saw her running with niggers."

Mozelle didn't believe her. "Who killed her?" she demanded. Kelly looked at the three women. She could see that Onzell was terrified. "You deserve to know what really happened," she said, focusing on Onzell and sounding kind. "So I'm going to tell you the truth."

Kelly said she had been walking down the street on the Thursday night when Vickie Lynn had disappeared. Two men in a pickup truck had offered her a ride. Ralph Myers was driving, and Vickie Lynn was sitting between them. Kelly got into the pickup, and the four of them drove into the woods, where they began drinking and smoking dope. Suddenly the two men attacked Vickie Lynn with their fists and then with a pipe. Kelly claimed that she had watched helplessly while Myers and the other man beat Vickie Lynn to death.

"Who was he?" Mozelle asked. "Who was with Ralph? You got to tell us!"

"You really don't want to know," Kelly said coyly.

"Oh yes we do," Mozelle replied.

"Are you sure you can stand the truth?" Kelly asked. She was clearly enjoying this, Mozelle thought.

"You bitch," Mozelle said. "You tell me the truth or you are going to roast in hell no matter how many times you and that sheriff preacher pray."

Kelly smiled at her, just as she had when she was being led from the courtroom. "It was Vic Pittman," she said. "Your brother helped kill his own daughter."

"*Why?*" Mozelle asked. "Why would Vic do that?"

"They killed her," Karen answered without any show of emotion, "because she knew something and she was going to the police with it."

"The bank robbery? Drugs?"

"No," said Kelly. "She knew that Ralph and Vic were the ones who really robbed Jackson Cleaners and killed Ronda Morrison."

Chapter 32

The three women drove from the jail to Onzell's house, where they hurried to check the calendar hanging near the telephone in the kitchen. On November 1, the Saturday when Ronda was murdered, Vic Pittman had been confined in an alcohol detoxification center a hundred miles from Monroeville. It would have been impossible for him and Myers to have robbed Jackson Cleaners as Karen Kelly claimed they had. "That bitch was lying to us," Onzell said. "She's lying to protect that nigger."

Mozelle had no choice but to admit that Kelly had lied, but she did not agree with Onzell. She had never believed that Johnny D. had robbed the cleaners. The newspapers had described him as a major drug kingpin. Why would a drug lord bother with such a petty crime? She did not argue with her sister, however. "One thing you never do down here in the South," she said later, "is protect a nigger or even act like you believe him—not even in private to your own kin." Instead she announced that she was going to contact Ralph Myers.

"Why?" Onzell asked.

" 'Cause only he and Kelly really know what happened and if she won't tell us, maybe he will."

She sent a letter to Myers at the jail in Brewton, where he was now being held awaiting his trial in the Pittman murder. A few days later she received a letter from him written by another inmate, since Myers could neither write nor read. Myers was willing to meet Mozelle, but only if his court-appointed attorney was with him. Mozelle didn't want that. She wanted to confront him one-on-one, so she contacted a friend who worked at the jail and asked if he would get Myers to telephone her. Two weeks later Mozelle was awakened at two A.M. It was the jailer calling. He had taken Myers out of his cell and had him standing next to him waiting to talk. Before he put Myers on, the jailer wanted Mozelle to swear she would not tell anyone about the call. Otherwise he might lose his job. Mozelle agreed.

Still groggy, she suddenly realized that she didn't know what to say, but as soon as she heard Myers utter "Hello," her anger took charge.

"Before we start," she said, "I want you to know that I hate you. I hate your guts." Myers didn't respond, and for a moment Mozelle was worried that she had offended him so much that he wouldn't talk to her. "Ralph, if you believe in God, then you know in your heart that you owe me the truth," she continued. "Please tell me what happened." Her voice was heavy with emotion, and she was about to cry. Seconds passed in silence, and then he spoke.

"Well, whatd'ya wanna know?"

They talked until four A.M., and Myers told her the identical story he had originally told investigators. He said he had loaned his truck to Kelly and Johnny D. on the night Vickie Lynn vanished. He had found out only later that they had killed her and used his truck to carry her body into the woods.

Mozelle did not interrupt. She did not question him. She also did not believe him. "Please call me again," she said when it was time for him to return to his cell. Myers said he would if she sent him five dollars' worth of postage stamps, which he could trade for cigarettes.

Mozelle called Onzell.

"He's lying to you," Onzell warned.

"I know," replied Mozelle, "but at least he's talking."

Late that night Myers called again. This time he told her that Kelly and Johnny D. had forced him to go with them into the woods after they had already killed Vickie Lynn. They had made him help hide her body. Mozelle still didn't believe him. The next night he said that he had watched Kelly and Johnny D. beat Vickie Lynn but had not taken part in the killing. Each night he was getting closer to telling her the truth, Mozelle decided.

On the fourth night she told him she had a tape recording she wanted him to hear. She held a cassette player close to the phone's mouthpiece. Over the line Myers heard a country-and-western singer's voice. It was a song about a man who was lonely because his true love had been killed. "That's how I feel," Mozelle said. She played the tune again. "I want you to think about them words."

As he had on the previous nights, Myers again changed his story. This time he said Vickie Lynn had been alive when the four of them drove into the woods. A fifth person, whom he did not identify, had driven into the woods a few minutes after they did, and it was this mystery man who had ordered them to kill Vickie Lynn.

"Who was he?" asked Mozelle. "Was it Vic?"

"This man will have us both murdered," he replied, "if I tell you his name." He hung up the phone.

When Myers called the next night Mozelle tried to make him feel as guilty as she could. He had become emotional whenever he spoke about his own three children, so she asked him how he would react if his youngest son were abducted and beaten to death. How would he like to find the boy's corpse in the woods half eaten by animals? Mozelle bore down so hard that Myers began to cry. "I'm going to hang up," she said. "Don't call me back until you are ready to tell me what happened. But if you tell me the truth, I will forgive you for what you did and God will forgive you too. You would like that, wouldn't you, Ralph? Wouldn't you like to know that God has forgiven you?"

Mozelle put down the phone and took a deep breath. She had sensed during their earlier talks that Myers wanted her forgiveness. Five minutes passed, and then ten. Five minutes later the phone rang.

"I'm going to tell you something that is going to shock you," he said. Then he blurted out, "I murdered your niece."

"Good, Ralph," Mozelle said, surprising herself. Her voice was calm, though her emotions were churning. "Doesn't it feel good to finally tell the truth?"

"Yes," Myers said. She could hear him crying. The line went dead, and Mozelle panicked. Then she heard the voice of her friend the jailer. Myers had dropped the receiver and run into a bathroom to vomit. A few minutes later he came back on the phone. He said he had not wanted to kill Vickie Lynn. The mystery man had forced him to beat her. He had threatened to kill Myers if he didn't follow his orders.

"It was my life or hers," Myers said. The mystery man made him and Johnny D. take turns hitting Vickie Lynn with a tire tool from the trunk. He then made Kelly stab the body. That way all three of them were involved.

"Tell me, Ralph," Mozelle said. "Who made you do it?"

"He's a sheriff."

"*Who?*"

Myers hung up the phone.

The next morning Mozelle hurried into the district attorney's office.

"Ralph's admitted to me over the telephone that he killed Vickie Lynn, and I want that son of a bitch tried for capital murder and put in the electric chair," she said.

"You've been talking to him?" Godwin asked, startled.

Mozelle realized she had made a mistake. She had forgotten that no one was supposed to know about her late-night calls. "How I got to him don't matter. What's important is Myers has confessed."

That night Mozelle waited for Myers to call, but when the telephone finally rang it was the jailer. Benson had come to the jail that afternoon and grilled Myers about the calls. Sheriff Hawsey was furious that Myers had been allowed to use a telephone, and Myers's court-appointed attorney was livid too. Mozelle acted dumb. She didn't want to admit that she was the one who had let slip about the calls.

"Can you get Ralph to call me tonight?" she asked.

He promised he'd try, but when the phone rang that night it was the jailer's voice she heard.

"They moved Ralph out of here," he said. "I think they're going to fire me."

"They're shutting Myers up," Mozelle said when she called Onzell the next morning. "I was getting too close to the truth. This is bigger than we think. Ralph told me there is a sheriff involved."

Onzell was skeptical. "He's lying to you just like she did."

Mozelle didn't argue. She knew that was possible, that Myers might be lying about the sheriff for reasons only he knew. Still, Mozelle was pleased with what she had learned.

"At least we now know for sure Ralph is one of the killers. At least he admitted that much and we can finally force Godwin to make him pay. We can force him to execute Ralph for what he done."

PART FOUR

Arrival of the Stone-Catcher

"Well, Dill, after all he's just a Negro."

—Harper Lee
To Kill a Mockingbird

Chapter 33

They were coming to kill him. He could see them walking down the tier toward his cell, and he could even hear their footsteps. Had death row ever been this quiet before? He couldn't remember such a silence. There were four guards, the warden, and a minister carrying a copy of the Holy Bible. They opened his cell door and called him out by his real first name: Walter. How strange it sounded. How respectful they seemed. They led him down the narrow passageway, and he could see the other death row inmates looking through the bars of their cells as he passed, and he made eye contact with the men who were willing to look into his face, but none of them said a word, not even goodbye. What was there to say to a man who was walking to his execution? Were they wondering about him? Were they wondering if he would scream out and fight or cry or beg for mercy or ask for forgiveness? Were they wondering if there was a heaven and a hell or simply nothing on the other side but a void like the blackness that was there before you were born when you remembered nothing? Or were they thinking of themselves and how they too might someday be taken down this same corridor just as he was now being taken? How would they react? What do you do in the final minutes of your life?

Inside a small room they put a dab of shaving cream on the right side of his head, just above the ear, and they shaved a spot there until it was smooth and soft to the touch. They shaved the hair on the calf of his left leg too because these two spots had to be completely clean, since this was where the electrical wires would be attached, and if they were not clean, then the hair would burn like tinder and the skin would be scorched the blackest black. If the skin was clean, however, the 1,900-volt electrical charge would shoot through his skull down his neck through his heart and into his leg, magically exiting by the other wire, sailing through his entrails with lightning quickness, baking the organs but not searing his flesh, as if he were a human entrée tucked into a microwave, completely cooked inside yet cool to the touch. Would it hurt? How long would the pain last? Who could tell him for sure? The death chair was bolted onto the floor in a room where watermelons were often stored during the summer because there was not enough space for them in the prison kitchen. The room was usually kept dark and cool, and prison officials knew there was less chance of a watermelon's being stolen if it was kept in the same room as Yellow Mama, the chair on which 115 men had been executed by the state since 1927. Only once had Yellow Mama failed to squeeze the life out of one whom she kissed. A technician had mismatched two wires, thereby reducing the charge by half. When the doctor listened to the man's heart, it was still beating after the first series of jolts, so another round was quickly ordered as soon as the wires were correctly aligned. No one could tell if the condemned man had suffered during the delay because his body had slumped forward after the first burst and he had not moved, not even twitched, until the second jolt had snapped him to attention as if he were a puppet suddenly called to life by unseen strings.

They were in the death room now, and they were strapping him into the chair, and he looked up and through the glass window that was used by those outside to watch him die, and he could see Simon Benson and Larry Ikner and Tom Tate and Judge Key and Ted Pearson and Charles and Bertha Morrison. All of them were staring at him. There was another person in the very back row, but he couldn't make out the face, and as the red minute hand swept around the clock dial and moved closer to 12:01 A.M. and the warden prepared to let loose with the surge that would kill him, he peered frantically through the window to make out the face, and at last, just as the electricity was racing toward him with its blue heat of death, he saw clearly who it was. Karen Kelly was laughing—laughing and pointing at him and smiling and shaking her head. It was she who was killing him. Of this he had no doubt.

Johnny D.'s face was covered with sweat. It was not the first time this particular nightmare had come to him, yet when he was asleep and it came to haunt him it always seemed to be happening for the very first time and was real until he snapped himself awake. Sometimes, even after he was certain it was only a dream, he would still swear that he could smell the stink of burned flesh and hot feces in his nostrils. It was a stench that he would later claim he had first smelled shortly after he was put on death row. He had been a newcomer then, an outsider. Everyone else on the row had been condemned, but he was convinced that he was not going to be found guilty and the murder charges filed against him were going to be dropped. The State of Alabama had executed Wayne Eugene Ritter fifteen days after he arrived. Ritter hadn't murdered anyone, but his partner had killed a store owner during a robbery, and both thieves had been sentenced to death. Johnny D. had watched as the guards took Ritter from his cell twenty-four hours before his scheduled execution. He had been led to a special holding area where his head and leg were shaved and he was fed his last meal. Although the warden would later deny that it was possible, Johnny D. would insist that moments after Ritter was electrocuted, the odor of seared flesh and feces had drifted through death row, coming like a fog through the night.

Chestnut and Boynton assured Johnny D. that they would appeal his case, but he no longer trusted either man. He told Minnie during a visit that he wanted a new attorney, someone who would be willing to find the two white "FBI men" who had stopped at the fish fry or some other evidence that would prove him innocent. Minnie's face went blank and he knew instantly she was hiding something, so he demanded to know what it was. "We ain't gots no more money!" she declared. Chestnut and Boynton had bankrupted them. She couldn't imagine how she would pay all the bills they owed. After Minnie was gone Johnny D. was led back to his cell. He had lived on death row for sixteen months, but it was as if he were seeing it for the first time. Always before he had seen himself as merely passing through. He had told himself: As soon as they realize I'm innocent, they will let me go. Not now. The State of Alabama is going to kill me! he thought. And there is nothing I can do to stop it. A copy of the Holy Bible was in his cell, and although he could barely read, he picked it up and began studying a few passages. He closed it and prayed.

It had been a long time since he had called on God for help, but as he sat on his bunk, he realized there was no one else for him to ask.

Bryan Stevenson turned his Toyota Corolla onto Interstate 65 and pushed down on the accelerator, merging the well-traveled import into the parade of cars hurrying south from Montgomery. It was mid-January 1989, and Stevenson was en route to Holman prison, where he planned to interview three inmates on death row. He had never met any of them. The last name on his list was Walter "Johnny D." McMillian.

Stevenson was not from the Deep South. He had been born and reared in rural Delaware, and he often found life in Alabama depressing. He stayed only because of his work. As a civil rights lawyer who specialized in death row appeals, Stevenson was right where he belonged. More than half of the nation's death row inmates are imprisoned in Alabama, Georgia, Mississippi, Louisiana, Texas, and Florida. Nearly eighty-five percent of all executions take place in those six states. Among attorneys the states are known as the Death Belt. Stevenson was the newly hired director of the Alabama Capital Representation Resource Center, and it was his job to do everything he could to prevent Alabama from executing a single inmate.

Despite its grand-sounding name, the nonprofit Resource Center was a fledgling two-month-old operation based in a Victorian row house not far from the state capitol in Montgomery. The driving force behind the creation of the Center was a no-nonsense white woman in her late twenties named Eva Ansley, who had waged a one-person campaign against the death penalty in Alabama for several years. Ansley was not an attorney, but she was highly respected in Alabama legal circles and despised by death penalty proponents. She had first visited Alabama's death row in 1981 while doing research for a college term paper, and she had been shocked by what she found. Like other states, Alabama had been forced to stop executions in 1972 after the U.S. Supreme Court effectively declared all capital punishment laws unconstitutional. The court said defendants were being sentenced to death arbitrarily and often in ways that were clearly discriminatory. But in 1976 the court decided that states could begin executing criminals once again if they established stricter guidelines. Alabama responded by drafting a new death penalty law that was just about to take effect when Ansley visited death row.

After years of aimless waiting, the inmates "on the row" were in a panic. Few of them, Ansley learned, were still being represented by lawyers. Many had thought they would never be killed. One inmate near the top of the execution list begged Ansley to telephone his attorney. When Ansley called, the lawyer admitted that he had done nothing for several years to help his client, nor did he plan to do anything. "He deserves to fry for what he's done," the attorney said. Aghast, Ansley found a new lawyer for the inmate, and others on death row immediately began pleading with her to help them find legal help too. She persuaded a public-interest group to give her an office, a telephone, and a bare-bones salary after she graduated from college so that she could help the inmates. But matching them with attorneys proved nearly impossible. Under Alabama's new law, whenever someone was sentenced to death, the case was automatically appealed. If the defendant was poor, the state paid a set fee to his attorneys for filing the appeal. But as soon as the Alabama Supreme Court ruled that the defendant had received a fair trial and denied the appeal, the state stopped paying the attorneys' hourly legal bills, and most lawyers began abandoning their clients—though they were entitled to a second round of appeals. These secondary appeals, commonly called postconviction relief, often required hundreds of hours of work by an attorney, and few were willing to take on such an arduous task knowing that they might never be paid, or would receive only a $600 fee from the state. Ansley worked the telephones every day, calling lawyers and begging them to handle postconviction appeals. Sometimes she picked the names of lawyers out of the yellow pages. "I expected the first ten to say no." At one point she became so frustrated that she quit, but after the state executed a man whom she had befriended, she returned to her job.

In early 1988 Bryan Stevenson heard about Ansley's efforts in Alabama and called to offer his help. Back then he was working for the Southern Prisoners' Defense Committee in Atlanta, another nonprofit group opposed to the death penalty. Stevenson agreed to represent Ansley's most hard-pressed clients, and he also began offering other lawyers in Alabama advice on how to file death row appeals. With Stevenson's help, Ansley convinced the Alabama Bar Association that something had to be done to assure the condemned men legal representation up until the point of their execution, and the bar association agreed to help her apply for various federal grants. In November 1988 the federal funds started to arrive, the Resource Center was organized, and Stevenson agreed to move to Montgomery temporarily to run it. He and Ansley were now in the process of hiring a staff and unpacking files.

As he drove south Stevenson thought about the three men he planned to meet. With more than a hundred cases to choose from,

Stevenson's decision to pick out McMillian's might have seemed odd. There were lots of other prisoners much closer to being executed. But Johnny D.'s case had stuck out. Nearly everyone on death row had a long criminal record. Johnny D. didn't. Nearly everyone on death row had been linked to a murder by fingerprints or some other physical evidence. He hadn't. And few death row inmates had alibis as strong as Johnny D.'s. Why hadn't jurors believed his six alibi witnesses? Stevenson thought he already knew the answer. They were black, and that made them less credible than Ernest Welch, a white man. Part of the reason Stevenson assumed this was that he was black. He knew what it was like not to be taken as seriously in an Alabama courtroom as a white attorney.

At age twenty-eight he was a handsome man, standing just under six feet tall, with cropped hair and a closely trimmed black beard. He was athletically lean. Whenever he appeared in court or visited a prison, he wore a dark suit, the expected uniform of an attorney, but on most days he could be found in worn denim jeans and a faded T-shirt. His choice of dress, like everything he did, was deliberate. He had decided early in his life that he wanted to help poor people, particularly blacks, and he had taken an unspoken vow of poverty. When the Center's newly established board of directors offered him a starting annual salary of $60,000 to direct it, Stevenson turned them down. All he needed, he explained, was $18,000 per year—a wage that undoubtedly made him one of the lowest-paid graduates in the history of the Harvard University Law School.

Stevenson spent longer at Holman prison talking to the first two death row inmates than he had planned. It was after five o'clock when Johnny D. was finally brought into a tiny room in handcuffs. Because he was angry at Chestnut and Boynton, Johnny D. viewed Stevenson with suspicion and did not say much. Stevenson expected this. He had seen it before. So he began by explaining how the appeals process worked and what he could and couldn't do as an attorney. Stevenson knew that lawyers often considered it a waste of time to discuss the process with their clients. They simply told them they would take care of the legalities. But when all that was preventing a man from being strapped into Yellow Mama was the law, even the slowest and most uneducated inmate suddenly found his interest in procedures and legal statutes sparked.

Johnny D.'s case would automatically be reviewed by the Alabama Court of Criminal Appeals and the Alabama Supreme Court, Stevenson told him, but both courts would look *only* for procedural errors. If they decided, for example, that Judge Key had made a serious mistake during the trial, then the justices would order the state to give him a new trial. That usually did not happen, however, Stevenson warned. More than likely the courts would rule that Johnny D. had received a fair trial. At that point an execution date would be scheduled and the clock would begin ticking. The state would pay Chestnut and Boynton to represent Johnny D. up until then. During the postconviction relief stage, however, it would pay only $600 to his attorneys regardless of how much work they did. This was when most lawyers quit. It was also when new evidence could be introduced and new legal issues raised. "If you want the Center to take over as your legal counsel," Stevenson continued, "we will investigate this case from scratch." The Resource Center had just hired its own full-time investigator, and that detective would be sent to Monroeville to interview witnesses and gather evidence.

"Would your investigator find them two FBI men?" Johnny D. asked.

"Our investigator will certainly try."

That was all Johnny D. needed to hear. He agreed to terminate Chestnut and Boynton as his attorneys and hire the Resource Center. Now that Johnny D. was formally his client, Stevenson moved to the next stage of his standard speech. "I am going to do everything I can to save your life," he said. "It doesn't matter to me whether a person has killed nine hundred thousand people or one person or if a person has never killed anyone. The objective is still the same. I don't want to see you executed." Stevenson always told death row clients this because he knew they often were afraid to tell the truth about what they had done—even to their attorneys. They were worried that their crimes were so heinous that even their lawyers would be appalled if they knew the truth and would not defend them.

"The bottom line is, your life is of value regardless of what you have done," Stevenson concluded.

Johnny D. looked shocked. "I didn't kill that little Morrison girl," he said solemnly. "I knowed everyone in here tells you they is innocent. Now maybe they is, maybe they ain't. That ain't up to me to decide, but I'm telling you I didn't kill that little girl."

"That doesn't matter to me," Stevenson replied. He started to explain once again that he was going to work just as hard regardless of Johnny D.'s guilt or innocence, but Johnny D. interrupted.

"It do matter to me," he said. "I want you to believe me. I didn't kill that girl. You got to believe that."

It was Stevenson's turn to be surprised. He had never encountered anyone on death row who was so insistent.

"I always believe what a client tells me unless I later learn that it is wrong," Stevenson said.

"So you believe I'm innocent?"

"If you say you are, I believe you."

During the next hour Johnny D. answered every question he was asked, and when they finished, Stevenson told him that he was going to handle his case personally. He would not simply turn it over to one of the new attorneys the Center was hiring.

"So then you really do believe I'm innocent?" Johnny D. asked.

"I really do," Stevenson replied.

Relief swept across Johnny D.'s face. "Good," he said. "Good."

Although it was getting late, Stevenson drove to Monroeville, where he had already arranged to meet Minnie and Johnny D.'s relatives. Minnie had given him directions to her house, but Stevenson couldn't find it, so he stopped at a gas station south of Monroeville and asked for directions from an older black man who was filling his truck with gas. The man told Stevenson how to find the McMillians' house, and then, just as Stevenson was about to drive away, he added, "Johnny D. ain't home right now, you know, on account they done framed him up for a murder."

Stevenson stopped. "Does everyone in this town think Mr. McMillian was framed?"

"Only some," the man replied, "but everyone who be black know it true."

Most lawyers handling appeals do not bother to meet a defendant's family. The appellate courts make their rulings based on a review of the court transcript, not on emotional conjecture. There didn't seem to be much point in a lawyer's getting involved with relatives. Stevenson thought differently. He wanted Johnny D.'s family to know, as he later put it, "that I care about them and Johnny D. as people, not just clients." This kindness also masked a shrewdness. Stevenson knew that if he became friends with the family it could help him. He wanted them to become his eyes and ears in Monroeville. No matter how insignificant a rumor about Ronda Morrison's murder might seem, he wanted to hear it.

Minnie had been waiting nervously for him, and when he pulled into the driveway she hurried to explain that she had arranged for everyone to meet at Johnny D.'s oldest sister's house. Minnie gave him directions as they drove. When they turned off the main highway and entered the woods, Stevenson felt as if he were leaving civilization. The blacktop ended just past a mailbox that marked the last house on the road owned by a white family. From that point on the unpaved, rutted road led past farms and houses owned by blacks. Eventually they came to a rickety log bridge built over a mosquito-infested swamp of moss-covered water and cattails. To the right of the road was an old wooden shack with windows not covered by shades. Inside Stevenson could see a gaggle of kids, and bare walls. "That be where Johnny D.'s mama lived," Minnie explained. "One of his sisters lives there now." Ahead on the left, Stevenson saw a new, well-maintained three-bedroom house. It was the home of Johnny D.'s oldest sister, Armiller Hands, the matriarch of the family. Thirty-five of Johnny D.'s kinfolk were waiting inside. Stevenson noticed that few of them seemed friendly.

Stevenson was convinced that Johnny D.'s race was part of the reason why he was in jail, and he was blunt when he spoke to the group. "I'm not going to tell you that I will get Johnny D. out of prison. You know and I know that we are dealing with a lot of things here that have nothing to do with the law or what's right and wrong. We are dealing with a black man and corrupt white officials who have framed him."

"That's right," one of the relatives declared.

Stevenson talked a bit about himself and the Center, but within a few minutes he was interrupted.

"How much you gonna charge?" a woman demanded. Like the others in the room, she had loaned Johnny D. and Minnie money to pay Chestnut and Boynton, and she was angry because they had not been able to keep Johnny D. from being convicted.

"I don't want a penny for what I am going to do," Stevenson replied.

"You ain't gonna charge us anything?" a man asked skeptically. "Well then, what are you gonna do that them others didn't?"

Before Stevenson could reply, Minnie spoke out. "He's already here talking to us, ain't he? That's more already. Now let the man speak."

Everyone laughed, and for the first time Stevenson saw several smiles. As he talked and answered their questions, he realized that many of the people in the room felt ashamed. "In some ways, it would have been better for them if Johnny D. had not been home when the murder happened," he later said, "because then there might have been some question in their own minds about his innocence or guilt. But the people in the room had seen him at the fish fry. They knew he didn't commit that murder and yet they had seen the justice system take him and find him guilty and put him on death row—even though many of them had come forward and testified that he was innocent. That had said something incredibly powerful to these people, and what it told them was: 'You don't matter. We don't believe what you tell us. You live in the fringes, you black and poor people don't count, you are invisible. So no matter what you say, we do not believe you.' "

As he listened to them talk about Sheriff Tate and justice in Monroe County, Stevenson decided he had entered a time warp. "For generations, blacks in this community had been held down and then—when the sixties came along and the schools were integrated and black people were allowed to vote and they took down the 'Colored Only' signs—it was as if someone had taken one heel off these people's necks and they were so pleased to breathe with only one boot heel still on their necks that basically they constructed their lives to protect that. They hadn't thought about getting rid of that other boot heel. Instead, they had learned to accommodate whites and had accepted the day-to-day racism. Walter McMillian's conviction had suddenly jolted them back into reality. They realized that any of them or their sons or their daughters were vulnerable, that if a white man accused them of murder, they too could be convicted."

It was well after midnight when Stevenson began his drive back to Montgomery. He had another thought as he traveled through the blackness. If Johnny D. hadn't killed Ronda, then her killer was still free, and he was not going to welcome Stevenson and the Center's staff's poking around.

Chapter 34

A few days after he notified the court in Monroeville that he was Johnny D.'s new attorney, Bryan Stevenson received a telephone call from Judge Robert E. Lee Key.

"Who are you?" the judge asked.

Stevenson said he was the director of the Alabama Capital Representation Resource Center, a federally funded agency that defended poor death row inmates.

Key wasn't impressed.

"Do you know who Johnny D. McMillian is?" the judge asked. Without waiting for a reply, he continued. "He is one of the biggest drug mafiosos in this part of the country . . . I wouldn't think that any self-respecting attorney would want to have anything to do with the likes of Walter McMillian."

Never before had a judge called Stevenson to warn him about representing a client. He considered it a violation of judicial ethics. "Judge," he replied, "he still needs a lawyer and I plan to represent him."

"Well, that just may not be possible," Key declared, "because this man McMillian is reputed to have money buried all over southern Alabama."

Stevenson understood what Judge Key was implying. The Resource Center was supposed to represent indigent inmates. If Johnny D. had money, he didn't qualify for free help. But the attorney also knew that the judge was bluffing. There was nothing he could do to stop Johnny D. from asking the Resource Center to defend him. What he could do, however, was throw hurdles in front of the Center by making it pay for copies of all trial transcripts, as well as future court filing fees. Poor death row inmates are usually exempt from paying such fees; this could easily cost the Center thousands of dollars.

"Well, if he does have money buried, Judge," Stevenson said, "he certainly can't get to it while he is in prison, can he? So I guess that makes him poor."

Judge Key did not reply immediately, and Stevenson thought he was irritated and had hung up. But Key hadn't, although from the tone of his voice when he spoke again, he was indeed annoyed. If Stevenson was intent on representing McMillian, the judge said, then he should be prepared to spend a lot of time in his car. Again Stevenson thought he understood what Key was implying. He was warning him that he was going to hold a court hearing on the case every chance he could. That meant Stevenson would have to drive to Monroeville and make an appearance each time he or the prosecution asked the court for a ruling, even on routine motions. Obviously Key was going to make representing Johnny D. as difficult for Stevenson as possible.

"If you hold a hearing," Stevenson replied, "I will be there."

Before hanging up, Judge Key once again suggested that Stevenson reconsider his decision to defend Johnny D. The evidence presented at the trial had been overwhelming, Key said. Johnny D. was clearly guilty, and a prolonged appeal would be a waste of everyone's time.

Stevenson called District Attorney Ted Pearson. He wanted to introduce himself and learn whether the Monroe County prosecutor was as biased against his client as Key seemed to be. To his surprise, Pearson didn't seem too concerned about Johnny D.'s appeal, and he laughed off the judge's telephone call. "Judge Key is a very fair man," Pearson said. "I've known him for years. Don't worry. He'll treat you right." Pearson would probably see the judge later that evening, he added, because they often ate at the same restaurant. "I'll talk to him for you."

As Stevenson put down the receiver, he felt a flash of anger. "I could just see Pearson and Judge Key eating dinner together at the local country club," he later said. "Two white good old boys deciding how justice would be dispensed in Monroe County."

It was impossible for Stevenson to picture himself in that same scene—at a country club, eating dinner with a white judge. He had always thought of himself as an outsider. It was a role he had found himself forced into early in life. He had grown up in the country outside Dover, Delaware, where his mother, Alice, worked as an accounting clerk and his father, Howard, as a lab technician at a food plant. The family lived in a modest house along a county road, and as a young child Stevenson had been insulated from racism. That had changed dramatically when he started school in 1965. His mother refused to send him and his older brother, Howard, Jr., to the shabby all-black school nearby and insisted that they attend an all-white public school farther down the road. With forced integration looming, the school reluctantly accepted the two black brothers, but they were not welcomed. No matter how frantically Bryan waved his hand in the classroom, his teachers would not call on him. At recess he and his brother would dash out onto the playground, where they teamed up with Joe, the son of a Mexican migrant couple. The three of them spent their recesses fighting a steady stream of white boys who taunted them with racial slurs. School officials never stepped in. Once a teacher told her students that they should avoid the monkey bars if Stevenson was on them because "blacks are dirty."

"I learned early on that I had to make my own judgments about what people told me," Stevenson explained later. The yardstick was not the white community. It was his family and the congregation at the all-black Prospect African Methodist Episcopal Church. "If people in my church had been saying things like 'You are too dirty to play on the monkey bars' or 'You are too stupid to be in a white school,' then perhaps I would have listened, but they didn't."

When the all-black schools were closed and other blacks were bused to his elementary school, Stevenson was put in the black "slow learners' class." His mother demanded that her son be returned to the regular class with white children. Reluctantly the principal agreed but warned that Stevenson wouldn't be able to keep up. Stevenson earned the highest marks in the class. By the time he was a senior at Cape Henlopen High School, he was president of the student council, a star soccer player, a straight-A student ranked number one in his class, and an accomplished public speaker. He was also extremely popular. His teachers and principal now bragged about him, but he did not take their praise seriously. "Many of these people were the same ones who had been saying 'Wait a minute, you shouldn't even be in our schools.' " His measuring stick remained the charismatic church his family attended.

After graduation Stevenson attended a small Baptist college in Pennsylvania because his brother went there. He was determined to find a profession in which he could help poor black people. Although he had never met a lawyer, he decided to become one, and he applied to Harvard University's law school. On the first day of classes Stevenson and his classmates were told to look around the room. What they were seeing, they were told, were the faces of future congressmen, Supreme Court judges, and the leading partners of all the most important law firms. Only the best and brightest made it to Harvard. Stevenson almost laughed out loud. Such elitism made him feel uncomfortable, especially when he began to notice that "success" was narrowly defined at Harvard, usually in terms of how much money an attorney earned. His mentors were Martin Luther King, Jr., and Frederick Douglass, not Wall Street legal tycoons. On Sundays he attended a church in a depressed black Cambridge neighborhood, where he gave kids free piano lessons and helped adults with their legal problems. One day when he walked through a tough segregated Boston neighborhood, Stevenson was harassed by a gang of whites. Rather than reacting with hate and anger, he told his classmates he felt sorry for the gang members. "It sounds mushy," a classmate said later, "but Bryan radiated a sense of goodness and kindness. He had an inner peace."

The summer before he graduated Stevenson worked as an intern at the Southern Prisoners' Defense Committee and was impressed by the dedication of the lawyers there. He was also touched by the plight of the inmates. "When I looked at the faces of these men on death row," he later explained, "I could very easily see my own." That notion seemed far-fetched to his Harvard classmates, but not to Stevenson. One night after driving home late from work during his internship in Atlanta, he stayed in his parked car outside his apartment complex for a few minutes, listening to a new song being played on the radio. Suddenly a police car appeared and two white officers jumped out. When Stevenson opened his car door, one of the officers grabbed his pistol and yelled, "Move and I'll blow your head off." Stevenson froze. The other officer rushed forward, pulled him from the car, and pinned him against its hood. He was quickly frisked and questioned. There had been a number of burglaries in the area, and a tenant had called the police when she spotted "a suspicious black man" sitting in his car outside the building.

It was a painful reminder. Despite all his accomplishments, he was still just another "suspicious black man."

"Had I been a few years younger, my reaction probably would have been to run, and if that had happened, I could have very easily been arrested or shot or taken to jail."

There were plenty of other signs that race mattered. White clerks put change on the counter because they didn't want to risk touching his black skin. He was told that an apartment was for rent, but when the landlord saw that he was black, she announced that she had "just rented it." But it was in the justice system that Stevenson saw the most blatant discrimination. In Alabama, Mississippi, and Georgia, three out of every four people who were executed were black. Alabama's white population was nearly three times the number of its black residents, yet in its prisons the ratio was reversed: two black prisoners for every white one. A black man was four times more likely than a white man to be sentenced to death even if both were convicted of similar crimes. In one of his first court victories as an intern in Georgia, Stevenson appealed a case in which a black defendant was found guilty and sentenced to death in less than twenty-four hours. The trial started in the morning, and the prosecution rested that evening. The defense had not bothered to call a single witness. The jury had deliberated for four hours before it became deadlocked by an eleven-to-one vote. Rather than declare a mistrial, the judge had simply replaced the obstinate juror with a new one, who voted guilty. By two A.M. the defendant was condemned to death.

To his horror, Stevenson discovered that rushed "justice" like this was common, particularly in death row cases involving poor blacks. One death row inmate had been represented by a defense attorney who came to court drunk; another lawyer had been caught snorting cocaine during a recess in a murder case, and one condemned man had been represented by a court-appointed attorney who had spent his entire legal career as a real estate broker and had never tried a criminal case.

When Stevenson returned to Harvard after his internship, he was grilled by other students. How could he defend cold-blooded killers? After all, not everyone on death row was there by mistake. Some surely deserved to die. A few close friends reminded Stevenson that his own grandfather had been murdered in Philadelphia by two thugs who broke into his apartment and stabbed him repeatedly when he refused to let them take his television set. Didn't Stevenson want revenge?

Stevenson's reply never changed. Killing someone solved nothing, he argued. "Before I even get to the question of whether or not the death penalty is moral, I get to the question of is it racist? If it is racist, then we shouldn't be doing it. Is it biased against people who are poor? If it is, we shouldn't be doing it. That is not to say the death penalty is morally wrong. It is saying that if the death penalty is administered on the basis of race or class, it is morally wrong. Or if we have a death penalty because of politics and we have a situation where a judge is running for reelection so he chooses the death penalty for political gain, that is wrong. When I look at these things, that is when I say that we shouldn't be executing people—because this country is not morally fit to decide who should live and die."

His classmates would reluctantly agree: The system is corrupt. But what if it were not? What if there were a foolproof way to guarantee that only murderers were executed—the Richard Specks, the John Wayne Gacys? How would he feel then?

"I would probably still be opposed to the death penalty," he always replied, "because I do not believe that human beings are good at judging the worth and value of other human beings . . ."

Stevenson graduated from Harvard Law School in 1984. A year later he finished at Harvard's John F. Kennedy School of Government. With two advanced degrees from that prestigious institution, he could have gone to work at any number of the nation's best law firms and earned a six-figure salary. But he returned to the South to defend death row inmates. Whenever he was asked why, Stevenson always spun the question around. "Why do I do what I do?" he replied. "How can anyone do anything else?"

Chapter 35

While Stevenson was wrestling with Johnny D.'s fate, Ralph Myers was reviewing his own legal problems. In return for his testimony against Johnny D., the capital murder charge filed against him in the Morrison murder had been dismissed and he had been allowed to plead guilty to a lesser charge. Judge Key had sentenced him to thirty years in prison. At first glance the sentence seemed harsh, especially given Myers's original demand that he not spend a day in prison for his role in the killing. But the plea bargain was actually a tremendous coup for the star witness. Myers would be eligible for parole in six years and would serve no more than ten. The real payoff, however, was hidden. Under Alabama's habitual offender law, any criminal who committed four felonies was supposed to be automatically sentenced to life in prison *without* parole. Myers already had three felony convictions on his record when he was charged with the Morrison murder. It looked as if he were doomed. But after he agreed to help the prosecution, District Attorney Pearson reduced the murder charge to "third-degree robbery," and that crime was not a felony. On Myers's record, he still had one strike left before he would automatically be declared a habitual criminal and shipped off to prison for life.

That was what was preoccupying Myers now. All his maneuvering in the Morrison case would be wasted if he ended up being tried and found guilty in Escambia County of murdering Vickie Lynn Pittman. A fourth conviction would bring with it the dreaded automatic life sentence. He had to find a way to get this second murder charge reduced.

It did not take Myers long to concoct a plan. Because he was illiterate, he used a cassette recorder to send messages to the court-appointed attorney who had been assigned to defend him in this case. In his first cassette Myers told George B. Jones that he wanted him to negotiate a plea bargain with Escambia County Prosecutor Michael Godwin. If Godwin would agree to reduce the murder charge against him to a misdemeanor, then he would help investigators catch an even bigger prize than Johnny D. Continuing with his tape-recorded explanation, Myers said he was willing to provide evidence and also testify against a "corrupt sheriff" who, he claimed, was involved in drug trafficking, gun dealing, and numerous murders, including Vickie Lynn's. This lawman was so dangerous and cunning that he could easily arrange for a contract murder, even inside a prison. Despite the dangers, Myers said he was willing to talk, and had taken the precaution of recording his entire criminal history on eleven cassettes, each eighty minutes long. "If this dude has me killed in prison, you can turn my tapes over to the D.A. and he will have plenty of evidence to go after this sheriff," Myers said, adding with ample drama, "You'll hear my voice from the grave."

A few days later Jones received the eleven tapes. He slipped one of them into a player. As soon as he finished listening to it, he telephoned Godwin and told him what Myers was offering. The tapes were phenomenal, Jones said. Myers was naming names and offering to help solve a slew of robbery, arson, and murder cases that were still unresolved. The biggest disclosure, however, involved Myers's claim that a "dishonest sheriff" had been present when Vickie Lynn was murdered and had forced Myers, Johnny D., and Kelly to kill the teenager.

Godwin sent Simon Benson and an FBI agent to question Myers in prison, and he told them a tantalizing tale about the "corrupt lawman."

"We can't deal with you unless you tell us his name," said Benson.

Myers began to squirm. Then he leaned close to the two men and in a voice that was barely audible said, "The corrupt lawman is none other than Conecuh County Sheriff Edwin Booker."

Sheriff Booker was the drug kingpin behind Johnny D.'s dope dealing, Myers alleged. Booker had also used Karen Kelly as a mule to transport drugs and had ordered Myers to burglarize several businesses. "Vickie Lynn was going to tell on him. That's really why she was murdered."

Had Myers said any other sheriff's name, Benson and the FBI agent might not have believed him. But Benson and other ABI and FBI agents had been trying for years to link Sheriff Booker to some sort of criminal activity. He was the most controversial sheriff in all of southern Alabama. Now Myers was willing to testify that he had personally committed crimes under Booker's direct orders, including drug trafficking and murder. Benson and the FBI agent scurried back to brief Godwin.

A short time later Mozelle and Onzell received telephone calls from Godwin's office. Myers was going to be sentenced the next morning, they were told. Just as he had done with Karen Kelly, Godwin had negotiated a plea bargain with Myers's attorney.

"Not again!" Mozelle screamed into the receiver. "You're not letting him off just like you did Karen Kelly, are you?"

The clerk on the phone said she could not reveal what the plea bargain was, only that one had been made. For a moment Mozelle thought she was going insane. Ever since Myers had admitted to her on the telephone from jail that he had helped beat Vickie Lynn to death, she had thirsted for his trial and eventual execution.

The next morning both twins were waiting in the courtroom when Godwin and defense attorney Jones arrived. Myers was hurried in minutes later. Godwin announced that he was reducing the murder charge filed against Myers to second-degree assault, a misdemeanor. He was doing this because Myers had agreed to provide crucial information to law enforcement officials. In return for his help, Godwin recommended that Myers be sentenced to thirty years in prison, just as he had been in the Morrison murder case, and that the two sentences be served concurrently.

Mozelle whispered, "What's that mean?" Onzell wasn't sure.

The judge asked Myers if he understood Godwin's recommendation. Myers said he did. He then pleaded guilty, and the judge followed Godwin's suggestions to the letter. Both thirty-year terms would be served at the same time, the judge explained.

Mozelle and Onzell were dumbfounded. Myers had beaten Vickie Lynn to death, hitting her in the face until she was unrecognizable, and he had admitted doing it. Yet he was not going to serve one extra day in prison. Vickie Lynn's death simply didn't matter. He was being punished only for his role in the Morrison killing!

By the time the sisters had regained their composure, the hearing was over and Myers was being led away. Mozelle raced toward Godwin, who was still at the front of the courtroom, just as she had done when Kelly was sentenced.

"You didn't give him a damn day!" she yelled. "Not one damn day!"

Onzell grabbed her sister's arm and tugged her toward the door. She was afraid Mozelle was going to physically attack the young prosecutor.

"C'mon," Onzell pleaded, "before you get us both put in jail."

Outside in the hallway, the sisters spotted Myers being escorted down the corridor by deputies. Mozelle broke free from Onzell and ran toward him. Onzell ran after her. The deputies were about to lead Myers into a room when Mozelle screamed at him from ten feet away.

"Myers! You cold-blooded killer!"

Myers spun around as the deputies, now panicking, pushed him into the room. The last thing he saw was Mozelle's face. It was twisted with hate. When he glanced at her, she had stopped running and had raised her right arm in front of her chest, curling back all the fingers in her hand except for the middle one. Mozelle's hand trembled as she pointed her finger at his face.

The deputies shut and locked the door.

Onzell put her arms around Mozelle.

"C'mon, hon," she said quietly. "It's time to go home."

Chapter 36

Bryan Stevenson studied the 730-page transcript of Johnny D.'s murder trial. He jotted down notes as he read. Most were questions about obvious contradictions in the testimony. He began with Myers.

1. Hurt Arm?
   Myers says he met Johnny D. in Evergreen at a car wash and agreed to drive him to Monroeville because his "arm hurt." Yet they stopped at a filling station and Johnny D. pumped gas into his truck with his "hurt arm." Later he used that same arm to tote a gun, stuff money into a bag, shove Myers against the wall, and lift the hood and repair the engine of his truck after it stalled as they were fleeing. If Johnny D.'s arm was hurt, how could he do all of these things?

2. Stalled Truck?
   Myers says the engine in the truck stalled as they were leaving

the cleaners. But Bill Hooks, Jr., testified that he saw Johnny D. and Myers "speed away."

3. Blue LTD?
   Myers says that while he was waiting outside the cleaners for Johnny D., two men in a blue LTD sedan arrived and left a bundle of laundry. Yet the prosecution says Jan Owen was the last person to see Ronda alive at 10:15 A.M. Why weren't there any records in the cleaners if two men were the last to leave laundry there? Who are these two men?

Stevenson continued making notes as he read the testimony of Bill Hooks, Jr.

4. John Dozier?
   On the night of the murder, Hooks was arrested for urinating in public and was taken to jail where he tried to tell the police what he had seen. Hooks says no one in the jail believed his story because he incorrectly identified Johnny D. as "John Dozier." It took Hooks six months to figure out the connection. Yet at the trial, Hooks admitted that he had known Johnny D. for several years, had periodically worked at his house on cars, and had gone to school with his daughter. Why hadn't the police asked Hooks to show them on the night of the murder where John Dozier lived? Why hadn't they shown Hooks mug shots? How come Hooks is the only person who ever knew Johnny D. by the nickname John Dozier?

5. Low-Rider?
   Hooks says Johnny D.'s truck was a "low-rider," but Jimmy Hunter said the truck wasn't converted into a low-rider until several months after Ronda's murder. Joe Hightower identified the truck as a low-rider too. If both men had actually seen Johnny D.'s truck parked outside Jackson Cleaners, then they would have known it was not a low-rider when the murder was committed.

6. Rewards?
   Hooks says he was not promised or offered anything in return for his testimony. What has happened to the $18,000 in rewards?

Stevenson moved ahead to Joe Hightower's testimony.

7. Surprise Witness?
   Why had it taken Hightower so long to come forward? Why had he been reluctant to testify? Was he really afraid of Johnny D. or was there another reason?

8. Different Parking Spots?
   Hightower says he saw Johnny D.'s truck parked directly in front of Jackson Cleaners. But Myers says he parked the truck in the lot at the Piggly Wiggly grocery store "a fairly good ways . . . from the cleaners."

As he continued reading, Stevenson scribbled down some general questions.

9. Body Moved?
   How did Ronda's body get from the front lobby where Myers saw it into the back room? Where was the trail of blood?

10. No Testimony?
    Why did Myers refuse to testify the first time Johnny D. was scheduled to be tried? Myers was sent to a state mental hospital. What happened there that made him change his mind about testifying?

11. Missing Witnesses?
    Jerrie Sue Dunning and Coy Stacey said a black woman, Florence Mason, was with them when Ronda was found. Why wasn't she called to testify?

12. FBI Visitors?
    Johnny D.'s sister, Everline Smith, says two white FBI agents stopped at Johnny D.'s house during the fish fry after Ronda was murdered. Who are they?

Finally Stevenson wrote down two words: "OPPORTUNITY—MOTIVE?" These are the two primary elements every investigator tries to prove in a murder investigation.

OPPORTUNITY?
Johnny D. produced six alibi witnesses who testified that he was at home during the murder. The prosecution produced one witness who said he had seen Johnny D. inside the cleaners and two who said they had seen Johnny D.'s truck parked outside. But the critical witness who had rebutted Johnny D.'s alibi was Ernest Welch. Why had the alibi witnesses said that they had seen Welch that Saturday morning? Surely they would have known better than to choose one of Ronda Morrison's uncles to corroborate a lie. Why mention him at all? Why take the chance that the prosecution would contact him?

This doesn't make sense, Stevenson thought, unless Johnny D.'s witnesses are telling the truth. Then they would have assumed that Welch was going to back up their testimony.

MOTIVE?

Stevenson couldn't think of any reasons why Johnny D. would want to kill Ronda Morrison or go to the cleaners that morning. He had heard whispers about drug dealing, but Johnny D. had assured him that he only sold marijuana occasionally and never anything harder. Besides, there was no evidence that drugs were linked to the murder. No drugs or traces of them had been found at the store; no testimony showed its owners were engaged in trafficking.

The entire case against Johnny D. was circumstantial, and there was really only one witness, Ralph Myers, who could actually link Johnny D. to the killing. Hightower said he had seen Johnny D.'s truck parked outside the cleaners. That was not a crime. Hooks said he had seen Johnny D. and Myers leaving the cleaners. That was not a crime either. Only Myers had been able to put Johnny D. inside the building, standing over a dead Ronda Morrison.

Stevenson wrote another phrase on his legal pad.

WITNESSES' MOTIVES/WHY THEY MIGHT LIE

Myers—To avoid being tried in the Pittman murder.
Hooks—Reward?
Hightower—Reward?
Welch—Pressure from relatives?

He finished writing and thought about his notes. Then he called Brenda Lewis into his office. She was a former police officer whom he had hired to work as the Resource Center's criminal investigator.

"I need you to go to Monroeville," he said. "Find out what you can about Myers, Hooks, and Hightower."

After she was gone, Stevenson telephoned J. L. Chestnut in Selma and asked him for copies of all the police records, witness statements, and any other documents the prosecution had provided to the defense before Johnny D.'s trial. Chestnut said he didn't have any. He had sent all his records to Bruce Boynton. Stevenson telephoned Boynton, and Boynton promised to send him everything he had, but he warned that there wasn't much. Benson, Ikner, and Tate had given him only a handful of documents. Stevenson typed up a new discovery motion. In it he demanded copies of every report and witness statement taken by the police. When he finished he wondered: Would the prosecution send him the same documents they had provided to Chestnut and Boynton or would they be more forthcoming? He made a note to himself. He would want to compare the two packages as soon as they arrived.

A week later investigator Lewis returned from Monroeville with a thick packet. She had conducted background checks on Myers, Hooks, and Hightower, mostly by examining court records in Monroe, Conecuh, and Escambia counties, and she had unearthed some curious finds, particularly about Hooks.

Stevenson already knew that Hooks had been in the Conecuh County jail awaiting trial on a burglary charge when he saw Ralph Myers's photograph in the newspaper, began crying, and called Benson, Ikner, and Tate. Their all-important meeting, the one at which Hooks had first realized that John Dozier was actually Johnny D., had happened on June 4.

"Look what happened next," Lewis told Stevenson.

Immediately after that meeting Hooks was transferred from the jail in Evergreen to Sheriff Tate's jail in Monroeville. On June 9 Hooks signed a sworn statement identifying Johnny D. as the man he had seen fleeing the cleaners. The very next day, June 10, Hooks was taken before Judge Key for a hearing. The burglary charge filed against him was reduced to trespassing; Hooks was sentenced to "time already served" and was immediately released from jail. He was neither fined nor required to pay any court costs.

Stevenson was suspicious. Hooks had been accused of a burglary in Evergreen, in Conecuh County, not in Monroe County. Yet his hearing had been held in Monroeville. He had been waiting for six months to go to trial, and his case had not been scheduled to be heard until late July, yet on the day after he signed a statement against Johnny D., his case had suddenly been hurried up, the burglary charge filed against him had been reduced to simple trespassing, and he had then been freed without having to pay any of the normal costs or fines.

"It looks as if Mr. Hooks was treated rather special after he agreed to testify against Johnny D.," Stevenson said.

There was nothing illegal about the prosecution's showing Hooks preferential treatment in return for his help, but it was improper to keep any such help a secret. The defense and jury were entitled by law to know if Hooks had been rewarded for his help. Stevenson had already checked to make sure Chestnut and Boynton had filed a standard Motion for Disclosure of Impeaching Information, which required the prosecution to reveal "any and all consideration or promises" it had made to its witnesses. That motion had been filed, and the prosecution had said that none of its witnesses had been "enticed" to testify or had been rewarded for their help.

"Didn't nobody pay me to say nothing," Hooks had testified at the trial. "Didn't nobody pay me to do nothing."

The records Stevenson was now holding in his hands, however, seemed to suggest otherwise. If Stevenson could prove that Hooks had received favorable treatment in return for his testimony, then there was a good chance the appeals court would be forced to overturn Johnny D.'s conviction and order a new trial.

There was more.

Brenda Lewis had learned that Hooks had owed twenty-five dollars in police fines and thirty-two dollars in court costs in a Monroeville city court case. Yet after he agreed to testify against Johnny D., those fines and costs had been set aside. A note in the file said the fines and costs had been dismissed "upon the request of D.A. Larry Ikner, Deputy William Gibson, Chief Bill Dailey and the judge." Larry Ikner had no jurisdiction over city court cases. Neither did the sheriff's office. So why had Ikner and Deputy Gibson gotten involved? Why had they recommended that the city drop its case? Again Stevenson thought the answer was obvious. Hooks was being rewarded.

There was still more.

Between the time when Hooks was released from jail and Johnny D.'s murder trial, records showed that Hooks had been issued $446 in traffic fines in Monroeville alone, yet he had not been required to pay any of them within the required thirty days. At one point an arrest warrant had been issued automatically because his fines were overdue. But Monroeville Police Chief Bill Dailey had not arrested Hooks. Instead Hooks had been allowed to ignore the fines for more than one year. Why?

Finally Lewis showed Stevenson the record she considered her most important find. When Hooks had eventually gotten around to paying the $446 in traffic tickets, he had used money given to him by Sheriff Tate as a *reward* for his help in solving the Ronda Morrison murder. Lewis had found copies of canceled checks in the city's general fund files that showed Hooks had received $5,000 in reward money at the recommendation of Sheriff Tate.

"For someone who supposedly did not benefit from testifying against Johnny D.," Stevenson said, "Mr. Bill Hooks, Jr., certainly did all right."

As Stevenson studied the records, he made another intriguing find. He had always wondered why it was so important for Sheriff Tate to arrest Johnny D. on Sunday, June 7, on the sodomy charge. Why had that particular day been so crucial? Suddenly Stevenson figured out the reason. On *June 4* Hooks had told investigators that he had seen Myers and Johnny D. "speed away" from Jackson Cleaners in Johnny D.'s pickup truck. On *June 7* Johnny D. was arrested while driving home in that same truck. Sheriff Tate had confiscated it and parked it directly in front of the Monroe County jail. On *June 9* Hooks had been transferred from the jail in Evergreen to the Monroe County jail. That same afternoon Hooks had given Benson, Ikner, and Tate a sworn statement against Johnny D. that included a detailed description of the pickup truck.

"They weren't after Johnny D. that Sunday," Stevenson announced. "They were after his truck. They needed to confiscate it and show it to Hooks so that he could be sure to describe it accurately in his statement. That's why they parked it in front of the jail. They showed it to him!"

Something else now became clear to Stevenson. The reason why Hooks had mistakenly described Johnny D.'s truck as a low-rider in his sworn statement and later at the trial was because Johnny D.'s truck *was* a low-rider when it was shown to him outside the jail on June 9. Hooks and the investigators had not realized until Hooks had already signed his sworn statement that the truck had only recently been converted. By that time, Hooks's statement was already part of the court record, so he had to stick with it even though it was wrong.

Based on the documents he now had, Stevenson decided that Sheriff

Tate, Police Chief Dailey, Larry Ikner, and even Judge Key had to have known that Hooks had received special treatment before the trial. None of them had said anything, and that bothered him. "These men are all law enforcement," he told Lewis. "They are supposed to make sure the laws are kept, not ignored."

Chapter 37

Based on his review of Johnny D.'s trial transcript and the records Brenda Lewis had uncovered, Bryan Stevenson filed a seventy-eight-page appeal before the Alabama Court of Criminal Appeals. He cited seventeen examples of what he claimed were errors that had prevented his client from receiving a fair trial. His best shot was his claim that prosecutors had rewarded Bill Hooks, Jr., for his testimony without telling anyone. "Even if there were no formal deal, jurors still should have been told that Hooks was a known police informant who stood to benefit greatly by testifying against our client," Stevenson wrote.

The Alabama attorney general's office, which is obligated to represent the state in death penalty appeals, responded with a seventy-two-page legal brief of its own. It countered each of Stevenson's charges. William D. Little, an assistant attorney general, wrote that Stevenson's accusation about a secret deal with Hooks was not really relevant. Neither of Johnny D.'s original attorneys had raised the issue at the trial, and since the appeals court was supposed to review only evidence that had been presented at the trial, Stevenson's claim was immaterial.

Seven months later the appellate court ruled that Stevenson's accusations about Hooks needed to be investigated. However, the court said its decision did not mean that it thought anyone had done anything wrong. Rather, it wanted the charges about Hooks to be investigated for "judicial expedience." It did not want Stevenson bringing them up later in an attempt to delay Johnny D.'s execution. Because he had been convicted in Baldwin County, the appeals court ordered a judge there to hold a special "remand" hearing to investigate the charges. The court gave both sides five months to prepare.

Stevenson asked Michael P. O'Connor, a new lawyer hired by the Resource Center, to help him on the case. O'Connor was white, a short man in his early twenties with a weight lifter's build and a tough, street-wise Irish manner. Although he was a recent graduate of Yale University Law School, O'Connor felt that he had more in common with some of the men whom he defended in court than with his former Ivy League classmates. At age twelve he had started drinking alcohol and using drugs, and by his own admission he had soon become addicted to both. When he was eighteen he was arrested and charged with two felonies. He hired a lawyer, but his attorney left him stranded minutes before a hearing when O'Connor disclosed that he didn't have enough money to pay his legal fees. "I will never forget how it felt to walk into that courtroom without a lawyer, knowing that I was innocent and knowing that it probably didn't matter." Luckily for O'Connor, the prosecution's main witness didn't show up, so the judge dismissed the case. With his parents' help, O'Connor entered a drug rehabilitation program, beat both of his addictions, and later graduated with honors from college and law school. "I got a second chance," he said. "Most of the people I see every day in prison didn't."

O'Connor was not the only lawyer newly becoming involved in Johnny D.'s legal battle. In 1990 Ted Pearson abruptly resigned as district attorney. On the very same day, Alabama Governor Guy Hunt named Tommy Chapman to replace him. Stevenson knew that Chapman had previously represented Johnny D., Myers and, most recently, Karen Kelly. Now that Pearson was gone, Stevenson wondered if the new district attorney might be willing to take a more favorable view of the case. He telephoned Chapman and suggested they meet. Chapman invited him to Monroeville. O'Connor went along.

The selection of Chapman as the new district attorney in Monroe and Conecuh counties came as a surprise because he was a staunch Democrat; it seemed odd that a Republican governor would choose him. The story of how he got appointed tells much about him and about the way political power is often wielded in south Alabama. Pearson and Chapman had been eating lunch at the country club in Brewton in mid-1990 when Pearson complained that he was tired of his job. "I wouldn't mind doing it," Chapman replied, "but Governor Hunt will never appoint a Democrat." By the time the two men had finished their desserts, they had a plan. Pearson said he would recommend Chapman as his replacement, and also promised not to resign unless the governor agreed to appoint his pal. Chapman, meanwhile, began pulling strings. He had been thinking about entering an upcoming race for a state Senate seat and had recently paid for a poll that showed he could defeat the incumbent. Chapman called several of his Democratic friends at the statehouse in Montgomery and told them about the poll results. He then mentioned that he would not campaign for the state Senate seat if Governor Hunt appointed him to replace Pearson. Word spread quickly, and the state senator whose job was in jeopardy went to talk to the governor. A few days later Pearson resigned and Hunt appointed Chapman. Chapman had no idea what the senator had traded Governor Hunt to protect his job. It was not his problem. All he knew was that his backroom politicking had worked.

During the short time he had been in office, Chapman had proved an aggressive and controversial prosecutor. He had inherited six murder cases from Pearson, all in Conecuh County, and had won every one. He also had hired a black secretary to work in his office at the Monroe County Courthouse. Pearson had never hired any blacks, and Chapman received several nasty comments from white voters. He shrugged them off. The new district attorney opposed racism, but he was a shrewd enough politician to know that he had to be careful about what he said and did. He did not invite blacks, even those who were Democrats, to dinner in his home.

Chapman greeted Stevenson and O'Connor cordially when they arrived at his office. After he closed the door, he told them that he personally had serious doubts about whether Johnny D. was guilty. He mentioned that his brother, Terry, was convinced that Johnny D. was innocent, based on their knowing each other in the woodcutting business. Besides, Chapman said, there were things about Myers's testimony that didn't add up.

Stevenson and O'Connor felt relieved. At last it looked as if Johnny D. was going to get a break. But before either of them could speak, Chapman added that despite his personal feelings, he was obligated as district attorney to "defend the integrity of the jury's verdict." He was going to argue against Johnny D.'s appeal at the upcoming remand hearing. Any hope that the two defense attorneys had felt quickly vanished. Both suspected that Chapman was simply bending to political pressure: He was not about to help a black man convicted of killing a white girl. By this time they had also learned that a long-standing rivalry existed between Monroe and Conecuh counties. Former prosecutor Ted Pearson had always lived in Monroe County and had spent most of his time at the courthouse in Monroeville. Chapman lived in Evergreen and preferred to work there. What better way to appease the voters in Monroeville, who believed they were getting less attention with Chapman replacing Pearson as district attorney, than to uphold the conviction of the black man who had murdered one of the town's most beloved teenagers?

"Why are you obligated to defend the jury's verdict?" Stevenson asked. "Your job is to defend justice, not a wrongful prosecution."

"A jury found your man guilty," Chapman replied. The question offended him. What right did Stevenson have to lecture him about justice?

"Yes, but that jury was not told the truth," Stevenson said. "This man's fate should not be decided based on what the popular thing to do is or what the political thing to do is, but what the right thing to do is. Everyone knows the truth hasn't come out, and you can either assist in helping present the truth or act in denying the truth, but there is no in-between. You are either for the truth or against the truth, whether or not you admit it, the judge admits it, or Larry Ikner and Simon Benson admit it. The truth will come out, and you have to make a moral choice about which side you are going to be on."

Chapman was really irked by now, but he concealed it and politely told the two attorneys that he disagreed. It was part of his Southern rearing to be cordial even when he was furious. Chapman had his secretary call Benson, Ikner, and Tate into his office so that he could introduce them to Stevenson and O'Connor. He also told Ikner to give the two defense attorneys copies of all the police and witness statements they had demanded in their new discovery motion. They walked back with Ikner to his office, where he opened a file drawer and handed them three documents: Ralph Myers's two confessions and the sworn statement by Bill Hooks, Jr., implicating Johnny D.

"Is this it?" asked a surprised Stevenson, looking at the three documents. Most murder investigations generate hundreds of pages of reports and witness statements.

Ikner nodded. "That's all there is."

Once that was done, Stevenson and O'Connor left. Everyone had been friendly on the surface, but both sides were now angry. Stevenson and O'Connor believed Chapman cared more about politics than justice. Chapman thought they had come across as big-city know-it-alls. "Stevenson didn't know me or anything about me, and yet he comes in here and he has this attitude of 'I'm a Harvard-educated lawyer and I'm going to come down here and tell these honkies how to do their job,' " he said later. "Well, I'm just as smart as that guy, even if I didn't go to Harvard. And just because we don't see things eye to eye doesn't mean that I'm not a moral person. What right did he have to come lecture me about morals?"

Chapman was a firm believer in the death penalty. Some crimes were so horrible that capital punishment was the only appropriate way for society to resolve them. He had not always thought this way. When he had graduated from the University of Alabama law school in 1975, he had returned home to Evergreen eager to defend the wrongly accused. As time passed, however, he found himself becoming uncomfortable defending local riffraff. "Ninety-eight percent of the people who came into my office were clearly guilty," he recalled, yet he used his skills to get them off. "This is my community, and I was helping these criminals go free to prey on my friends and neighbors. That bothered me."

One night in 1988 Chapman and his wife, Patsy, were awakened by a noise. "There's someone in the house," Patsy said. Chapman told her she was imagining things, but the next morning they discovered that their home had been ransacked while they slept. Two men were later arrested and confessed. They had been traveling on the nearby interstate highway and had chosen Chapman's house at random. Patsy had nightmares. What if she had gotten out of bed to investigate when she heard that noise? Chapman started sleeping with a loaded pistol near the bed, and thereafter began turning away some potential clients, burglars in particular. That was part of the reason he had switched to the prosecution's side. He felt more comfortable there.

When Stevenson and O'Connor left the courthouse, they went to see George K. Elbrecht, the attorney who had been appointed by the court to defend Hooks against his 1986 burglary charge. If anyone knew whether or not Hooks had been "enticed" to testify, the two defense attorneys figured it would be Elbrecht. Usually Stevenson didn't trust local lawyers. In a small town they had too much to lose financially and socially by helping defend a convicted killer. But Elbrecht, who was white, was considered Monroe County's most liberal defense attorney, and he prided himself on not being a bigot. He had grown up in a deeply religious Lutheran family, and his parents had welcomed blacks into their Selma home at a time when that was apt to invite ostracism or a firebombing. Elbrecht had represented a number of unpopular blacks in Monroe County, and whenever attorneys for the NAACP Legal Defense Fund came to town, he let them use his office. He was the only white person in Monroeville who regularly used the new politically correct term "African American."

Although Stevenson, O'Connor, and Elbrecht would recall their meeting that day as friendly, they would later strongly disagree about what happened. Elbrecht claimed he had been unable to answer most of the questions Stevenson and O'Connor asked about Hooks because of the attorney-client privilege, which prohibited him from discussing Hooks's legal affairs without his permission. But Stevenson and O'Connor would insist that Elbrecht had discussed the case freely and had told them he had a letter in his file that would prove Hooks had been rewarded for his testimony against Johnny D. Both men later quoted Elbrecht as saying their appeal was as good as won.

After meeting with Elbrecht, they went to see another helpful witness. Clay Kast was the white mechanic who had converted Johnny D.'s truck into a low-rider. He confirmed that he had worked on the truck nearly seven months after Ronda's murder. He said he had always wondered why Chestnut and Boynton had never bothered to interview him, particularly since his testimony could have helped Johnny D. And then Kast said something that surprised his visitors. He told them Sheriff Tate and Simon Benson had come to see him before the trial and that he had told them that Hooks and Hightower were lying if they said Johnny D.'s truck was a low-rider at the time of the murder.

"You mean Sheriff Tate and Benson *knew* it wasn't a low-rider?" Stevenson asked.

Kast nodded.

"Do you know if they wrote up a statement about what you told them?"

Kast wasn't sure.

"I wonder," Stevenson said to O'Connor as they were driving out of town, "how many people in Monroeville were interviewed by the police without anyone ever writing up the results—especially if what they said would have helped Johnny D."

By the time they got back to Montgomery, O'Connor was feeling confident. "We should win this appeal based on the Bill Hooks material alone," he predicted. Stevenson was not so certain.

"You need to remind yourself what we are asking this judge to do," he said. They were, in fact, asking a locally elected judge to set the stage for Johnny D.'s conviction to be overturned. They were asking him to help an unpopular black man who had just been convicted by a local jury of brutally murdering a white teenager.

"I'm not certain that we will ever win at the local level," Stevenson told his colleague, "no matter what we prove."

Chapter 38

The Julia Tutwiler Prison for Women sits atop a hill north of Montgomery, a drab compound of five gray buildings encircled by miles of chain-link fencing topped with curls of razor wire. Karen Kelly was assigned a bunk in an open dormitory in the oldest building. Within two weeks she had befriended the fiercest black woman in the eleven-hundred-inmate population, a known lesbian and trouble-maker. "I've never seen any white woman who wanted to be one of them more than Karen Kelly did," a white guard said later. "She even spoke like a nigger."

Mozelle wrote to Kelly right away. She didn't want to lose contact, even though Kelly had lied about Vic and Myers's robbing the cleaners.

Onzell couldn't understand why. "Why are you doing this?" she asked.

"We still don't know the truth," Mozelle said.

"And you think that whore will tell you it?"

It was the start of a hectic exchange. Kelly answered Mozelle's letter a few days later, but she offered no new information. Instead she complained that she had been pressured into pleading guilty by her mother.

She also accused Myers of lying about her and Johnny D. "There's an innocent man on death row," she wrote. In a postscript she asked if Mozelle would send her the issue of the Brewton newspaper that had published her photograph and a story about her plea bargain. She was keeping a scrapbook.

Mozelle's reply was thoroughly mean. She called Kelly several obscene names and drew a picture at the bottom of the letter that showed two stick figures hitting and stabbing another figure on the ground. "KAREN KELLY MURDERER" was scrawled above one of the standing figures.

In answer Kelly protested that she had barely known Vickie Lynn and was not responsible for her death. The girl had already been involved in drug trafficking, she claimed, and she didn't care whether or not Mozelle believed her because Jesus had forgiven all her "mistakes."

"I don't call putting cocaine up your nose and going with goddamn niggers a mistake and then naming it all after God," Mozelle wrote back. "You will go to hell . . . just like the rest of them."

In her response Kelly insisted that she was a "victim"—just as much as Vickie Lynn was. She had gotten into trouble because of drugs and because she had, in her own words, "fallen in love with the wrong man." All the "ugly things you wrote," Kelly added, only made her "pray a little harder for you."

Mozelle noticed that in this letter Kelly had changed her story about what had happened. In her first letter she had claimed she barely knew Vickie Lynn. Now she was saying they were best friends.

A long letter came from Kelly a few days later in which she announced that she was finally ready to tell Mozelle the "entire truth." She and Vickie Lynn had decided to tell the police the names of several drug dealers, but at the last minute Kelly had changed her mind. That left Vickie Lynn on her own, and a few days later someone saw her talking to an FBI agent. On the night she was abducted she had known she was going to be murdered, and moments before she was beaten to death, she had made Kelly promise that someday she would tell her aunts who had killed her. Kelly had always wanted to tell the truth, she wrote, but she had been afraid of Johnny D. and what he would do. Now that he was on death row, she felt safe.

"Mozelle," the letter said, "when they hit Vickie Lynn I was standing close to her and her blood went all in my face."

Kelly's letter ended by proclaiming that Jesus had forgiven her. She asked whether Mozelle and Onzell were willing to do the same. "I am innocent," Kelly wrote. "I never stabbed that girl." She signed the letter "Love Karen."

Ralph Myers was enjoying himself. Whatever he asked for—a package of cigarettes, candy, a sandwich, soda pop—an agent would hurry outside the prison interrogation room and fetch. Of course, he was giving the various federal and state agents who came to interview him plenty in return. He admitted that he had been responsible for starting at least four house fires in Evergreen and for performing several burglaries. None of them, however, had been his idea. He had been forced by Sheriff Booker to commit each of the crimes. "Booker would drive me to a store or house or business and give me a damn portable two-way radio. I'd break in and be stealing left and right and he'd sit outside, and if a police car came by, why, he'd mash the mike button on the radio, one time long and then let go, and then hit it twice fast again—bing, bing—so I'd know to keep low."

Myers claimed that he had personally witnessed two drug-related murders: One was a simple shooting, but the other involved a dealer who had been dropped into a wood-chipper, a sharp-bladed device that shredded tree limbs within seconds. He also described numerous trips to Florida that he had made to pick up thousands of dollars' worth of drugs. He said he had carried a suitcase to Miami for Booker that was filled with half a million dollars in counterfeit bills. He had given it to a man who had bragged about being "in the Mafia." Johnny D. was the second-in-command under Booker, he told the agents, and was a major drug dealer.

Initially both the ABI and the FBI agents who came to see Myers believed his accusations, but they soon noticed that whenever they asked for specifics, he became evasive. "Goddamn, man, how stupid do you think these people are?" Myers would reply when asked the name of an accomplice. "No one uses their real names when they is laundering money or dealing dope." After six months most of the agents had wearied of this and stopped coming to interview him.

Simon Benson and Larry Ikner stuck with it longer, but eventually even they became suspicious. Finally they demanded that Myers produce some sort of evidence they could use to arrest Sheriff Booker. Myers put them off for a week, then confided in them. He had secretly taped Booker telling him to burglarize a business in Evergreen, he said, and had hidden a copy of the tape, with a pistol, in a box underneath an abandoned house in Evergreen. Myers drew a map for Benson and Ikner and told them that if they crawled underneath the house, which was built on concrete pillars about two feet above the ground, and looked up between the floor joists, they would find all the evidence they needed to prosecute.

With Myers's instructions in hand, Benson and Ikner went to Evergreen and located the old house. It looked exactly as he had described it. Eager to find proof that would help convict Booker, Ikner crawled under the building to search for the box. All he found were cobwebs.

They raced back to the prison and confronted Myers. "Someone must've stolen it," he replied glibly. "Booker must have caught wind of what you were doing and got out there first."

Benson and Ikner decided to give Myers a lie detector test. They had not required him to take one before the Morrison murder trial, but now they thought it might be useful. When the polygraph examiner finished, he told them that Myers had been a difficult subject because he had frequently refused to answer questions with a simple "yes" or "no"—he had rambled. Nonetheless, the examiner believed Myers was fabricating all his stories about Sheriff Booker. "He's lying to you," the examiner said.

Myers had wasted their time. Benson and Ikner were angry. They thought about nullifying his plea bargain. For all his promises of evidence against Booker, he hadn't come up with a single thing they could use. Meanwhile, of course, he had dodged a sentence of life without parole. They thought about taking him back to court but decided against it. It would have been embarrassing for them to acknowledge that Myers had snookered them. They would also have been forced to admit in court that Ralph Myers, their prime witness against Johnny D., had clearly been lying to them. If he had lied about Sheriff Booker to save his own neck, how could they be certain he had not lied about Johnny D. too?

The two men returned to Monroeville and cut off all communication with Myers.

Chapter 39

Rumors that Johnny D. had hired a black, Harvard-trained, Yankee lawyer spread across Monroeville. How could he afford another new attorney? It had to be drug money. Hadn't the Morrison family been through enough? On January 14, 1991, a line of cars left town for Bay Minette and the court-ordered remand hearing. Everyone wanted to see this new hotshot lawyer who had been quoted in *The Monroe Journal* as saying he was going to prove that Johnny D. had been falsely accused and wrongfully convicted.

Before the hearing started, Bryan Stevenson felt confident, and when deputies brought Johnny D. into the courtroom, the defense attorney greeted him with a reassuring smile. The records the Center's investigator, Brenda Lewis, had found in Monroeville contained four separate examples of what Stevenson considered "special enticements" given to Bill Hooks, Jr., in return for his testimony against Johnny D. All Stevenson needed to do to win his client a new trial was prove one of them.

The bailiff called the courtroom to order as soon as Judge Charles Partin walked in and motioned the attorneys to begin. Larry Ikner was the first witness. He sauntered to the witness stand with a bored expression.

Holding copies of various city court records in his right hand, Stevenson announced that he had found evidence that a city court judge had dismissed a twenty-five-dollar fine and thirty-two dollars in court costs owed by Hooks. Those costs had been forgiven at the request of Larry Ikner a few weeks after Hooks had agreed to testify against Johnny D. Turning toward the witness, Stevenson demanded to know why an investigator for the district attorney's office, which had no jurisdiction over a city court case, had bothered to concern himself with such a trivial matter.

Ikner's answer came with a shrug. Hooks had come to his office and asked for his help, he said. He had felt sorry for the black youth because he had spent the previous six months in jail and had not been able to find a job. "It is not unusual to ask a judge to give somebody credit for time served." He had done nothing for Hooks that he hadn't done a dozen times for others in town.

Then why, Stevenson continued, hadn't his investigator found other examples in the city records of times when Ikner had interceded?

Maybe she hadn't looked hard enough, Ikner replied.

Behind him Stevenson could hear chuckles from the spectators. He realized that no matter what he said, Ikner was not going to testify that Hooks had been enticed. He decided to call his next witness.

Attorney George K. Elbrecht represented Stevenson's best shot at winning the remand hearing. Stevenson and O'Connor had thought Elbrecht seemed eager to help when they had talked to him in his Monroeville office only a few weeks before. Based on that meeting, both believed that Elbrecht was, as O'Connor later put it, "someone who was going to help us blow this case wide open, especially with the letter in his files that he had mentioned to us." They planned to use him as their star witness when it came to proving their second example of enticement: that the prosecution had rewarded Hooks by reducing the burglary charge filed against him and releasing him without imposing a fine or assessing court costs.

Elbrecht was indeed a star witness—but for the other side. As Stevenson and O'Connor listened in disbelief, he assured the court that Hooks had not received any special enticements. Under gentle questioning by Tommy Chapman, he said the burglary charge filed against Hooks had been reduced to trespassing because that was what his client should have been charged with originally. Hooks and a friend had gone to burglarize a house in Evergreen, but it was the friend who had actually gone inside the building. Hooks, who had been drinking, had stayed outside to urinate. As soon as prosecutor Pearson had learned that Hooks had never entered the house, he had agreed to reduce the burglary charge to trespassing. In fact, Elbrecht said, he and Pearson had decided this at least two months before his client identified Myers and Johnny D. as Ronda's killers. Hooks had been ready to plead guilty to trespassing back on March 24, but Judge Key had nixed the deal. "Judge Key was not in the best of moods," said Elbrecht, so they had decided to wait.

On June 10 Elbrecht had received a telephone call from the courthouse. He couldn't remember who had called him, but he had been told that Judge Key was in a better humor. "We had, like, settlement days. Judge Key would say, 'Get as many clients as you can over here,' and we'd try to settle cases." Elbrecht had dashed to the courthouse, and Key had been in such a good mood that he had not only agreed to let Hooks plead guilty to trespassing but also had turned him loose without fining him or charging him court costs.

All this had happened wholly independently of the Morrison murder case, said Elbrecht. As far as he knew, the decision to release Hooks from jail and his decision to testify against Johnny D. were not linked.

Stevenson thought Elbrecht's testimony was the most far-fetched story he had ever heard. How could anyone believe it was just a coincidence that, after languishing for six months in jail, Hooks had suddenly been freed six days after he had agreed to cooperate—and *one* day after he had signed a sworn statement implicating Johnny D. in the murder?

When it was his turn to cross-examine the witness, Stevenson asked whether Elbrecht had any letters in his file about the Hooks case.

Hooks had written him one letter from jail, Elbrecht replied, but he was reluctant to read it because it was protected by the attorney-client privilege. As soon as he heard that, Stevenson demanded that Elbrecht provide a copy of the letter to the court. After a heated debate, the judge ordered the witness to read the letter. In it Hooks wrote that Sheriff Tate had just visited him in the Evergreen jail and had told him that arrangements were being made to bring him to Monroeville and free him.

Stevenson asked Elbrecht when the letter had been postmarked.

"June eighth," Elbrecht replied.

That was two days before Elbrecht had received his June 10 telephone call from the courthouse informing him that Judge Key was having one of his "settlement days."

How was it possible, Stevenson asked, that Sheriff Tate—who had no jurisdiction in an Evergreen burglary case—had known two days in advance that Key was going to turn Hooks loose? Did Tate have some crystal ball that told him when the judge was going to be in a good mood? Or had Tate known because a deal had been cut?

Elbrecht didn't respond to this. He simply continued to insist that there had never been any quid pro quo deal.

Stevenson still had two more examples of alleged enticements, but they were quickly explained by the next two witnesses. Police Chief Bill Dailey claimed that there was nothing unusual about his decision to let Hooks wait more than a year to pay $446 in traffic tickets—his department often gave residents extra time to raise the cash to pay their fines, he said. Tate acknowledged that Hooks had been paid a reward for his help, but that money had been given to him *after* Johnny D. was convicted. Tate said he had never promised Hooks a reward before the trial.

"We've got the entire white establishment going against us," O'Connor whispered to Stevenson, "and every one of them has their story down pat."

By this point in the hearing, Stevenson realized that there was only one way left for him to prove that Hooks had been rewarded for his testimony, and that was by getting Hooks himself to admit it. But when Hooks took the witness stand, he merely parroted what everyone else had said.

Stevenson refused to give up. He asked Hooks whether Benson, Ikner, or Tate had ever told him that they would get him out of jail in return for his testimony against Johnny D.

"No," Hooks said.

Stevenson repeated the question. Had they offered him any help at all?

"Sho' didn't," Hooks snapped.

For a third time Stevenson asked Hooks if his testimony about Johnny D. was linked to his release from jail.

Irritated, Hooks said they were completely separate matters.

Stevenson had been setting a trap. He had remembered that during Johnny D.'s trial, Hooks had been asked why he had been released from jail on June 10. Picking up a copy of the trial transcript, Stevenson read his answers:

Q: What happened when you went before Judge Key?

HOOKS: . . . They told me that the evidence—that I had done—the statements that I had done gave them—

Q: Wait. What statements . . . ? You mean statements in reference to what you saw at Jackson Cleaners?

HOOKS: Yes, sir . . .

Q: . . . You mean the only thing they talked about before the judge is not a crime you were charged with committing [burglary] . . . but the fact that you had given information in the Ronda Morrison murder case . . . ?

HOOKS: Yes, sir.

Lowering the transcript, Stevenson asked Hooks if the Morrison murder case had ever been mentioned during his June 10 hearing on the burglary charge.

Hooks was trapped. If he said that it hadn't, he would be contradicting his own trial testimony. But if he said that Ronda's murder *had* been discussed, he would be admitting that he had just lied about the two cases' not being linked. After a long pause, Hooks said that he had been mistaken at the trial. No one had ever mentioned Ronda's murder at the June 10 hearing.

"At least we got the fact that Hooks is a liar into the record," Stevenson whispered to O'Connor when he sat down at the defense table. "He either was lying at the trial or is lying now."

Chapman called Ted Pearson to testify next, and Pearson not only backed up the testimony of the state's other witnesses but also managed to turn the spotlight away from Stevenson's accusations and back onto Johnny D. The retired prosecutor said that just before the trial, he had been approached by J. L. Chestnut, who had asked what sort of deal Ralph Myers was getting in return for his testimony.

"Now this is paraphrasing, but it's pretty accurate. I said, 'Well, I think he's gonna plead, get life, and he's gonna testify for us,' and Mr. Chestnut said, 'Why are you gonna give him life when you're trying to give my man the death penalty?' And I said, 'Well, Ralph Myers says your man is the man that had the gun and killed the girl.' Chestnut said, 'Well, what if my man testifies that Ralph is the one that had the gun and killed the little girl? Would you give him life?' I said, 'Well, Mr. Chestnut, you know, your man has always maintained he wasn't there, didn't have anything to do with it.' Chestnut just kind of laughed. He said, 'You know, he might could change his mind on that.' "

As soon as Pearson quoted Chestnut's saying Johnny D. "might could change his mind," gasps rose from the spectators. Johnny D. glanced back at where Minnie and his friends were sitting. He shook his head. "I never said nothin' like that," he protested. The judge demanded silence.

Stevenson had to counter Pearson's testimony. But how? He had subpoenaed Chestnut to testify, but the attorney had been involved in another trial and hadn't come to the hearing. Stevenson asked the judge for permission to question Chestnut over the telephone in the judge's chambers. The judge had his bailiff arrange the call, and within a few minutes Chestnut's voice could be heard over a speaker phone.

"I'm not prepared to stand on this record and call Ted a liar," Chestnut replied when told about Pearson's accusation, "but I have to say to you that I don't remember that conversation."

Stevenson relaxed. It was not a strong repudiation, but it would do. And then Chestnut's voice came back on the line: "But I'm not prepared to say on my oath that it didn't happen either."

Stevenson seethed.

Back in the courtroom, he announced that he wanted to call Ralph Myers as a witness, but Chapman told the court that through an oversight, no one had arranged to have Myers brought from prison to the hearing. Stevenson had no choice but to rest his case. The judge announced that he would make his decision as soon as possible.

Johnny D. felt dejected. He had come into the hearing certain that his new attorneys would prove that his right to a fair trial had been violated. Instead Pearson's testimony and Chestnut's statement had made him look even guiltier. As the deputies stepped forward to handcuff him and return him to his cell, he heard Stevenson's voice whispering gently in his ear.

"Don't worry, Walter," Stevenson said. "This is not as bad as it may seem. We are going to get the truth out. Be patient."

Johnny D. felt as if he had been betrayed by his first two attorneys, but though the remand hearing had not gone as he had hoped, he still trusted Stevenson and O'Connor. He believed in them. He told himself he had to.

Outside the courthouse Chapman was surrounded by reporters and supporters from Monroeville. He was visibly pleased, and he publicly criticized Stevenson and O'Connor for making "outrageous" accusations without providing the court with a shred of evidence. No one had done anything improper in prosecuting Johnny D. No one had enticed or paid off anyone for their testimony. Under the glare of the television lights, Chapman said he deeply regretted that the Morrison family was being forced to relive their daughter's tragic death simply because a pair of clever defense attorneys were seeing conspiracies where there were none. The hearing was nothing but an attempt to drag out the death penalty process, he declared.

Stevenson and O'Connor slipped past the media unnoticed. Both knew they had failed to show that Hooks had been paid off. They decided they had underestimated the prosecution. Both were also furious at Elbrecht. They believed he had betrayed them. "The next time we go back to court," said O'Connor, "we'll know better than to count on help from any of them."

Stevenson didn't respond. He was praying that there would be a next time for his client.

Chapter 40

Five days after the remand hearing, Judge Charles Partin ruled that Stevenson had failed to prove his accusations. "There was no agreement between Bill Hooks, Jr., and the state with respect to his testifying in the McMillian trial," Partin told the Alabama Court of Criminal Appeals. The fact that Hooks had been released from jail one day after he had agreed to testify against Johnny D. "appears to be happenstance."

Stevenson had never wanted to be a detective, but he knew the only way to save his client now was to find irrefutable evidence that proved Johnny D. was innocent. The seventeen examples of alleged errors by the court that he had cited in his first appeal were simply not going to be enough. He suspected that the appeals court would knock them down one by one. He called O'Connor and the Center's investigator, Brenda Lewis, into his office and announced that he wanted them to track down and interview every witness in the case. He wanted them to investigate Ronda's murder as if they were the police and had just been called to the murder scene.

In early 1991 Stevenson and O'Connor drove to the state crime lab in Mobile and asked to see the autopsy report on Ronda Morrison. They could have had a copy mailed to them, but Stevenson wanted to examine the "raw data" and any letters or memos in the medical examiner's file that might not have made it into the final copy. They struck pay dirt. A "memo to the file" written by criminalist Elaine Scott seventeen days after Ronda's murder described a pair of shoes that had been sent to the crime lab by Monroeville investigators. The right shoe had a bloodstain on it and belonged to Carlos Roquellera, who was identified by Scott as "suspect—Ronda Morrison murder." Another internal memo written one month after the murder disclosed that hair and blood samples taken from "suspect Carlos Roquellera did not match hair and blood samples taken from Ronda Morrison." A third internal document showed that Roquellera's clothing had been examined and that Roquellera had been held in jail during December 1987 as the prime suspect in the Morrison killing.

This was the first time Stevenson and O'Connor had heard the name Carlos Roquellera. There had been no mention of the Cuban in any of the papers that Benson, Ikner, and Tate had been required by the court to provide to the two defense attorneys. They had always been told that Johnny D. had been the only suspect.

Back in Montgomery, O'Connor began searching for Roquellera. Stevenson, meanwhile, drove to the Julia Tutwiler Prison to interview Karen Kelly.

"Johnny D. didn't have nothing to do with that Morrison girl being killed," she told him. "Ralph made all this up and I was crazy to help him." Kelly told Stevenson that she and Myers had been interrogated about the murder "two or three days" after Myers was arrested, in the same room at the Monroe County Courthouse.

"Wait a second," Stevenson said, interrupting her. "Are you sure it was that soon after he was arrested?" He had always been told that Myers had not talked to the police until June 9, nine days after he was arrested.

"Yes," said Kelly. "I'm positive."

"And they interviewed you both together?"

"They took me into a room with Ralph and he and I got into an argument and called each other all sorts of names."

"And who was there?"

"They all were—Larry Ikner, Simon Benson, and Sheriff Tate."

Stevenson made a note. He had never been given any transcripts of interviews that indicated Kelly and Myers had been questioned together. He had never been given any copies of *any* statements made by Kelly.

Stevenson asked Kelly what had happened next. Benson, Ikner, and Tate had taken them out of the interview room, and for about ten minutes she and Myers had been left alone in a hallway. "That's when Ralph told me that we was both going to go down for Vickie Lynn's murder. I said, 'You're crazy, Ralph. I didn't kill that girl.' And he says, 'It don't matter 'cause I'll say you did unless you do what I say.' Then he tells me that we got to give them someone to put it off on, otherwise they are gonna get us. He says, 'Let's put it off on Johnny D. Let's tell 'em that he did Vickie Lynn and Ronda Morrison'—'cause they had been asking Ralph all about the Monroeville murder. I said, 'Ralph, you are one sick, crazy bastard,' but he says, 'You bitch, you do what I tell you or I'll say you and Johnny D. killed Vickie Lynn and Ronda Morrison.' I was in Monroeville when that girl was killed, and he said that he'd blame me and Johnny D. so I said I'd do what he told me."

The next time she talked to Ikner and Benson, Kelly said, she told them that Johnny D. had bragged to her on the day after the murder about how he had killed Ronda. "It was a damn lie," she said. "I made it up, but it was what they wanted to hear."

Stevenson was excited by what Kelly was saying, but he also knew it was not really going to help. No one was going to believe her now, not after all the stories she had told, and especially since she still claimed to be in love with Johnny D.

He said so. "Karen, no one is going to believe you."

"Then I'll tell you something you can prove," she answered.

Five months after Ronda had been killed, Kelly and Myers had gone to the Crispy Chick in Evergreen to eat lunch. While they were there, she noticed that Johnny D.'s truck was parked at a garage across the street. He had been avoiding her, she said, so she wrote a note on a paper napkin and asked Myers to take it across the street and give it to Johnny D.

"When he went across the street, he walked right by Johnny D. and asked the garage owner if he knew a Johnny D. McMillian," she explained. "Everyone laughed and said, 'He's standing right behind you.' Now you tell me something. If Ralph Myers and Johnny D. McMillian had killed the Morrison girl in November 1986, how come Ralph Myers can't even recognize Johnny D. five months later at that repair shop?"

Stevenson drove to Evergreen, found the garage Kelly had described, and interviewed its owner. He did indeed remember the day when Myers had come across the street with a note for Johnny D. Myers had walked directly past him, the owner said. He didn't have a clue who Johnny D. was.

Stevenson's investigator, Brenda Lewis, found Florence Mason living in Florida. "I wondered if anyone was ever going to ask me what I seen that day at the cleaners," Mason volunteered. "You know, I was the first one to see that dead girl and it seemed like I would have been the first one for the police to talk to."

"Did the police take a statement from you?" asked Lewis. If they had, she wanted to know why Stevenson had not been given a copy of it.

"No, they never did," Mason replied. Along with Jerrie Sue Dunning and Coy Stacey, Mason had been told to wait outside Jackson Cleaners. An hour or so later, a white police officer had come outside and taken down her name. Mason said she had seen this same officer give Jerrie Sue Dunning a piece of paper and had heard him ask her to write down everything that had happened in the cleaners, "but he didn't ask me nothing." She also saw another officer interviewing Coy Stacey. "But no one ever asked me nothing."

The first Mason knew about Johnny D.'s trial was when she read about it in the newspapers. "They said that white lady was the first person in the cleaners that morning, but that ain't true."

"It isn't?" asked a surprised Lewis. At the trial the prosecution had said that Dunning had arrived first, followed by Mason, and finally Stacey.

"Well, that ain't right," said Mason. "I will go to the top and tell anyone who asks me that that white lady did not come to the cleaners first that morning. I was there first, unless she come and then went and then come back. Otherwise I was the first somebody there and then he, Mr. Stacey, he come in and then she comes in."

"What time did you get there?" Lewis asked.

Mason said she hadn't been wearing a watch but it had been at least five minutes before Stacey and Dunning arrived. That meant she had arrived at the cleaners at about ten-forty, or five minutes earlier than the trial testimony indicated.

"I thought about them not contacting me a lot," she replied. "It woulda been easy to find me. The only reason I think they didn't want me to testify is because I'm black and them other two is white."

Michael O'Connor couldn't find Carlos Roquellera, but he tracked down Randy Thomas in Tuscaloosa. The former owner of the cleaners was reluctant to meet with him, but he finally agreed. As soon as O'Connor began questioning him, Thomas broke into tears. "No one was involved in drugs at the cleaners," he said. "I never did anything wrong there."

O'Connor asked Thomas if he had ever noticed anything suspicious at the store, and Thomas replied that the only thing he thought was odd was how all of the girls who worked there were frightened of Miles Jackson.

Had Thomas ever mentioned this to the police? O'Connor asked.

"Of course," Thomas replied. "They talked to Mr. Jackson and took a statement from him."

O'Connor made a note. No one had ever given them any statements from Jackson.

Stevenson and O'Connor were hesitant to contact Monroeville police lieutenant Woodrow Ikner. After all, he was the police department's chief investigator and had testified for the prosecution against Johnny D. But in May 1991 *The Monroe Journal* reported that Woodrow Ikner had been found guilty of perjury and sentenced to five years in prison for fabricating evidence against a black burglary suspect. He was appealing the verdict and was allowed to remain free on bond while the appeals court reviewed his case. As soon as Stevenson and O'Connor read the article, they drove to Monroeville. According to the newspaper, Woodrow Ikner had been prosecuted by Tommy Chapman, based on evidence gathered by Larry Ikner and the sheriff's department. At the time of the Morrison trial, Woodrow Ikner had been part of the prosecution's team. Both attorneys suspected that he no longer was.

Ikner agreed to meet them and answer their questions, but first, he said, there were two things they needed to understand. "I'm innocent," he declared. "I never did anything dishonest in my life as a police officer." He had never been part of the "right" crowd in Monroeville, he said. "I've put some influential people in jail around here—a doctor, a lawyer—and I think the people in power just wanted to get rid of me. I've seen the people who run things around here do that to other people. They can charge anyone with anything and get a jury to convict them."*

The second issue Ikner wanted Stevenson and O'Connor to under-

* Eleven months after Woodrow Ikner was found guilty of perjury, the Alabama Court of Criminal Appeals overturned the verdict and in a biting opinion declared that no evidence presented at his trial showed he had committed perjury. All charges against him were subsequently dismissed.

stand was that he believed Johnny D. was guilty. "I think he murdered that little Morrison girl."

"All we are after is the truth," Stevenson assured him. "We don't want you or anyone else to lie."

Woodrow Ikner seemed to relax. "I tried to do everything by the book in the Morrison case," he said. "We ran down every lead. I know we took over thirty-five statements from witnesses and we had most of them write them out themselves—"

"You did?" O'Connor interrupted.

"Sure we did," Woodrow replied. "Every time we met with a suspect, we made a record of it." Spreading his right thumb and forefinger about four inches apart, he said, "I had an accordion file this thick with witness statements and documents."

"Where are those records now?" Stevenson asked.

"At the police department. The FBI also has a copy."

Stevenson asked Ikner whether he could get copies of the reports for them. No, Ikner replied; because of his perjury conviction, he was no longer on the police force. But he could call a friend and make certain the records were still there. He was surprised, he added, that Stevenson and O'Connor hadn't been given copies of the files.

"We asked for all of them," said O'Connor, "but they haven't given us them. They have only given us three statements."

"One thing that has always troubled me," Ikner said, "is that we thought this was a sex crime when we first found her body, not a robbery and not a drug deal. I've always wondered what would have happened if Ronda Morrison had not been so religious. Whoever it was who killed her was trying to rape her, and I figured that Ronda would rather have died than have someone rape her. That was just the kinda girl she was. I kept asking myself what if she had not been so religious and had not fought? Would she have still been alive?"

The first time he had heard about Johnny D. being a suspect, Woodrow Ikner said, was after Benson, Larry Ikner, and Sheriff Tate had arrested Johnny D. "They promised they would keep me informed of their investigation, but they never did."

Stevenson asked Ikner if he had seen any drag marks in the cleaners at the place where Ronda Morrison's body had been moved from the lobby.

"Weren't no marks there," Ikner said firmly. "That little girl died right where we found her. That body was never moved. Listen, before the trial, Ted Pearson asked me to testify that the body had been drugged across the floor. I said, 'No sir, I will not testify, because I saw no evidence that the body had been drugged.' "

"The district attorney asked you to testify that the body had been dragged?"

"Yes sir, he sure did. And I said no. I wasn't going to say that."

Back at the Resource Center, Stevenson, O'Connor, and Lewis reviewed their findings:

- The state crime lab reports showed that a Cuban named Carlos Roquellera was the first suspect questioned by the police.
- The owner of the garage in Evergreen said Ralph Myers did not recognize Johnny D. five months after the Morrison murder.
- Karen Kelly said she and Ralph Myers agreed to frame Johnny D. to save themselves.
- Florence Mason said she was the first to arrive at the cleaners at about ten-forty A.M., five minutes earlier than had been reported.
- Woodrow Ikner said Ronda's body had not been dragged from the lobby into the back room. He said at least thirty-five witness statements about the murder had been collected.
- Randy Thomas said there were no drugs at the cleaners, but that the girls had felt uncomfortable whenever Miles Jackson came into the building.

Stevenson, O'Connor, and Lewis all agreed that there was one witness in Monroeville whom they still needed to interview. O'Connor and Lewis drove to Miles Jackson's house the next day. They were afraid he might refuse to meet with them if they telephoned first, so they waited until they saw him come outside. Jumping from their car, they hurried across the driveway and introduced themselves. Jackson seemed pleased to see them. He invited them inside, where Doris was watching television in the family room.

"I wondered when you'd come see me," Jackson said excitedly. "You know, of course, that I was the last person to see that little girl alive?"

O'Connor and Lewis glanced at each other.

"You didn't know, did you?" said Jackson, reacting to the startled looks on their faces. During the next few minutes, he explained that he had gone to the bank on the morning of the murder. "The police have my bank slip. It has ten-nineteen stamped on it," he volunteered. From there he had driven directly to the cleaners, where he had spoken to Ronda, picked up his laundry, and left the building at approximately ten-thirty.

"You were at the cleaners at ten-thirty that morning?" O'Connor asked.

"Yes, I was," Jackson replied.

"And the police know this?"

"Of course they do, young man. All of this is in my statement."

"So you did give the police a written statement?"

"My Lord, yes," said Jackson, adding that he had also submitted to a polygraph test that had proved he was innocent.

"Miles was supposed to testify at the trial," Doris explained. The prosecution had subpoenaed him, and the two of them had driven to the courthouse in Bay Minette. Because he was a witness, they were told that Jackson couldn't go into the courtroom, so Doris had waited with him in a room with other witnesses. But no one ever called him to testify. It wasn't until after the trial ended and they were reading about it in the newspaper that they learned that Ted Pearson had identified Jan Owen as the last customer to see Ronda alive, at ten-fifteen A.M. Both of them knew that was wrong, and Doris had decided that the prosecution had kept her husband's name out of the case on purpose.

"We think it was because they thought that the nigger lawyers would immediately pounce on Miles," she recalled later in a tape-recorded interview. "They would have spent so much time trying to destroy Miles that it would have clouded the issue."

"They tried to keep me out of it," Miles Jackson added. "They slurred over the fact that my fingerprints were all over that place. The way they worded it was there were 'no fingerprints of any importance found' because they didn't want anything to sidetrack and put the spotlight onto me, and I thank them for that."

O'Connor and Lewis were astounded. They headed for a pay telephone as soon as they left the Jacksons' house, but then O'Connor worried that it might not be safe. He was beginning to feel paranoid about the power of law enforcement in Monroeville. Instead they drove directly to Montgomery. Although they arrived after midnight, Stevenson was still in his office.

"Jackson was at the cleaners at ten-thirty on the day of the murder!" O'Connor blurted out. "He was the last person to see Ronda alive, not Jan Owen!"

Stevenson picked up his copy of the trial transcript and found Owen's testimony. He wanted to make certain he knew exactly what had been said in court. Owen had testified that she was at the cleaners at ten-fifteen. Pearson had then called Jerrie Sue Dunning to the witness stand, and she had testified that she arrived at the cleaners at about ten-forty-five. There was no mention of Miles Jackson's going into the store at ten-thirty.

Flipping to the end of the trial transcript, Stevenson read the prosecution's closing arguments to the jury.

Assistant prosecutor Lynn Stuart had gone first, outlining the facts of the case. Pearson had then delivered his remarks.

STUART: I think it is without dispute that at approximately ten-fifteen on Saturday morning, November first, Ronda Morrison was fine . . . I think it is also without dispute that approximately thirty minutes later, at a quarter to eleven, additional customers came to Jackson Cleaners and . . . found her lifeless body. . . . The facts that are essential to this case occurred in a thirty-minute period.

PEARSON: I don't think there is any doubt Ronda was alive somewhere around ten-fifteen. I don't think there is any doubt she was dead at about a quarter to eleven. That is about a thirty-minute period . . .

Neither of the prosecutors had mentioned that Miles Jackson had come into Jackson Cleaners at ten-thirty A.M.

Next Stevenson turned to Myers's testimony and read his account of the murder. Myers said he had stayed in the pickup truck when they got to the cleaners, but Johnny D. had gone inside. He had come outside about four minutes later to apologize for taking so long and then had gone back into the building. Around five minutes later he had come outside again. This time he suggested that Myers drive to a gas station and buy some cigarettes.

QUESTION: Do you know approximately how long you were gone?

MYERS: Probably about, I say about, probably about ten or fifteen minutes, if that long.

When he returned, Myers waited outside the cleaners for another five minutes. That was when he saw two men in a blue LTD sedan drop off their clothes. A few minutes later he heard "popping noises" and raced inside. He and Johnny D. spent at least five minutes in the building arguing before Myers returned to the truck and waited two or three more minutes for Johnny D. to come outside. They then fled. According to Myers's testimony, Johnny D. had spent a minimum of thirty minutes inside the cleaners.

"The prosecution wasn't protecting Miles Jackson when they kept his trip there that morning a secret," Stevenson told O'Connor and Lewis. "They were protecting Ralph Myers and their case." If the jury had been told that Miles Jackson had been inside the cleaners at ten-thirty, then it would have known that the murder had to have happened within a *fifteen*-minute period—between ten-thirty and ten-forty-five—and that meant Ralph Myers's *thirty*-minute account was simply impossible. Myers had clearly lied.

Lewis reminded them that Florence Mason had said she was the first to arrive at the cleaners, at about ten-forty. That narrowed down the killing to about a ten-minute period, which meant Ronda had been murdered between ten-thirty and ten-forty.

It was obvious that Benson, Ikner, and Tate had known that Jackson was at the cleaners that morning. Stevenson also suspected that prosecutor Pearson had known, simply because the state had subpoenaed Jackson as a witness. But not one of those men had said anything during the trial, nor had they told the defense about his visit.

"They sat there and didn't tell the jury what really happened that morning," Stevenson declared. "How could they have done that? How could they have sat there and allowed the jury to believe a lie?"

Chapter 41

In June 1991 Ralph Myers called J. L. Chestnut from prison. "I lied on the witness stand about McMillian killing Ronda Morrison," he said. "I put an innocent man on death row."

"I know you lied," Chestnut replied. "I knew you were lying then. Why have you suddenly found Jesus?"

Myers didn't want to talk about it on the telephone. He asked Chestnut to come see him at the state prison in St. Clair, northeast of Birmingham. Chestnut said he was too busy. He gave Myers the telephone number for Bryan Stevenson. Two weeks later Chestnut happened to be talking to an attorney who worked for Stevenson and asked whether Myers had ever called. He hadn't.

"Well," Chestnut told the attorney, "Ralph Myers has admitted to me that he lied about McMillian. He made up the entire story."

The attorney scrambled into Stevenson's office. "Myers wants to recant!" she exclaimed. "He called Chestnut two weeks ago!"

Stevenson and O'Connor went to see Myers at prison the next morning.

"Them sons of bitches in Monroeville don't want me talking to you,"

Myers declared. "They never told me about your hearing down there in Bay Minette because they didn't want you to know what I'm about to say."

Myers paused and took a long drag on his hand-rolled cigarette. He had talked to so many attorneys and law enforcement officers through the years that he was an expert at pacing his stories for dramatic effect. "Everything I said at the trial was a goddamn lie," he proclaimed. "Your man was framed."

Because Myers rambled as always, it took him several hours to outline what had happened. His story came out in fragments, diverted by tangents and sprinkled with excuses. But when they finished talking that night, Stevenson and O'Connor were both pleased. Myers had admitted that he had concocted his entire testimony about how Johnny D. had killed Ronda Morrison. He also told them one of the most incredible tales about corruption in law enforcement that either of them had ever heard. "You got to get me out of here!" he pleaded. "A sheriff is trying to have me killed."

During the next several days Stevenson and O'Connor met continuously with Myers. They wanted him to sign an affidavit admitting that he had lied; they were afraid he might change his mind or, worse, might be killed. But Myers was not in any hurry now that he had an audience coming to see him. He enjoyed the attention, and he would not be governed by anyone's schedule but his own.

First he wanted them to help him determine whether a murder contract had actually been put out on his life. Another inmate at the prison, Robert Johnson, had told Myers that he had been offered a contract to kill him. Myers suggested that O'Connor interview the alleged hit man. Johnson told O'Connor that he had recently gone to the Julia Tutwiler Prison to perform with an inmate musical band and had been approached by Karen Kelly. Kelly, he said, had told him that a "certain sheriff" wanted Myers killed. In return for the murder, this "sheriff" would arrange for Johnson to be transferred to a county jail and would then let him escape. Johnson had considered the offer, but decided it was too risky. Kelly could be lying, and even if she was telling the truth, there was no guarantee that Johnson wouldn't be murdered himself once he was transferred to the county jail. Rather than accept the contract, he decided to tell Myers about it.

O'Connor and Stevenson thought the two inmates were telling the truth. That made Myers happy. He asked if they could find someone in the FBI or Justice Department outside Alabama who would be willing to help him. In return for immunity and an early parole, he would be willing to testify about the "corrupt sheriff." They promised to help.

Stevenson and O'Connor had no idea, of course, that much of what Myers was saying was a repeat of the unsubstantiated stories he had already told about Sheriff Booker. He did not mention the polygraph examiner who had already determined that his accusations were lies, nor did he tell the same story he had told before. When Myers had talked to Benson and Ikner, he had identified Johnny D. as Sheriff Booker's second-in-command, but now that he was talking to Johnny D.'s lawyers, ABI agent Simon Benson had that role. Years later Myers would become upset when he was asked during an interview about the way he had played each side's fears and suspicions against the other's—always to his advantage. After several uncomfortable minutes, he blurted out a comment that revealed much about him and his skill at manipulating others. "What the hell is the truth? I'll tell you what it is. It is whatever damn well the person listening to you wants to hear. If it agrees with what they've been wantin' for you to tell 'em, then, by golly, they say, 'Oh, Ralph is telling us the truth.' But if they don't want to hear it, then bingo, 'Oh, Ralph is a-lying to us.' So what is the truth? You tell me."

Although Myers was clearly a con man and a liar and was a self-confessed murderer, the two attorneys found it hard to dislike him. He had compensated for his inability to read and write by developing extraordinary skills as a storyteller. He could make an experience as mundane as trying to buy a soft drink from a broken vending machine sound as if it were some grand adventure that required hours to explain. He never stopped talking. When he couldn't find anyone to speak with in person, he made collect calls on the prison's pay phones. One afternoon he announced that he had called the White House and had been connected directly with President Ronald Reagan. The fact that Reagan was no longer in office didn't prevent him from insisting that he was telling the truth and quoting at length what he claimed Reagan had confided to him. It was obvious to Stevenson and O'Connor that Myers was a compulsive liar—something that Benson, Ikner, and Tate had to have known. Myers was also lonely and insecure. They soon learned that he always had been.

Myers had been an unwanted baby, the first child born to Ruth Myers, an unwed teenager. Four years later Ruth married Donald Morgan, an army private, and the family settled in Coffee Springs, Alabama, population three hundred, where Ruth gave birth to seven more children.

Years later neighbors would still remember the family as being totally out of control. "No one had ever locked their doors in Coffee Springs," said Dick Smith, a mail carrier who lived next door to the Morgans, "until Ralph and his parents moved to town." Ralph stole money from the Smiths' house, the school principal's house, and a parsonage. Once he was spotted pulling a red wagon overflowing with stolen booty down Main Street. Yet despite such shenanigans, most townfolk seemed to forgive him. "He was such a good-hearted kid," said Smith. "He stole a silver dollar from my house one day, but he spent it on candy for himself, my children, and others in the neighborhood. He wasn't mean-spirited. You could tell that he just didn't get any attention or guidance at home. He seemed desperate for someone to love him."

When he was eleven years old, Myers started running away. A year later the state put him in a group home in Birmingham. His parents claimed that he had been such a hellion that the entire family had been forced to leave town. He charged that his stepfather beat him, fed him dog food, and kept him locked in a dark closet for punishment—charges the stepfather later denied.

When Charles Gilmore was elected sheriff of Barbour County in 1969, he found Ralph, then fourteen, living at the county jail at Eufaula, Alabama, a resort town on the Georgia border, where his parents had relocated. "My predecessor turned all of the prisoners loose on the day that I took office, but he left little-bitty Ralph locked up there," Gilmore recalled. "The boy hadn't been charged with any crimes. He was simply a throwed-away kid with nowhere to go. No one wanted him—including his parents. So he was living in the jail."

Gilmore got a welfare worker to put Myers into a foster home. Just before Christmas in 1970, he stepped too close to a gas heater and his pajamas burst into flames. "His nightgown lit up like it was gasoline," recalled Gilmore, who drove the screaming teenager to the hospital. "It was so hot that Ralph's chin was welded onto his chest." More than half of his body was covered with third-degree burns. He underwent sixty-three skin grafts at various burn centers. He was sixteen when he was finally allowed to return home, but he didn't stay there long. He had only completed the fifth grade and felt awkward going to school with children six years younger than he. Because of his burn scars, particularly on his chin, he frightened other children. A social worker would note that Myers was attacked by several high school boys one afternoon and was tied to a tree. The boys ripped open his shirt so that they could see his scarred skin, and when he began cursing at them they hit him. Myers left town. He hitchhiked to New York state, where he lived briefly with relatives.

In 1980 Myers was arrested three times for burglary and sentenced to fourteen months in prison. For a short period after his release, he worked for a paving crew putting down asphalt and stayed out of trouble. Through a cousin he met Jennifer, a twenty-two-year-old girl with a son aged two. She lived in Evergreen with her parents, a poor white family. "He asked me to marry him seven times before I finally agreed," Jennifer said later. They got along well until he lost his job. "He began staying out all night drinking." Without any income, they were forced to move in with her parents. One afternoon Myers took his stepson to a fast-food restaurant, and when they returned, the boy was crying. Jennifer took off her son's shirt and found bruises. She hurried the boy to the hospital for X rays, and the doctors called the police. Uncertain about what had happened, a child welfare worker took custody of the boy away from Jennifer. Myers, who had never gotten along well with his in-laws, was kicked out of their house. He began spending his nights at the Waffle House restaurant near the Evergreen exit on Interstate 65. He would stay there all night, nursing cups of coffee.

Off and on, Myers and his wife would get back together, but it never lasted more than a few weeks. He couldn't keep a job, and there was never any money. During one of their on-again periods, Jennifer got pregnant. Ralph moved back home after the baby was born, but Jennifer kicked him out the night she found him holding a pillow over the baby's face because its crying was getting on his nerves. A despondent Myers slashed his wrists. A few days later he jumped in front of a truck. That was in April 1986, when Tommy Chapman was appointed by the court to represent Myers at a sanity hearing. Myers was sent by a judge to Searcy Hospital, where he complained of recurring nightmares, most of them about his experiences in prison. After he was released, Myers befriended Karen Kelly. He also began using drugs.

During their meetings in prison, Myers told Stevenson and O'Connor that he had never heard about the Ronda Morrison murder until Benson and Ikner arrested him and drove him to the jail in Monroeville. "They slowed down in front of the cleaners and began talking about how a girl had been killed there," he said. "Every time we got together, they told me a bit more about the Morrison case. I knew what they were doing."

Myers said the officers told him he would not be allowed to visit with his wife or children until he told them who had killed Ronda Morrison. "They kept asking me about Johnny D., asking if he killed her, putting his name in my mind."

One morning while he was in the Monroe County jail, he spotted a mouse scampering across the floor. He began leaving it food, and eventually the mouse became tame enough for him to hold. He talked to it and let it sleep under the blanket with him at night. Lillie Falkenberry, an elderly and deeply religious Monroeville resident who regularly visited jail inmates, would later remember that Myers had showed her his pet mouse. He named the mouse Midnight. "I think that the mouse filled a little of the vacuum in his life," Falkenberry said. "I have never met anyone who was so desperate for someone to care about him."

Myers began drawing cartoons, first of Midnight and then of Midnight's imaginary family, which included his mouse wife and "Baby Mouse." In the cartoons Midnight always took care of and protected Baby Mouse. Myers drew pictures of Midnight tucking Baby Mouse into bed, telling him that he loved him, telling him what a good mouse he was and how he made his father proud. One morning Myers's real mouse disappeared. "The truth is that nobody really gives a damn about anyone else in this world," Myers said later, recalling the incident. "People say they do and they might for a short while, but they always end up leaving you. Even that goddamn mouse left me."

Myers told Stevenson and O'Connor that after he had spent a few days in jail, he was under so much pressure that he finally cracked and lied about Johnny D. "But I tried to get out of it before the trial. I told 'em I wasn't going to testify because I didn't want to be responsible for putting an innocent man on death row." That was when Judge Key sent him to the Taylor Hardin Secure Medical Facility for observation. While there, he began having hallucinations. "One day I looked up from my bed and there was Simon Benson and Judge Key sitting in my room with me. I wasn't on any dope but I was so scared of them and they pointed at me and said, 'Just do what you are told to do' and it pissed me off so I jumped off the bed and I swung at them to hit them and my fist hit the wall because they weren't really there. I said, 'Jesus, I'm going crazy.' "

At the mental hospital a few nights later, he woke up drenched with sweat. "I looked over and there was the devil. He was the ugliest creature you could ever imagine, with crooked horns and long black teeth and bloodred skin. He began laughing at me because that evil son of a bitch knew exactly what I was going to do. He knew I was going to lie about Johnny D. McMillian, which is what I did."

On August 28, 1991, Myers signed an affidavit that Stevenson had prepared for him based on their conversations. Among other things, it contained these statements:

1. I never saw McMillian on the day that Ronda Morrison was murdered . . .
2. I was not at the cleaners when Ronda Morrison was killed and I did not see McMillian at the cleaners . . .
3. I was shown pictures of the crime scene that helped me make up the testimony about the Morrison murder and McMillian . . .
4. I was told to make up allegations about McMillian sexually assaulting me so that local law enforcement could arrest McMillian . . .
5. I was heavily pressured to testify falsely against McMillian . . .
6. I'm sorry for what I've done . . .

Chapter 42

"We've had a major breakthrough in your case," Stevenson told Johnny D. over the telephone, "but I don't want to talk about it until we can meet in person." All Myers's stories about corrupt law enforcement had made him leery. He didn't know who might be monitoring the prison telephones. "I'll be at the prison tomorrow."

Back in his cell, Johnny D. got out his dictionary and looked up the word "breakthrough." He was relieved to learn that it wasn't something bad.

"Myers is admitting that he lied about you," Stevenson told him the next morning. O'Connor, who had come to the prison with Stevenson, showed Johnny D. a copy of Myers's recantation.

"God has answered my prayers," Johnny D. said, his face a huge smile. Two years earlier a minister from Mobile had visited death row and had offered to pray with its inmates. "I told that preacher: 'A man lied on me and put me in prison.'" Together they had asked God "to make Ralph Myers tell the truth."

"Some might not believe it," Johnny D. continued, "but I believe the Lord made Ralph talk."

From Holman prison, Stevenson and O'Connor drove northwest to Monroeville, parking outside the courthouse. They had called ahead and told Tommy Chapman they needed to meet with him. Though Chapman had been hostile toward them during the remand hearing, they were hoping he might change his attitude once he learned that Myers had recanted. Chapman was all smiles when they arrived, but when they handed him a copy of Myers's recantation and he read that the inmate was now claiming that Benson, Ikner, and Tate had pressured him to lie, his mood changed.

"Ralph Myers is a bald-faced liar," Chapman said. "You can't believe anything he tells you."

"Then why do you believe what he has said about Johnny D. being at the cleaners?" Stevenson replied. "You can't have it both ways, Tommy."

"You're forgetting that two other witnesses testified that they saw your man at the cleaners," Chapman said.

Those two witnesses, Stevenson replied, were hardly credible. "Hooks was given favorable treatment and a reward and—"

Chapman cut him off. "We've been over all that at the remand hearing and you couldn't prove any of it." Returning to Myers's recantation, he said, "Bryan, you and I both know that it is not uncommon for someone who has testified against a codefendant to change his story once he gets into prison. No inmate wants to be known as a snitch. That's all Ralph is doing. He's feeding you a bunch of bull."

Stevenson disagreed. "He's told us the truth about Johnny D. and he has told us some other things that you need to hear." Stevenson told Chapman about Myers's charges against Sheriff Booker, including his claim that the sheriff had personally ordered Vickie Lynn Pittman's execution.

"I've been hearing accusations against Sheriff Booker for years," Chapman replied. "If any of those charges were true, don't you think the FBI or ABI would have proven them by now?"

Stevenson realized that he was getting nowhere, so he changed the subject. Several witnesses had told him they had been interviewed by the Monroeville police about Ronda's murder, but the defense had not been given copies of their statements. "We know they exist," he said, "and we want copies of them."

"You have been given everything you are entitled to get," Chapman replied coldly.

Stevenson and O'Connor left the courthouse empty-handed and annoyed. Chapman called Larry Ikner and Benson into his office.

"Ralph Myers says you forced him to testify against Johnny D.," Chapman said. He showed them a copy of Myers's recantation. Both immediately denied any wrongdoing. Chapman felt better. But he later recalled just how angry the incident had made him. "Stevenson and O'Connor came into my office and basically claimed that Sheriff Tate and Larry Ikner and Simon Benson were so corrupt that they had framed Johnny D. because he was black and because he was dating a white woman and because he was linked to Sheriff Booker—and I knew that none of that was true. And then I find out that they are basing all of these charges on Ralph Myers! They don't have one single piece of evidence that he has given them, not one thing to corroborate this fairy-tale stuff about Booker threatening him, making him kill somebody, running drugs. There is just no reason to believe this stuff."

The more Chapman thought about it, the more it bothered him. He decided someone needed to tell Sheriff Booker what Myers was saying, so he picked up the telephone and dialed the sheriff's number.

Chapman didn't know exactly what he believed about Booker. Benson and Larry Ikner didn't trust Booker, and there were plenty of others in law enforcement who refused to deal with him. During his sixteen years in office, Booker had been successfully sued by an inmate for using prisoners as slave labor on his cattle ranch, had feuded with a local judge, and, by his own admission, had been under almost continual surveillance by federal and state drug agents. Before Chapman was appointed district attorney, he had defended Booker's chief deputy, Jerome Boykin, who had been charged with knowingly buying a stolen Cadillac. A horde of FBI agents had come to see Chapman before the trial with offers of immunity for his client if he was willing to turn against Booker and tell them what he knew. But Boykin had refused to cooperate and had eventually been acquitted of the Cadillac-stealing charge. He still worked for Booker.

None of Chapman's other clients had ever been offered such lucrative deals by the FBI. It was clear to Chapman that the government was eager to arrest the sheriff. Still, he couldn't help wondering: If Booker was dishonest, then how come no one had ever caught him doing anything wrong?

Booker had his defenders as well as his critics. He was extremely popular among blacks, in part because he had been the first sheriff in Conecuh County to hire a black deputy. Tommy Chapman's wife, Patsy, worked at the local elementary school, and she told her husband that two or three times each week Booker ate with the children in the lunchroom and lectured them about staying out of trouble. He was also an active leader in the town's tiny Reorganized Church of Jesus Christ of Latter-Day Saints. Those activities certainly didn't seem to fit with his rogue image.

When Chapman told Booker about Myers's latest charges, the sheriff laughed. "Hey, if I wanted to kill someone," he said, "don't you think I'm smart enough to do it without Ralph Myers's help? . . . Only a fool would murder someone in front of the likes of Ralph Myers or Karen Kelly."

Chapman was relieved. He felt even better a few days later. Without being asked, Simon Benson had gone to the prison in St. Clair, where Myers was being held, to investigate Myers's claim that Booker had tried to hire another inmate to kill him. "Benson tells me that he talked to this Robert Johnson in prison and, sure enough, Johnson admitted to him that he had been approached by Karen Kelly at Tutwiler Prison to kill Ralph Myers," Chapman said later. "But Benson tells me that Johnson says it was Johnny D. who wanted Ralph dead. He's the one behind the contract to kill him, not Sheriff Booker."

Benson also told Chapman that Stevenson and O'Connor had met with Myers in prison more than ten times. "You got to wonder why they have been meeting with Ralph so often," Chapman said to Benson. "You got to wonder if they aren't pushing Ralph to change his story."

Chapman telephoned Larry W. Burton, the warden at St. Clair prison, and asked him for two favors. He wanted Myers moved to a more remote facility to make it difficult for Stevenson and O'Connor to continue meeting with him. Chapman also asked for the warden's help in running a scam on the inmate. He asked Burton to tell Myers that the FBI wanted to talk to him, but that before it could, the agents needed to confer with his lawyers. "I want to know who Myers says is representing him," Chapman told Burton. A few hours later the warden telephoned with an answer. Myers had identified his attorneys as "Mr. Bryan Stevenson and Mr. Michael O'Connor."

That was exactly what Chapman had hoped to hear. It was a conflict of interest for Stevenson and O'Connor to represent Johnny D. and Ralph Myers, the state's main witness against him. Stevenson had accused the prosecution of unethical conduct. Now it was time, Chapman decided, to turn the tables with an accusation of his own.

Chapter 43

A few days after their fruitless meeting with Tommy Chapman in Monroeville, the telephone rang in Stevenson's office. The caller said he was an FBI agent. He wanted to meet Stevenson to discuss Ralph Myers's accusations against Sheriff Booker. Stevenson quickly agreed. He believed the stories he had heard about Booker, and he was worried that Myers was going to be murdered in prison unless something was done to protect him. The agent suggested that they get together late the next evening at a rest stop along Interstate 65.

"Why meet there?" Stevenson asked. "I have an office and you have an office, why do we need to meet at a rest stop?"

The agent said he lived in Mobile. The rest stop was halfway between Mobile and Stevenson's office in Montgomery. "It will make it easier on both of us," he explained.

Stevenson was suspicious. The rest stop was in Conecuh County, only a few miles from the Evergreen exit. That meant it was right in the middle of Sheriff Booker's home turf.

"Come alone," the agent said.

Stevenson put down the receiver. Why would an FBI agent want to meet him alone late at night at a highway rest stop in Sheriff Booker's county? "That's one meeting," he told O'Connor, "I'm not going to make."

As usual Stevenson worked late the following night and didn't leave the Center until nearly four A.M. Exhausted, he fell asleep instantly when he got home, but was awakened within minutes by the ringing of his telephone.

"Hello," he said. There was no response. "Hello," he repeated. Again nothing. He put down the receiver. Ten minutes later the phone rang again. This time he heard a muffled voice.

"Are you the Bryan Stevenson who represents Walter McMillian?"

"Yes. Who is this?"

Click. The phone went dead. He suddenly remembered that the front door to his apartment was not locked. As he hurried toward it, the beams from a car's headlights flashed through his front window. He thought he heard footsteps. He reached the deadbolt, locked it, and peeked out. The car was gone.

The next morning there was another call. A man who refused to identify himself asked Stevenson to meet him along a rarely traveled road outside Montgomery to discuss the McMillian case. When he declined, the man hung up. That afternoon Stevenson and O'Connor decided that they would begin using rental cars whenever they drove to Monroeville or passed through Conecuh County. They would keep their schedules as secret as possible. Both were afraid the McMillian case was getting dangerous.

On September 20, 1991, the Court of Criminal Appeals formally rejected all seventeen points Stevenson had raised in his initial appeal. The court ruled that Bill Hooks, Jr., had not received any special enticements to testify. Stevenson reacted by doing something unthinkable in a death row case. He asked the courts to speed up the appeals process. He told the Alabama Supreme Court that Myers was now admitting that he had lied at the trial. He also said he had found examples of "extraordinary law enforcement misconduct" that needed to be exposed. Technically the recantation and new evidence could not be introduced during Johnny D.'s first round of appeals. The State Supreme Court still had to review Stevenson's seventeen-point appeal and reject it before any new evidence could be considered. But Stevenson didn't want to wait that long. His client had already spent nearly six years on death row, so he asked the court to put aside his original appeal and skip ahead in the process. The Alabama Supreme Court agreed and ordered Thomas B.

Norton, Jr., a locally elected judge in Baldwin County, to investigate Stevenson's latest charges. Norton scheduled a hearing for April 1992. At the hearing he would review Myers's recantation, as well as Stevenson's claims that the prosecution had concealed evidence.

Once that date was set, Stevenson filed a twenty-two-page discovery motion. He demanded the release of "all prosecution files, records, and information" pertaining to the Ronda Morrison *and* Vickie Lynn Pittman murders. He specifically asked for written statements made by Miles Jackson, Carlos Roquellera, Randy Thomas, the Morrisons, and Sheriff Edwin Booker. He also demanded copies of all statements made by Myers and Kelly.

"We are going to force them to give us everything they collected about these two murders," he told O'Connor.

In a reply to the motion, Chapman claimed that his office had already given Stevenson all the documents he was entitled by law to receive.

On December 18, 1991, Judge Norton held a hearing in Bay Minette to review Stevenson's demand for documents. Chapman arrived ready for a fight. As soon as the hearing was called to order, Chapman objected to what should have been a routine matter. Stevenson had asked the judge to appoint the Alabama Capital Representation Resource Center the attorney of record for Johnny D. so that the Center could receive the standard $600 fee that the state paid lawyers representing indigent death row clients. Chapman said he did not believe the Center was entitled to the money. Without explanation, Judge Norton agreed.

"This judge isn't going to do us any favors," O'Connor whispered to Stevenson. "Here we go again."

Chapman told the judge that Stevenson's demand for witness statements was an outrageous fishing expedition, especially since he was asking for police statements from both murders. "Your Honor, the Vickie Lynn Pittman murder is a totally unrelated case. . . . Quite frankly, we do not have the foggiest idea why those records . . . would pertain to this appeal."

Judge Norton said he didn't understand the connection either, so Stevenson offered an explanation. His client, he said, had been accused of killing Vickie Lynn Pittman as well as Ronda Morrison. The main witness against him in both cases was Ralph Myers. Stevenson wanted to make certain that the state had given him copies of every statement Myers might have made regardless of whether he was being questioned about Ronda or Vickie Lynn.

Judge Norton turned toward the prosecutor's table. "Mr. Stevenson says Mr. McMillian and Mr. Myers were both indicted in the Vickie Lynn Pittman murder. Is that correct?"

Stevenson felt a flush of embarrassment and anger. The judge was asking Chapman to verify something he had just said. "He was asking them if I had lied to him." Stevenson wondered: Is the judge asking them because I represent Johnny D., because he doesn't know me, or because I'm black?

"Well, I'm not sure whether Johnny D. and Myers were indicted together or not," Chapman told the judge. He turned to Ted Pearson, who was seated next to him at the table. "Mr. Pearson was the district attorney at that time, Judge," he said, passing the buck.

Norton asked Pearson: Had Johnny D. and Myers both been accused of killing Vickie Lynn Pittman and Ronda Morrison?

"I couldn't tell you for sure, Judge, whether they were or not. I don't know," Pearson said. ". . . It could have been . . . I think they were, maybe. I don't know. I just don't know."

Stevenson was dumbstruck. "I couldn't believe what I was hearing," he said later. Chapman had been Karen Kelly's attorney in the Pittman murder case. He *knew* that Johnny D. and Myers had both been accused of that murder. Pearson had persuaded Escambia County District Attorney Michael Godwin to let him prosecute Johnny D. first in the Morrison case. He also knew the answer to the judge's question. "Chapman and Pearson basically sat there at the discovery hearing and lied to Judge Norton," Stevenson said. "They acted as if they didn't know. It was simply outrageous conduct!"

At first Stevenson thought Chapman and Pearson were both acting "incredibly stupid." It was going to be easy for him to prove that his client had been charged in both murders. All he had to do was get a copy of the murder indictment. But then he realized that they could afford to dodge the judge's question without worrying about the consequences. "They knew they could get away with it because no one would care that they were lying," Stevenson said. "When I heard Tommy Chapman and Ted Pearson avoid answering the judge's question, I suddenly realized that it really didn't matter what I said or did in court. If it had been Tommy Chapman's son or Sheriff Tate's son whose life was on the line, then Chapman and Pearson never would have suffered such an obvious memory loss. But Johnny D. wasn't really part of their world, their community, their circle of friends. He wasn't one of them. He was invisible because none of them really knew him or cared about him. He wasn't important, and because of that, they saw nothing wrong with not answering truthfully. It did not matter how they answered because Johnny D. did not matter and I did not matter. I could put on a suit and tie and sit down with Tommy and Larry Ikner and Tom Tate and the judge, and I could talk their language, talk European without any hint of black slang. I could go to Harvard University and I could become a lawyer just like them and I could put on the best European airs possible, but the truth was that I was black and I was not like them and they knew it and they also knew that it mattered."

Chapman would later admit with some embarrassment that he had dodged Judge Norton's question. "I was irritated at Bryan Stevenson and the way he was pushing us," Chapman said, "so I played with him a bit with my answer and acted like I couldn't remember."

After listening to a short debate between the lawyers about Stevenson's demand for documents, Judge Norton decided that the defense was entitled to witness statements from both the Morrison and Pittman case files. He ordered the prosecution to provide them. Stevenson had won. But before the hearing ended, Chapman jumped from his seat and announced that he had a motion of his own that he wanted to introduce. Judge Norton asked what it was, and Chapman said he was formally accusing Stevenson and O'Connor of unprofessional conduct and was demanding that they be immediately disqualified from serving as Johnny D.'s lawyers. The two defense attorneys were not only representing Johnny D., he said, but also providing legal advice to Ralph Myers, and that was an obvious violation of the Alabama bar's ethical code.

Judge Norton agreed to hold a hearing to determine whether they should be disqualified. A few days later Stevenson retaliated by accusing Chapman of unethical conduct. He asked the judge to disqualify Chapman from the case because he had represented Johnny D., Kelly, and Myers in legal matters before he was appointed district attorney. Stevenson claimed that was a conflict of interest.

Several weeks later Judge Norton held a hearing on the two motions, and for more than one hour the two sides bickered. Finally Judge Norton slammed down his gavel. "Gentlemen," he said, "I'm tired. I'm not going to put up with any of this." He threw out both motions.

After the hearing Ikner and Tate gave Stevenson a package that contained four tape-recorder cassettes and a few typewritten sheets of paper. This was everything the prosecution had gathered as evidence in the Morrison murder case, they told him. Stevenson glanced at the materials and shook his head in disgust. There were no statements from Miles

Jackson, the Morrisons, Randy Thomas, Carlos Roquellera, or any of the thirty-five witnesses Woodrow Ikner had claimed had been interviewed by the police. Once again Stevenson suspected that the prosecution was hiding information from him. But later that day, after he began listening to the tapes, he wondered whether Ikner and Tate realized exactly what they had just given him.

Chapter 44

On April 16, 1992, another parade of cars and pickup trucks made its way from Monroeville to Bay Minette to watch Johnny D.'s two attorneys try once again, in yet another court-ordered hearing, to prove that he had been framed. By this time word had spread throughout Monroeville that Myers was now saying he had lied about Johnny D. Everyone had also heard that Stevenson was claiming to have found new evidence that had been kept secret during the trial. Despite such revelations, the coffee drinkers at the City Cafe were confident that the "Harvard nigger," as Stevenson was now being called, and his "hippie sidekick" were going to suffer another embarrassing defeat just like the one at the remand hearing.

When the two defense attorneys arrived at the Baldwin County Courthouse, they found Minnie McMillian and a dozen of Johnny D.'s supporters waiting in the hallway outside the courtroom.

"They won't let us in," Minnie said.

A metal detector stood in front of the door. Behind it was a sheriff's deputy.

"Why can't these people go inside?" Stevenson asked.

"Security," the deputy replied. But he waved O'Connor through the detector.

"I'm Mr. McMillian's attorney," Stevenson said, "and so was that man you just let through."

"Oh," said the deputy. He hadn't realized that the two men, one white and one black, were together. "Uh—just a minute."

A few seconds later the court bailiff appeared, eyeballed Stevenson, and then motioned him through the metal detector. Inside, the Morrison family and several others were already seated. All were white. Only the blacks who supported Johnny D. were being kept in the hallway.

"What about the people waiting outside?" Stevenson asked.

"I guess it's okay for them to come in now," the bailiff replied.

Johnny D. was led into court a few seconds later bound in leg irons and handcuffs. As soon as Judge Norton entered, Stevenson complained, "My client was not handcuffed in earlier proceedings." Judge Norton had the handcuffs unlocked.

"This may sound like a very strange question," the judge said, "but other than sworn officers, is there anyone in this courtroom who has a weapon?" And then, looking directly at the defense table, he asked, "Any of you have a pistol?"

Stevenson and O'Connor stared blankly at the judge.

"If you are found later to have one, uh, if you're an officer, no problem," Judge Norton said. "Anyone else?" No one replied.

Leaning close to Stevenson, O'Connor whispered, "What is going on? What's all this talk about pistols?" Stevenson wasn't sure, and then it came to him. It had been rumored in Monroeville that he and O'Connor were Mafia lawyers. He had thought the charge so absurd that he hadn't bothered to answer it, but now he wondered whether some people in the courtroom, perhaps even Judge Norton, believed it was true.

Stevenson called Ralph Myers as his first witness and immediately asked him to repeat the testimony he had given at Johnny D.'s trial. After he finished, Stevenson said, "Now, Mr. Myers, was any of the testimony that you gave at Mr. McMillian's trial true?"

"No," replied Myers, "not at all."

Stevenson methodically led Myers through each of the accusations he had made against Johnny D. One by one Myers said that each had been a lie.

"Why did you testify falsely . . . ?" Stevenson asked.

"I was kept under a lot of pressure," Myers answered. "I kept telling these people that I didn't have anything to do with the murder of Ronda Morrison. They kept asking me . . . 'Was Walter McMillian there?' They kept asking me . . . 'Did I do this? Did I do that?' I kept telling them 'No, no, no.' And it seemed like the pressure got more and more, worse and worse, and the next thing I knew, it had got so bad until I went ahead and started saying anything they wanted to hear . . . if they would say something and then turn around and say, 'Ain't that right,' I said, 'Yeah.' "

"Who pressured you?"

Without hesitating, Myers looked directly at the prosecution table. "Mr. Larry Ikner right there and . . . Mr. Thomas Tate, Simon Benson . . ."

In a voice laced with skepticism, Tommy Chapman began his cross-examination by asking Myers why he had waited nearly five years to recant. Myers said he wasn't sure. Chapman fired off a string of questions. Why hadn't Myers ever told anyone that he was being pressured? Why hadn't he told his wife or his minister? Why hadn't he told Judge Key? Why had he accepted a thirty-year jail sentence for a crime that he now said he never committed? Myers said he wasn't sure. Chapman said *he* was.

"You have been under a lot of pressure since you have been in prison, haven't you? . . . And you had eight, ten, twelve meetings with these lawyers . . . didn't you? They were coming to see you all the time, weren't they? . . . And you knew that a murder contract had been let on you, didn't you?"

Without waiting for a reply, Chapman asked Judge Norton for permission to play a tape recording of a telephone call Myers had made from prison to Sheriff Tate on September 9, 1987, shortly before Johnny D.'s trial. The district attorney explained that the recording had never been made public because Tate had been caught off guard by the call and had not properly warned Myers about his constitutional rights before taping it. For this reason, it could not be used as evidence at the trial. However, Chapman said, he believed that Judge Norton needed to listen to the tape now so that he could judge for himself whether Myers had been pressured by Tate to lie about his trial testimony. Norton told Chapman to play the recording, and within seconds Ralph Myers's voice echoed through the hushed courtroom. He was crying, sobbing uncontrollably.

"Do you know what it is like to see someone dead?" Myers asked Tate on the recording.

"Yes sir, it's tough . . . ," Tate replied sympathetically.

For the next several minutes Myers could be heard confessing his role in the Ronda Morrison murder. He described how he had driven Johnny D. to the cleaners and had seen Ronda Morrison lying dead on the lobby floor. "Johnny D. was behind the counter and he was picking up money and dope and putting it in a damn brown bag," Myers could be heard saying. "Johnny D. says to me, 'You open your goddamn mouth and you'll look just like her.' " On the tape Myers said he was terrified of Johnny D. and was having nightmares. He was certain Johnny D. was going to hunt him down and kill him and his family. Myers begged Tate to help him.

Chapman shut off the tape player.

"Now, Ralph," Chapman said, stepping close to the witness stand and dropping his voice as if he were chatting to a close friend, "you were in prison when you made that phone call . . . and the sheriff, Mr. Ikner, and Mr. Benson—none of them were there to intimidate you or pressure you in any way when you called—were they?"

". . . That's right," Myers said. He had called Tate entirely on his own.

". . . The truth . . . Mr. Myers . . . ," Chapman continued, "is that the pressure you were under during this period was pressure that was coming because you thought your life was in jeopardy. And your life was in jeopardy because of what you knew about this murder, isn't that right?"

"No," Myers said. He knew what Chapman was leading up to.

"Well," said Chapman, raising his voice and turning away from Myers to face the spectators, "that's what you told Sheriff Tate. That's what you told law enforcement officers on other occasions—that your life was in jeopardy!" And the person who had threatened Myers and scared him, Chapman continued dramatically, was *not* Sheriff Tate, *not* Simon Benson, and *not* Larry Ikner. It was Johnny D. McMillian. Before Myers could disagree, Chapman said he had no more questions and sat down.

Stevenson rose slowly. He asked Myers whether any of the statements that they had just heard him making on the tape were true.

"Absolutely a lie—all of them," Myers said.

"Did you see Mr. McMillian standing over the victim's body . . . ?"

"No."

"Are you scared of Johnny D.?"

"No."

"Has Johnny D. ever threatened you?"

"No."

Stevenson reminded the court that Chapman had mentioned that a murder contract had been put out on Myers. The prosecutor had implied that it had come from Johnny D. He had implied that Myers had decided to recant because he was afraid Johnny D. was going to have him killed. "Who do you think put a murder contract on your life?" Stevenson asked.

"I object," yelled Chapman. "Judge, he can't testify about hearsay."

Myers had learned about the alleged murder contract from another inmate, Chapman explained, and that made it secondhand information.

"Judge . . . they're the ones that started this business about a murder contract," Stevenson replied. "I need to establish that this threat has nothing to do with Walter McMillian."

Judge Norton told Myers to answer the question.

"I was told that the murder contract was coming from the Conecuh County sheriff's department," Myers said, ". . . from the sheriff there."

"And who is that sheriff, please?"

"Edwin L. Booker," Myers replied.

"I have no more questions for this witness," Stevenson said triumphantly. As Myers left the courtroom, he flashed a smile at the defense table. "I wanted McMillian to know," he said later, "that I tried to do him right."

Chapter 45

Now that Myers's recantation was part of the court record, Stevenson set out to prove that the prosecution had hidden information from Johnny D. and his attorneys that could have helped them prove his innocence. He began by calling Larry Ikner to the stand. Stevenson thought Ikner had been evasive during the earlier Hooks hearing. He assumed that he would be just as uncooperative this time around, so he decided to drop all pretenses and asked Judge Norton to declare Ikner a hostile witness. The judge was startled. Ikner had not said anything yet, Norton pointed out. How did Stevenson know that he was going to be a hostile witness? Stevenson simply looked at the judge and said he knew. Judge Norton shrugged and granted the request.

During the next few minutes Stevenson laid a trap for Ikner. He began by asking him how many times he and Benson and Tate had interrogated Myers.

Ikner said they had tape-recorded two interviews with Myers. The first was on June 9, the next on September 14. The defense, Ikner added, had been given transcripts of both of those interrogations, as was required by law. Nothing had been hidden from McMillian's attorneys.

Ikner's answer was exactly what jurors at the trial had been told, Stevenson said to the court. Ted Pearson had emphasized that Myers had made only *two* statements. On June 9 he had admitted driving to the cleaners but had denied going inside the shop. On September 14 he had finally admitted he had actually gone into the building. In both statements he had positively identified Johnny D. as the man who had killed Ronda Morrison.

"Do you recall interviewing Myers prior . . . to June ninth?" Stevenson asked.

"No, sir," Ikner replied. "I don't."

Stevenson handed Ikner a document and explained to the court that it was a transcript of an interview with Myers. He had found it in the Vickie Lynn Pittman case files at the courthouse in Brewton. He asked Ikner to read the names of the officers who were conducting the interrogation.

"It says two officers were present," Ikner said, "Simon Benson . . . and . . . myself."

"And when was this interview conducted, please?" Stevenson asked.

Looking down at the transcript, Ikner replied, "June the first."

Obviously that was before June 9, Stevenson observed. It also proved that Myers had been interviewed at least three times, not two, as the jury had been told. Ikner disagreed. The reason he had not mentioned the June 1 interview before, he explained, was that he and Benson had been questioning Myers about the Vickie Lynn Pittman murder, not Ronda's. The June 1 interview had nothing whatsoever to do with the Morrison killing, so there had been no reason for the prosecution to provide a copy of it to Johnny D.'s defense team or mention it to the jury.

Stevenson acted as if he didn't quite understand what Ikner had just said, so Ikner repeated it. He and Benson and Tate had interrogated Myers only twice about the Ronda Morrison murder. Those interviews were conducted on June 9 and September 14.

Stevenson smiled. That was exactly what he had expected Ikner to say. He stepped over to the defense table and picked up another document. He showed it to Ikner and explained to the court that it was a verbatim transcript of one of the four tape cassettes Ikner and Sheriff Tate had been ordered to give him only a few weeks earlier. The first two cassettes were recordings of Myers's June 9 and September 14 sessions. The third was a recording of the September 9 telephone call Myers had made from prison to Sheriff Tate—the one that had just been played in court. But the fourth tape had never been made public.

Stevenson told the court that the cassette was a recording of an interview that Benson, Ikner, and Tate had conducted with Ralph Myers on June 3, 1987. Its existence proved that Myers had talked to the three investigators specifically about the Ronda Morrison murder at least *three* times. Its existence also proved that the prosecution had not given the defense all the tape-recorded interviews it had been required to disclose before the trial.

After Ikner had a chance to glance at the transcript, Stevenson asked him if he recalled interviewing Myers on June 3.

"I don't recall it personally, no, sir," Ikner said.

Stevenson offered to refresh his memory by reading a part of the interview for everyone to hear.

"Question by Simon Benson: 'Did you kill Ronda Morrison on your own?'

"Reply by Ralph Myers: 'I did not kill Ronda Morrison.'

"Question by Benson: 'You would take a polygraph to the fact that you did not shoot Ronda Morrison in the dry cleaners?'

"Reply by Myers: 'That's right. Yes, sir. I certainly will.'

"Question to Myers: 'That you do not know who killed Ronda Morrison?'

"Reply by Myers: 'That's right.' "

Stevenson reminded Judge Norton that the prosecution had insisted during Johnny D.'s trial that Myers had always identified Johnny D. as Ronda's murderer. Yet here was evidence showing that on June 3, Myers had repeatedly denied knowing anything about the murder. Nor had he admitted on June 3 that he could identify the killer.

"You don't dispute, do you," Stevenson asked Ikner, "that Mr. Myers told you during the June third interview that he did not go to Jackson Cleaners, he did not take Johnny D. McMillian to Jackson Cleaners, and that he had no information incriminating Johnny D. McMillian in the Morrison murder?"

"I don't deny that is what he said on the tape," Ikner replied.

Had the prosecution ever transcribed the June 3 tape recording? Stevenson asked.

"No, sir," Ikner said. "Not that I know of."

"What Myers told you on June third directly contradicted the testimony he gave at the trial . . . isn't that true?" Stevenson asked.

Ikner paused and then replied, "Yes, sir."

Satisfied, Stevenson changed the subject. He wanted to get Ikner to admit that the prosecution had kept quiet at the trial about Miles Jackson's ten-thirty A.M. trip to the cleaners. But he soon discovered that Ikner was not going to make that admission unless he was forced.

"At the trial, the prosecution presented evidence that the crime in this case took place in a thirty-minute period . . . do you recall that?" Stevenson asked.

"I remember it was a time period between ten and eleven o'clock, yes, sir," Ikner replied.

Stevenson wanted Ikner to be more specific. He continued to press him until Ikner acknowledged that Ronda had been seen alive for the last time at ten-fifteen and that her body had been found by Jerrie Sue Dunning at ten-forty-five—a thirty-minute period.

"Now, you had other information about people being at that cleaners in that thirty-minute time period, didn't you?" Stevenson asked.

"No, sir . . . ," said Ikner.

"Mr. Ikner," Stevenson said, "do you ever recall talking to a Miles Jackson?"

"Yes, sir, I do."

"And did Mr. Jackson tell you that he was at the cleaners at ten-thirty that morning?"

"Mr. Jackson told us he was at the cleaners. He even volunteered—he said, 'I will take a polygraph. I went there. I left. That girl was alive'—"

Stevenson cut him off. "Mr. Jackson told you he was there at ten-thirty that morning, didn't he?"

"I can't—off the top of my head I cannot tell you," Ikner replied.

"Did you take a statement from Mr. Jackson?"

"I did not, no," Ikner said.

"Well, did anyone in your investigation take a statement?"

"I'm sure somebody took a statement," Ikner said. "I did not, no."

"Where is that statement?"

"I don't know."

Was Miles Jackson ever given a polygraph test? Stevenson asked.

Ikner said he thought Jackson had been given a test, but he certainly hadn't given him one.

"Did you receive a report from that polygraph examination?"

"Not that I can recall."

"Was there a report?"

"Well, if there was a polygraph," Ikner replied, "there would have been a report . . ."

"Well, where *is* the polygraph report?" Stevenson persisted.

"I have not seen it. I do not have it."

"Do you recall Mr. Jackson giving you a bank statement verifying that he was at the cleaners at ten-thirty that morning?"

"Mr. Jackson did not give me a bank statement," said Ikner. "Mr. Jackson gave me a bank deposit slip . . ."

"Well, you used that to establish that Mr. Jackson had been at the cleaners at ten-thirty, is that correct?"

"No, sir, you couldn't use the bank slip to say he was at the cleaners at ten-thirty. He was at the bank at ten-thirty or . . . whatever time was on his receipt. He wouldn't have been at the cleaners."

Stevenson was growing tired of this cat-and-mouse game. He switched tactics. Had Miles Jackson ever lied to the police? he asked.

"Not that I can recall," Ikner replied.

"So if Jackson told you he was at the cleaners at ten-thirty, you accepted that?" said Stevenson.

Ikner thought for a second. Stevenson finally had him cornered. "Yes, sir. I mean we verified whatever he had told us."

"All right, if he told you he was at the cleaners at ten-thirty, you accepted that?" Stevenson repeated.

"If that's what we established," Ikner replied with a smile, "yes, sir."

At best Ikner's answer was a weak admission, but Stevenson was not worried. If necessary he would call Jackson himself as a witness to prove that he had been at the cleaners at ten-thirty and that the prosecution had known about it.

When Simon Benson was called to testify, Stevenson once again produced a newly discovered document. This one also came from the Vickie Lynn Pittman case files. It was a copy of an interview Benson had conducted on August 27, 1987, with Tyrone Patterson. But as soon as Stevenson showed the document to Benson, the ABI agent announced that he could not comment on it. Addressing the judge, Benson said that whenever the ABI transcribed an interview it always put an official agency stamp at the top of the first page. The document that Stevenson was now showing him did not have an ABI stamp on it. Because that stamp was missing, Benson said he couldn't be certain that the transcript was an accurate account of what had been said during the interview and therefore couldn't testify about it.

Stevenson assured the court that the transcript had come directly from the Pittman case files. But Benson refused to budge.

"I cannot identify this and cannot testify about it," he reiterated.

Stevenson thought Benson was simply being difficult. The two sides argued for several minutes, and then Benson revealed that he kept his files about the Pittman murder case in the trunk of his car. If the judge would allow it, Benson said, he could walk outside and fetch a bona fide copy of his interview with Tyrone Patterson. Judge Norton sent Benson to get it, and he returned moments later holding a copy with an official ABI seal emblazoned on the front sheet. Stevenson compared the two documents. They were identical except for the missing ABI stamp.

Now that Benson was content, Stevenson read a specific passage from the transcript. "Tyrone Patterson is speaking: 'I was in the presence of Ralph Myers . . . there were two more people [there] . . . when Myers bragged about the part he played in the Pittman murder. He related to us that he and Karen did the killing and . . . plotted together to put it off on Johnny D.' "

Stevenson glanced up. "Do you recall Mr. Patterson saying such a thing to you?"

"I can't recall it right off . . . ," Benson said.

Stevenson suggested that Benson refresh his memory by reading the paragraph again. Benson did, but said he still couldn't recall whether Patterson had ever made such a statement. For the next several minutes Stevenson tried unsuccessfully to force Benson to acknowledge that Patterson had warned him about a plot by Myers and Kelly to frame Johnny D. in the Pittman case. He was trying to prove that Benson had been given plenty of warnings about how unreliable Myers and Kelly were as witnesses, yet had ignored these warnings and believed their stories. But instead of answering Stevenson's questions, Benson delivered several long-winded speeches describing how he had investigated the Pittman murder. Finally Judge Norton intervened.

"The question . . . is fairly simple," the judge told Benson. "He is asking you, 'Do you recall that statement [where] Ralph Myers said they . . . "killed Vickie Lynn Pittman and were gonna lay it off on Johnny D."?' "

Benson looked at the judge. "Yes, sir," he said. He remembered that Patterson had warned him about the plot by Myers and Kelly to frame Johnny D.

Stevenson thanked the judge for his help. He then asked Benson whether he or anyone else in the ABI had ever interviewed the other two people who were with Patterson when Kelly and Myers discussed the plot.

"No, sir," said Benson. The ABI had never made any effort to find out if Patterson was telling the truth.

"Did you ever provide this statement to Mr. McMillian's trial counsel before his trial?" asked Stevenson.

"No, sir," said Benson. He had never told them that Myers and Kelly had been overheard discussing ways to frame Johnny D.

Stevenson showed Benson a copy of the June 3 interview with Myers. Did Benson remember Myers's saying during that interview that he hadn't killed Ronda and had not been hired by Johnny D. to kill her?

"I don't recall him saying that he did not kill her or saying that Johnny D. McMillian did not kill her . . . ," Benson said.

Stevenson opened the transcript and read from it. "This is Ralph Myers talking: 'I didn't kill Ronda Morrison and Johnny D. didn't get me to kill Ronda Morrison.' "

He closed the transcript and looked up at Benson. Again he asked Benson if he remembered Ralph's denying that he had killed Ronda or had been paid to kill her.

"Well," said Benson grudgingly, "it is here in the statement so it must be true."

Stevenson read another excerpt. "This is Simon Benson addressing Myers: 'You said, no one can put you at the cleaners when Ronda Morrison was killed?'

"Myers: . . . 'I was not at no cleaners.'

"Benson: 'You didn't make a statement at the Waffle House, in the presence of Karen Kelly and two other people, that Vickie Lynn wasn't the first girl that you was hired to kill? That you was hired to kill Ronda Morrison too?' "

"Myers: 'That's a damn lie.' "

Stevenson paused. He wanted everyone in the courtroom to understand the importance of what he was about to read.

"Benson: 'You will take a polygraph test that Karen is lying, these two other witnesses is lying. . . .' "

Looking up from the transcript, Stevenson asked, "Mr. Benson, who are these other two witnesses?" Who, he asked, besides Karen Kelly, had told the ABI that they had overheard Myers bragging about girls he had killed?

"Okay," said Benson, "the witnesses that we were referring to, uh—this goes back to . . ." For the next several minutes he rambled. When he finally stopped, Stevenson was still waiting for the names of the two witnesses.

"My question, Mr. Benson," Stevenson repeated, ". . . is did you have information that Mr. Myers had admitted killing Ronda Morrison? Had two people given you statements to that effect?"

Once again Benson gave a long, confused speech but did not answer the question.

"Mr. Benson," Stevenson asked again, "my question is, did you have a witness statement where two persons said they heard Ralph Myers say, 'I killed Ronda Morrison'?"

Benson talked for another five minutes, still not answering the question.

"These two witnesses," Stevenson said in an irritated tone, "either told you that they heard Myers say that or they didn't tell you they heard that. . . . Yes or no. Which is it?"

Benson looked at Judge Norton. "Judge, I can't answer that as a yes or no question."

But this time the judge refused to be drawn in. Benson was clearly cornered. If he said there were two witnesses, Stevenson would ask why their statements had never been made public and why they had never been called to testify. If he said there were no such witnesses, he would be admitting that he had lied to Myers during the interrogation and had intentionally misled him into thinking there were two other people, besides Kelly, willing to testify that he had admitted killing Ronda.

"We had information concerning a conversation that went on at the Waffle House," Benson said at last.

Stevenson waited for Benson to continue. He didn't. "I don't really care about the conversation," Stevenson said curtly. Raising his voice, he asked, "I want to know, did somebody tell you that they heard Ralph Myers say, 'I killed Ronda Morrison'? Did somebody tell you that?"

Benson looked at Judge Norton and then back at Stevenson.

"No, sir," he admitted.

"What?" Stevenson asked.

"No, sir. No one told me that," Benson said a bit more loudly.

"So when you told Mr. Myers in this interview that you had a statement that someone had heard him say, 'I killed Ronda Morrison,' then that wasn't true, was it?" asked Stevenson. He wanted the record to show that Benson had lied to Myers during the interrogation.

Judge Norton interrupted. "Were you fishing, Mr. Benson?" he asked.

"It was my way of interviewing Mr. Ralph Myers," Benson answered.

"Sort of a fishing expedition?" the judge repeated.

"Yes, sir!" said Benson, beaming.

Stevenson wasn't certain why Judge Norton had decided to help Benson get off the hook, but he didn't agree with his casual characterization of what the agent had done. Benson had told Myers that he had Kelly and two other witnesses ready to testify that he had admitted killing Ronda Morrison. That was enough to send Myers to the electric chair. In Stevenson's view, this was not a mere fishing expedition. It was intimidation, bordering on a threat.

When it was his turn to question the ABI agent, Chapman was brief, and Benson suddenly became succinct.

"Did you ever intimidate Ralph Myers, threaten him, drug him, promise him anything in any way to get him to tell you a lie about the Ronda Morrison murder?" Chapman asked.

"No, sir," Benson replied.

"Did you ever tell him what to say when he was interviewed and when he was giving statements to anyone?"

"No, sir."

Under the rules of the court, Stevenson was allowed to cross-examine Benson one last time. He asked the judge for permission to show Benson another document. Norton granted it, and Stevenson handed the agent a two-page report. Benson recognized it immediately. Earlier in the hearing, when he had gone outside to get the "official" ABI copy of the Patterson statement, he had also picked up another document. It was a report that he had written for his bosses at the ABI when Johnny D. had first been arrested. In it Benson had outlined the evidence that he believed showed Johnny D. was guilty. Benson had brought this two-page summary back with him into the courtroom because he thought it might be helpful to Chapman. But once he handed it to him, Chapman became obligated under the rules of the court to provide Stevenson with a copy. Stevenson was now going to use it to embarrass Benson.

Stevenson asked Benson to read aloud the list of witnesses who were identified in the summary. Benson began reading names. Stevenson stopped him when he said "Miles Jackson."

"What did you write about Miles Jackson in your report?" he asked.

" 'Witness Miles Jackson stated that he was in the cleaners at ten-thirty A.M. and that Ronda Morrison was alive and that . . . no one else was in the cleaners,' " Benson read.

Stevenson turned and looked at Tommy Chapman. Larry Ikner had refused to admit that he and the other investigators had known that

Jackson had been in the cleaners at ten-thirty. Unwittingly, Benson had just given Stevenson the documentation he needed to prove that the prosecutors had indeed known about Jackson's visit. It was right there in Benson's report.

"Thank you," said Stevenson. "No more questions."

Chapter 46

As in the earlier hearings, J. L. Chestnut was busy and couldn't attend, but Bruce Boynton had come to this hearing eagerly and was prepared to testify. Stevenson began his questioning of Boynton by having the witness assure the court that he had filed the prerequisite motions every attorney files before a murder trial, including one that required the prosecution to give him a copy of every statement Ralph Myers had made to investigators.

"I got two statements that were given by Ralph Myers," Boynton testified. He had brought a large accordion file with him into the courtroom. Fishing through it, he withdrew copies of Myers's June 9 and September 14 statements.

"Did the state give you any other statements by Ralph Myers?" Stevenson asked.

"No," Boynton answered; he was not aware that Myers had made any other statements to the police.

How important were the two statements that he and Chestnut had been given?

Boynton said they were crucial and explained that he and Chestnut had scrutinized both, looking for inconsistencies that could help them discredit Myers. They had found only one.

"According to Mr. Myers, this whole sequence of events took place in something like thirty minutes," Boynton said. ". . . We attacked his testimony and his credibility on the basis that it could not have occurred within that length of time."

"Mr. Boynton, do you know who Miles Jackson is?" Stevenson asked.

"It doesn't ring a bell right now," Boynton replied.

Had prosecutors ever told the defense that Miles Jackson had stopped at the laundry at ten-thirty A.M. on the day of the murder?

"No!" Boynton exclaimed. He had never heard anything about Miles Jackson's being at the cleaners that morning.

"Would that information have been helpful?"

"Of course it would have!" Boynton said. ". . . It would actually have contradicted what Myers was stating did occur."

Stevenson showed Boynton a copy of Myers's June 3 statement and explained that Myers was repeatedly quoted in it denying that he knew anything about Ronda's murder.

"I've never seen this before," Boynton said.

Would having that statement have helped the defense?

"Yes, sir," Boynton said. "There's no doubt about that. We would have considered that to be information of the highest order of assistance."

Pleased, Stevenson sat down.

Chapman had watched Boynton carefully. He assumed that Stevenson had gone over his questions with Boynton before the hearing and that Boynton was not nearly as surprised by the revelations as he seemed. Still, Boynton had been a good witness for Stevenson, and Chapman was beginning to feel uncomfortable with the way this hearing was going. He thought he had done a good job undercutting the importance of Myers's recantation. Playing the recording of his conversation with Sheriff Tate had been both dramatic and effective. Myers had come across as terrified of Johnny D., and that had helped substantiate Chapman's theory that Myers was now recanting out of fear for his life. But Stevenson's second round of charges was proving much more difficult to undermine. Chapman suspected that his discovery of the June 3 statement and Miles Jackson's unreported visit to the cleaners were going to be enough to cause the appeals court to overturn Johnny D.'s conviction. He either had to prove that Boynton and Chestnut had actually been told about both pieces of information, or he had to explain why the prosecution had not been obligated to share that information with them.

Chapman began by asking Boynton a series of questions about how he and Chestnut had divided their duties as Johnny D.'s cocounsels. He was searching for some crack he could exploit, and he soon found one. Boynton said that he and Chestnut had kept separate case files.

Was it possible, Chapman asked, that Chestnut might have talked to the prosecutors without telling Boynton about it?

"We lawyers say that anything is possible," Boynton replied, "so I would have to certainly say yes."

Then wasn't it also possible, Chapman continued, that Chestnut might have received documents from the prosecution without telling Boynton?

"We both kept separate files because we have separate offices," Boynton said. However, Chestnut had given all his files to Boynton after the trial, and he had read through them. There was nothing in Chestnut's files that Boynton had not known about.

Chapman glanced down at the accordion file in Boynton's lap. A murder case, with all its motions and trial testimony, would fill more than one file, he thought. Now it was his turn to set a trap.

"You have been practicing law how long now, please, sir?" Chapman asked.

More than thirty years, Boynton replied.

"And you have had thousands of criminal cases?"

Boynton chuckled. "Oh yes."

So it would be safe to assume, Chapman continued, that you know the defense is supposed to be given a list of the prosecution's witnesses before a trial?

Boynton nodded. That was something every first-year law student learned.

Did the prosecution give you and Chestnut a copy of a witness list before Johnny D.'s trial? Chapman asked.

Yes, Boynton answered.

Pointing at the file in Boynton's lap, Chapman said, "Please show us your copy of that list in your file."

Boynton paused. "I don't recall seeing it there."

Why? Chapman asked. Where is it?

Boynton said that when he had merged Chestnut's files with his own after the trial, he had decided to "cull" the material and had thrown away dozens of documents that he believed were unimportant.

Chapman seized the opening Boynton had just given him. "So there are other things that were given to you that are not now in your file?"

"Yes," Boynton said, ". . . that's true."

How, then, Chapman demanded, could Boynton be so certain that he had never been given Myers's June 3 statement or told about Miles Jackson's trip to the cleaners? Wasn't it possible that he had mistakenly discarded Myers's statement? Wasn't it also possible that the prosecution had told J. L. Chestnut about Jackson's ten-thirty visit and he had forgotten to mention it to Boynton?

"I've gone through Mr. Chestnut's file, as I have gone through mine . . . and again, I will tell you . . . I have never seen the June third statement before," Boynton declared.

Having raised what he thought was a reasonable doubt, Chapman sat down. Now it was Stevenson's turn to cross-examine Boynton. He approached the witness quickly. Had the prosecution ever given him a cassette of tape-recorded interviews that the police had done with Myers? he asked.

He had never been given any tape recordings, Boynton replied, only two typed transcripts. He was positive of that.

A satisfied Stevenson looked over at Chapman. He then reminded the court that Myers's June 3 statement had never been transcribed by prosecutors or investigators. It would have been impossible for Boynton to have carelessly discarded a copy of it; there had been no copies.

"The defense rests," Stevenson said moments later.

Chapman had guessed before the hearing that Stevenson would call Boynton to support his accusations. Now he set out to counter Boynton's statements by calling a witness of his own, attorney George Elbrecht.

As Elbrecht walked toward the witness chair, O'Connor whispered to Stevenson, "Here we go again." He was remembering Elbrecht's testimony at the Hooks hearing, when the attorney had effectively undercut all Stevenson's charges.

Chapman reminded the court that Elbrecht had not only been appointed to represent Bill Hooks, Jr., in his burglary case, but had also been appointed to represent Ralph Myers in the Ronda Morrison murder case. Chapman asked Elbrecht how he had been treated by the prosecutors. "Would you generally say that the prosecution maintained an open-file policy in regard to the Morrison case?" he asked.

"Absolutely," said Elbrecht, who volunteered that he had met numerous times with then prosecutor Ted Pearson, Ikner, and Benson to discuss the murder charge filed against Myers.

"Did you have an occasion to go through the prosecutor's file and review the file of the ABI, particularly Mr. Benson's?" Chapman asked.

"Yes," said Elbrecht. The prosecution had gladly opened all its files to him.

"Did you learn about other suspects—besides Myers and McMillian?" Chapman continued.

"I did," said Elbrecht, adding once again that Pearson, Ikner, and Benson had always been very cooperative and responsive to him. The prosecution, he volunteered, had shared everything with him that it legally could about the state's witnesses and their statements. Whenever he asked them for documents or information, they had provided them willingly.

Chapman asked whether Elbrecht had spoken to Chestnut and Boynton before the trial.

"Yes," said Elbrecht. He had talked to both men about how they were going to defend Johnny D.

Had either of them ever complained that the prosecution was hiding evidence?

"No," said Elbrecht. Neither man seemed to believe that the prosecution was concealing material from them.

O'Connor leaned close to Stevenson. "If the information was hidden from them," he said wryly, "how would they know they hadn't been given it?"

Chapman changed the subject. He asked Elbrecht about his relationship with Myers. Elbrecht told the court that he had spoken with his client nearly every day. In fact, he had spent more time talking with Myers than he had with any other client he could remember.

Why had Myers refused to testify at Johnny D.'s trial when it was first scheduled to begin? Chapman asked.

"Myers was scared of Mr. McMillian," Elbrecht said, "and he was scared for the safety of his family." That was why he had balked at testifying.

Had Myers ever complained that he was being pressured by investigators to lie? Chapman asked.

"Absolutely not!" said Elbrecht. Besides being scared, Myers had refused to testify because he was unhappy with his plea bargain, he said.

Had Myers ever admitted to Elbrecht that his testimony was a lie? "Absolutely not!" Elbrecht said. ". . . Mr. Myers has never told me at any time that the testimony that he gave was untrue."

Chapman thanked Elbrecht and sat down.

Stevenson had been caught off guard by Elbrecht at the remand hearing. But not this time. He had anticipated that Elbrecht would exonerate the prosecution. He had expected him to state that Myers had never been pressured—that he had refused to testify because he was scared. Rising from the defense table, Stevenson addressed Elbrecht. Had he ever received a report about Myers from the doctors at the Taylor Hardin Secure Medical Facility, where Judge Key had sent him after he balked at testifying?

"I don't recall," Elbrecht said.

Stevenson's face registered surprise. The judge had sent Myers to the mental hospital for an evaluation, he reminded the court. The doctors there must have done one, and assuming that they had, wouldn't they have sent a copy to Elbrecht? He was, after all, Myers's attorney.

"There was no one from Taylor Hardin at any hearing in Monroe County," Elbrecht said. "Therefore, there had to be some written document from the hospital. But I—just, like I said, I haven't looked in my file and I wouldn't—"

Stevenson interrupted. "Let me just ask you this, Mr. Elbrecht. If you got a written document or written report, it would have been your practice to review that before allowing your client to testify . . . isn't that correct?"

"Certainly," Elbrecht replied. As Myers's attorney, he would have been obligated to read such a report. Otherwise he would not have been properly representing his client.

Once again a witness had just told Stevenson exactly what he had wanted to hear. The doctors at the mental hospital had, in fact, issued a lengthy report about Myers, Stevenson announced; and he had a copy of it, which he was quick to submit in evidence. With much drama, he called the court's attention to several specific passages.

On May 10, 1988, Dr. Norman Poythress, a director at the hospital, interviewed Myers and wrote in a confidential report:

> Ralph Myers stated that after being arrested, he was kept in isolation, he was not allowed to visit or make telephone calls to his family and he stated that he did not have attorney representation for several weeks while being kept at the jail. He stated that police officers pressured him on a daily basis to give a statement about a murder and indicated to him through leading questions the kind of "statement" that they wanted him to make. He stated that because of this psychological pressure and coercion, he eventually parroted back to the officers what they had indicated he should say. In summary, the defendant stated that his prior "confessions" are bogus and were coerced out of him by the police through keeping him physically and psychologically isolated.

On May 12 Dr. Bernard Bryant, a staff psychiatrist, wrote:

> The patient stated that he did not commit the crime and that at the time he was incarcerated . . . he was threatened and harassed by the local police authorities into confessing.

On May 24 Dr. Omar Mohabbat wrote:

> Ralph Myers categorically denied having anything to do with the alleged crime. He claimed, "I don't know the name of this girl. I don't know the time of the alleged crime. I don't know the date of the alleged crime. I don't know the place of the alleged crime." Mr. Myers was very much angry mostly toward the authorities and in more particular towards his attorney, as well.

In early June Dr. Kamal Nagi wrote:

> Mr. Myers said that the "police and also my lawyer want me to say that I had driven these people to the laundromat and they shot the girl, but I won't do it."

Stevenson reminded the court that earlier in the hearing, prosecutor Chapman had asked why Ralph Myers had never told anyone before Johnny D.'s trial that he was being forced to lie. Holding a copy of the medical records before him, Stevenson declared that Myers had tried repeatedly to warn the court that he was being pressured. But no one had listened to him.

According to the mental hospital's records, copies of the hospital's evaluation of Myers had been sent to Judge Key, to the district attorney's office, and also to the Monroe County court clerk's office for distribution to Elbrecht.

This time after he finished questioning Elbrecht, Stevenson felt triumphant.

Although Judge Norton had said at the beginning of the hearing that there would be no closing statements, he changed his mind. Both sides were told that they would now have a chance to summarize their arguments. Stevenson went first. Under Alabama law, he said, a defendant is entitled to a new trial if he can prove that he was convicted by false testimony. Ralph Myers had admitted that he had lied about Johnny D.; the Taylor Hardin records corroborated Myers's claims that he had been pressured to lie; and Myers's testimony at the trial about the murder's taking thirty minutes did not make sense, now that the court knew about Miles Jackson's ten-thirty A.M. visit. All these things showed that Myers's original testimony was clearly not true, and that meant Johnny D. deserved a new trial.

Moreover, Stevenson said, even if the judge rejected Myers's recantation, Johnny D.'s conviction should still be reversed because the prosecution had concealed evidence from the defense. The jury had never been told about Myers's June 3 statement. It had not been told that Myers had initially denied knowing anything about the killing. Neither the defense nor the jury had been told about Miles Jackson's ten-thirty trip to the cleaners. The prosecution had withheld the June 1 statement later found in the Pittman case files, as well as the Tyrone Patterson statement and the Taylor Hardin medical records. Even now, Stevenson said, he was certain that prosecutors were still keeping witness statements secret. The fact that Simon Benson had gone out to the trunk of his car during the hearing and had returned with a report that the defense had never seen before was prima facie evidence that the prosecution was still concealing records.

"Mr. McMillian is an innocent man," Stevenson said. "He is entitled to a trial where the full evidence can be presented to a jury which is not misled about the time of the crime, the circumstances of the crime, and the reliability and nature of the only witness who can convict Mr. McMillian."

When he began his summation, Chapman was visibly angry. "There has been absolutely no evidence of any extraordinary law enforcement misconduct in this case," he said. "Mr. Myers had plenty of opportunity to recant but he never did it until . . . another inmate comes to him and says, 'I've got a contract on you.' " Despite what the defense and Myers now said, Chapman continued, Simon Benson had been told that the murder contract had come from Johnny D. McMillian, not Sheriff Booker.

Pointing toward the defense table, Chapman said, "These gentlemen, these attorneys in this case, actually met with Mr. Myers . . . numerous times, and after meeting with him three or four times, he signed a recantation." Was it a coincidence, Chapman asked, that Johnny D.'s two attorneys had showed up wanting to talk to Myers only a few days after he had received a death threat? Or had the death threat and their visit somehow been linked?

Chapman then attacked the state mental hospital's records. He said he doubted those records had ever been sent to or seen by Pearson, Judge Key, and George Elbrecht. But even if they had, did it really matter? Myers had refused to testify because he was scared of Johnny D. and was unhappy about his plea bargain. What better way to stall than to go into a mental hospital and accuse the prosecution of trying to make you lie?

What was important, Chapman declared, was what had happened after Myers had gotten out of the hospital. Myers had gone on the witness stand voluntarily and had identified Johnny D. as Ronda's killer, and despite a vigorous interrogation by Chestnut, Myers had been credible enough to convince the jury that Johnny D. was guilty.

Finally, Chapman said, Stevenson had failed to prove that the prosecution had intentionally hidden documents. Elbrecht had had no trouble getting information from the prosecution. Also, Boynton had admitted that he had "culled" his records, making it impossible for anyone to now know what he had once had in his files. In regard to Miles Jackson, Chapman said that Boynton had admitted that he had been given a witness list, and since Jackson's name was on that list, the prosecution had not been trying to hide him or his ten-thirty visit. Any competent attorney would have interviewed Jackson to find out why he was being called to testify. "I submit that Boynton and Chestnut knew all that information [about Miles Jackson] and had dismissed it as not important."

Chapman then tackled the toughest evidence Stevenson had presented: Myers's June 3 statement. Was it really that important a document? he asked. Of course Myers had denied when he was first interviewed that he had known about the murder. Every criminal denies knowing about a crime the first time he is questioned. Would jurors really have changed their minds if they had been told that Myers had originally denied knowing anything about the murder? Chapman said he didn't think so. Remember, he told the judge, there were two other witnesses at the trial who testified that they had seen Myers and Johnny D. leaving the cleaners.

"There has been no new evidence presented here today other than that Ralph Myers, a convict who is unhappy about his predicament, has decided that he wants to change his testimony . . . ," Chapman concluded.

Under the rules of the court, Stevenson was permitted to give a short rebuttal.

"The question about Miles Jackson is not just a simple question of: 'Was he on a witness list?' " Stevenson said. "The prosecution sat in the courtroom and allowed the jury to believe a lie. They knew the thirty-minute time period was not true."

Judge Norton promised to issue his decision quickly.

As he was leaving the courthouse, Stevenson saw Charles and Bertha Morrison. He had never spoken to them. He knew they believed Johnny D. had murdered their daughter. He knew the family of the victim always sides with the prosecution. But he very much wanted to tell them he hoped the real killer would be caught soon. "I'm sorry about your loss," he said. "But Mr. McMillian did not kill your daughter."

Charles and Bertha did not reply. Nothing he had said or done during the hearing had convinced them that he was doing anything but dragging out the appeals process. They turned and walked away.

Chapter 47

Judge Norton ruled against Johnny D.

In a three-page report to the appeals court, the judge said he could find no proof that Ralph Myers had lied at the original trial. The judge did not comment on whether or not the prosecution had concealed evidence. He said that the appeals court's instructions to him were not completely clear about whether or not he was supposed to rule on that issue, so he had decided not to.

"There is absolutely no evidence in the trial record or the recantation testimony that places Ralph Myers somewhere other than the scene of this crime at the time it was committed," the judge explained. "There is ample evidence that pressure has been brought to bear on Ralph Myers since his trial testimony which would tend to discredit his recantation."

When he read Norton's comments, Stevenson was incredulous. "Why should we have to prove that Ralph Myers wasn't at Jackson Cleaners when the crime happened?" he asked. "We don't know *where* Ralph Myers was on November first! All we know is that Walter McMillian was not with him!"

Stevenson considered Norton's comments about Myers's being pressured to recant equally stupid. "Clearly this judge thinks we are some sort of Mafia lawyers," he said. But it was Judge Norton's refusal to rule on whether or not the prosecution had concealed information that most outraged him. "This judge knows perfectly well that the prosecution erred by not giving us Myers's June third statement. He knows the prosecution should have told the defense about Miles Jackson. But rather than following the law and enforcing it, he is simply ignoring it. Meanwhile, an innocent man sits on death row for who knows how long? This isn't right. Unfortunately, it is exactly how small-town justice works and why we can't expect to be treated fairly until we get this case into the federal courts. That's why the current effort by the U.S. Supreme Court to limit death row appeals scares me. We can't get justice in a local court!"

Johnny D. took the news better than his attorneys.

"What do we do next?" he asked.

The Monroe Journal announced Judge Norton's decision in a front-page story. It quoted Tommy Chapman as saying he was "definitely" going to file perjury charges against Myers to punish him for retracting his statement. If convicted, Myers would be sentenced to life in prison without parole under the habitual offender statute, Chapman explained, which would serve him right for the trouble he had caused.

"Bryan Stevenson and Mike O'Connor came down here and made a bunch of serious and libelous accusations about how they were going to expose corrupt prosecution and corrupt officials," Chapman charged, "and they couldn't produce a single fact in court to support those ridiculous claims. As far as I am concerned, they have acted irresponsibly and owe an apology to Ted Pearson, Larry Ikner, Sheriff Tate, and Simon Benson. Unfortunately, Stevenson is protected because he made those charges in court."

Chapman, Ikner, and Benson celebrated the judge's ruling by eating lunch with a journalist at Radley's Deli, one of the town's best restaurants. "When all this started," Chapman said between bites of a Reuben sandwich, "it was not personal. But then Bryan Stevenson makes all these outrageous accusations and it did get personal because I want people to realize that there is another side to this story other than this crap about Mr. Bryan Stevenson being a white knight, crusading on the side of justice.

"What I dislike is Stevenson trying to make us look like a bunch of racist, corrupt bad guys while he paints this picture of his client being some poor innocent who is framed for murder because he is black and sleeping with a white woman," Chapman continued. "That is simply not true. Race has nothing to do with this case. Absolutely nothing. Mr. Stevenson would like us just to forget about what happened in that cleaners, but somebody murdered Ronda Morrison and a jury decided that somebody was his client and all the legal tricks in the world aren't going to change that."

Ikner agreed. "The fact that McMillian was sleeping with Karen Kelly did come into play," Ikner said. "Not because she is white and he is black, but because Karen Kelly is one of the ones who said that Johnny D. killed Ronda Morrison. If he wants to blame someone, how about her? She was the one who brought up his name first to us. We didn't set out to get him. She told us he done it." Ikner paused and then said, "As far as I'm concerned, Johnny D. was lowering himself when he slept with Karen Kelly, not the other way around."

Benson nodded. "This don't got nothing to do with racism. It's got to do with murder. And Johnny D. done that murder and lots more."

In Montgomery, Stevenson immediately began work on an appeal of Judge Norton's decision. Late one night, after all the other employees at the Center had gone home, he sat quietly in his office thinking about his next move. The only sounds were the hum of his computer and of the fluorescent ceiling lights. It was completely dark outside. The streets were empty except for an occasional cat walking among the metal garbage cans set along the curb for collection. In the same issue of *The Monroe Journal* as Norton's ruling, there was a story announcing auditions for a local production of the play version of *To Kill a Mockingbird.* It would be presented in the old courthouse, and several of Monroeville's most prominent residents were expected to compete for parts. Stevenson wondered: Was he the only person who saw the parallels between Tom Robinson, the falsely accused black man in Harper Lee's famous novel, and Johnny D. McMillian?

"Because I am black, I am automatically accused of seeing racism in every problem, and that is interesting to me because I spend most of my time desperately trying to find a way to see something other than race," Stevenson explained. "It doesn't make you any more hopeful to always have to see the problem in terms that you had thought you had solved twenty years ago. I mean, I keep looking for a place where race *isn't* an issue, where you can rule out race as being responsible for anything bad that happens to you and also discount it for anything that is good. A place where you can live like any normal human being. The tragedy is that you spend a lot of time trying to deny things that are race-based because you would rather not believe it. I would rather believe that the investigators and the Monroeville community just made a mistake and if Walter McMillian were white, he would be in the same situation as he is in now—if Ronda Morrison had been black, that the same thing would have happened. I would think more highly of that community if that were true, but the bottom line is that I can't convince myself that it is true, and it doesn't help black folks or white folks to act like it is true if it is not."

Stevenson had kept track of the murders that had happened in Monroe and Conecuh counties since Ronda's. He updated it regularly, and over time his findings had confirmed what he had already suspected. If the victim was white and the murderer was black, the sentence was nearly always death. But if the victim and killer were both black or if the victim was black and the murderer was white, then the death penalty rarely came into play.

"I don't believe that Johnny D. was framed for this murder simply because he is black or because he was sleeping with a white woman," Stevenson said. "But both of those contributed." The fact that Johnny D. was black made him one of the community's "invisible people." The fact that he was having an affair with a white woman made it easier for the white establishment to see him as a threat.

Three decades had passed since *To Kill a Mockingbird* was published, and yet, Stevenson believed, the same prejudices still flourished in Monroeville. He recalled how much he disliked the novel. "What that book is really about is the South, a small town, the criminal justice system, a lawyer, and white people. The blacks in it really play no significant role and the struggle in the book isn't about how you make black people, who are invisible, visible and bring them from the margins into the mainstream of the community. The issue was could Atticus Finch, a white lawyer, still be a true Southern gentleman if he went against the community and defended an invisible person. The reason I dislike that book is because it contributes to the 'invisible legacy.' What did Atticus Finch do to change his community? The Tom Robinsons of the world, and the black community from which he came, were still left in the margins. It doesn't change things because there is one white Atticus Finch out there ready to represent you, willing to stand up against the other whites. It may make you *feel* better to believe there is someone out there like Atticus Finch, but it didn't keep Tom Robinson from being killed.

"The problem is that too many people in the justice system define their contribution as being like a modern-day Atticus Finch. Well, that is not enough! What you should care about is creating a society and a legal system where people are not forced to have an Atticus Finch represent them, where people who do not have enough money or who are black or who are not well educated do not have to be in a position where they pray for an Atticus Finch to step forward.

"What I am talking about is the next level up from *To Kill a Mockingbird*, a higher level where what Atticus Finch did is not seen as extraordinary but as normal—the everyday way that things should be done. That is the level where the people in the margins are made part of the entire community, and that not only benefits the invisible people but also the community. It makes for a better community because it makes for real justice.

"What is sad about Monroeville is that they understand the novel and are preoccupied with putting on their little drama and are content bragging about how their town is where the book was written. But the truth is that the people who live there are not even prepared to play the real role of an Atticus Finch, and that is what is both amusing and terribly sad about that town."

Stevenson had tried to free Johnny D. by going through the proper legal channels. He would continue to do that. But he also decided to do something more. A producer for the CBS television show *60 Minutes* had once asked him to telephone if he was ever involved in a case in which he knew that an innocent man was facing execution. The producer had a New York telephone number. As soon as daylight came, Stevenson dialed it.

PART FIVE

His Eye Is on the Sparrow

"Dill?"
"Mm?"
"Why do you reckon Boo Radley's never run off?"
Dill sighed a long sigh and turned away from me.
"Maybe he doesn't have anywhere to run off to . . ."

—Harper Lee
To Kill a Mockingbird

Chapter 48

When a CBS producer telephoned him, Tommy Chapman was puzzled: Why was *60 Minutes* interested in a local murder case that was several years old? He assured the caller that there was nothing newsworthy about the Morrison case. But correspondent Ed Bradley came to town despite that assurance, and Chapman and Sheriff Tate met separately with him on June 25, 1992, to discuss the case. The next edition of *The Monroe Journal* quoted the two men complaining about Bradley's visit. "CBS came down here with the preconceived idea that Johnny D. was framed," Chapman told the newspaper, ". . . and they focused the report from that perspective—sympathetic to the defendant!"

As proof of the network's bias, Chapman revealed that he had offered Bradley a copy of the police mug shot taken of McMillian after his arrest. In the photograph Johnny D. had a large, uncombed Afro, a menacing Fu Manchu mustache, and an angry look in his eyes. Bradley had not accepted the picture. "The person they interviewed at prison is not the same person arrested by Sheriff Tate for this murder," Chapman stated in the newspaper. "They did not see the real Johnny D. McMillian." The

Journal printed the unflattering mug shot. "What people in Monroe County fail to understand is that McMillian is a person who led two lives. On one hand, he was a person who worked hard and, according to the people he worked for in the wood business, he was a good worker," Chapman was quoted as saying. "But then there was the other side to Johnny D., and it wasn't good. He had been convicted of assault—he had cut a man up—and he had been convicted of possession of marijuana. He was charged with selling it but not convicted . . ."

"If a person is not involved in things they shouldn't be," Chapman concluded, "then they don't associate with the Ralph Myerses and Karen Kellys of this world."

Stevenson claimed that Chapman's quotes in the newspaper were racist and misleading. "Can you tell from a mug shot if someone is guilty of murder?" he asked. "What is Chapman really saying here: that because Walter McMillian is black and has a mustache and his hair is long that he is a killer? . . . Just look at his photograph and you can tell that! Unfortunately if you are part of the white community, you may not see the racism and unfairness in these statements. . . . But what if you put a white person's mug shot in the paper and said that just by looking at it, you could tell that person was guilty of murder? *Then* he would understand just how outrageous this is. If that photograph looked like someone he knew, someone in his family or a relative, he would be furious. What Tommy and the white community in Monroeville don't understand is that when the black community looks at that mug shot, they don't see a murderer, they see a photograph of a black man, someone they know, and that sends them a message. It tells them that just because they are black, they are vulnerable."

60 Minutes broadcast its story in late November 1992. It contained no new evidence. All the charges of misconduct and questions about fairness raised by Ed Bradley came directly from Stevenson's appeals. The prosecution and the Alabama judges who had heard the case were familiar with each charge and had rebutted them all. But in Bradley's skilled hands on prime-time Sunday-night television, stripped of courtroom protocol and confusing legalese, the injustice of the case against Johnny D. suddenly seemed clear and overwhelming.

Bradley began by pinpointing the obvious flaws: how Ralph Myers had testified that he had seen Ronda lying faceup in the lobby of Jackson Cleaners, yet her body had been found facedown in the northeast corner of the back room; how Bill Hooks, Jr., had seen Johnny D.'s low-rider truck parked at the cleaners, yet the truck had not been converted until six months after the murder. From prison Johnny D. told viewers that he had never met Ronda or been inside the cleaners. Jimmy Hunter recounted how he was helping Johnny D. replace the transmission in his truck on the morning of the murder. Ralph Myers admitted framing Johnny D. From the prison yard at Julia Tutwiler, Karen Kelly said Johnny D. had been railroaded because he was a "nigger" sleeping with a white woman. But while each of these statements was unsettling, it was the appearance of Hooks and Chapman on camera that disturbed viewers most.

Bradley bushwhacked Hooks by arriving without warning at the junkyard where he worked. The cameras recorded a startled and then terrified Hooks as he fumbled to answer questions. When Bradley asked Hooks about the reward money he was paid, Hooks tried to dart past him, but Bradley stepped in front of him, temporarily blocking his exit. Hooks wiggled by Bradley and fled off camera like a frightened rabbit.

Chapman's appearance was less confrontational but even more unnerving. With the Great Seal of Alabama rising behind him on the wall, his skin a pasty white in stark contrast to the chocolate-brown leather chair and dark wood paneling of the office, Chapman tried unsuccessfully to discredit Myers and defend the ABI, Hooks, the prosecution, the jury's verdict, and the entire community of Monroeville.

Near the conclusion of the segment, Bradley asked Chapman what he thought was wrong with the criminal justice system.

"What is wrong with the justice system is the fact that people want to come back sometimes and second-guess juries . . . ," Chapman replied icily.

"If an execution date is set for McMillian and that date comes, and it is time for him to go to the electric chair, would you be comfortable with that?" Bradley asked.

For thirteen minutes viewers had been bombarded with nagging questions about the way the case against Johnny D. had been handled, yet as soon as Bradley asked his question, Chapman's reply was instant. "Yes!" And then he added, with a chilling certainty, that if McMillian were being electrocuted the very next day "I'll be comfortable with it."

Sitting at home with his wife, watching the program, Chapman himself was startled at how cold and uncaring his final words on film had seemed. "I am not a bigoted person," he said moments after the end of the program. "I have worked hard in my community to improve race relations." But his closing comment on television seemed to send just the opposite message to viewers.

His telephone rang seconds later. The first caller was a longtime friend who berated Chapman at length for sounding so racist on national television. The next caller was just as hostile. Chapman took the phone off the hook. Waiting for him at his office in Evergreen the next morning was the black secretary whom he had hired to work in the Monroe County Courthouse. She had driven over to warn him. The entire black community in Monroeville was furious, she reported. Moments later Chapman was reprimanded by the most influential black politico in Conecuh County. "All my support from the black community was vanishing."

So when a reporter from *The Mobile Register* telephoned Chapman and asked about the broadcast, he exploded. "For them to hold themselves up as a reputable news show is beyond belief and irresponsible," he charged. Ted Pearson and Sheriff Tate also lambasted *60 Minutes*. "I think there was more than sufficient evidence to convict McMillian," said Pearson, who announced that he had not even bothered to watch the program. Tate posed for a newspaper photograph with a clearly uncomfortable Charles and Bertha Morrison. They had been interviewed by Bradley and were shown on television speaking to him, but their comments were not broadcast. Instead Bradley had explained in a voice-over that the Morrisons believed McMillian was guilty and wanted him executed. "There were not two sides shown," Charles protested to the Mobile newspaper. "What's the need of interviewing someone if you don't intend to use it?"

The program deepened the growing racial divide in Monroeville. Blacks thought it fair; most whites didn't. When Chapman went to lunch on the Monday after the broadcast, one white diner thanked him for "sticking up for our side." Tate received a rousing round of applause when he condemned the program at a local men's civic club luncheon. He confided to the group that he had offered to shake Ed Bradley's hand when they first met, but the correspondent had turned his back. "That tells you how impartial he was!" At the City Cafe, the regulars blistered CBS and cited the program as just another example of the liberal dogooder media from up North rushing into the South to tell the world that it is filled with, as one regular put it, "ignorant rednecks anxious for a lynching."

In its lead editorial on December 3, 1992 *The Monroe Journal* accused *60 Minutes* of showing only part of the evidence. "Many points presented as fact on television could have been refuted with information gathered during the investigation," the newspaper declared. Nothing shown on the broadcast, the editorial concluded, convinced the newspaper's editors that Johnny D. had been wrongfully convicted.

"*The Monroe Journal* has not done one bit of independent investigative reporting on its own about this case," Stevenson observed when the editorial appeared. "And yet its editor feels comfortable attacking *60 Minutes* and declaring that he is certain Walter McMillian is guilty. Why does the newspaper automatically side with the district attorney and sheriff? They should be siding with the truth. The newspaper simply doesn't want Monroeville to look bad to the rest of the world, so they circle the wagons. That may send a reassuring message to the chamber of commerce, but not to people who want justice, and certainly not to the black community."

The furor continued into the next week, when *The Monroe Journal* printed a letter from two CBS producers, David Gelber and Amy Cunningham, who chastised the newspaper for its editorial. "The politicians in Monroe County are mouthing platitudes to get around tough questions," the letter stated. "We think it's the job of the press not to let them get away with it." Responding on the same page, the newspaper printed another editorial in which it took credit for publishing more stories about the Morrison murder than any other publication. It then criticized *60 Minutes* for suggesting that racism was behind McMillian's conviction without telling viewers that the chief investigator on the case, Simon Benson, was black.

This last bit of reasoning caused chuckles in the black community. "Whites always have some Uncle Tom doing their dirty work," one of McMillian's supporters said.

The *60 Minutes* segment was the first salvo in a media campaign Stevenson planned to orchestrate. "I had appealed to Tommy on a personal basis, on a moral basis, and on a legal basis and it had not worked," he explained. "I truly wanted the courts to do the right thing. But I decided I had no choice but to hit him and the white community with something it could understand—raw power and threats. If Chapman suddenly realizes that he is not going to get a single black vote, then he might do something."

The day after *60 Minutes* aired, Stevenson began calling black ministers in Monroe County. He told them he wanted to speak to their congregations about the McMillian case and justice in Monroeville. He also began telephoning out-of-state reporters. "I don't expect the Alabama media to help us," he explained. "But if *The New York Times* comes down here and tells what is going on, then it might shame the other papers into doing what is right. Believe me, if Tommy and the others think *60 Minutes* was bad, they haven't seen anything yet. Wait until they have two hundred black people surrounding the courthouse demanding equal justice."

Chapman's telephone rang nonstop for days after the broadcast, and he finally decided he had heard enough. In mid-November he telephoned Major Jerry Shoemaker, chief of the ABI's investigative unit, and asked him to reopen the Ronda Morrison investigation. Shoemaker was dead set against it. A jury had found McMillian guilty, he said, and there was nothing new in the broadcast that merited reopening the investigation. Besides, he didn't think the ABI had done anything wrong, and he was not going to reopen the case just because a local prosecutor was feeling some heat and *60 Minutes* had gotten a few viewers excited.

"Taking a fresh look at this thing is not an admission that Benson or anyone else did anything improper," Chapman told Shoemaker. "Look, there's a very good chance that the court is going to overturn McMillian's conviction because the defense wasn't given Myers's June third statement. If that happens, I'm going to have to prosecute McMillian again, only this time I won't have Ralph Myers to help us. Your agent is going to look like a total fool if I don't get some help and *60 Minutes* comes down here again for the next murder trial."

Shoemaker understood what Chapman was saying. After the television broadcast he had been briefed by his top two aides, and both had warned him that there were, as they described it, "several holes" in Benson's investigation. Shoemaker told Chapman he needed time to think about his request. Unhappy with this response, Chapman decided to call Jimmy Evans, Alabama's attorney general. "I told the attorney general's people, 'Hey, look, when *60 Minutes* called, you told me that the attorney general didn't want to get involved and that Ted Pearson was refusing to talk to CBS and you needed me to go on camera and I said, 'Whoa, this isn't my case. I don't want to defend this.' But you guys begged and pleaded and so I did it and now I'm way out on a limb on this thing, looking like a complete fool on national television, and now when I need some help, you guys are turning your backs. I want, no, I *demand*, some help here. You got to reopen this case and find me some new evidence.' "

It took Chapman two weeks of insistent telephone calls, but he finally got what he wanted. Shoemaker agreed to assign two new agents to the Morrison investigation. However, there were conditions. If the media asked, everyone would be told that this was not a new investigation.

Rather, these agents were simply continuing to investigate Ronda's murder. Myers had testified that there was a third man in Jackson Cleaners during the murder, and they were simply looking for this man.

Shoemaker also insisted, and Chapman agreed, that the agents were not going to investigate whether or not Benson, Ikner, or Tate had done anything wrong. This was not an internal review. "The assumption was that these two new agents would come in, take a fresh look at the facts, and arrive at the same conclusion that Benson, Ikner, and Tate had: that Johnny D. McMillian was the killer," Chapman explained later. "In the process, they would find me new evidence that I could use to prove McMillian was guilty."

No one, of course, knew at the time what was going to happen next.

Chapter 49

Chapman felt relieved. Now that he had two new ABI agents coming to Monroeville to reinvestigate the Morrison murder, he was confident that he could convict Johnny D. a second time if the appeals court overturned his conviction. "The truth is I know the court is going to demand that we give him a new trial," Chapman admitted in private in early December 1992. "There is no way the court can overlook the fact that the defense wasn't given a copy of Myers's June third statement."

Assuming a new trial would be ordered, Chapman holed up in his office and began reading all the files the investigators had gathered about the case. Although he had read the trial transcript, he had never studied any of the reports the Monroeville police department and Benson, Ikner, and Tate had compiled. By the time he finished, Chapman felt as if he were going to vomit. That night he told Patsy he was scared. "I'm beginning to think that a terrible mistake has been made," he said. "I think Johnny D. really may be innocent."

Patsy asked why. What had he read that had changed his mind? It was the text of Ralph Myers's September 14 confession, Chapman replied, the one in which he described how he had gone into the cleaners and seen Johnny D. standing over Ronda's body. "I don't think Simon, Larry, or Tate did anything improper," he said, "but it's clear if you read it with a skeptical eye that Myers was simply repeating back to them whatever they told him. He didn't have a clue what the interior of that cleaners looked like until they started asking him if he remembered seeing this or that."

Chapman told Patsy they had to keep quiet about his doubts, at least for now. But during the coming weeks he began to feel like a traitor whenever he was around Pearson, Benson, Ikner, and Tate. He also began having trouble sleeping. Pearson was his close friend and had helped him get appointed as district attorney. Chapman and Ikner were buddies too. How were they going to feel if he stuck up for Johnny D.? Chapman decided to tell another close friend, a fellow lawyer, about his doubts. His pal warned him that his political career would be over if he publicly defended McMillian.

"Wait and see what the ABI investigators come up with," the friend urged. "They might find something that will change your mind."

Just before Christmas Chapman thought of a safe way to satisfy his conscience and avoid the political heat that was sure to come if he announced that he no longer believed Johnny D. was guilty. "I've decided," he told Patsy, "that if the court overturns Johnny D.'s conviction, I am going to recuse myself and withdraw from the prosecution." Stevenson had already accused Chapman of having a conflict of interest because he had once represented Johnny D., Myers, and Kelly. "I will simply tell everyone that I agree that there is a conflict and turn it over to another prosecutor," he said. "Then I'll be off the hook."

Patsy said she understood why he thought that was a good idea. She was aware of the political consequences. "But, Tommy," she asked, "can you really do that if you think he's innocent?"

His wife's question irritated him. "Right now I can't be certain that he is innocent," he snapped.

Patsy told him she was sure he would make the right choice.

That night as they were getting ready for bed, he said, "Patsy, isn't this strange? At this moment, I am probably one of the best allies that Johnny D. has, but I'm sure that he and Bryan Stevenson think I'm just a terrible person."

There was only one question about the case that still nagged him. Bill Hooks, Jr., had told the police on the night of the murder that he had seen a white man with burns on his face and a black man fleeing Jackson Cleaners. "If Johnny D. is really innocent," Chapman asked, "then how in the hell was Hooks able to say on the night of the murder that a black man named John Dozier—Johnny D.—was the killer?"

The next morning Patsy said she had dreamed about the Ronda Morrison murder case. "A white man was the murderer and you prosecuted him and were a hero," she said, laughing. "Wouldn't that be great if that happened?"

Chapman did not reply. He had not slept at all.

The first threatening telephone call came into Bryan Stevenson's office early one morning not long after the *60 Minutes* broadcast. Legal aide Sharon McCormick answered the phone.

"I'm going to see to it that you are no longer in business," an angry male voice declared.

"Why would you do that?" McCormick asked.

The caller spat out expletives and slammed down the receiver.

At ten A.M. the same man called again.

"I'm going to make sure that y'all will be in business no longer."

About an hour later Eva Ansley was smoking a cigarette on the front porch of the row house where the Center's office was when she noticed a white man glancing at her several times as he walked down the opposite side of the street. When he got to the corner he crossed the street and made his way back to the porch.

"I wonder if you could give me directions," he said.

"Where are you trying to go?"

"Uh—well," the man replied. It seemed to Ansley that he was trying to think of a place. Finally he mentioned a nearby street, and Ansley told him how to get there. Instead of listening, he seemed to be examining the porch and front door.

Another call came at noon.

"You don't have long now," the voice said.

"Why?" asked McCormick.

" 'Cause I put a bomb in your place!"

Trying to remain calm, McCormick asked where the bomb was hidden.

"You must think we're fools," said the caller, laughing. "I'm tired of seeing that nigger killer and his nigger attorney on television. . . . It's always the niggers helping niggers . . ."

The Center was evacuated and the police called, but no bomb was found. Stevenson warned his staff not to open the front door to strangers. A schedule was posted. No one was allowed to work late at the Center without a "buddy."

A few days later the caller dialed the Center again. "The clock is ticking," he warned. "Boom!" he yelled. Then he laughed and hung up.

Chapter 50

Corporal Thomas G. Taylor of the ABI had just finished watching a football game and was about to switch off the television when CBS ran a teaser for *60 Minutes.* He heard only part of it, something about an innocent man on death row in Alabama, but it was enough to keep him watching. Taylor knew nothing about the Morrison murder—he lived in Huntsville, in the northern part of the state—nor was he a fan of *60 Minutes.* He'd had enough experience as an agent to know that the media often sensationalized stories. But he had to admit that Ed Bradley made a convincing argument during the program that Johnny D. McMillian was innocent. Still, Taylor didn't think much more about the news story until a call came from Major Jerry Shoemaker ordering him to report to ABI headquarters in Montgomery. When he got there Shoemaker told him he was being put in charge of reopening the Morrison murder probe. Taylor wasn't surprised. He had spent most of his career tackling cases the ABI considered "extremely sensitive."

At age forty-three, Taylor had twenty-two years' experience as an Alabama cop. He had been captain of his high school football team and had married his high school sweetheart, Karen, the homecoming queen.

Although he had come of age during the counterculture 1960s, he kept a portrait of John Wayne hanging in his ABI office. "The Duke" represented everything Taylor thought was good in a man.

"Who would you like to work with on this?" Shoemaker asked. He suspected he already knew whom Taylor would ask to be paired with, and he was right.

"You'd better give Greg a call," Taylor said.

Technically Lieutenant Thomas Greg Cole outranked Taylor, but Shoemaker knew Cole wouldn't mind being Taylor's subordinate on this assignment. The two men were close friends, and they were considered two of the finest criminal investigators in the state.

Cole's father had also been an ABI agent, and he couldn't remember a time when he hadn't wanted to follow in his dad's footsteps. He had joined the ABI as a dispatcher on his eighteenth birthday, the moment he was eligible. He was now forty-two, and he had spent much of his career as a supervisor. He was a stickler for organization, charts, and making certain that every step of an investigation was thoroughly documented. The two agents were an odd couple. Taylor looked like the football player he once had been, while Cole was thin, with short, reddish hair and wire-rimmed glasses. Where Taylor often operated on gut instinct, emotion, and adrenaline, Cole depended on logic. Taylor was an in-your-face, kick-ass investigator who asked tough questions and didn't care if the person being interviewed was furious by the time they finished talking. Cole was quiet, unassuming, sympathetic, a good listener. In the twenty years the two men had known each other, they had never exchanged an angry word.

They had first been paired ten years earlier, when they investigated a mayor suspected of looting city funds. The mayor had been under investigation for a decade, but no one had been able to prove that he was a thief. It took the two agents four months of digging through city records before they discovered how he was pocketing some $25,000 annually. It took them another two months to prove it. The break came when they confronted him. Usually investigators try to discourage suspects from having a lawyer at an interview, but Taylor and Cole encouraged the mayor to call his attorney. They thought it probable that he had not told the attorney the truth about what he had done. "When we would ask for specific documents or receipts, the attorney would say, 'Sure, why not?' because he thought the mayor had nothing to hide," Taylor recalled with a chuckle. As a result, the agents got the records they needed to put the mayor in prison.

Some four years later they were reunited to investigate the highly publicized murder of a Roman Catholic priest whose body had been discovered on fire in a field. The local police had arrested a drifter and had obtained several incriminating statements from him. It turned out, however, that they had arrested the wrong man. Their suspect had an alibi. He had been locked in jail when the murder happened. His "confessions" turned out to be fabrications by the police. Taylor and Cole solved the case when they arrested a man who had not even been considered a suspect until they began their probe.

Cole had not seen the *60 Minutes* segment, but, like Taylor, he was skeptical about the media. Both knew Simon Benson, but not well. Neither had ever worked with him or been in Monroeville.

A few days before Christmas of 1992, Cole and Taylor drove to Evergreen, where Chapman had called together every investigator who had played a role in the Morrison murder case except for ousted former police lieutenant Woodrow Ikner. They met in a conference room at the Holiday Inn, and each investigator brought copies of all his records to the meeting. Although Stevenson and O'Connor had been told repeatedly that there were only three witness statements, Taylor and Cole were given two large cardboard boxes crammed with papers. No one had ever taken the time to catalog or make a single all-inclusive file about the case. What startled the two agents, however, was how little information the various officers in the room had shared with one another.

It soon became apparent that there had been two separate investigations. The first was a cooperative effort that had begun on the day of the murder. It had involved the local police, the sheriff's office, and the ABI, and had been coordinated by ABI case agent Mike Barnett and Woodrow Ikner. But after two months of dead ends that effort had fizzled out, and Benson, Ikner, and Tate had taken charge. Those three investigators were the only ones who could explain why and how Johnny D. had become a suspect.

Shortly after the meeting began, several troubling facts surfaced. Taylor and Cole were told that no one had ever given a polygraph test to Bill Hooks, Jr., or Joe Hightower. Then they learned that Myers had never been asked during his polygraphing about his testimony against Johnny D., nor had Karen Kelly been given a comprehensive polygraph test. Thus, although the three witnesses responsible for Johnny D.'s arrest—Myers, Kelly, and Hooks—were known to have lied to the police in the past, their statements had been blindly accepted as the truth without the aid of a polygraph.

Moreover, there were pieces of evidence that could not be found. For example, Benson, Ikner, and Tate said they knew Hooks had been driving by Jackson Cleaners on the morning of Ronda's murder because he was returning from an errand at Taylor Parts, where he had signed a receipt. Yet no one had a copy of that receipt, although Ikner said he had seen it in a file.

At one point during the meeting, Taylor and Cole asked whether anyone had any information about the two "FBI agents" who Johnny D.'s sister claimed had stopped at the McMillian house on the day of the murder. Benson and Ikner quickly explained their theory about the two white men. Ikner was certain that the description of the "FBI agents" matched that of the two "white men armed with shotguns" who Myers claimed had broken into the Conecuh County jail. He and Benson were positive that the men were hired killers from New Orleans, sent to murder Johnny D. because of a bad drug deal at Jackson Cleaners.

But as soon as they told the group their theory, ABI agent Mike Barnett made a jarring confession. Until that moment, he said, he had never heard about the two "FBI men." Unlike the others, he had not been involved in Johnny D.'s trial, and he was not familiar with much of the testimony. But he knew who the "FBI men" were.

"They weren't from the FBI," he announced. "It was me and my partner."

Shortly after Ronda's body had been found, the ABI had received a report that a service station near Interstate 65 had been robbed. Thinking the murder and the robbery might be related, Barnett and another agent had sped east from Monroeville on State Highway 84, en route to the service station. As they were crossing the Monroe-Conecuh County line, they spotted a car that matched the description of the robber's. It was headed toward Monroeville. Barnett and his partner made a U-turn and followed the car to a house on the edge of "the projects." They had stopped at the house and had questioned the driver, a young black woman, but decided that she was not a suspect in the robbery.

Barnett said he had completely forgotten about the wild-goose chase but remembered it now because there had been a large number of blacks at the house and he recalled that they were having a fish fry. He was the one, he was sure, who had been at Johnny D.'s house that day.

Chapman was stunned. He asked Barnett if he had identified himself as an ABI agent to the black woman. Barnett said he had. Obviously, said Chapman, she had misunderstood and thought he was from the FBI.

"Did you see Johnny D. there?" Chapman asked. Barnett couldn't be certain. At the time he had not known who Johnny D. was.

Everyone had assumed that Johnny D.'s witnesses were lying about the fish fry. Now it was clear that they weren't. They were indeed having a fish fry on the Saturday when Ronda was killed.

Chapman was worried. If Bryan Stevenson found out that the two unidentified "FBI men" were actually ABI agents, he would be outraged and would claim that the ABI had hidden crucial evidence. It was quickly decided that Barnett's disclosure should be kept secret.

Despite Barnett's admission, Benson, Ikner, and Tate remained convinced that Johnny D. was guilty. All three insisted that he had murdered Ronda. During the next hour they described to Taylor and Cole what they believed had happened at Jackson Cleaners. Johnny D. had arrived while Ronda was in the bathroom. She had had only enough time to pull up her pants, not to button them. Johnny D. had tried to force open the bathroom door, but she had thrown herself against it. He had managed to stick his hand with the gun inside, but she had pushed it upward, causing him to fire a round into the ceiling. Unable to hold the door, she had tried to run past him, but he had grabbed her throat, and during the struggle her gold necklace had been broken from her neck, her blouse had been ripped open, and her bra had been pushed up. She had freed herself and started toward the lobby. That was when Johnny D. had shot her. She had managed to keep going, and he had shot her two more times. She had collapsed in the lobby just moments before Myers came running inside.

That was when Myers had seen Ronda lying faceup on the floor and had spotted the "third man" hiding in the back room. Johnny D. had threatened Myers and ordered him back outside. Either by himself or with the help of the "third man," Johnny D. had carried Ronda's body into the northeast corner, where he tossed it under a rack of clothing. He had then cleaned out the cash register and fled. What he hadn't known, of course, was that Hooks was driving past—nor had he known that Hightower had spotted his truck.

That was how Ronda Morrison had died, said Benson, Ikner, and Tate. And they were confident that Taylor and Cole would reach the identical conclusion as soon as they completed their own investigation.

Chapter 51

Taylor and Cole read. They sequestered themselves in Room 101 of the Econolodge in Monroeville and spent the first week of their investigation examining every witness statement, police report, and scrap of paper they had been given. They put each document in alphabetical order, copied them all, arranged the copies in chronological sequence, and cataloged the complete transcripts of Johnny D.'s trial and the appeals Stevenson had filed. They studied Simon Benson's notes about the Pittman murder and the statements Myers, Kelly, Vic Pittman, Mozelle, and Onzell had made to investigators. Neither agent discussed the cases while he was reading and filing the documents.

After they had completed their examination of the documents Taylor and Cole drove to the state crime lab, where they studied the photographs of Ronda's body, examined her clothing, inspected the five shell casings, and peered through a microscope at the tiny blood spot found on the lobby wall in Jackson Cleaners. From there they drove to the cleaners itself, where they carefully measured the area where Ronda's body had been found and drew an extensive diagram of the entire place, showing where each shell casing had been located and the body had lain.

"The crime scene is generally the most important clue you have," Cole explained later. "It is very difficult for a killer not to leave something behind, something that will tie him or her to the murder."

Despite all they had heard about Johnny D., both agents avoided thinking about him or any other potential suspect. They had learned from past investigations that if they had a suspect in mind when they examined the crime scene, there was a good chance that their preconceptions would lead them to overlook something. "A murder investigation is like climbing a mountain," Taylor liked to say. "If you take it step by step, you will eventually get to the top. We were not worried about who we were going to find at the top of the mountain. All we were worried about was making certain that we took the first few steps correctly, so that we would end up starting off on the right path."

The two agents stood in the cleaners and tried to visualize what had happened to Ronda. Each man walked from the front counter to the bathroom at the rear, from the bathroom to the northeast corner where the body had been found, and then back again. They asked themselves what Ronda had seen, what the killer had seen. Finally they returned to their motel room and ended their self-imposed silence. Taylor spoke first.

"I don't think this was a robbery," he said.

"Neither do I," replied Cole.

"I think it was a sex crime," Taylor continued.

Cole agreed. Neither was surprised. To them it seemed obvious.

"Everyone wants to make this more difficult than it is," said Taylor. "A girl is found with her blouse open, her pants unbuttoned, and her bra pushed up. That is a sex crime."

From the start of the investigation, Pearson, Benson, Ikner, and Tate had each insisted that robbery or drugs had brought Johnny D. to the cleaners—not sex. But the physical evidence simply did not support those statements. Taylor and Cole had used a magnifying glass to examine Ronda's clothing. None of the buttons on her blouse had been torn from the fabric. There was no evidence of stress—no pulled straps or tears. Ronda's blouse had not been ripped open during a struggle, as Benson, Ikner, and Tate claimed. It had been unbuttoned. Nor did the so-called bathroom theory make sense. The other girls who worked at the cleaners had said in their statements to the police that whenever they or Ronda were working alone and needed to use the bathroom, they always locked the front door of the building. How could they do their job if the only employee in the cleaners was in the bathroom when a customer came inside? There was other evidence as well. The autopsy showed urine in Ronda's bladder. She had not gone to the bathroom anytime shortly before she was murdered. Taylor and Cole both agreed that there was no credible evidence to show that Ronda had been in the bathroom when she was surprised by her attacker. She had been led there, probably at gunpoint.

The initial investigators had also assumed that Ronda had simply been unlucky: that she had been in the wrong place at the wrong time. If the killer's motive was robbery, perhaps that was true. But if this was a sex crime, the odds were against its being a random killing. Someone had wanted Ronda sexually, and there was a good chance that she had known her attacker. That was part of the reason why he had killed her. She could have identified him.

Over the years the two men had fallen into a pattern when it came to investigating homicides. Each would throw out different scenarios of how a crime might have happened and then do his best to explain why that theory was right or wrong. Sometimes they would spend hours trying out comments and asking each other questions. This night was no different. The questions came rapidly and were often answered as quickly as they were posed. Later Taylor and Cole would recall the questions but not remember who had asked them because they had offered and rejected them so quickly.

- What sort of idiot robs a dry cleaners on a busy Saturday morning in broad daylight on the busiest street in town? Everybody knows that the most you are going to get is a hundred bucks.
- What sort of idiot rapes someone in a dry cleaners on a busy Saturday morning in broad daylight?
- Maybe the sexual attack was done on impulse by a customer.
- The intruder brought a .25 caliber pistol with him. This wasn't a sudden whim.
- Maybe he was paranoid and always carried a handgun? Or perhaps he carried a gun as part of his job?
- What if the criminal came in to rob the cleaners and then decided to rape Ronda when he saw how pretty she was?

Something was bothering Taylor, but he wasn't certain what it was. He began looking at the photographs of the crime scene again. He believed he and Cole were missing something obvious. He stopped when he got to an eight-by-ten black-and-white photograph of the cash register. The photograph had been taken by Steve Stewart, the editor of *The Monroe Journal*, ten or fifteen minutes after Ronda's body had been discovered. Handing it to Cole, Taylor asked, "Notice anything funny about this photograph?"

"An empty cash regis—" Cole started to reply, then caught himself in midsentence. "No, this register is not empty."

"Exactly," said Taylor.

The picture showed that there were no bills in the cash register, but the change drawers were filled with coins—at least twenty-five dollars' worth. "If a robber is so desperate he holds up a dry cleaners knowing that he's going to get only about a hundred bucks, then why doesn't he take the twenty-five dollars' worth of change?" Taylor asked.

"He was in a hurry," Cole replied.

"Then why'd he take time to go into the back room and try to rape Ronda Morrison?"

Cole suddenly remembered something he had read in the trial transcript. Jerrie Sue Dunning had been asked if she had looked into the cash register when she had first arrived at the cleaners and found the lobby empty. Cole pulled her testimony from his indexed file and read it aloud.

"Question: 'You say there was both currency, that is, paper money, and change in the cash register?'

"Dunning: 'Yes, sir.' "

Another witness had also told the police that he had seen both coins and bills inside the register.

"What if there never was a robbery?" Taylor asked. "What if the killer came into the cleaners, attacked Ronda, and then fled without taking any money from the cash register?"

"Then who took the paper bills?" asked Cole.

"Someone who wanted this to look like a robbery," Taylor replied. Both men knew of instances in which police officers had stolen valuables at crime scenes. According to the trial testimony, the police had done a poor job of sealing off the cleaners. Numerous people had walked through the lobby, including several curious onlookers. Anyone could have helped themselves to the bills—including a police officer who had simply decided to take advantage of the situation.

Taylor thought of another possible explanation. Under Alabama law, a defendant accused of murder does not automatically face a death sentence. However, if a defendant is accused of murdering someone while committing another crime, such as robbery, then prosecutors can seek the death penalty. "Everyone loved Ronda," Taylor said. "Maybe someone took that money to ensure that her killer was going to end up in the electric chair."

Room 101 of the Econolodge was soon transformed into an office. The agents brought in a folding table for their laptop computers and printers. They propped four large portable files on the dresser and compiled a minute-by-minute breakdown that showed who had been at the cleaners on Saturday morning. On another chart they listed all the witnesses who had been questioned and the names of every suspect. Each time they completed a chart they tacked it to the wall.

As Taylor and Cole tried to reconstruct the crime, they kept running into an important discrepancy in the trial testimony. It was the same flaw that prosecutor Pearson had first noted six years earlier. Myers had testified that he had seen Johnny D. standing over Ronda's body as it lay faceup in the lobby. Monroe County sheriff's deputy William Gibson had testified that he had seen drag marks next to the body that led into the northeast corner of the building. But the autopsy suggested that Ronda had actually died in the northeast corner, and ousted police lieutenant Woodrow Ikner had claimed on *60 Minutes* that Pearson had pressured him to testify that her body had been dragged when there was no proof that it had. Pearson had denied the charge. Who was telling the truth?

The two agents decided to interview Gibson. He had moved from Monroeville and was now working for another Alabama police department. When the agents located him and asked him about his testimony, he told them he had made a mistake. There had been no drag marks on the floor of the cleaners. "She died right where we found her," he said.

"As soon as we heard that," Taylor said later, "we were fairly certain that Ralph Myers's entire testimony had to be a lie. He had never been inside that cleaners and had never seen Ronda as he had claimed."

By late December Taylor and Cole had developed their own theory about how Ronda had been murdered. It was based on their "reading" of the crime scene. The killer had come into the lobby and had found Ronda working behind the counter. Because of the location and time of the crime, neither investigator was convinced that the murderer had come into the cleaners specifically to rape Ronda. Rather, they believed that something had happened that had made him snap. If this assumption was correct, then the murderer was the sort of man who routinely carried a pocket pistol, since he clearly had a .25 caliber handgun with him. As the agents knew, this was true of a good many men in southern Alabama.

The killer had led Ronda at gunpoint back through the area behind the lobby and into the bathroom at the rear of the building, where he had told her to begin undressing. The autopsy showed that Ronda had been slapped in the face. Based on what they had read about her, the agents theorized that she had refused to disrobe, so the killer had gotten tough with her. Ronda had undone her pants and had unbuttoned her blouse as ordered. But when the killer actually reached over and lifted her bra off her breasts and then touched her skin with his hand, Ronda had panicked. The agents presumed that it was simply too much for the deeply religious girl to take. That was when she and the killer had struggled. Her gold necklace had been ripped off and had fallen to the floor. A shot had been fired into the ceiling. The two agents had discovered traces of Ronda's makeup on the outside of the bathroom door, which opened inward. Her face had been pressed against it with such force that six years later these traces were still embedded in the white paint when Taylor and Cole examined it. Although it would have been difficult for them to prove that the marks had come from Ronda's makeup because so much time had passed, the imprint could still be seen by the naked eye, and employees told them that it had appeared there after the murder. Based on those statements, Taylor and Cole felt confident that Ronda's face had been pressed against the door by the killer. They guessed that he had grabbed her neck and pinned her against the door with her back to him. That was when he fired into her right shoulder. Because the bullet had gone downward into her chest cavity, the agents suspected that he was taller than Ronda, probably more than six feet in height, and was right-handed.

After firing that round, the killer had probably stepped back and loosened his hold on her neck. It seemed likely that he had been shocked at what had happened. That was when Ronda had broken free. She had run toward the northeast corner of the building, and the killer had chased her, firing as he ran, until she fell. Then he had stood over her and fired a final shot into her back.

The killer had then run through the lobby and out the front door, leaving it open and abandoning Ronda to die a slow death. Neither agent believed there had ever been a robbery. Someone else had taken the paper bills.

Their theory was, of course, exactly that, a theory. But both men believed it was how Ronda Morrison had spent the final minutes of her young life. Now it was time to move to the next step: finding her killer.

Chapter 52

Taylor and Cole had been told to take a fresh look at the case, so they decided to proceed as if they were the first agents called to the murder scene. If they found evidence that implicated Johnny D., they would pursue it. Until then, however, they would start with the more obvious suspects, eliminating them one at a time until they reached one whose name they could not remove from their list. Cole called it the onion approach—they peeled back the layers until they reached the core.

Carlos Roquellera and his girlfriend, Maria, had been seen strolling past the City Cafe moments before the murder. The agents began with them. Based on police interviews in their files, they determined that the Cubans had passed the cafe at ten-thirty-five A.M. Maria had told the police that she and Roquellera had continued to walk down South Alabama Avenue for another five minutes (until ten-forty) and then had returned to the Lynam Apartments complex—a trip that took Taylor and Cole three minutes to reenact (ten-forty-three). The couple had stayed in Roquellera's room for another five minutes (ten-forty-eight) before deciding to leave. It was at this point that Roquellera had realized he was out of cigarettes and had gone to find some. Jerrie Sue Dunning had arrived at Jackson Cleaners at ten-forty-five. That meant Roquellera couldn't have killed Ronda. There simply wasn't enough time for him to have gotten to the store and murdered her before Dunning arrived.

The next obvious suspect was Miles Jackson. The agents knew that initially he had not told the police about his ten-thirty trip to the cleaners. They became even more suspicious of him when they interviewed Chuck Sadhue, one of the deputies who had been called to the store when Ronda's body was found. Sadhue had resigned after Thomas Tate took office as sheriff, but he remembered taking a statement from a man who had claimed that Jackson had made *two* trips to the cleaners on the Saturday when Ronda was killed. According to Sadhue, this witness had seen Jackson go into the store at ten-thirty A.M., wearing a hat. He had then seen him running from the store to his car without his hat and speeding off. The witness said Jackson had returned a few minutes later, gone back into the cleaners, and then come out wearing his hat. However, there was no way to check this account, Sadhue said, because the witness had died of old age a few months after Ronda's murder.

Taylor and Cole decided to confront Jackson. He welcomed them into his home and promised to cooperate. During the interview he insisted that he had been to the cleaners only once that morning, and although he had already passed a lie detector test, he agreed to take another one to prove he was innocent. The next morning he reported to the Econolodge, where the ABI's best polygraph examiner quizzed him about every possible aspect of the murder. The polygraphing took more than two hours, and when it was over the examiner assured Taylor and Cole that Jackson had "absolutely nothing" to do with Ronda's murder. They removed him from their list of suspects and sent him home.

The agents' third obvious suspect, Randy Thomas, had an alibi: He had been in Tuscaloosa visiting his parents when Ronda was murdered. Still, the men had heard rumors that Thomas had been spotted at Jackson Cleaners shortly before the murder. They were also curious about why he became so emotional whenever he was asked about the killing. They began tracking down the "witnesses" who reportedly had seen him in town that morning. Their search proved both frustrating and revealing. When confronted, the alleged witnesses admitted they had not actually seen Thomas—they had simply been repeating gossip.

It was Cole who found proof that Thomas had been in Tuscaloosa with his parents as he claimed. The agent obtained copies of the telephone records for Jackson Cleaners, Thomas's apartment in Monroeville, and his parents' house in Tuscaloosa. They showed that no one had made any calls from the cleaners or from Thomas's apartment that Saturday morning. But there was a record of one call *to* the cleaners from his parents' house in Tuscaloosa, made at 9:26 A.M. When asked, Thomas remembered making the call and apologized for having forgotten to mention it earlier. Whenever he was out of town on a Saturday, he said, he always telephoned the store to make certain it was open and that the Friday-night bank deposit had been made. Taylor and Cole compared one year's worth of telephone records against the dates when Thomas had been away on weekends. The records confirmed his statement. He had always called the cleaners on the Saturdays when he was in Tuscaloosa. There was no way he could have telephoned Ronda from his parents' home at 9:26 and gotten from Tuscaloosa to Monroeville before her body was discovered. He was eliminated as a suspect.

It was now January 1993, and Taylor and Cole had cleared the three most obvious suspects. They were now at the same point in their investigation as the first wave of investigators had been in January 1987, when they reached a dead end and quit. At this juncture Benson, Ikner, and Tate had taken charge, eventually arresting Myers and then Johnny D.

Nonetheless, Taylor and Cole believed there was at least one more obvious suspect who had been overlooked the first time around. Bill Hooks, Jr., had admitted that he had been driving by Jackson Cleaners that morning. If Ralph Myers had lied about being inside the store, then Hooks was lying when he said he had seen Myers and Johnny D. leaving the building. What reason did Hooks have to lie? In fact, why had he even come forward? Was he after a reward, or was there another reason?

"Maybe he was trying to keep the police from suspecting him," said Taylor. The agent had found one comment in Hooks's testimony at the trial that had struck him as odd. Hooks testified that he had heard an ambulance siren a few minutes after he returned to work from his errand to the auto parts store. This occurred after he had supposedly seen Johnny D. and Myers racing away from Jackson Cleaners. As soon as he heard the siren, Hooks had turned to a coworker named William "Nappy" Tidmore and said, "Something has happened down at Jackson Cleaners."

"How did Hooks know the ambulance was going to the cleaners?" Taylor asked Cole. "All he saw was two men sped out of a parking lot, and just from seeing that, he knew something terrible had happened at the cleaners. That's pretty amazing detective work."

Taylor offered Cole a new scenario. Ronda's friend Lisa Odom had told the agents that a pistol was kept in the desk drawer behind the counter at Jackson Cleaners. This was the handgun Odom had used to frighten away the black youth who had sexually harassed her one Saturday when she was working alone. Odom said that she and Ronda had laughed about the incident. What if Hooks had stopped at the cleaners to pick up his laundry and had made a suggestive remark to Ronda? What if she had reacted—just as Odom had done earlier—by pulling the pistol from the desk drawer? What if Hooks had not run away but had instead yanked out his own .25 caliber pistol? Taylor asked. What if Hooks had then decided to teach the beautiful white teenager a lesson?

It was worth checking, Cole replied, and within an hour he and Taylor had learned that Hooks was not only a customer at Jackson Cleaners but had been known, according to his friends, to carry a pistol.

Instantly Hooks's role in the investigation changed. He went from being a leading witness for the state to becoming the agents' prime suspect.

Chapter 53

Simon Benson and Larry Ikner hurried into Tommy Chapman's office in early January 1993 with alarming news. Bryan Stevenson, they said, was trying to bribe Bill Hooks, Jr. Stevenson had offered Hooks an undisclosed amount of cash, an airplane ticket to Mexico, and a house there with a clear title in return for his changing his testimony about Johnny D. The two investigators wanted Chapman to issue an arrest warrant for Stevenson at once.

Who had told them about the bribe? Chapman asked.

Hooks had, they replied.

Had Stevenson made Hooks an offer in person?

Not directly. He had sent William "Nappy" Tidmore and Brenda Armstrong, two blacks who knew Hooks, to make the deal.

If Chapman had heard this story two months earlier, he would have issued an arrest warrant, he said later. But he was beginning to have doubts about Benson and Ikner's judgment. He had believed them when they told him that Johnny D. was a major drug dealer—even though Terry Chapman, his own brother, had laughed at those charges. He had believed them when they told him that Johnny D. had killed four or five people—even though there was no proof that he had. He also had been convinced that Stevenson and O'Connor had threatened Ralph Myers in prison and had forced him to recant. But now Chapman wasn't so sure. He told Ikner and Benson he would have Taylor and Cole investigate Hooks's story about the bribe.

The two ABI agents had been discussing their newest theory about Hooks's being the murderer when Chapman telephoned the Econolodge and asked them to look into the alleged bribe. They found Tidmore at his home a short time later. Tidmore admitted that he and Armstrong had gone to see Hooks but denied that they had tried to bribe him.

"All we told him was he needs to begin telling the truth," Tidmore said, "and stop all his lying in court about Johnny D."

The agents asked Tidmore why he thought Hooks was lying.

" 'Cause I was with Hooks that Saturday morning at Blanton's Used Cars and Bill Hooks never left the car lot that morning. He never went on any errand to the parts store."

"He never left the car lot—never went to the parts store?" Taylor repeated.

"That right."

Tidmore said he and Armstrong had warned Hooks that they would go to the police if he did not admit he was lying. He had reacted by threatening to get them into trouble. "That's what all this bribe stuff is about," said Tidmore. "He's trying to get us arrested now."

Taylor and Cole were no longer interested in the bribery charge. It was Tidmore's statement that Hooks had never left the car lot that Saturday that interested them. They asked Tidmore three times if he was absolutely certain that Hooks had not left the lot that morning.

"I done told you that boy never went nowhere," Tidmore replied.

If Hooks never left the lot, then he obviously was not the killer. But even more important, Hooks was clearly lying about having seen Johnny D. and Myers at Jackson Cleaners.

"Of course he's lying," said Tidmore. "Me and him didn't even hear about that murder until around five o'clock that Saturday night." They had gone to wash their clothes at a coin-operated laundry and overheard some black women there discussing it. Hooks had been arrested for urinating in public a short time later. The next morning Hooks had come to Tidmore to get the clothing he had left behind at the laundry. "He never said nothing about the cleaners when he got his clothes," Tidmore said.

Taylor and Cole drove to Brenda Armstrong's house, and she too said Hooks was lying about Johnny D. Several weeks after the murder she and

Hooks had been riding around Monroeville when they spotted a reward poster. She had made a joke about wishing she had some information on the Morrison murder so that she could collect the $18,000. Hooks, she said, had told her he was going to get himself some of that reward, and when she laughed at him he had said he was not joking.

Back in their motel-room-cum-office, Cole dug through the trial records and pulled out a statement by a young black man named Darnell Gregory Houston. After Johnny D. had been found guilty, Houston had contacted defense attorney Boynton and had accused Hooks of lying. Houston had claimed that he, not Hooks, was the employee at Blanton's Used Cars who had driven to Taylor Parts on the Saturday of the murder. Boynton had immediately notified Judge Key and a special hearing had been held, but Key had not believed Houston's testimony, and after the hearing Pearson had charged Houston with perjury. Cole noted that Bill Hooks, Jr., had not attended the special hearing, though he had been subpoenaed by Boynton and Chestnut. The sheriff's office had said it couldn't find him.

"It looks as if everyone assumed Houston was lying," said Taylor, "when he may have been the one telling the truth." To Cole it also looked as if Hooks had conveniently chosen to disappear at the time of the hearing.

Benson, Ikner, and Tate had told the two ABI agents that Hooks had signed a receipt that proved he had been at the parts store that Saturday. However, no one had been able to produce the receipt. Taylor and Cole drove to the store and asked the manager for a copy but were informed that the receipts from 1986 had been destroyed. Unwilling to give up, they went to the Monroeville police department. They were looking for any evidence that Hooks had been questioned on the night of the murder and, if so, whether or not he had mentioned the name John Dozier to the police, as Benson, Ikner, and Tate claimed. They were told that there was no written record of Hooks's ever having been interviewed, and no one in the station could recall any mention on that Saturday of someone named John Dozier.

Monroeville Police Chief Bill Dailey said he thought former lieutenant Woodrow Ikner had talked to Hooks that night in the jail, but he wasn't certain of it.

Next Taylor and Cole went to see Woodrow Ikner. Questioned at his house, Ikner assured them that he had indeed interrogated Hooks that same night and that Hooks had told him about "John Dozier" and about a white man with burn marks on his face. Ikner also said that he had written down the names of everyone he had interviewed and had kept careful records about what he had been told. All his records, he added, were in Chief Dailey's office. He was fairly certain that his interview with Hooks had been tape-recorded, and he gave them the name of another police officer who he said had been present in the room when he had questioned Hooks.

Back at the Monroeville police station, Taylor and Cole examined both the police logs and Woodrow Ikner's personal notes made on the night of the murder. There was no mention of any John Dozier, nor any notation about Hooks's being interviewed. Then they questioned the officer who Ikner said had been with him during the Hooks interview. "I never saw Woodrow talk to Hooks that night," the officer said. "I don't think anyone interviewed Hooks that Saturday. We were all too busy."

Back in their motel room, Taylor and Cole reviewed what they had learned. They could not find any record of Hooks's having signed a receipt at the parts store; there was no record at the police station of Hooks's ever having been interviewed on the night of the murder; there was no record of a John Dozier's ever having been mentioned; at least two witnesses claimed that Hooks had never left his job that morning; a third witness said Hooks had told her he was going to get some of the reward money for himself.

When the two agents searched through their own files, they discovered that the first written mention of "John Dozier" was in a note Larry Ikner had jotted down while interviewing Hooks—five months after the murder. They also noted that Hooks had not been able to describe "John Dozier" until after Ikner asked him whether John Dozier and Johnny D. were the same person. Only then had Hooks been able to connect a face with a name.

On January 18 Taylor and Cole brought Hooks to the Econolodge for questioning. He denied that he had ever lied, but when the agents asked him specific questions about the murder, he began contradicting himself. A polygraph test that afternoon showed that his entire testimony at Johnny D.'s trial had been false. When he was confronted with the test results, Hooks broke down and admitted that he had made everything up in an attempt to collect the reward. At nine-fifty that night, in the presence of Taylor, Cole, and three other ABI agents, including Simon Benson, Hooks signed a sworn statement that outlined what he had admitted earlier to Taylor and Cole. After this session, the two men wrote a brief report. It read in part:

1. Bill Hooks, Jr., stated that he didn't see anybody at Jackson Cleaners on the day of Ronda Morrison's murder. . . .
2. Hooks said he did not see Johnny D. or Ralph Myers at all that day, but the police said that they had been there. . . .
3. Hooks never identified the officer who "put the info in his head" about Myers and Johnny D. being the killers.
4. Hooks said that Sheriff Tate and Larry Ikner told him that he did see . . . Johnny D. and Ralph there.
5. Hooks wanted to know if he had to pay back the $5,000 [reward].

Two days later Taylor and Cole questioned Joe Hightower about his last-minute testimony at the trial. Their interview with him lasted only twenty minutes. It ended when Hightower voluntarily gave the agents this handwritten statement:

> I don't know if I saw Johnny D.'s truck there at the cleaners on the day Ronda Morrison was killed. It could have been another day.

While Taylor and Cole had been busy interviewing Hooks and Hightower, as many as seven other agents had been checking Johnny D.'s alibi. Taylor and Cole had asked Major Shoemaker to send them extra help when they first began to suspect that Hooks had lied. Within a few hours the additional agents collected statements from nearly two dozen blacks who said they had seen Johnny D. at home on the Saturday of the murder. "All we did," one agent said later, "was what the police should have done the first time around—gone out and interviewed people. It was clear that Johnny D. was innocent. It was also clear that no one had ever bothered to check his alibi."

On January 22 Taylor and Cole drove to Evergreen and briefed Tommy Chapman. They explained that none of the evidence used to convict McMillian was credible. Myers's testimony did not fit with known facts; Hooks had admitted fabricating his testimony; Hightower had issued a statement saying that he could no longer be certain his testimony was accurate. Moreover, Johnny D.'s alibi had been corroborated by dozens of witnesses. ABI agent Mike Barnett's disclosure that he had been to the McMillians' house and had seen the fish fry seemed additional proof that Johnny D. and his witnesses had been telling the truth all along.

Chapman would later recall that as he was listening to Taylor and Cole, everything that had happened during the Morrison investigation suddenly seemed to fall into place. Because he knew them well and they were his friends, Chapman could not bring himself to believe that Benson, Ikner, and Tate had set out to wrongfully convict Johnny D. of murder. But in their eagerness to catch Ronda's killer, he decided, they had allowed themselves to be manipulated by Myers, Kelly, and Hooks; and, for a variety of reasons, they had ignored several telltale signs that Johnny D. was innocent. Could he really blame them? Hadn't he been duped as well? It had been his face millions of television viewers had seen and his words they had heard on *60 Minutes* proclaiming with certainty that Johnny D. was guilty and ought to die. Nor had he been alone. *The Monroe Journal* had editorialized about Johnny D.'s guilt; nearly every white person in Monroeville had been convinced of it. The thought scared him. An entire community had been willing to condemn a man, demand his execution, and he was innocent!

"Are you absolutely certain that Walter McMillian didn't kill that girl?" Chapman asked. Taylor and Cole both said they were positive.

"Then who did?" asked Chapman.

After a brief pause Taylor and Cole told Chapman that they had been investigating a new suspect for several days. With any luck, they might be able to arrest him within a week, but they did not want to say anything further until they were certain they had the right man. Chapman said he understood, but he warned them that this time he wanted everything carefully documented. Then, although he knew it was obvious, he felt compelled to add, "I don't want anyone arrested unless you are absolutely positive that he is the killer."

Under Alabama law, a district attorney is not only legally bound to prosecute criminals, but also is compelled to right any wrongful convictions. Chapman knew this, but he asked that Taylor and Cole keep quiet about their findings until he could decide what needed to be done next.

After the two men left, Chapman sat quietly in his office. He felt ill, just as he had on the night when he had first started to doubt that Johnny D. was guilty. Part of him wished he had never heard of Johnny D., yet another part of him felt proud. He honestly believed that if he had not pushed the ABI to reopen its investigation after the *60 Minutes* broadcast, nothing would have been done. For six years Monroe County officials had insisted McMillian was a cold-blooded killer who deserved to die. Charles and Bertha Morrison had been told repeatedly that he had killed their daughter. Chapman thought about all the lives that had been damaged by this case. Miles Jackson's reputation had been destroyed—the old man had prided himself on being an upstanding citizen, and now he was afraid to leave his house because of the whispers that followed him. Randy Thomas had sold Jackson Cleaners and returned to Tuscaloosa, and was still so devastated by the murder that he wept whenever he was questioned about it. The Morrisons had been betrayed. They had trusted the police to catch the right man. They had believed in the system. And then there was Johnny D. himself. His family had been bankrupted, his name forever tarnished, and for six years he had been sitting on death row without knowing whether or not he would be executed.

Chapman suddenly found himself smiling at the tragic irony of the case. The best thing that had ever happened to Johnny D., he decided, was that Judge Key had sentenced him to death. If Key had accepted the jury's recommendation of a life sentence, then the case never would have attracted the attention of Bryan Stevenson or the spotlight of *60 Minutes*. Johnny D. would still have been in prison, a convicted murderer, without any hope of parole.

How many other Johnny D.'s were out there? Chapman wondered.

Chapman had high political aspirations. Someday he hoped to be the attorney general of Alabama. He knew his political future hinged on what he was about to do. Calling for the release of Johnny D. would be political suicide. Socially he would also pay a huge price. Judge Key had always been Chapman's mentor; the judge was convinced Johnny D. was guilty. Ted Pearson was Chapman's friend; Key and Pearson would be publicly humiliated. So would Benson, Ikner, and Tate. Chapman would be alienating all of them. For a brief moment Chapman wondered what would happen if he simply kept quiet. The ABI did not have the authority to prosecute or free anyone. All it could do was turn its findings over to him. Under state law he was required to right wrongful convictions, but he could always stall and claim to be studying the ABI's findings or conducting his own private probe. No one could really force him to free Johnny D.

Chapman kept a photograph of Patsy in a gold frame on his desk. She had been the one who had first asked the question that now kept pricking at him: Could he really keep quiet, knowing Johnny D. was innocent? Chapman knew the answer. He also understood that he and Patsy were about to have their lives turned inside out, and he had no way of knowing what the final outcome would be.

Chapter 54

Taylor and Cole had come upon their newest murder suspect entirely by chance. They had been interviewing Lisa Odom, Ronda's high school friend and former coworker, when she suggested they contact Howard K. Denmar. The agents had been asking her about the pistol that she said was kept in the metal desk at Jackson Cleaners, but she couldn't remember much about it. Denmar came into the store nearly every day, she said, and he had been there once when she was handling the gun. "He can tell you what caliber it was and all that good stuff," she assured them. Denmar collected guns as a hobby and was well known around town for his skill at appraising weapons.

Both agents recognized Denmar's name, but they couldn't remember exactly why until they dug through their records and found the witness statement he had given to the police four days after the murder. Denmar was the insurance agent who had initially told the Monroeville police that he had seen a black man leaving the cleaners at the time of the murder. He had later launched his own private probe of the killing.

The agents knew from Denmar's statement to the police that he had worked out of an office directly across the street from Jackson Cleaners, so they went there to speak with him. A secretary told them, however, that Denmar had shut down his office and was now living in a trailer park south of town. She gave them directions, but as they turned and started to leave the office building, both men stopped. From the lobby of the building, they had a clear view through the windows of Jackson Cleaners across the street. They could even see the clerk working behind the counter.

At the trailer park Taylor and Cole located a neglected trailer that they thought belonged to Denmar, but they didn't get out of their car. The trailer was surrounded by three formidable fences. There was a wire fence around the lot, another fence just inside it, and a third fence, which looked as if it were electrified, enclosing the trailer itself. All the gates in the fences were locked, and barbed wire was strung behind the trailer.

The two agents decided to check with the park manager before they tried to make their way through the series of blockades. The manager, a heavyset, friendly woman, told them they had come to the right place. Howard Denmar lived in the fortified trailer. He was a recluse, she said, who left his trailer only at dusk, when he drove to his mother's house a few miles away to eat dinner. Sometimes he stayed cooped up in his trailer for days, and his mother would leave food for him outside the barricades. The manager suggested that they wait for Denmar to come outside rather than trying to get to his front door. "He has guns in there," she warned. "People around here are scared of him."

It was almost dinnertime, so Taylor and Cole parked down the street from the trailer to see if Denmar would come out and drive to his mother's house for dinner. An hour or so later a tall man stepped from the trailer, made his way through the fences, and got into a car. The agents pulled alongside him.

"Excuse me, but we are trying to find where Howard Denmar lives," Taylor said innocently. "Can you help us?"

"I'm Denmar," the man replied.

Taylor identified himself and told Denmar they wanted to talk to him about a gun that they had been told was kept at Jackson Cleaners. He suggested that they follow him to his mother's house. "We can talk there," he said. "There's a lot you need to hear."

Howard K. Denmar would later recall in tape-recorded interviews the encounters he had with Taylor and Cole over the next several days. On that first night, he said, he had been excited about talking to them because he was convinced that Johnny D. was innocent. He also believed he knew the identity of the real killer. As soon as the agents were seated in the living room of his mother's house, Denmar told them he had already briefed the Monroeville police, Larry Ikner, and Sheriff Tate about what he knew, but that none of them wanted to do anything about it. At first Taylor and Cole thought Denmar was talking about his original witness statement. They knew he had told the police that he had seen a black man hurry out of the cleaners at precisely 10:38 A.M. on the morning of the murder. They also knew that a hypnotist had tried unsuccessfully to question Denmar. But Denmar told them that he was not referring to his original report. He was talking about the results of his own investigation into Ronda's death.

As soon as he began talking about the Morrison murder, Denmar became emotional. His voice choked up and he began to chain-smoke. Before the murder, he said, he hadn't had "a care in the world." In November 1986 he had had a good job, was well respected, and was happy. Now all that had changed. He was afraid to come out of his trailer. He had become an alcoholic and had suffered a nervous breakdown, he said, all because of what he had learned. For two hours Taylor and Cole listened as Denmar spun out his story. Neither interrupted.

Denmar said that about two weeks after Ronda was murdered, he had been working in his office across the street from the cleaners when Lieutenant Woodrow Ikner had come inside. "Woodrow wanted to know if anyone who worked in the building had seen anything—you know—been at work on the morning Ronda was killed." Besides Denmar, two other people happened to be in the building when Ikner came in. Both Carol Smith, a secretary, and Kurt Kramer, a real estate salesman, said they had not been at work on the day of the murder. Ikner had thanked them and left. A few minutes later Kramer had also left. As soon as he had gone, Smith had turned to Denmar and exclaimed, "Kurt just lied to Woodrow! I know he was in the office on Saturday." Hurrying over to Kramer's desk, she had found his appointment book and showed it to Denmar. "It clearly said 'ten o'clock—meeting at office,'" Denmar told the agents. "Carol also told me that she knew that Kurt had been in that Saturday because he had left some papers on her desk which she had found on Monday. I asked myself: 'Why would Kurt lie to Woodrow like that?'"

A few days later Denmar learned from the police that Ronda had been shot with a .25 caliber semiautomatic pistol. His first thought, he said, was "Kurt owns a twenty-five!" Kramer had showed him the gun once. "I got to thinking, maybe if I worked across the street from where a girl was just murdered and I was in possession of a weapon in the caliber of the murder weapon, maybe I wouldn't have said anything to Ikner either."

At that point Denmar had decided to play detective. He invited Kramer to come by his apartment for a few drinks after work one afternoon. He intended to get Kramer drunk. After they both had put away several shots, Denmar nonchalantly asked if Kramer still owned a .25 caliber handgun. Much to his surprise, said Denmar, Kramer insisted that he had never owned such a gun. "You showed it to me, Kurt," Denmar told him. The two men had then gotten into an argument, and Kramer had left. Several days later one of Denmar's life insurance clients called to say she had heard some gossip about him that she thought he should know: People were saying he was selling drugs. Although he couldn't be sure, Denmar suspected that Kramer had started the gossip. He began to worry. "By this time the rumor was already flying around town that it was a drug-related murder at Jackson Cleaners . . . [and] I didn't want my name linked to buying drugs or whatever." Denmar said he drove to the police station and assured Police Chief Dailey that any rumors he might hear about him and drugs were not true.

About two months later Denmar walked into his office and caught Kramer standing at a window peering through a pair of binoculars. "What the hell are you doing?" Denmar demanded. He said Kramer offered him the binoculars and when he looked through them, he discovered that Kramer had been watching a woman in tight shorts as she bent over to scrub her car at a self-service car wash down the street. "I realized that all Kurt had to do was move his head a few degrees and he would be looking directly at Jackson Cleaners," Denmar told the agents. "When I left him that morning, the hairs on the back of my neck were standing up."

By now Denmar had become so suspicious of Kramer that he decided to share his misgivings with others. Another employee told him that Kramer kept hard-core pornography hidden under the sink in the men's room in the office building. His barber told him that Kramer lived near the Morrisons and had been seen watching Ronda while she jogged. The more he learned, the more certain he felt that Kramer had become fixated on Ronda. He believed this in part, he told Taylor and Cole, because he and Kramer had once argued over a woman. Both of them had tried to date her, but she had snubbed Kramer and had gone out only with Denmar. "After I went out with her, Kurt became obsessed with her," he said. He began calling her every day, sending her gifts, driving by her apartment. Eventually he harassed her so much that she had to quit her job and leave town to get away from him. "Kurt thinks he is God's gift to women and he assumes that all women are attracted to him."

By itself that incident seemed insignificant, Denmar continued, but something had happened a few weeks before Ronda's murder that had made Kramer's jealous behavior worth remembering. Once again, Denmar recalled, he had been in the office with Kramer and Carol Smith when Lisa Odom called from the cleaners to tell Denmar his clothes were ready to be picked up. Smith had answered the phone, and she had begun teasing him in front of Kramer.

"She said, 'Howard, I think that the cute little girl at the cleaners is flirting with you,' " Denmar recalled. "She made a big deal out of it. She was having fun at my expense . . . but now that I look back on it, it would fit. To Kurt this was like a competitive sport."

Because Smith had only identified the caller as "the cute little girl at the cleaners," Denmar theorized that Kramer mistakenly thought she was describing Ronda, not Lisa. He further suspected that if Kramer was already interested in Ronda sexually, having watched her jog and looked at her through binoculars, then the telephone call might have made him jealous.

In May 1989, more than two years after the murder, Denmar told his suspicions to a Monroeville attorney, who in turn contacted Sheriff Tate. The sheriff had questioned Kramer and tracked down a .25 caliber pistol he had once owned. Ballistic tests showed, however, that the gun was not the murder weapon. Kramer, quite naturally, had been furious when he learned that Denmar suspected he was the person who had killed Ronda, and the two men had gotten into a violent argument. Tate had gotten upset at him as well, Denmar said. "He told me to quit spreading gossip."

One year later, while Denmar was getting his hair cut, his barber mentioned that Charles Morrison had hired a private investigator to look into his daughter's death. Denmar wanted to contact the investigator, so he called one of Bertha Morrison's sisters, who was one of his insurance clients, and asked her if she knew the investigator's name. She didn't, but Denmar said she had given him several interesting clues. The Morrisons had been receiving mysterious telephone calls right before and after the murder. "She also said that much to Mrs. Morrison's displeasure, Ronda sometimes used to sunbathe topless in the backyard," Denmar recalled. "I immediately thought to myself, 'That is something that would gain the attention of a neighbor.' " Again he was thinking of Kurt Kramer.

In April 1990 Denmar worked up his courage and went to see the Morrisons. "I told them that I had run across some things that I just felt like they needed to know . . . I had tried the local authorities but they didn't want to listen. At that point, the Morrisons told me that . . . they had gotten nothing but a runaround from the authorities and that they didn't believe Walter McMillian had killed their daughter."

Denmar said that just as he was about to tell the Morrisons about Kurt Kramer, they disclosed that they had not hired a private detective. In that case, he decided, his story would only upset them, so he left. Two months later Denmar read in the newspaper that Bryan Stevenson was representing Johnny D., so he called Stevenson and later mailed the attorney three tape-recorded cassettes about Kramer.

Denmar said that his suspicions about Kramer had started to wear on him, so much so that he had trouble concentrating at work. He began drinking heavily. He was scared of Kramer, he said. He had started to feel paranoid. Eventually he had become so terrified that he had closed his business and moved into the trailer. He was afraid to venture outside except to go to his mother's house. "If people would listen to me and give me the benefit of the doubt, then they could find the truth . . . ," Denmar said, "but no one seems interested in Kurt Kramer."

After Denmar finished his story Taylor and Cole promised that they would interrogate Kramer and, if he was involved in the murder, do their best to bring him to justice. Denmar thanked them and shook hands as they left.

As soon as they were out of earshot, Taylor asked Cole what he thought.

"I think," said Cole, "that we had better hear what Kurt Kramer has to say about all this."

Chapter 55

Kurt Kramer said Howard K. Denmar was a liar. Moreover, Kramer had an excellent alibi. On the Saturday of the murder, he had been in the northern part of Monroe County with two other people, both of whom vouched for him. Just to make certain, the two ABI agents gave Kramer a polygraph test. The examiner said it showed that Kramer knew nothing about the Morrison murder. Kramer then offered them his thoughts about what had happened. He had never been infatuated with Ronda, he said, but Howard K. Denmar had been. All the stories that Denmar had told them about Kramer—how he had watched Ronda jog, had kept pornography in the men's room at work, and had been so jealous that he had driven another woman from town—were actually stories about himself.

When Taylor and Cole ran a routine background check on Denmar, they discovered that in July 1990 he had been prosecuted by Tommy Chapman on charges of reckless endangerment and harassment. A woman, identified at the time by the police as Denmar's girlfriend, had claimed that he had held her at gunpoint for several hours and had threatened to kill her and commit suicide because she was trying to end their relationship. A short time later, according to the woman's complaint, Denmar had become so angry that he had circulated a flyer around Monroeville that contained a nude photograph of the woman printed next to her name, her telephone number, and a copy of her bank deposit slip. The woman told authorities that Denmar had mailed the flyer to her parents, the principal of her child's school, her boss, her minister, and more than a dozen of her friends.

When the agents began interviewing former employees at the office building where Denmar worked, they found several other women who claimed that he had sexually harassed them. Two women told the agents that Denmar had sexually attacked them during dates. One of these alleged attacks had taken place about one month before Ronda was murdered. It was particularly brutal, the woman claimed: "I thought he was going to kill me." Neither woman, however, had ever told the police about the incidents. Both women also told the agents that they would not cooperate with the ABI or repeat their stories in public if Denmar was arrested. His family was too well respected, the women said, and each was afraid that no one would believe her. Taylor and Cole knew they couldn't use the women's accusations against Denmar, but both believed they were significant. If true, they suggested that Denmar had a history of sexual problems with women, problems that often ended in violence.

The agents drove to the City Cafe and interviewed the coffee klatch there. One regular remembered that Denmar had acted "very nervous and . . . strange" on the morning of the murder. Rather than sitting in his regular chair, he had taken a seat alone by the window and had stared out in the direction of the cleaners. Denmar had been so distracted that when he left, Hazel, the waitress, complained that he had forgotten to pay his tab. After they finished at the City Cafe Taylor and Cole went to see Sam Crook, the lone white man who had defended Johnny D. Crook told them that Denmar had come to see him shortly after Johnny D. was arrested. He said Denmar had told him that Kurt Kramer was the real killer and had tried repeatedly to get him to blame Kramer for the murder. He had been suspicious of Denmar, Crook said. "I kept wondering why he was so sure that Kramer was the killer."

The two agents decided to ask Charles and Bertha Morrison about their encounter with Denmar. Ronda's parents said Denmar had started telephoning them a few days after the murder, and insisted on meeting them. When they finally agreed, he had come to their house and pelted them with a series of personal questions. Bertha had become so distraught that she had burst into tears. Charles asked Denmar why he was tormenting them. Denmar's continued barrage made the couple so suspicious that Charles confronted him in a loud voice, saying: "Did you kill Ronda?"

That question, the Morrisons told the agents, had "rattled" Denmar and he had left their home.

Back at their motel room–office, Taylor and Cole decided to reread all the statements the Monroeville police had taken on the day of the murder to see if they might have overlooked something. Sure enough, they found a report that had gone unnoticed. It had been written by a Monroeville man who had told the police that he had been driving by Jackson Cleaners and had nearly hit a "white man running across the street" toward the office building where Denmar worked. The motorist said the man was tall, had dark hair, and was wearing a blue sweater. According to a notation on the report, the Monroeville police had never bothered to follow up on the man's statement because investigators had assumed that he was describing Dr. Ed Lee, the dentist whom Jerrie Sue Dunning had asked for help as soon as Ronda's body was discovered. Lee's office was also across the street from the cleaners but was in a different building than the one in which Denmar worked.

The two agents tracked down the motorist and asked him to tell them exactly what he had seen. He told them he could still describe the man. "I saw him eyeball to eyeball," the motorist said. "I never could figure out why the police didn't ask me about him." When the agents told him that the police had assumed that he was describing Ed Lee, the motorist looked startled. "Why, I know Dr. Lee," he said, "and it wasn't him."

Taylor and Cole arranged for an ABI agent whose specialty was preparing police lineups to meet with the motorist. The agent showed the motorist six photographs taken from Alabama drivers' licenses. One of the men in the photographs was Denmar; the other five were chosen because they looked similar to him. The motorist said none of the men looked exactly like the person whom he had seen seven years earlier, but when the agent asked him to pick out "the one who looks most like him," he chose the picture of Denmar.

Taylor and Cole had nothing but bits and pieces. Two women claimed that Denmar had sexually attacked them; a regular at the City Cafe said Denmar had seemed nervous on the day of the murder; the Morrisons thought Denmar had acted strangely; the motorist said he had seen a man who could have been Denmar running across the street from

Jackson Cleaners at the time of the murder. These clues proved nothing, yet both agents thought they were pointing them in the right direction.

Denmar's actions after the murder made them even more suspicious of him. In the privacy of their motel room, Taylor and Cole began discussing Howard Denmar. Why had he told the Monroeville police that he had seen a black man leave the cleaners at precisely 10:38 A.M.? When he made the statement, the police had not yet established the actual time of the murder. Now, however, Taylor and Cole knew that Ronda had been killed sometime between ten-thirty and ten-forty or ten-forty-five, depending upon whether Jerrie Sue Dunning or Florence Mason was the first woman to arrive at the store. (Each woman continued to insist that she was the first to arrive, and the matter had never been settled.) Denmar had picked a time that was very probably close to when Ronda's killer would have been leaving the building. How had he known that? Had he really seen someone or had he been giving the police a clue?

There were other questions. Why had Denmar become so obsessed with Ronda's murder? At various times he had approached Chief Dailey, a local attorney, the Morrisons, a relative of the Morrisons, Sam Crook, and Bryan Stevenson. It seemed that every time someone new got interested in the case, Denmar showed up at his doorstep. Why had he been so intent on finding a killer?

Denmar's rapid slide into alcoholism, his paranoia, and his decision to close down his business and seclude himself in a trailer also struck them as strange. If Kurt Kramer wasn't the killer, and neither agent thought he was, then why was Denmar hiding out in his trailer?

The two agents decided to ask for help from the FBI's behavioral sciences unit, renowned for its work in tracking down serial killers. The ABI agents did not tell the FBI they had a suspect, nor did they tell the agency anything about Howard Denmar, because that might have skewed the analysis. They simply sent the FBI a brief description of the murder and several photographs of the body and the crime scene. A short time later an FBI agent briefed them verbally in Mobile.

Ronda's murder was clearly a sex crime, not a robbery, the agent said. That was obvious because her blouse had been unbuttoned, her bra pushed up, and her pants unzipped. Based on the materials Taylor and Cole had provided, as well as information the FBI had learned over the years about sex offenders, the agent said several assumptions could be made.

The killer was probably a white man between the ages of twenty-seven and thirty-three at the time of the killing, the agent said. He was an only child, had probably been married once or twice, with both marriages ending in divorce, and had trouble dealing with women his own age, particularly women in authority. The killer had probably engaged in a series of progressively worse sexual acts, leading up to the murder itself. These could include making obscene telephone calls, exposing himself in public, or even rape.

Some event on the morning of November 1 had sparked the killing. This could have been an argument between the killer and a woman. It could have been with Ronda or with someone else—his mother, his boss, even a rude salesclerk—who had humiliated him and made him decide to lash out at another woman. The killer showed signs of being paranoid. Because of that, there was a good chance that he had talked about the crime to others. It was unlikely that he had confessed, but the FBI agent told Taylor and Cole they should look for someone who was obsessed with the case. He might even have volunteered to help the police solve the murder while secretly trying to keep tabs on their investigation. There was a good chance that he had met personally with the Morrison family. This was common, the agent said. Observing the family's pain and suffering was a way for the killer to prolong the thrill of what he had done, just as becoming obsessed with the crime enabled him to continue focusing on his own act. The killer might even have divided feelings, the agent said. Part of him might want to be caught while the other half did not. The FBI agent concluded with a warning: If the killer was not caught, he would probably kill again.

Taylor and Cole left the briefing astounded. They were convinced that the FBI agent had just described Howard K. Denmar. A few days later they became even more certain. During an interview a woman told them that she and Denmar had gotten into a bitter argument on the morning when Ronda was murdered. Denmar had left her office fuming, she claimed.

"About what time did this altercation happen?" Cole asked.

"Just before ten o'clock," the woman replied.

Taylor and Cole decided that they now had enough circumstantial evidence to confront Denmar. They called his mother's house at dinnertime and asked Denmar if he would take a polygraph test. "I certainly will," he said. "I am not a murderer. From day one, I've had only one intention and that has been to help find the man who did this."

At one P.M. on January 20, 1993, Denmar reported to the Econolodge, where the ABI, with its extra agents still in town, now occupied four rooms. The ABI polygraph examiner asked Denmar if he had murdered Ronda Morrison. Denmar said no. When the test ended, the examiner went into an adjoining room, where he briefed Taylor and Cole. A few minutes later the two agents returned.

Denmar would later recall what happened next. "They told me, 'Howard, you may as well confess because we know you did it. We have evidence. You failed the polygraph and we have enough evidence to arrest you right now.' I said, 'Gentlemen, I did not kill Ronda.' . . . They said, 'Howard. . . . We got a sworn statement that on November first at the approximate time of the murder . . . an individual had to slam on the brakes of his car and swerve to keep from hitting you as you ran across the road from the cleaners.' I said, 'Gentlemen, it is impossible.' "

For several hours Denmar talked to the agents without a lawyer present. "Everything that I had told them about Kurt Kramer's peculiar behavior . . . was turned on me. . . . I had the binoculars in the office. I was watching Ronda from across the road. I was making hang-up phone calls to the Morrisons . . ."

The agents told him a witness had seen him acting strangely at the City Cafe. "I said, 'Gentlemen, that is impossible . . . I believe what you are telling me is a lie.' "

Taylor and Cole told Denmar that Chief Dailey had denied that he had ever spoken to Denmar about rumors that Denmar was selling drugs. The Morrisons, they said, had denied that they had ever told him they thought Johnny D. was innocent. The agents told him that Sam Crook had been suspicious of him. They also told him that they had interviewed several women who claimed he had sexually assaulted them. About two hours into the interrogation, the agents suddenly turned sympathetic. "They said to me," Denmar later recalled, " 'You didn't mean to kill her. You didn't go over there to kill her. You went over there, things got out of control, and it just happened.' I told them, 'Gentlemen, I am not going to confess to anything that I did not do.' "

At this point the agents asked Denmar if he would tell them what he thought had happened. Flattering him, they said they were obviously not smart enough to figure it out, but he probably was. "Tell us what happened to Ronda that morning, Howard," Cole asked. "We're not saying you did it. Just tell us what you think the murderer did and why that little girl was killed."

Howard Denmar smelled a trap. He said later that he knew the agents were hoping he would say something incriminating. But he also said he simply could not resist telling them what he thought had happened to Ronda.

Chapter 56

"This was not a robbery," Howard Denmar said.

Why? Cole asked. Neither agent had told Denmar they believed Ronda's murder was a sex crime. Denmar looked at them incredulously. "Who robs a cleaners on a Saturday morning?" he replied. Pausing, Denmar asked the agents if they knew for certain whether money had been taken from the cash register. The question surprised them. Neither had said anything to him about their theory that someone other than the killer had grabbed the paper money. They refused to answer his question. They wanted him to tell them his theory. They weren't interested in sharing information.

Denmar told them that after Ronda was murdered, he had learned from one of Monroeville's more prominent real estate agents that several women had received strange telephone calls during the summer of 1986. These were not obscene calls, Denmar explained carefully. "They went something like this:

" 'Hey, how are you?'

" 'Okay, who is this?'

" 'You know who I am.'

" 'What do you want?'

" 'I wish you could meet me in a place to be selected.'

" 'I'm not meeting anyone, especially someone I don't know.'

" '. . . You will know me when you see me and you won't be concerned when you know who I am.' "

Denmar said he immediately suspected that the caller was Kurt Kramer because of the wording. "It goes back to his ego—that all women would find him attractive once they saw him in person."

Denmar said the Morrisons had told him they had been receiving mysterious telephone calls just before the murder. "Mr. and Mrs. Morrison told me in fact . . . that if they answered the phone, the party calling said nothing and eventually would hang up, but if Ronda answered, Mrs. Morrison told me she could tell . . . someone was communicating to Ronda."

Because Ronda was young and naive, she had probably found the calls amusing, Denmar explained. Maybe she thought one of her classmates at the junior college was calling her—a shy boy who was interested in dating her but didn't have the courage to ask. There was no way to tell. But he added, "These were not obscene calls."

"Okay," Denmar now said, having set the stage, "here is my theory." On the morning of the murder, the caller had been more direct when he telephoned Ronda. "He comes on to Ronda," Denmar explained. "Maybe this call is obscene." She gets upset and is trying to figure out who has been telephoning her. "I told the agents, 'Let's just say maybe the caller walked into that place of business on that Saturday morning and Ronda . . . suddenly puts a voice to the face. She suddenly knows who has been calling her. . . ."

At that moment Ronda would have become angry, Denmar theorized. She would have verbally confronted her caller. Maybe she had even threatened to call the police or tell her father. An argument had started. Maybe she had reached for the telephone.

"I'm saying it wasn't premeditated," Denmar told the agents. The caller had not intended to pull out his pistol. But suddenly he did exactly that. Lots of men in southern Alabama carry pocket pistols. The killer had then ordered Ronda into the back of the store. Maybe just to talk, to try to cool down the situation without passing motorists' seeing the two of them arguing at gunpoint in the lobby. It was impossible to know for sure what had happened next. Maybe the gunman had gotten angry and lost control. Maybe he thought Ronda would enjoy having sex. Maybe "it just happened," Denmar said. "Someone panicked."

Denmar paused and then announced that he was finished. That was his theory. Taylor and Cole pounced on him. "They told me they wanted me to put my theory on paper," he recalled later, "and I told them not 'No' but *'Hell no!'* " Denmar said he immediately regretted having told the agents his theory about the telephone calls. "They threw it all back at me. They twisted my theory around and said, 'You killed her because she was going to call her daddy and tell him. She was going to call the police.' I said, 'Gentlemen, you got it all wrong. The reaction that would result in someone killing someone like that are the actions of someone who is clearly deranged—and also married. A single man is not going to kill a woman over some obscene calls, but if a married man gets confronted, let's say he has been drinking and he is already a little shaky and she puts a voice to the face and confronts him . . . then a person might kill in order to keep their wife, their job. . . .' " Denmar reminded the agents that he was twice divorced but that Kurt Kramer had been married.

Denmar asked them if they really thought he would kill someone over a few obscene telephone calls. When neither replied, he pointed out that he had a deep, distinctive voice. When he telephoned, people knew immediately who was calling. He also reminded the agents that he had gone into Jackson Cleaners at least two or three times each week for more than a year. "Ronda would have recognized my voice instantly," he said, "if I were the caller."

Taylor and Cole switched tactics.

"At first they wanted me to confess . . . I said, 'Gentlemen, I am not going to confess to anything that I did not do' . . . Then they wanted me to confess—not that I killed her, but that I just went into the cleaners and found her body. . . . Then it went to 'I just went in there and no one waited on me so I left.' . . . They were trying to get me to say I had gone into the cleaners that morning and I said, 'I didn't go in there. . . . Gentlemen, I am not going to confess.' "

By this point the agents had been interviewing Denmar for nearly seven hours without a break. They were all getting tired. Without being asked, Denmar suddenly offered to let Taylor and Cole search his trailer without a warrant. They rode to the trailer together and made their way through the fences. Inside, there were two rifles but no pistols. There was hardly any furniture, no television, radio, or other indulgence. Denmar told the agents that his monthly bills were thirty-five dollars for rent, five dollars for electricity, and eight dollars for water. He paid them with the few premiums that were still coming in each month from life insurance policies he had sold years before. He ate only one meal a day, and that was the one he got free from his mother each night. "I don't call this living," he later recalled telling Taylor and Cole. "I call this subsistence."

Denmar said he had suffered a nervous breakdown in 1990 after breaking up with his girlfriend, the one who had charged him in court with harassment. He told them he had cut off contact with everyone except his mother. He had moved into the trailer, he said, because he knew he was an alcoholic and was trying to stop drinking. "I told them there are only two things that are going to help me . . . psychiatric care . . . which is extremely expensive . . . or time, which costs me nothing." It had been one month since he had last taken a drink of alcohol, he said.

The agents left, but at eight-thirty that evening they telephoned Denmar at his mother's house, where he had gone to discuss what had happened. He was an only child, and she was worried that he was being too cooperative with them. Cole asked Denmar if he would take another polygraph test the next morning. Despite his mother's warning that he should hire an attorney, Denmar agreed. He arrived at the Econolodge the next day several minutes before the scheduled time. He was ready, he said, for another session.

Once again he was given a polygraph test, but this time he was told that the test results were "inconclusive." He didn't believe Taylor and Cole. He was convinced that he had passed the test and they were lying to him. Still, for nearly two hours he answered their questions, and then they stopped interrogating him. Unknown to Denmar, this was prearranged. The night before, they had decided that Denmar was, in Taylor's words, "toying with us." They suspected that he was getting a vicarious thrill out of telling them his theory about the murder, so they had planned to stop asking him questions. What would he do, they wondered, if they told him they were through with him? Would he run for the door or continue to talk?

Denmar stayed on. He sat there for another sixty minutes, rambling on about the killing. When he gave no indication that he was ready to leave, Taylor and Cole told him that he was free to go. He didn't. Fifteen minutes later they told him he had to go because they had other appointments. He talked for another fifteen minutes before they escorted him to the door. Both agents saw this as a sign that Denmar was relishing the moment, but he later claimed that he had simply felt trapped. "I agreed to talk to them because I didn't kill her . . . then they accused me of killing her and pretty soon, you start thinking: 'I got to convince these people that I did not kill her' so you just keep talking."

As he stepped outside, Denmar turned and confronted Taylor and Cole. He told them he knew they thought he had killed Ronda, but he said he was not afraid of either of them. Regardless of whom they interviewed or how long they stayed in Monroeville, they would never be able to prove in court that he was the murderer.

"What makes you so sure?" said Taylor, who was irked by the arrogant tone of Denmar's remarks.

"Oh, there is no doubt in my mind," Denmar replied, "because I know I am innocent."

Chapter 57

"You gotta help me!" Bill Hooks, Jr., cried over the telephone to Bryan Stevenson. "Sheriff Tate is gonna be mad at me!" He explained that he had just signed a sworn statement recanting his trial testimony and now he was afraid he would be charged with perjury. He asked Stevenson if he would come to Monroeville to meet with him. "No," said Stevenson, who had heard about Hooks's abortive attempt to get him arrested for attempted bribery. Instead Stevenson suggested that Hooks hire himself a good attorney and start telling the truth.

Howard Denmar called next. He told Stevenson that the ABI had accused him of killing Ronda. What should he do? Stevenson suggested that he hire an attorney too.

Thanks to those telephone calls and others from his black contacts in Monroeville, Stevenson knew that the ABI agents had decided Johnny D. was innocent. Yet no one had made any effort to free Johnny D. from death row. Finally, on February 3, 1993, Alabama Attorney General Jimmy Evans notified the appeals court in a letter that his office had discovered new "exculpatory" evidence that might prove helpful to

Johnny D. The attorney general told the court, however, that he did not wish to reveal what he had discovered because his investigation was not yet complete. Instead he asked the court to postpone issuing a decision in Johnny D.'s appeal until his office could finish its probe.

Stevenson promptly objected. If Evans had unearthed new evidence that proved Johnny D. was innocent, then the attorney general should make that proof public and release Johnny D. immediately. Why should Stevenson's client have to stay on death row until the state figured out who the real killer was?

When a copy of Evans's letter came out of Tommy Chapman's fax machine in his Evergreen office, Chapman too was outraged. Who had told the attorney general about Bill Hooks's recantation and Joe Hightower's new statement? These were supposed to be kept secret. And why had Evans decided to tell the court about them without first consulting Chapman? This was still his case. Angry, Chapman called the state capitol. An aide to Evans filled him in. The attorney general's letter had been prompted by politics. The top brass at the ABI had started to worry. Three weeks had passed since Taylor and Cole had proved that Hooks had lied, yet no one had notified Stevenson. The ABI was afraid that if he found out, he would sue the state for allowing his client to languish in jail when it knew he was innocent. To protect itself, the ABI had briefed the attorney general, in effect passing the buck to him. A skilled politician, Evans knew it was bad politics to free a death row inmate, particularly a black one, without first arresting the real killer. The ABI had assured him that Taylor and Cole were on the verge of making an arrest, so Evans had come up with what seemed like a brilliant way to stall. His letter satisfied the requirement under the law that he reveal that exculpatory evidence had been found. But he could still keep Johnny D. safely on death row until someone else was arrested by claiming that his probe wasn't finished.

During his telephone calls Chapman learned something else. When the ABI had passed the buck to the attorney general's office, it had also agreed to let him take full credit for the investigation. Evans had appointed a member of his staff to be the chief investigator on the Morrison case. This investigator was not actually going to *do* anything, but he would act as the media liaison and make certain the attorney general received full credit when Johnny D. was freed and the actual murderer was put behind bars.

"I cussed them out!" Chapman said later. "I mean I used old-fashioned south Alabama yellow-dog cussing. These were the same people who didn't want to say a word when *60 Minutes* came to town, but now they were jumping into this case trying to take credit for what Taylor and Cole had found and notifying the appeals court without even consulting me."

Chapman threatened to hold a news conference and announce to the public that Hooks had recanted and Johnny D. was innocent. "I told them that before they did anything further . . . they needed to consult with me . . . because if there was a new arrest, I was going to be the one who ended up prosecuting the case."

Evans's staff promised not to make any more announcements without first consulting with Chapman, and that week, in a front-page banner story in *The Monroe Journal,* Chapman announced that he and the attorney general's office had jointly discovered new evidence in the Morrison murder case. Chapman revealed for the first time that he had asked the ABI to reopen its investigation into Ronda's death shortly after the *60 Minutes* broadcast. Although he continued to believe the CBS program was slanted, he said it had raised several new questions that he had wanted resolved. Chapman did not disclose that Hooks had admitted lying, but the prosecutor did assure the newspaper's readers that no law enforcement officers were being investigated and "nothing has come to light, as far as I know, that would indicate any misconduct by anyone."

In the midst of all this, Agent Cole telephoned Stevenson and asked for his help. Cole wanted copies of the three tape recordings Denmar had mailed him several months earlier. The ABI agent thought Denmar might have said something incriminating on them. Stevenson was amazed. "No one seems concerned that my client is languishing on death row and that every day he spends there is another day of his life that is wasted," he told Cole. "All you care about is making another arrest." Stevenson offered the agent a deal. He was willing to give the ABI copies of Denmar's tape recordings under two conditions: Denmar had to approve the release of the tapes, and the attorney general's office had to give the defense the "exculpatory evidence" that it was keeping secret. Cole said he would check with his bosses.

A short time later, Stevenson received a letter from Attorney General Evans. "Our investigation into this matter has not yet been completed," Evans stated. "However, we feel obligated to provide the following documents to you . . ." Attached to the letter were seventeen separate witness statements collected by Taylor and Cole. Hooks's recantation and Hightower's new statement were among them. As soon as Stevenson got the package, he received a telephone call from Cole asking about tapes.

Stevenson had already checked with Denmar, who had said he didn't object to Stevenson's giving copies to the ABI. Stevenson agreed to send them to ABI headquarters.

He then telephoned an assistant attorney general in Evans's office. "You have five days to confess error and free Johnny D.," he declared. Otherwise, Stevenson said, he was going to announce that the three men —Myers, Hooks, and Hightower—who had testified against Johnny D. at his trial had all recanted, yet the state was still refusing to release Johnny D. from death row. Stevenson said he would make the announcement at a press conference on the steps leading to the old *To Kill a Mockingbird* courthouse in Monroeville, and he would guarantee that there would be hundreds of angry black demonstrators waving placards behind him. *60 Minutes*, he added, would be invited to attend.

On Tuesday, February 23, Stevenson drove to Holman prison and briefed Johnny D. He told him it might be a week, a month, or even a year before he was released. It all depended on how tough the state wanted to be, but eventually, Stevenson said, "you are going home."

"The mainest thing is they ain't gonna kill me," said Johnny D. "I can wait a bit longer now that I knowed that."

After he left the prison Stevenson stopped at a pay phone and called his office. An excited legal aide told him that the appeals court was just about to issue its ruling in Johnny D.'s case. This was totally unexpected. The court generally released its decisions only on prearranged days. Obviously the justices had decided to ignore Evans's letter. All of a sudden everyone seemed eager to get involved in Johnny D.'s case.

The Alabama Court of Criminal Appeals began its thirty-five-page ruling with a short explanation. Stevenson had raised two legal issues, it stated. The first was Myers's recantation; the second was Stevenson's claim that the prosecution had concealed evidence. Judge Norton had been told to rule on both questions, the court wrote, but he had initially ruled only on the recantation. Because of that, the court had been forced to send the appeal back to the judge. Norton had just delivered his second opinion to the court, the justices said. The Baldwin County judge had declared that Monroe County officials had not hidden any documents from Chestnut and Boynton. Norton had ruled that Johnny D. did not deserve a new trial and had suggested that his execution take place on schedule.

Having revealed Norton's decision, the appeals court methodically delivered its own. It said that it was impossible to tell whether Myers had lied at the trial or was now lying in his recantation. That decision was best made by the actual judges who had heard him testify. Accordingly, the appeals court ruled against Stevenson's first complaint.

The court then issued separate rulings on each of the five examples Stevenson had cited as proof that the prosecution had hidden evidence.

- Myers's June 3 statement, in which he denied knowing anything about Ronda's murder, was not only "clearly . . . favorable" to Johnny D. but was extremely significant, the court said. "Had Myers's statement been disclosed to the defense prior to trial, the results of the proceedings would have been different. A reasonable doubt might well have been created." The judges specifically chastised prosecutor Ted Pearson for telling jurors in his closing argument that Myers had never denied being at Jackson Cleaners. The court had no choice, the justices said, but to overturn Johnny D.'s conviction and demand that he be given a new trial.
  Stevenson had won.

- The justices said the prosecution had also violated Johnny D.'s rights when it failed to tell jurors about the August 27 statement by Tyrone Patterson. "The information that the state's key witness, Ralph Myers, was willing to frame Mr. McMillian for a murder that he did not commit [the Pittman killing] . . . would have cast grave doubt upon Myers's credibility," the court said.
  Again Stevenson had won.

- The court then declared that it was particularly outraged by the prosecution's failure to reveal that Miles Jackson had been at the cleaners at ten-thirty A.M. on the day of the murder. "Had the jury heard his testimony, there is a reasonable probability that the results of the trial would have been different." Once again the court ruled that Johnny D.'s rights had been violated.
  Stevenson had won a third time.

- In regard to Ralph Myers's mental records, the court said that doctors at Taylor Hardin had sent the Monroe County Circuit Court clerk a detailed report for review by the prosecution. That report clearly stated that "Mr. Myers denied any involvement in the alleged offense . . . and believes that he has been framed." In strong language, the court declared that "the prosecution suppressed this evidence," once again denying Johnny D. a fair trial.

Stevenson had won a fourth time.

- There was only one statement the court said was immaterial. Ralph Myers's June 1 interview, which was part of the Vickie Lynn Pittman murder case and did not directly have anything to do with Ronda's murder, was not something the prosecution was required to provide to the defense before the Morrison murder trial.

The five-judge panel had voted unanimously to overturn Johnny D.'s conviction. They had rebuffed Norton's opinion and had severely scolded Pearson and other members of the prosecution. The state now had eighteen days before it was required either to free Johnny D. or bring him to trial again.

It was late by the time Stevenson raced back from the appeals court building in Montgomery to Holman prison.

"We won," Stevenson declared as soon as Johnny D. was brought from his cell.

Johnny D. did not speak. He did not have to. Stevenson could tell by his smile and the tears in his eyes how he felt.

"Thank you," Johnny D. finally mumbled. "You saved my life."

Chapter 58

Tommy Chapman had the flu and a headache and had just finished asking a jury to sentence a young white man to death for the murder of an elderly Evergreen schoolteacher when he learned that the Alabama Court of Criminal Appeals had overturned Johnny D.'s conviction. During a recess in the trial Chapman telephoned the state attorney general's office and asked what Jimmy Evans planned to do. He was told that Evans had decided to let Chapman handle the matter. His office was no longer interested in the case.

Chapman was not surprised. No one had expected the appeals court to issue its ruling. Taking credit for unearthing new evidence, tracking down the "real" killer, and freeing an innocent black man from death row made for great publicity. But releasing a black convicted murderer because of procedural errors in the trial, without offering the public someone to take his place, was bound to be risky. For six years the state had argued vehemently that Johnny D. was a cold-blooded killer. Now someone would have to take the blame, and the attorney general wanted no part of that. Chapman felt trapped. He could demand that the court reconsider its ruling—that would waste sixty to ninety days. But Chapman knew the justices would simply reaffirm their decision. He was going to be forced either to free Johnny D. or to try him again. The politically popular move would be to go ahead with another trial. But what evidence did he have? Myers, Hooks, and Hightower had recanted. Worse, agents Taylor and Cole had warned him that if he held another trial they would testify on behalf of Johnny D.

And then there was the matter of Chapman's conscience. He knew Johnny D. was innocent.

Stevenson reached Chapman by telephone late Friday, February 26. He asked the district attorney what he intended to do. "I am not going to oppose your motion to free Johnny D.," Chapman said. "I want to do everything I can so that your client will not have to spend a single day more than he has already on death row." And then Chapman added, "I feel sick about the six years that Johnny D. has spent in prison and the part that I played keeping him there."

Chapman's apology and the tone of his voice surprised Stevenson, but he let it pass without comment. "I've already drafted a motion demanding that the murder charge be dismissed," he said, adding, "I want Johnny D. released at the courthouse in Monroeville."

"Monroeville?" Chapman repeated. He reminded Stevenson that Johnny D. had been convicted in Bay Minette. Besides, he said, he wasn't certain he would be able to find a judge in Monroeville who would be willing to sign an order turning Johnny D. loose. He didn't elaborate. He figured he didn't have to. Stevenson knew Monroe County well enough by now to know that no locally elected judge would want to risk outraging white voters by signing a motion to free his client.

"Judge Key sentenced my client in Monroeville," Stevenson said. "He was found guilty in Bay Minette, but Key arranged it so that everyone could watch him slam down that gavel and sentence Walter to death in Monroe County. The press was there taking pictures and the prosecution team was clapping hands and hugging each other and celebrating. I want McMillian's family and supporters to have their moment of celebration in that same courthouse. I want the press there recording their celebration." Chapman promised to try to find a willing judge, but he doubted he could. Judge Key had retired, and his replacement had shown no interest in the case.

All that weekend, the Resource Center was besieged by telephone calls from reporters. Now that Johnny D. was being set free, everyone wanted to talk to him. This included reporters from Alabama newspapers that had blindly accepted everything Pearson, Benson, Ikner, and Tate had said. When Stevenson was told that a reporter from a newspaper that had been particularly ugly toward Johnny D. was now demanding an exclusive interview, he nearly laughed out loud.

Stevenson telephoned the Atlanta bureau of *The New York Times* and arranged for one of its writers to interview McMillian that weekend in prison. "I was worried . . . not only about what some vigilante might do, but also what Sheriff Tate and others in Monroeville might do once Walter was released," Stevenson said. "I wanted them to know that the entire nation would be watching them."

On Monday, March 1, Chapman telephoned Stevenson and told him that none of the judges in Monroe County was willing to oversee the release of his client. Chapman had spent most of the day searching for a friendly judge and had finally persuaded a newly elected Baldwin County judge, Pamela W. Baschab, to hear Stevenson's motion. The hearing was scheduled for ten-thirty the next morning.

Late that night Johnny D.'s fellow prisoners held a church service for him in the chapel to say their goodbyes. He was about to become the first man in Alabama's history to be freed from death row. When it was over he could not fall asleep. He was too excited. Seven men had been executed since he had arrived. He had known all of them except for the first. Two had been close friends. The only other nights on death row when he couldn't sleep were the nights when there were executions. Now he couldn't sleep because there was not going to be one.

Early on Tuesday Stevenson brought Johnny D. a dark suit, white shirt, socks, and shoes, and he changed out of his all-white prison-issue uniform for the last time. They were alone for only a few minutes, and Johnny D. started to thank him, but Stevenson sensed how uncomfortable he felt and told him there was no need. They had won his freedom together.

Minutes before the court hearing began in Baldwin County, Chapman asked to speak with Stevenson privately outside the courtroom. "Tommy assured me that he was not going to object to my motion," Stevenson said later. "He said he had already spoken to Judge Baschab and she was going to grant my motion without asking a bunch of questions. Tommy said he just wanted me to know that there was no reason to drag anything out. At first I thought he was trying to be helpful, but then I realized what was going on. The reason he was telling me this was because he and the judge were genuinely afraid that I was going to act out in court—that I was going to give some speech about how Walter had been mistreated or talk about race or misconduct by the prosecution. Frankly, that would have been fun and entertaining, particularly with all of the national press there, but it wasn't in Walter's best interest. He simply wanted to go home, and I wasn't going to delay that. I told Tommy that I was not going to carry on in court, and he was clearly pleased."

As they were returning to the courtroom, Chapman said there was something else he needed to mention. "Tommy says to me, 'I hope you understand that I was the one who asked the ABI to do this investigation.' And I said, 'I know you asked for it, but it was too little too late.' He looked at me strangely and then he says, 'Well, I really did want the truth to come out.' And then Tommy said to me, 'Bryan, I hope you talk to Jerome Gray for me and set things straight.' Gray is the head of the largest black political conference in Alabama and is influential in deciding who gets the black vote in Conecuh County. I said, 'Well, Tommy, that will depend on a lot of different things.' "

When Johnny D. was brought into the courtroom he noticed that for the first time it was filled chiefly with blacks. It was also the first time he had been in court without seeing Charles and Bertha Morrison. Stevenson introduced his motion. Chapman said he didn't object. Judge Baschab granted the motion without comment. The hearing had lasted less than eight minutes. Johnny D. was a free man.

Chapman raced over to the defense table and stuck out his hand. Johnny D. shook it.

"Good luck, Johnny," Chapman said.

Family members and well-wishers enveloped Johnny D. and Stevenson as soon as they walked outside the courthouse. They were met by television cameras and reporters shouting questions. Behind them Johnny D.'s relatives unfurled a banner that read GOD NEVER FAILS.

"I'm happy," Johnny D. said. "I've done forgiven the people that lied on me and put me in prison. I'm not bitter at all . . ."

As best he could, Johnny D. answered the media's questions, but he clearly felt uncomfortable. "I'm innocent, and God knows I'm innocent," he kept repeating. "I just want to go home." Whenever he could, Stevenson helped him with answers. "I clearly feel that the state owes Mr. McMillian an apology," Stevenson declared, pointing out that neither Chapman nor the judge had mentioned that McMillian had spent six years in prison unfairly. Some of the questions irritated the attorney. "Who killed Ronda?" one reporter asked. "What did you learn from being in prison?" asked another. What did they expect Johnny D. to say?

It was Minnie McMillian, standing next to her husband, who proved the most eloquent. "You'd just have to go through it to know what it has been like," she replied when asked her feelings. "It's been so long since I had any feelings at all . . . now I am just bursting with happiness." Minnie asked the media to remember the Morrisons. "They've put them through this for six years, tormenting them over and over again completely unnecessarily. It's been hard on them and should never have happened."

When the news conference ended, reporters and family members followed Johnny D. to his house, where his oldest son, Johnny, was waiting. Minnie had made Johnny stay home because of the trouble he had had with Sheriff Tate after the trial, when he was arrested for making threatening remarks. Father and son hugged for several minutes.

Stevenson had been so determined at the hearing and news conference to make certain everything went well that he had not really paused to enjoy himself. Now, as he watched Johnny D. and his family celebrating, he started to relax. "People were coming from everywhere because they wanted to be part of what was happening. A woman came walking out from the woods. She was old and she didn't have any teeth and she didn't have any shoes but she hugged Walter and she cried and cried and cried and she said that she just wanted to touch him. For the first time, you could see that these people felt a sense of empowerment. For the first time, they were the guests of honor. They were the ones who had to be seated first in the courtroom. They were the ones who now were in front of the television cameras. They were the ones the reporters all wanted to interview. For those brief moments, they were not invisible people."

A few hours later, Johnny D. was driven to a dentist's office in Montgomery. Six of his teeth had been pulled in prison and a metal plate had been put in his mouth, but the prison dentist had never finished the job, and Johnny D. had been unable to chew properly for eight months. Stevenson had arranged for his own black dentist to help Johnny D. The dentist and his partner worked on him until three in the morning without charge. When he returned the next afternoon for some final dental work, a dozen people were waiting. "All of these people were black professionals, but that didn't matter. They wanted to shake Walter's hand," Stevenson explained. During the coming weeks that scene was repeated often. "Black people stopped whatever they were doing when they saw Walter and came rushing over to congratulate him."

The CBS Morning News interviewed Johnny D. and Stevenson. *The New York Times* published a follow-up story under the heading "Fresh proof from Alabama that prosecutors can win convictions with bent rules, racial stereotypes and no valid evidence." *60 Minutes* took credit for Johnny D.'s release. *USA Today, The Washington Post,* and other national publications printed stories and editorials about the case. A black Alabama state legislator introduced a bill that called for Johnny D. to receive $9 million in restitution from the state: $1.5 million for each year he had served in prison. The U.S. Senate Judiciary Committee flew him and Stevenson to Washington, D.C., to testify at a hearing about death row inmates who had been falsely accused. When an Alabama senator suggested during the hearing that Johnny D.'s release was actually proof that the justice system worked, Stevenson quickly objected. "Walter McMillian never received justice," he replied. "What he received was injustice." His client was an innocent man who had been fortunate enough to beat the odds, Stevenson testified. It had taken the state only forty-eight hours to convict Johnny D. and sentence him to death. It had taken four and a half years of litigation and thousands of hours of investigation to free him. That, he told the senator, was certainly nothing to brag about.

Only one newspaper did not portray Johnny D. as a wrongfully convicted man. In its front-page story, *The Monroe Journal* explained that the appeals court had not exonerated Johnny D. or ruled on whether he was innocent or guilty. Rather, the court had overturned the conviction because of errors by the prosecution. It quoted Chapman as assuring readers that regardless of what the higher court said, no one who worked in the district attorney's office, for the ABI, or for the sheriff's office had done anything "intentionally" wrong.

Stevenson was not surprised when he read the article. "No one is going to get fired or be punished for what they did to Walter," he predicted. "These people still don't understand the horrible injustice that they inflicted on this man."

Chapter 59

Larry Ikner had always thought the worst day in his life was in 1967, when he was in Vietnam and his platoon got pinned down. By late afternoon the temperature was more than a hundred degrees, no one had any water left, and each man had only a few rounds of ammunition. They were encircled by the enemy. "I had in my mind that when the sun went down that night," Ikner said, "I would never see it come up again." Someone found a bottle of Worcestershire sauce in a mail pouch and the men passed it around. "We ended up drinking that entire bottle." Luckily reinforcements arrived. Ikner survived.

As he sat in the Baldwin County Courthouse and watched as the murder charge against Johnny D. was dismissed, Ikner decided he had been wrong. This was his lowest point. "I have been going over and over and over everything in my mind," he said later, "looking for where I made a mistake, where I went wrong, but I can tell you if there were mistakes, they were honest ones. I genuinely believed that Johnny D. had been in that cleaners. I honestly believed Ralph and Karen Kelly and Bill Hooks were telling the truth."

Ikner felt certain he had spoken to Hooks about "John Dozier" on the night of the murder. He could not explain why there were no notes from that meeting. "I would never put anyone on death row I thought was innocent," he said. "I haven't been able to sleep thinking about this. My wife is afraid to move in bed because she might disturb me once I fall asleep, but I just lie there. I can't sleep."

What he disliked most was the looks he got from Johnny D.'s family and supporters. "Many of these folks are black people I have known all my life but now they look at me differently. All of my life they have thought of me as a good person and friend and I have thought of them that way. But now . . ." His voice trailed off.

Unlike Ikner, the other three men directly involved in the prosecution expressed no self-doubt. "I did what I thought was right at the time," Pearson told reporters, adding somewhat flippantly, "The jury did the convicting." The ABI had ordered Simon Benson not to comment on Johnny D.'s release, but he had trouble following the order. "I have no personal feelings about McMillian. I can live with what the court does," he said afterward. But then he whispered, "The whole truth hasn't come out and when it do, the public is gonna know Johnny D. is the man. He was involved in the murder. You just wait and see."

Sheriff Tom Tate was more vocal. He was tired of Stevenson's constantly harping about "law enforcement misconduct" and racial prejudice. "This doesn't have a damn thing to do with race and frankly no one gives a damn how many blacks Karen Kelly was screwing." Tate said he had not done anything improper, and he accused Chapman of being gutless. "It seems to me that we had a pretty airtight case until those two ABI boys rolled into town. They came riding in here determined to show us how to investigate and how they were big shots and Mr. Chapman just let them sell him a bill of goods."

How could agents Taylor and Cole be so certain that Johnny D. was innocent when they had never even bothered to speak to Myers or Kelly? Tate asked. "Them boys told me this was such a friendly community that they could call up women at ten-thirty at night and ask them to come to their motel room to be interviewed and they would do it," Tate said sneeringly. "Now you tell me what sort of investigator asks women to come to a motel at ten-thirty at night?"

Tommy Chapman soon learned from friends in the courthouse that Sheriff Tate was angry at him for not forcing Johnny D. to be tried a second time. "I've always thought of Tom Tate as a friend," Chapman said, "but he is really out of line on this. He knows there is no evidence that ties Johnny D. to that murder." Chapman called Captain John

Cloud at the ABI and asked him to personally brief Tate "before he makes a damn fool of himself."

On March 18 Tate's complaints about Chapman made the front page of *The Monroe Journal.* The sheriff accused the ABI of "keeping him in the dark" and Chapman of acting too quickly to release Johnny D. If the ABI had evidence that proved he was innocent, Tate said, then it should have revealed that evidence in court, rather than simply telling Chapman about it in private. Word soon spread that Charles and Bertha Morrison shared Tate's view. "McMillian may be innocent, but a jury convicted him and a jury should have set him free, not one man," Charles was quoted as saying in a Montgomery newspaper. Tempers flared even more when a hostile letter was published in *The Monroe Journal.* The author accused Monroeville of being a racist community. "Alabamians, you may now hang your heads in shame!" the writer declared. He also described Judge Key as a "bigot" and said the police were "corrupt." The letter was signed by a resident of Paris, France, but many in town suspected that the name and address were fake and the letter had been written by someone local. The *Journal* defended the community in a long editorial. "Monroeville and Monroe County have no reason to be ashamed . . . ," it declared. The editorial then joined Sheriff Tate in tweaking Chapman. "The district attorney says he is convinced of McMillian's innocence, but many questions have to remain in the public's minds about what really happened because details of the latest investigation have not been released."

Chapman figured that as soon as Taylor and Cole arrested Howard Denmar the criticism would end. Meanwhile, he began leaking scraps of information to *The Monroe Journal.* The killer's motive, he said, was "not robbery . . . as some have contended from the start [a thinly veiled slap at Tate] . . . This was a sexual assault." The ABI was close to making an arrest, Chapman promised, and once that happened he would be able to tell the public why he was certain Johnny D. was innocent.

While Chapman worked at quelling rumors, Taylor and Cole began running into dead ends. They had learned nothing new from the three tapes Denmar had made for Stevenson, nor had they found any compelling evidence linking Denmar to the murder. Denmar, meanwhile, paid $350 to a private investigator in Mobile to give him a polygraph test. The examiner told him that the test showed he was being truthful when he denied shooting Ronda Morrison. Denmar sent a copy to the ABI. "I knew those agents had to be lying about the tests they gave me," Denmar charged. He decided to stop cooperating with the ABI. "I don't like being accused of murder. . . . I told those two agents, 'You know I'm a past drunk. You know I had a nervous breakdown. You want to tie all this to me . . . but I didn't kill her. I'm not a Boy Scout,' I said. 'I have done things that I am ashamed of. I'm a drunk and you name one drunk who hasn't done things he is ashamed of . . . but on November first, 1986, I didn't have a care in the damn world. My reputation was spotless. I had a good life. Now you want to tie my drinking, you want to tie my nervous breakdown, you want to tie my troubles that happened in 1990 to what happened in 1986 and I don't like it worth a damn!' "

Finally taking his mother's advice, Denmar hired Richard D. Horne, an aggressive, tough-talking defense lawyer from Mobile, to represent him, and Horne immediately sent a private detective to Monroeville to investigate. The detective soon learned the identity of the motorist who had picked Denmar from the photo lineup. Horne had the detective show the motorist a photograph taken of Denmar in 1986, and he said he did not recognize Denmar based on that picture. The detective tape-recorded the motorist's answer, and as soon as Horne heard the tape, he telephoned Chapman and told him about it. If Chapman tried to call the motorist as a witness in court, Horne would play the tape and discredit his testimony. The defense attorney then complained about Taylor and Cole. He accused them of being "guerrilla cops" with "Rambo mentalities." He claimed the ABI was trying to use his client as a scapegoat.

"If you ask Howard Denmar about the John F. Kennedy assassination, he will talk about it for hours and act as if he knows all sorts of intimate details about it," Horne said. "The same is true if you ask him about his theories about the Morrison murder. But my client damn well didn't kill President Kennedy and he did not kill Ronda Morrison either." The attorney said he was particularly outraged about the widespread whispers in Monroeville that suggested his client had sexually attacked two women. "You cannot believe the anguish that this man and his good family have gone through . . . ," he said, "particularly all this date rape crap being spread by whores."

Chapman reacted to Horne's statements by hiring a hypnotist to question the motorist about what he had seen on the day of the murder. While he was in a trance, the motorist described the man. The description fit Denmar perfectly. Still, Chapman didn't think he had enough to file a murder charge against Denmar. In late March Taylor and Cole decided they had done everything they could do. They suggested that

Chapman obtain blood and hair samples from Denmar on the chance that the lone blood spot found near the cash register at Jackson Cleaners was his. But Chapman declined. All the evidence against Denmar was circumstantial, and he was not going to launch another "Johnny D. debacle." The two agents were told to go home.

As they carried their suitcases from their room at the Econolodge, Cole was philosophical. "There are other murders to be solved," he said. But Taylor was angry. He wanted to arrest Denmar. Cole reminded his partner that they had not wasted their time. Their four-month investigation had proved that Johnny D. was innocent. The appeals court had overturned his conviction, but it was their probe that had convinced Chapman not to try him again. Still, Taylor felt as if they had failed. "This case is a keeper," he said quietly. Cole nodded. As long as they were ABI agents, both men would keep the Morrison murder file among their list of active cases. "I am never going to give up hope," Taylor said later, "that someday, some way, we will be able to bring Ronda's murderer to justice."

Word spread quickly in Monroeville that Taylor and Cole were gone, and with that news came the realization that no new suspect would be arrested. The women who had accused Denmar of sexual misconduct felt betrayed. Chapman found himself coming under renewed criticism. A rumor swept through Monroeville that he had asked to be appointed to the district attorney's job specifically to free Johnny D. Lies were told about payoffs from the Mafia. Other gossip had Chapman helping Johnny D. because Chapman's brother had been Johnny D.'s friend. Chapman was shunned at the country club. He was no longer invited to join golf foursomes. Local judges refused to speak to him. He heard from friends that Judge Key was outraged about what he had done. To his shock, Chapman found that he was also being criticized by blacks who did not believe that he had done enough early on to help Johnny D. One afternoon a weary Chapman heard that Larry Ikner had suggested to some friends that he still believed Johnny D. was guilty. Chapman called Ikner into his office. As long as he was district attorney, Chapman declared, the official policy would be that Johnny D. was an innocent man. Anyone who did not agree with that policy should quit, and if in the future he ever heard Ikner or anyone else from the D.A.'s office saying that Johnny D. was guilty, that person would be fired.

And then, in a moment of anger, Chapman turned on Ikner, a man whom he had always considered a friend, and blurted out, "The truth is that you and Benson and Tate just went out and found yourself a nig—" He stopped before he finished the sentence. Ikner was his friend, and deep down Chapman really did not believe that he had done anything wrong. Still, he could not stop wondering how Benson, Ikner, and Tate had been so blind.

Chapter

60

In the March 11 issue of *The Monroe Journal,* a reporter asked Tommy Chapman why Myers had lied about Johnny D. Chapman said the answer was obvious. Myers had "cut a deal" with prosecutors to avoid being sentenced to death in the Vickie Lynn Pittman murder. This was not news to Mozelle and Onzell. They had both known, in their words, that "Vickie Lynn's murder had been used as a bargaining chip," but seeing it in print rekindled their anger. Mozelle dialed Simon Benson's home telephone number. She got his answering machine, and as soon as the tape started recording, she blistered him with profanity. Before hanging up, she told him that she and Onzell had hired an attorney and were going to sue him and the ABI.

Mozelle was exaggerating—neither woman could afford a lawyer—but she hoped her threat would scare Benson. It did generate a response. A few days later Benson's supervisor, Captain Ken Hallford, telephoned to assure her that the ABI would be happy to listen to her complaints and to pursue the case if she had new evidence about Vickie Lynn's murder.

Over the next several months Mozelle and Onzell met not only with other ABI agents, but with a string of investigators from the U.S. attorney general's office and the FBI. Each time a new one came to Mozelle's house, she and Onzell sat at the kitchen table and patiently explained everything they had learned about their niece's murder. There were two questions the women wanted answered: Why was Vickie Lynn murdered, and who was present when she was beaten to death with a tire jack? Was the "why" a drug deal gone bad? A bank robbery? Had Ralph Myers been there? Karen Kelly? Johnny D.? Vic Pittman? Karen Ann Pittman? Sheriff Booker?

Each time the sisters conferred with a new investigator, they convinced themselves that they were finally going to learn the truth. But their two questions were never answered. Some of the investigators stuck with the case longer than others, but none was ever able to give them answers that satisfied them, and eventually the agents stopped coming to see them. Later most would complain that the sisters would not be happy until Vic and Karen Ann Pittman were in jail. That was not how Mozelle and Onzell saw it. They were sure the reason their questions were never adequately answered was that Vickie Lynn's death was tied in some way to corrupt law enforcement officers. That was a path, they were convinced, that none of the investigators wanted to travel.

Late one afternoon while she was in her kitchen, Mozelle heard a knock on the back door. It was Vic. He looked to her as if he was drunk. He was clearly upset. He had just been to the cemetery, and he claimed that someone had vandalized Vickie Lynn's grave. Mozelle shooed him away but decided to check for herself. The girl was buried in a family plot next to an old white-clapboard church. It was a familiar site to the sisters; when they were children, their mother had made them pull weeds there.

At the cemetery Mozelle walked over to the grave. Vickie Lynn lay under a six-by-three-foot concrete slab with a gray granite headstone incised with her name and the date of her birth. Because no one could be certain exactly when she had been murdered, the date for her death read "Feb. 22–23, 1987." It was difficult for Mozelle to come to the cemetery without crying. Try as she would to remember Vickie Lynn as a smiling teenage girl, it was hard not to think of the brutalized corpse abandoned in the woods.

She saw no sign of vandalism and silently chastised her brother. But there were some feces on the concrete, probably from some animal, maybe a stray dog—they didn't look human—so Mozelle removed them. Then she paused at the foot of the slab. It was beginning to turn dark, but from where she was standing the late-afternoon light struck the headstone, and Mozelle realized there was a scratch on the granite. She got down on her knees to examine it. There were other scratches as well. Someone had used a nail or other sharp object to make them. They formed two jagged words: "IM SORRY." A piece of folded white paper was tucked between the grass and the concrete slab near the headstone. It was not weathered, so she knew it had been put there recently. She pulled it out. "I love you Vickie Lynn," she read. "They will pay for what they done to you." Mozelle recognized the writing. It was Vic's.

When she got home, Mozelle read Onzell the note. Was this one of Vic's tricks? Had he left it there knowing that she would go to the cemetery and find it? Or was he making some sort of written pledge to Vickie Lynn, a grieving father's promise to his murdered child?

In the fall of 1993 Mozelle and Onzell sat at the dining room table in Mozelle's house with a tape recorder perched between them. Vickie Lynn had been dead nearly seven years. The sisters had broken off all communication with Karen Ann Pittman and also with Vickie Lynn's aunt, Eunice Flowers, because of squabbles about the murder. It was time to stop searching for answers.

Mozelle began speaking into the recorder. She stated her name, the date, the time. "This is what I believe happened," she said solemnly. Reading from her notes, she recounted everything she and Onzell had learned about Vickie Lynn's murder. Mozelle said she did not believe that Johnny D. was involved. Kelly and Myers had tried to frame him, just as they had done in the Morrison murder. Near the end of her statement, she said that she did not believe that Vic was present when Vickie Lynn was beaten to death, nor did she think Karen Ann was there. But she blamed both of them for introducing Vickie Lynn to people such as Kelly and Myers. And finally she said that although she did not wish any harm to Sheriff Tim Hawsey, prosecutor Michael Godwin, or Simon Benson, she did wish there was a way they could discover what it felt like to have a family member murdered and then watch as the killers smiled and smirked and laughed in court while cutting deals that spared their lives.

Onzell spoke more briefly. She told how much she loved Vickie Lynn and how sorry she was that on the night when the girl had disappeared, she had not somehow sensed what was going to happen. Both women had tears in their eyes when Onzell stopped talking. They put the tape cassette in a large brown envelope that also contained photographs of

Vickie Lynn. Then Mozelle tucked the envelope into the cardboard box where she kept all her notes about the murder, as well as a poem that Vickie Lynn had written as a school assignment before she was killed. Mozelle walked down the hallway to her bedroom and placed the box on a shelf in the closet. She closed the door.

Chapter 61

Walter "Johnny D." McMillian was free. Besides dismissing the murder charge, Chapman dropped the still unresolved charge of sodomy filed against Johnny D. in Conecuh County. Myers had admitted in his recantation that the accusation was a lie. The only remaining charge was the murder of Vickie Lynn Pittman, and Stevenson forced prosecutor Godwin to drop it for lack of evidence.

At the time, said Johnny D., "I really felt I could pick up and go right back when I got out of prison. I thought I could get my trucks and things and get right back to work just like it was. That was the plan, to go home."

But Stevenson was reluctant to let Johnny D. return to Monroeville; he was afraid someone might accuse him of another crime or actually kill him. So McMillian spent his first few weeks of freedom riding back and forth between a motel in Montgomery and his house in Monroeville. Before long he learned that there was an additional reason why Stevenson had suggested he not move back immediately. Johnny D.'s wife no longer wanted him to live with her.

Minnie had stuck by him faithfully while he was in prison, and by the time he was freed they had been married thirty years, but it had been an odd match from the start and they had spent more years apart than together. Neither was good at expressing feelings to the other. What Minnie really wanted now was an apology. She wasn't angry at him because he had been falsely accused of murder or because she had been forced to beg for money to pay attorneys' fees and her bills. But she had been publicly humiliated. Johnny D.'s affair with Karen Kelly had been repeatedly mentioned in the media during the six years he was in prison. In fact, the front-page article in *The New York Times* that Stevenson had orchestrated contained a fresh "revelation": It reported that Johnny D. had nine illegitimate children. Minnie was well aware that he had been unfaithful, but this particular story put her in a bind from which there was no escape. How could she possibly find out whether it was accurate? She certainly couldn't ask anyone about it—it was embarrassing enough on its own. "If he wants to move back in here, then he's got to convince me he is through with all this chasing around," she said. She had an ulcer. "My nerves have been through enough. I just can't take any more. It can't be like it used to be."

But Johnny D. did not believe he owed Minnie or anyone else an apology. He was a victim. He had been framed. His reputation had been ruined. All the years when he had scrimped and saved so that he could raise enough cash to start his own business were for naught. He had lost six years of his life. Hadn't he served enough penance for his marital infidelities?

Stevenson was worried about him. "You just don't walk off death row and pick up your life." He had known of three men in Georgia who had been released from death row. Two had committed suicide within three years. "I am afraid for Walter," he explained, "because I know he is not only going to have to deal with all that has happened but all that is about to happen too."

Stevenson suggested that Johnny D. and Minnie go on a trip together. They could talk about their future. Stevenson would help pay for it. Johnny D. asked Minnie if she wanted to go. "You best be going without me," she replied. She still owed more than $11,000 to creditors, and she didn't want to take any time off from work. Johnny D. reminded her that there was a bill before the state legislature that would compensate him for damages in the sum of $9 million. But Minnie laughed. "Them peoples ain't gonna help you," she said. Rather than argue, Johnny D. went by himself. As soon as he left, however, Minnie complained, "If he really wanted me to go, you would think he would have asked me twice."

When Johnny D. returned, Stevenson suggested that he live with one of his sisters in Florida for a while. If he found a job there, perhaps he could convince Minnie to join him. Johnny D. went to Florida and looked for work, but failed to find any. He was fifty-two years old and skilled at clearing trees, but that was a job linked to Monroe County. He had lived there all his life. He knew the land, who owned the trees, what kinds of trees they were, how to price them, who would buy them. Outside Monroe County that knowledge was useless.

He and Minnie continued to argue long distance. Their oldest son got a divorce and moved back home. Their youngest still lived at home and was unemployed, although it was now four years since he had graduated from high school. Johnny D. thought both sons should be on their own, but Minnie defended them. By late summer Johnny D. had run out of options and money. He came back to Monroe County and moved into a tiny trailer parked on the land his grandfather had bought years before. Whenever he could, Sam Crook found him work cutting trees.

Not long after Johnny D. settled in, Minnie heard rumors that he was seeing Thulani again. In a fury, she confronted Thulani at work one morning at Vanity Fair Mills. Within minutes the two women were screaming at each other. Minnie accused Thulani of trying to steal her husband, and Thulani charged Minnie with turning him away. Each accused the other of caring only about the $9-million settlement that was pending in the legislature. They barely avoided coming to blows, and both almost lost their jobs. Johnny D.'s relatives began to avoid Minnie. In turn, her friends told her that he was still a womanizer. In fact, they said, he had secretly corresponded and met with Thulani while he was in prison. One afternoon Johnny D. went to see his wife, hoping to resolve their problems. Instead they began to argue, and Minnie abruptly pulled out a pistol and ordered him to leave.

The state legislature adjourned without bringing the $9-million compensation bill for Johnny D. to a vote. That meant it was dead. Making a number of telephone calls, Stevenson learned that several influential white citizens from Monroeville had quietly lobbied against the bill. He was also told that Sheriff Tate and Simon Benson were still claiming that Johnny D. was guilty of murdering Ronda. "When I first became involved in this case, I kept thinking that it was sheer incompetence that was driving the prosecution," Stevenson said, "because anyone interested in justice could read the court record and see that there was no credible evidence that Walter was guilty. Now I know better. After all we have been through, we still have folks like Sheriff Tate running around claiming that Johnny D. is a murderer. That is not stupidity. It is meanness and hatred."

On a Sunday morning in November 1993, eight months after Johnny D. was freed from prison, Minnie McMillian stood in her kitchen preparing for a birthday party for her two granddaughters. They lived with their mother, her oldest son's ex-wife, but were spending the weekend with her. She had gotten up early to begin her cooking. All her relatives were coming after church for barbecued ribs and chicken. She wondered if Johnny D. would join them. He loved spending time with his grandchildren and had not seen them much since he was released.

It was unusually cold, and weather forecasters had warned it might even snow in Monroeville. That was a worry; there would not be enough room in her house for everyone if it got too cold for an outdoor picnic. She stood at the window and listened to the trucks and cars hurrying past on Highway 84. Occasionally she glanced up at the clouds. Sundays were special. From childhood, she had always enjoyed them. Her own children could never understand how she and her eight siblings had endured spending nearly all day in church, but that was because they did not understand how those services routed the bleakness from a poor person's life. She loved the singing. Besides, being in church had meant she did not have to work in the fields. As she stood peeling potatoes, she wondered again whether Johnny D. would drop by that afternoon.

Bryan Stevenson turned thirty-four on that same Sunday. He spent the morning speaking to a dozen men and women at a prayer breakfast in the basement of a well-established African Methodist Episcopal Church in Montgomery. His mother had called him earlier to wish him a happy birthday. She was worried about how hard he was working, and she wished he would move closer to home. "We hardly see you," she said. Her concerns had made him feel melancholy, but he put them aside at the prayer breakfast and spoke passionately, without notes, about how politics, racial bias, and money all corrupt the justice system. Much of his talk was about Johnny D. There was no mention of marijuana, no talk about an affair with Karen Kelly or weekends spent at nightclubs.

"Here was a man who had no significant prior criminal history," said Stevenson, "who worked two jobs to feed his family, who was at home with his family on the day of the crime with at least ten, fifteen, twenty black people around him . . . but despite all that, he was arrested, convicted, and sentenced to death. . . . And what is even more outrageous is that we believe many of those involved in the prosecution fully knew that Walter was innocent. . . . They knew he wasn't the kind of person who would commit this murder. . . .

"But charging him with murder was not enough. They had to create an environment where people could find it easier to see him as a person who would do this crime, so they also accused him of raping another man, a totally trumped-up charge, and even that wasn't enough. They sent him off to death row, even though his case had not yet gone to trial. . . . And they put him there three weeks before an execution. . . . His cell was less than fifteen feet from where people are executed. He could smell the excrement and other horrible odors. . . . There is no question in my mind that they put Walter there before his trial intentionally, in an attempt to coerce and intimidate him, to try to make him break, to make him say, 'I'll do whatever you like just to save my life. . . .' And yet Walter McMillian endured, he refused to give up, and that is why I hold him in such high respect and admire him so much. He never lost hope."

During his speech Stevenson recited a slew of statistics that proved the death penalty was administered unfairly. And then he said, "I often think about the story in the Bible where the people bring this woman accused of adultery before the Lord and they are about to stone her to death and the Lord looks down and starts drawing little figures in the sand and then He says very quietly and very humbly, 'Let you who is without sin cast the first stone.' The people drop the rocks and walk away embarrassed. We are living in an era today where people don't just think about what Jesus says and walk away. Instead, they just kind of thoughtlessly throw their stones. It is no longer enough to say, 'Hey, none of you are righteous enough or moral enough or fit enough to judge another human being,' because there are plenty of people in our society who *are* eager to decide who is fit to live and who is fit to die. That is why we must be the stone-catchers, the people who are willing to step in between and catch the cast stones . . .

"I am not saying that justice in every situation means freeing a man from death row. In some cases that would be injustice. There are people who should be locked up. But the criminal justice system is so corrupt, so filled with racism and unfairness, that we must ask ourselves: 'Who are we to decide who lives and who dies?' "

Johnny D. thought about going to his granddaughters' birthday party, but he was afraid of Minnie. "She mad and she gonna stay mad and ain't nothing I can do but go ahead with my life," he said. Stevenson had told him about some jobs in Mississippi that he might be able to get. He was going to go there and look. "No time like the present to go," he said. With some money from Stevenson, he had bought himself a beat-up old car. He tossed a secondhand suitcase in the back and started down the road.

By three o'clock, Minnie's sauce was simmering and there were three grills outside in the back ready for the ribs and chicken. Ten adults and at least that many children were gathered around them. The men were drinking beer and standing around talking. The women fussed over a new baby. Inside, Minnie was trying to decide if the sauce had enough spices. She liked it hot.

"I guess Johnny D. ain't coming," she said to no one in particular.

There was a song that she had enjoyed as a child in church on Sundays. She could still remember the first time she had heard it. It was sung by a young girl in a white-and-pink dress. The song was about sparrows and how God was so all-knowing and all-powerful that He knew even when a single sparrow fell dead. If God kept track of sparrows, then surely He kept track of people who loved Him, regardless of whether they were black or white, important or nobodies. That was what Minnie liked about the song: that God knew you, was watching you, cared about you.

Some of her relatives wanted her to divorce Johnny D. Some of his relatives said she was being stubborn and not treating him right. She was worried about how she would pay her debts. There were rumors that Vanity Fair might be cutting back. She was afraid she might be laid off. Her ulcer was bothering her.

She started humming the song about the sparrows.

Did she really think God was watching her? she was asked.

"Oh Lawd, I know He is. Without Him, I couldn't have made it through this mess." A few minutes later she added, "I don't know why all this mess happened, but I got to believe something good will come out of it. I got to believe God is watching me and the Morrison family and even Johnny D. I don't understand. I really don't. But we is like them sparrows, every one of us. And I know He's watching. I know He cares. That He surely do."

• • •

Charles and Bertha Morrison observed the anniversary of Ronda's death that November by publishing a memorial in *The Monroe Journal.* Under her picture they wrote:

> Ronda, it is that time of the year again—Nov. 1. It has been seven years now. We go to your grave and place fresh flowers several times a year and each time it seems to be sadder. May the person who killed you see these flowers and may it affect him so badly that he will have to confess.
>
> Ronda, we will always miss you and we pray that those responsible will someday be arrested.

Author's Note

This book is a factual account based on interviews, court records, newspaper articles, and personal observations. Nearly all the persons whose names appear in these pages were interviewed face-to-face. Several others who are not specifically named also provided me with useful information about Monroeville and Alabama. A few names in the book have been changed to protect the privacy of the persons involved. With one exception, however, all the major characters are identified by their actual names. No one was paid for his or her cooperation, nor did any of the people who were interviewed read the text in advance.

I wish to thank the following persons for their cooperation: Charles Adkins, Eva Ansley, Kenneth Arrant, Mozelle Arrant, Michael Barnett, Simon Benson, Edwin Booker, Bruce Boynton, Carolyn Brantley, Doug Brown, Kathy Cain, Michelle Cain, Mike Cain, Patsy Chapman, Thomas Chapman, J. L. Chestnut, John Cloud, Thomas G. Cole, Claude Cosey, Marcia Coyle, Deedre Crane, Dawn Crook, Sam Crook, Gary Cumberland, Lynn Davis, Raymond Dudley, Beth Dunning, Jerrie Sue Dunning, Lee Dunning, George K. Elbrecht, Lillie Falkenberry, Eunice Flowers, Lola Flowers, Mac Flowers, Yvonne Frament, William Gibson, Charles Gilmore, Michael Godwin, Sheri Godwin, Raymond Haacke, Shirley Haacke, John Hale, Kenneth Hallford, Marilyn Handley, Armiller Hands, Jiles Hands, Doris Hansen, Tim Hawsey, Millard D. Helton, Arnold Holt, Bill Hooks, Jr., Richard Horne, Jimmy Hunter, Danny Ikner, Larry Ikner, Woodrow Ikner, Doris Jackson, Miles Jackson, C. E. Jones, George Jones, Ron Jones, Karen Kelly, Robert E. Lee Key, Brenda Lewis, Fred Lisenby, Onzell Lisenby, Shirlie Lobmiller, V. M. Lowell, D. MacKinnon, Ron Manning, Florence Mason, Sharon McCormick, Jackie McMillian, James McMillian, John McMillian, Minnie McMillian, Walter McMillian, Byron Merritt, Donald Morgan, Ruth Morgan, Marc Moss, Ralph Myers, John Nixon, Michael O'Connor, Evelyn Odom, Lisa Odom, Dennis Owens, Kathy Painter, Ted Pearson, David Pittman, Karen Ann Pittman, Vic Pittman, Chuck Sadhue, Lenwood Sager, Jerry Shoemaker, Wendell

Simmons, Dick Smith, Everline Smith, Grover Smith, Tina Smith, Coy Stacey, Steve Stewart, Darlene Stripling, Patricia Stumb, William Sunday, Thomas Tate, Michael Taylor, Thomas Taylor, Morris Thigpen, Jerome Turner, Luther Upton, and Walter Williams. Fifteen persons who granted me interviews asked that their names not be mentioned. I am grateful for their participation.

It would have been impossible for me to have written this book without the cooperation of Bryan Stevenson and the Alabama Capital Representation Resource Center. I owe both special thanks. Although the relatives of Vickie Lynn Pittman made themselves readily available, Charles and Bertha Morrison declined to be formally interviewed. I regret any heartache this book may cause them by the recounting of their daughter's tragic murder.

Much of the dialogue is based on court transcripts and personal observation. Other conversations were reconstructed based on the recollections of the participants. I found during interviews that people sometimes recalled the same events quite differently. I have noted significant disparities in the text of the book, usually by giving more than one account; but in minor instances I have chosen the version that in my judgment seemed most likely to be accurate.

I am grateful to two most valued friends and fellow authors: Walter Harrington, who introduced me to Bryan Stevenson, and Patricia Hersch. Both provided thoughtful advice on the manuscript and much-appreciated encouragement. At Bantam Books I thank my editor, Ann Harris, for her continuing support, editorial skills, and friendship. Thanks are also due Irwyn Applebaum, Harriette Dorsen, Lauren Field, and Barb Burg. Barbara Perris was an able copyeditor.

I am also indebted to the William Morris Agency, in particular my agent, Robert Gottlieb, and Debra Goldstein, Johnny Levin, Tracey Keyes, and Brett Smith.

My parents, Elmer and Jean Earley, helped proofread the manuscript and offered me their support. Others who helped me with this project include Terrance Alden, Barbara Cernio, Kristen Crooks, Nelson DeMille, George Earley, Linda Earley, Carolyn Hunter, Richard Miles, C. T. Shades, Thomas Silverstein, Lou Ann Smith, Lynn Smith, Donna Wolfersberger, and Wayne Wolfersberger.

Most of all, I thank my wife, Barbara, and my children, Stephen, Kevin, and Katherine, for their love.

ABOUT THE AUTHOR

Pete Earley's interest in prisons and the American justice system dates back to the 1970s, when he wrote a series of newspaper articles about the inhumane treatment of mentally ill convicts being held in the Oklahoma state prison system. He was formerly a reporter for *The Washington Post* and is the author of articles for other newspapers and national magazines. Like his earlier acclaimed books, the bestselling *Family of Spies: Inside the John Walker Spy Ring* and *The Hot House: Life Inside Leavenworth Prison*, *Circumstantial Evidence* shows Earley as the consummate reporter who lets the evidence of what he observes form the heart of the powerful story he has to tell. He and his family live in Virginia.

A000120049389 6